D1525209

FATAL REVOLUTIONS

Published for the
Omohundro Institute of
Early American History
and Culture,
Williamsburg, Virginia,
by the University of
North Carolina Press,
Chapel Hill

FATAL REVOLUTIONS

Natural History, West Indian Slavery,

AND THE ROUTES OF American Literature

Christopher P. Iannini

The Omohundro Institute of Early American History and Culture is sponsored jointly by the College of William and Mary and the Colonial Williamsburg Foundation. On November 15, 1996, the Institute adopted the present name in honor of a bequest from Malvern H. Omohundro, Jr.

All rights reserved. Designed by Kimberly Bryant and set in Miller by Tseng Information Systems, Inc. Manufactured in the United States of America. The paper in this book meets the guidelines for permanence and durability of the Committee on Production Guidelines for Book Longevity of the Council on Library Resources. The University of North Carolina Press has been a member of the Green Press Initiative since 2003.

Library of Congress Cataloging-in-Publication Data
Iannini, Christopher P.
Fatal revolutions : natural history, West Indian slavery, and the routes of American literature / Christopher P. Iannini.
p. cm.
Includes bibliographical references and index.
ISBN 978-0-8078-3556-2 (cloth: alk. paper)
1. West Indies—Intellectual life—18th century. 2. West Indies—History—18th century. 3. Natural history—West Indies. 4. Slavery—West Indies—History—18th century. I. Omohundro Institute of Early American History & Culture. II. Title.
F1609.5.I26 2012
972.9—dc23

2011046725

16 15 14 13 12   5 4 3 2 1

To Polly & Benjamin

Acknowledgments

Many people helped me write this book, and it is difficult to find adequate words to thank all of them. First thanks are due to William Kelly for introducing me to the literature of natural history in an exceptional seminar at the Graduate Center of the City University of New York and supporting my work on this project since its beginnings as a dissertation proposal. Katherine Manthorne and Joan Richardson were uncommonly generous and insightful readers. I was sustained throughout my time at CUNY by the intelligence and good cheer of Ira Dworkin, Duncan Faherty, Geoffrey Jacques, Cara Murray, Zohra Saed, and Paul Stasi, among many others.

I owe a large debt of gratitude to a number of people at the McNeil Center for Early American Studies at the University of Pennsylvania. Dan Richter took an interest in the project at a crucial early stage and provided steadfast support during my time as an Andrew W. Mellon Postdoctoral Fellow. During two eventful years, I benefited from conversations and exchanges of work with an extraordinary group of scholars, including Monique Allewaert, George Boudreau, Max Cavitch, April Hatfield, Chris Hodson, Benjamin Irvin, Julie Kim, John Larson, Bob Loughart, Michelle McDonald, Roderick McDonald, Jen Manion, Cathy Matson, Amanda Moniz, Cyrus Mulready, Justine Murison, Yvette Piggush, Jared Richman, Sarah Rivett, Robert Blair St. George, Martha Schoolman, and Mike Zuckerman. I also gratefully acknowledge the American Council of Learned Societies for providing a fellowship during 2008–2009 as I expanded the first section of the manuscript.

This book would not have been possible without the support of a vibrant community of early Americanists. I have delivered portions of this book at meetings of the Society of Early Americanists (2005–2010), the American Studies Association (2007), and the Modern Language Association (2007). I am also grateful for opportunities to present my work at the Colloquium Series at the Omohundro Institute of Early American History and Culture, the American Seminar at Brown University, the Center for the Americas at Vanderbilt University (at a conference on "Alexander von Humboldt and the Americas"), the Americanist Colloquium at Yale University, the Atlantic Studies Research Group at the University of Miami and Florida International University (at a symposium on "Atlantic Narratives"), and the

New York Eighteenth-Century Seminar at Fordham University. On these and other occasions, I have received invaluable questions and comments from scholars including Anna Brickhouse, Jen Brown, Ed Cahill, Elizabeth Dillon, Michael Drexler, Jim Egan, Patrick Erben, Sibylle Fischer, Sandra Gustafson, Philip Gould, Kay Dian Kriz, David Kazanjian, Thomas Krise, Vera Kutzinski, Barbara Ladd, Maurice Lee, Neil Safier, David Shields, Siân Silyn Roberts, Eric Slauter, Ezra Tawil, Laura Dassow Walls, Bryan Waterman, Ed White, and Karin Wulf. Roy Goodman at the American Philosophical Society and Phil Lapsansky at the Library Company of Philadelphia gave generously of their time and expertise.

An earlier version of Chapter 3 was published in the *William and Mary Quarterly* under the title "'The Itinerant Man': Crèvecoeur's Caribbean, Raynal's Revolution, and the Fate of Atlantic Cosmopolitanism," 3d Ser., LXI (2004), 201–234. I am indebted to Chris Grasso for his sage editorial guidance and to Sarah Pearsall and two anonymous readers for their expert reviews. Sections of an earlier version of Chapter 4 appeared in the *Mississippi Quarterly* under the title "The Vertigo of Circum-Caribbean Empire: William Bartram's Florida," LVII (2004), 147–155. I thank Jon Smith for editing the special issue on "Postcolonial Theory, the U.S. South, and New World Studies." Parts of Chapter 5 appeared under the title *"Notes on the State of Virginia* and the Natural History of the Haitian Revolution" in *Clio*, XL (2011), 63–85. I am thankful to Tim Watson for editing the special issue on "Atlantic Narratives," and to Ashli White for her insightful comments. I gratefully acknowledge the publishers for permission to reprint these articles in modified form.

Rutgers University proved the ideal place to complete this book. I am fortunate to work alongside a diverse and energetic group of Americanists. Brad Evans, Ann Fabian, Greg Jackson, Myra Jehlen, Meredith McGill, and Michael Warner read portions of the manuscript with care and understanding. Their generosity and insight has improved this book immeasurably, as has their advice about negotiating the demands of junior faculty life. I have been blessed with a series of hard-working and imaginative department chairs: Richard Miller, Kate Flint, Jonah Siegel, and Carolyn Williams. I am particularly indebted to Jonah and Carolyn for providing funds for the beautiful color plates in this book. My colleagues in the English Department have been a constant source of intellectual inspiration and practical advice. Special thanks are due to Ann Coiro, Lynn Festa, Billy Galperin, Colin Jager, Jonathan Kramnick, Ryan Kernan, John Kucich, David Kurnick, Carter Mathes, Michael McKeon, Dianne Sadoff, Michelle Stephens,

Henry Turner, Cheryl Wall, Rebecca Walkowitz, and Edlie Wong. Across the green in the History Department, Paul Clemens and James Delbourgo have been valuable interlocutors. Across campus, Ben Sifuentes-Jáuregui has offered me a home away from home in American Studies. My students in two challenging graduate courses enriched the readings at the core of this study. William Ryan was a superb research assistant with a sharp eye for detail and a deep knowledge of the field.

From start to finish, it has been a pleasure to work with my editor, Fredrika J. Teute, who understood the implications of the project earlier and more clearly than I did. Her assistant, Nadine Zimmerli, provided valuable guidance. Susan Scott Parrish and one anonymous reviewer read the manuscript in its entirety and helped me to extend and tighten its argument. My manuscript editor, Kathy Burdette, refined the prose and annotation, showing patience and good humor throughout.

My most personal thanks go to my family, especially my mother, Virginia Iannini, my father, Paul Iannini, my brother, Craig, and my sister, Beth. And finally to Benjamin and Polly, who sacrificed much for the writing of this book and were the light at the end of each working day. I dedicate this book to them, with love and gratitude.

Contents

Illustrations

Abbreviations & Short Titles

CJB   Edmund Berkeley and Dorothy Smith Berkeley, eds.,
        The Correspondence of John Bartram, 1734-1777 (Gainesville,
        Fla., 1992).

HSP   Historical Society of Pennsylvania, Philadelphia

LCP   Library Company of Philadelphia

PTJ   Julian P. Boyd, Charles T. Cullen, John Catanzariti, Barbara B.
        Oberg, et al., eds., *The Papers of Thomas Jefferson*, 36 vols.
        (Princeton, N.J., 1950–)

WTJ   Paul L. Ford, ed., *The Writings of Thomas Jefferson*, 10 vols.
        (New York, 1892–1899).

FATAL REVOLUTIONS

Introduction

In February of 1797, Pierre-Louis Baudry des Lozières, recently arrived from the turbulent port city of Cap Français, Saint-Domingue, delivered an address to the American Philosophical Society. Entitled "A Memoir on *Animal Cotton;* or, The Insect *Fly-Carrier*," his essay found a receptive audience. Philadelphians were hungry for all manner of news from Saint-Domingue, which, before the outbreak of a massive slave insurrection in 1791, had been a leading trading partner of the early Republic. The form and content of Baudry's address enhanced its appeal. Composed at a pivotal moment in the history of the Atlantic world, as people throughout Europe and the Americas adjusted to the new reality of slave revolution, the essay draws on a long and influential tradition of natural history writing from the Americas to interest its audience in the fate of a rare and valuable specimen. But, although its narrative and rhetorical techniques derive from earlier printed volumes on the West Indies by Gonzalo Fernández de Oviedo y Valdés, Jean-Baptiste Du Tertre, and Hans Sloane, among many others, the essay also transforms and departs from that legacy, reflecting both the cognitive distress of the author and his social class and key transformations within the genre of natural history writing in the Age of Revolution more generally.

The essay is immediately striking for its elaborate, figurative surface, overt theatricality, and copious empirical detail. Though the "Insect *Fly-Carrier*" has long wreaked havoc on crops including indigo and cassava (the latter raised by enslaved Africans in provision gardens as an important food source), and though prior naturalists have experimented with a variety of means for eradicating the pest, Baudry instead hopes to clarify its lucrative potential. The possible value of the insect relates to its curious seasonal life cycle. During its annual metamorphosis in August, when the worm exchanges its multicolored "robe" for one of an "admirable sea-green," it is assailed by a swarm of so-called "ichneumon flies." Covering the entire surface of the worm, the flies "drive their stings into the skin of their victim" to deposit their eggs just beneath the surface. A fortnight later, the hatching eggs subject the cassava worm to prolonged "tortures," rendered with grotesque precision. Once they have worked their way to the surface of the skin, the larvae weave "millions and millions of cocoons," which quickly envelop the body of the cassava worm in an *"animated robe"* of "dazzling" whiteness. From these cocoons, Baudry hopes to manufacture "animal cotton" as a new article of trade, one with considerable advantages over the more familiar crop he calls "vegetable cotton."[1]

Having proposed the cassava worm as the source of a "new branch of commerce with the West India colonies," Baudry concludes his talk with an extended apology:

> Had it not been for the troubles that have laid our colony waste, and which have prevented the necessary communication, I should have brought to you a fly-carrier in every one of the periods of his life. You would have seen the eggs, the magnificent robe with which he is decked at his birth, the kind of food that he is fond of, the simple but noble vestment in which he wraps himself up on the approach of his tormentors, you would have seen those covering his whole body as it were with points, you would have seen him covered with his shell, and that same shell carded, spun and ready for the weaver. I had in great degree already executed this design. But it is too well known that I have not been able to save any thing in my flight from home.

This climactic apology makes plain that the purpose of the essay goes far beyond empirical reportage. Through his meticulous description of the insect, the exiled planter argues the potential consequences of the Haitian Revolution for the propagation of knowledge, virtue, and refinement in the Americas, centering his argument, not on a graphic portrayal of insurrectionary violence, but on an elegiac commemoration of an absent specimen. In a period when sensational depictions of corporeal "savagery" in revolutionary Saint-Domingue were commonplace, the essay instead characterizes slave revolution primarily in terms of epistemological crisis. Insurrection has dealt a possibly fatal blow to a colonial enlightenment that had begun to flourish on the island during the ancien régime. By trafficking in vivid imagery of a lost West Indian specimen and by using that imagery as the basis of his appeal for sympathy, Baudry makes plain his assumption that the circulation of natural knowledge from the region was of cardinal import for his audience, not only as it concerned the economic development of the colonial and Revolutionary Americas but also, and perhaps even principally, for the future of Enlightenment science and letters. Such

1. M. [Pierre-Louis] Baudry des Lozieres, "A Memoir on *Animal Cotton;* or, The Insect *Fly-Carrier,*" American Philosophical Society, *Transactions,* V (1802), 150–159 (quotations on 152–153, 154).

assumptions were well grounded. As his audience knew well, Baudry had been a founding member of the Cercle des Philadelphes, a scientific society that, before the revolution, had been among the most active in the Western Hemisphere.[2]

We begin with "Memoir on *Animal Cotton*" because it aptly sets the stage for questions about the development of scientific and literary culture in the early Americas. Broadly conceived, this book is about the relationship between two dramatic transformations in the history of the eighteenth-century Atlantic world (primarily the British Atlantic, but not exclusively, as considerations of Saint-Domingue, Spanish Florida, Cuba, and French Louisiana will attest). The first entails the growth of the West Indian plantation as a new kind of social institution and economic engine, one integral to the rapid expansion of the commercial empires of Britain, Spain, Holland, Portugal, and France in the period and to the emergence of the Caribbean region as home to the most valuable and dynamic colonies in the New World by far. The second consists in the rise of natural history as a new scientific discipline, intellectual obsession, and literary form. This book's more particular argument is that these transformations were inextricably linked and that together they established fundamental conditions for what we might call "the practice of letters" in the eighteenth-century Americas, in ways that have significant, if surprising, implications for understanding the culture and literature of American Enlightenment.[3]

2. Ibid., 158. On the Cercle des Philadelphes, see James E. McClellan III, *Colonialism and Science: Saint-Domingue in the Old Regime* (Baltimore, 1992), 4.

3. As traditionally employed, the term "American Enlightenment" refers to the circulation of new political and moral ideals from Europe to colonial America in the eighteenth century, as increased communication with the metropole allowed learned provincials to participate more fully in the intellectual life of the British Empire, developing distinctive American expressions of Enlightenment ideas. Although differing over issues including the relative importance of secular and religious influences on American Enlightenment thought, earlier scholars of the subject have shared a primary interest in tracing the roots of American Revolutionary ideology and therefore have normally focused their analyses on the transformation of political and moral philosophy while also limiting their geographic scope to British North America. See, for instance, Henry F. May, *The Enlightenment in America* (Oxford, 1976); Ned C. Landsman, *From Colonials to Provincials: American Thought and Culture, 1680–1760* (New York, 1997); and Robert Ferguson, *The American Enlightenment, 1750–1820* (Cambridge, Mass., 1997). More recently, scholars have stressed the importance of new scientific ideas and experimental practices, especially in the areas of natural philosophy and natural history. See, for instance, James Delbourgo, *A Most Amazing Scene of Wonders: Electricity and Enlightenment in Early America* (Cambridge, Mass., 2006); Susan Scott Parrish, *American Curiosity: Cultures of Natural History in the Colonial British Atlantic World* (Chapel Hill, N.C., 2006); Nina Reid-Maroney, *Philadelphia's Enlightenment, 1740–1800: Kingdom of Christ, Empire of Reason* (Westport, Conn., 2001); Andrew J. Lewis, *A Democracy of Facts: Natural History in the Early Republic* (Philadelphia, 2011). The studies by Delbourgo and Parrish also exemplify a second trend. By incorporating the scientific culture of the Caribbean, their accounts begin to redefine American Enlightenment as a shared New World phenomenon. For the purposes of this book, "American Enlightenment" refers to

The phrase "practice of letters" is meant to evoke an expansive conception of literary culture in the eighteenth century as encompassing, in Michael Warner's description, "all of the forms of written discourse and the uses of literacy." As the period understood it, the category comprised not only belletristic genres such as novels, plays, and poems but also those forms of written discourse devoted to the cultivation of practical knowledge, including scientific knowledge. Indeed, so expansive was the period's definition that many scholars of early America have shifted away from "literature" as an explicit term of analysis (too laden with post-Romantic conceptions of literature as a special kind of aesthetic good to be consumed privately) and begun to speak, instead, of a broader "world of letters," committed to the public exercise of reason and civility for socially beneficial purposes.[4]

Studies by Ralph Bauer and Susan Scott Parrish, among others, have begun to establish the centrality of natural history to this world of letters as it coalesced in the early Americas. One important effect of the Baconian and Newtonian reforms of natural philosophy in the early modern period, as they have demonstrated, was that European intellectuals and readers began to attribute considerable value to firsthand written accounts of flora, fauna, climate, and natural processes from the colonial Americas, as new metropolitan institutions such as the Royal Society (London) and the Académie royale des sciences (Paris) undertook the "improvement of natural knowledge" through observation, experiment, and published description. Throughout much of the eighteenth century, the demand for factual eyewitness reports on New World nature provided one of the primary channels—in many cases, one of the only reliable channels—through which learned provincials could take part in the broader intellectual culture of the Atlantic world, refashioning themselves as enlightened authors

---

a hemispheric intellectual and cultural transformation centered on the circulation of natural knowledge around the Greater Caribbean and between the Caribbean and North America, both before and after the American Revolution. However, I use the traditional term "American Enlightenment" (rather than, for instance, "New World Enlightenment") in order to evoke a key tension within this hemispheric intellectual movement. By the late eighteenth century, North American authors had begun to employ the discourse of natural history in a sustained (and, for the most part, failed) attempt to define the early Republic as a distinct geocultural entity. "American Enlightenment," that is, describes a process of transnational exchange between learned communities in the Caribbean and North America that, however paradoxically, contributes to the development of intense expressions of protonationalist sentiment, especially in the work of Thomas Jefferson and John Audubon.

4. Michael Warner, *The Letters of the Republic: Publication and the Public Sphere in Eighteenth-Century America* (Cambridge, Mass., 1990), 122. See also Bryan Waterman, *Republic of Intellect: The Friendly Club of New York City and the Making of American Literature* (Baltimore, 2007); Jennifer J. Baker, *Securing the Commonwealth: Debt, Speculation, and Writing in the Making of Early America* (Baltimore, 2005).

and subjects. In so doing, such authors learned to negotiate complex imperial assumptions about the proper function and form of colonial reportage, whether by composing personal letters that demonstrated their command of metropolitan norms of politeness and sociability or innovative first-person narratives that frequently subverted and parodied metropolitan theories regarding the degenerate mental, physical, and moral constitution of creole settlers.[5]

Fatal Revolutions both builds from and challenges these studies. The rediscovery of natural history has shifted our understanding of the generic landscape of colonial American literature. But we have only begun to assess its sweeping significance for mapping not just the regional geography of eighteenth-century literary history but also the formal evolution of colonial prose narrative. We have yet to adequately register the primacy of the West Indies as an object of natural knowledge in the period and thus have yet to place the evolution of natural history writing within its most salient historical context—the rise of Atlantic slavery and slave-driven commerce as they occasioned new and difficult problems of epistemology and representation.

Throughout the long eighteenth century, the assumption that the colonial Caribbean was the site of the most significant and valuable forms of empirical knowledge to be derived from the New World was all but axiomatic. The curious and learned assumed a close and necessary relationship between the development of a global commercial system based on the explosive demand for Caribbean agricultural commodities, the emergence of the "improvement" of nature as a prevailing cultural ideal, and the new prestige of natural history as a scientific and literary endeavor. At the most basic level, this historical relationship meant that the colonial West Indies

---

5. Ralph Bauer, *The Cultural Geography of Colonial American Literatures: Empire, Travel, Modernity* (New York, 2003); Susan Scott Parrish, *American Curiosity: Cultures of Natural History in the Colonial British Atlantic World* (Chapel Hill, N.C., 2006). Parrish maps the culture of natural history primarily in terms of transatlantic relations between England and the British Americas, arguing that the colonial Americas made a substantial though largely unacknowledged contribution to the history of modern empiricism. Although she does not pursue connections between the Caribbean and North America in any sustained fashion, however, she does note the prominence of the Caribbean as a source of natural historical intelligence for Europe (19). Bauer charts the literary culture of the early Americas both in terms of an east-west dialectic between Europe and the New World, and a north-south axis linking the Spanish and British Americas. Reflecting the necessary limitations of a study already unusually expansive in its geographic reach, however, the Caribbean plays little role in his assessment of either of these dynamics. For other insightful studies of natural history writing in early America, see, for instance, Thomas Hallock, *From the Fallen Tree: Frontier Narratives, Environmental Politics, and the Roots of a National Pastoral, 1749–1826* (Chapel Hill, N.C., 2003); Christoph Irmscher, *The Poetics of Natural History: From John Bartram to William James* (Piscataway, N.J., 1999); Pamela Regis, *Describing Early America: Bartram, Jefferson, Crèvecoeur, and the Rhetoric of Natural History* (1992; rpt. Philadelphia, 1999).

were the source and subject of a vast and eclectic body of natural history writing from the Americas—indeed, the overwhelming majority of such texts devoted to the Anglo- and Franco-American worlds. More important, however, this relationship also meant that the genre of natural history was shaped formally by the long legacy of its practice in the West Indies. In the long and complicated history of modern empiricism, perhaps no place produced such recalcitrant facts as the colonial Caribbean. Natural history developed as a colonial genre through its efforts to describe, disseminate, and contemplate those facts.

Only by recovering this history of the genre can we properly incorporate the Caribbean within the literary history of the early Americas and the Atlantic world in general. Studies by Colin Dayan, Thomas W. Krise, Sean X. Goudie, Elizabeth Maddock Dillon, and Michael Drexler, among others, have done much to unearth a vibrant tradition of vernacular performance and belletristic writing in the colonial West Indies, charting pervasive patterns of cultural exchange between the sugar islands and North America that persisted long after the founding of the United States. Because they largely exclude the seemingly extraliterary genre of natural history, however, such studies risk mischaracterizing not only the nature of literary production in the colonial West Indies but also the terms of this cultural exchange. By the late eighteenth century, colonial authors worked within an established repertoire of prose and poetic genres (including travel narrative, captivity narrative, georgic, locodescriptive verse, and natural history, to name but a few) and drew from an array of representational strategies that derived fundamentally from the long-standing metropolitan obsession with empirical reportage from the West Indies. The provincial worldview of these authors had been fashioned through close engagement with previous representations of the region.[6]

These generic and formal conventions wielded a powerful, if unexpected, influence on the literary culture of British North America and the early Republic. As they focused their intellectual efforts on natural history by the mid-eighteenth century—as potential cornerstone of a renovated so-

6. Joan [Colin] Dayan, *Haiti, History, and the Gods* (Berkeley, Calif., 1995), 187–267; Thomas W. Krise, *Caribbeana: An Anthology of English Literature of the West Indies, 1657-1777* (Chicago, 1999); Elizabeth Maddock Dillon, "The Secret History of the Early American Novel: Leonora Sansay and Revolution in Saint Domingue," *Novel: A Forum on Fiction*, XL (2006), 77–103; Sean X. Goudie, *Creole America: The West Indies and the Formation of Literature and Culture in the New Republic* (Philadelphia, 2006); Michael Drexler, "The Displacement of the American Novel: Imagining Aaron Burr and Haiti in Leonora Sansay's *Secret History*," *Common-Place*, IX (2009); Leonora Sansay, *Secret History; or, The Horrors of St. Domingo and Laura*, ed. Michael J. Drexler (Peterborough, Ontario, 2007).

cial identity within the wider empire—the authors at the core of this study were compelled to negotiate a cultural marketplace organized around the primary demand for Caribbean curiosities and writings. Like cosmopolitan intellectuals elsewhere in Europe and the Americas, they assumed that the prosperity and, indeed, survival of their local societies turned on the question of West Indian "culture," meaning both the literal improvement of Caribbean nature and the refinement of those new empirical and literary techniques dedicated to the advancement of knowledge.

In the context of these assumptions, Baudry's "Memoir on *Animal Cotton*" makes a strong, albeit implicit, claim about the imperiled future of colonial literature. From its opening paragraphs, the essay employs a representational strategy that was integral to nearly all of the texts examined in this study. Since the early modern period, printed natural histories of the region had relied on sophisticated techniques of emblematic interpretation, requiring the reader to draw subtle connections between an image, its label, and accompanying linguistic descriptions as they discerned the hidden providential or socioethical significance of a natural object or human artifact.

Baudry's essay choreographs a modified version of this hermeneutic process. His description of the worm is punctuated by allegorical gestures that make clear reference to the ongoing social and political conflict in Saint-Domingue. The insect initially functions as a representation of the colony's revolutionary ex-slaves. Although the species is well known among Saint-Dominguan planters for "the mischief which it occasions" as it "devours their indigo and cassava plantations," and although much energy has been devoted to discovering "the means of destroying it," Baudry suggests a new approach: "It is indeed very natural to endeavor to destroy our enemy, but to compel him to be of service to us is by far the greater triumph." During a decisive phase of the Haitian Revolution, the point of his moral commentary could not have been lost.[7]

Almost immediately, however, the insect transforms into a representation of the besieged plantocracy. Not only does Baudry's description evoke familiar conventions for characterizing the sumptuary and sexual habits of creole planters, dwelling both on the "elegant livery" of the worm ("He is decked at his birth with a robe of the most brilliant variegated colours") and the "ardency" of the mature butterfly during "the season of his loves" in September ("the excess of this indulgence soon destroys him, he dies in the

---

7. Baudry, "Memoir on *Animal Cotton*," American Philosophical Society, *Transactions*, V, 150.

same month after violent convulsions"). More pointedly, Baudry's account of the "tortures" endured by the worm resonates with his concluding rhetorical appeal to his own emotional distress. The sufferings of this noble and elegant insect provide an emblem of the avowed tragic plight of the Saint-Dominguan exiles. So intense is Baudry's identification with the insect, and so elaborate the figurative surface of the essay as he chronicles the torments of the worm, that it risks troubling the author's claim to empirical transparency and accuracy. The essay thus exemplifies the complex interplay between scientific and literary epistemologies during a period when they were not yet clearly demarcated, but the long historical evolution leading to their divergence in the early nineteenth century had nonetheless begun.[8]

Baudry's essay marks a crucial transitional phase within a history of representation that will take us, in the chapters that follow, from two influential and innovative works of the new science by Hans Sloane and Mark Catesby through some of the most canonical writings of the eighteenth-century British Americas by some of the first colonial authors to achieve international distinction: William Bartram's euphoric vision of colonial Florida as ground for a new kind of "peaceable" plantation and his expressive drawings of the "West Indian weeds" he discovered flourishing in the region; J. Hector St. John de Crèvecoeur's encounters with the systematic brutality of New World slavery and nature in Jamaica and South Carolina and his ensuing, dystopic meditations on the planetary histories of commerce, colonialism, and political violence; Jefferson's pseudoempiricist inquiry into the nature of black minds and bodies and his prophecy of apocalyptic slave revolution in *Notes on the State of Virginia,* as refined in a long series of personal letters on the Haitian Revolution; John James Audubon's extravagant depictions of natural predation in lower Louisiana during the so-called "Americanization" of the region, where he resided during a formative phase in his artistic career. By any reasonable admission, this will at first seem an eclectic series of texts, ranging from some of the most expensive illustrated scientific folios of the long eighteenth century (by Sloane, Catesby, and Audubon) to more widely available printed narratives shaped by their interaction with a variety of popular prose genres, including travelogue, spiritual autobiography, and early novel (by Crèvecoeur and William Bartram). But, within the period's capacious definition of the genre, all but effaced by subsequent critical taxonomies, these texts were understood pri-

8. Ibid., 151. For the classic account of this process, see C. P. Snow, *The Two Cultures and the Scientific Revolution* (Cambridge, 1960).

marily as natural histories. Moreover, with one meaningful exception (discussed in Chapter 5, on Jefferson), each of these texts takes the natural history of the Caribbean as an explicit and, indeed, central subject, though the fact has been nearly lost on modern scholars for reasons that bear careful consideration.

This history of representation is divided into two main sections. The first, entitled "The Nature of Slavery," focuses on two of the most formally sophisticated and lavishly printed natural history books of their day—Hans Sloane's *Voyage to the Islands Madera, Barbados, Nieves, S. Christophers, and Jamaica, with the Natural History of the Herbs and Trees, Four-Footed Beasts, Fishes, Birds, Insects, Reptiles, etc. of the Last of Those Islands* (1707–1725) and Mark Catesby's *Natural History of Carolina, Florida, and the Bahama Islands: Containing the Figures of Birds, Beasts, Fishes, Serpents, Insects, and Plants* (1731–1743). Virtually ignored by modern literary historians, these texts were understood in their own day as signal contributions to the English literature of the Americas, during a period of epistemological and social turbulence stretching from the growth of the Royal Society in the late seventeenth century (amid the early stages of the "sugar revolution") through the rise of post-Newtonian natural philosophy in the 1730s and 1740s (amid the continued explosive growth of slavery, the slave trade, and the West India trade). Natural historians of the Caribbean in this period, with Sloane and Catesby preeminent among them, developed a rich repertoire of linguistic and pictorial techniques for cultivating a vivid understanding of the region and its natural productions—a virtual descriptive and narrative experience designed to instill a concrete idea of colonial environment and society in the minds of curious readers and to sharpen their interest in the fate of that portentous yet distant archipelago. As a result of their efforts, natural history emerged as a crucial medium not only for the circulation of natural knowledge among physicians, planters, botanists, gardeners, merchants, and investors but also, in ways exemplified by Baudry's essay, for assessing the moral significance of colonial slavery as a new and seemingly necessary dimension of modern social and economic life.[9]

The longer, second section of the book, entitled "Reaping the Early Re-

9. My use of the term "English literature of the Americas" follows Myra Jehlen and Michael Warner, eds., *The English Literatures of America, 1500–1800* (New York, 1997). For related reconsiderations of the category of early American literature, see William Spengemann, *A New World of Words: Redefining Early American Literature* (New Haven, Conn., 1994); Spengemann, *A Mirror for Americanists: Reflections on the Idea of American Literature* (Hanover, N.H., 1989).

public," pursues the ramifications of this genealogy of natural history for writers and thinkers in British North America and the early United States. But it also demonstrates the fluidity of these geographic terms as the period understood them. Among the more complicated questions addressed by natural histories of the West Indies was the problem of where the region began and ended. For eighteenth-century naturalists, much as for cultural geographers today, the location of a colony was determined by considering physical characteristics such as topography, temperature, moisture, soil, and quality of air, along with a range of social, cultural, and economic criteria. In a period marked by the near-fanatical conviction that human endeavor could "improve" the natural landscape, even the question of a colony's physical climate was far from simple. As we will see in chapters on Catesby in Carolina and William Bartram in East Florida, patterns of agricultural development, it was widely believed, could substantially transform the climate of a colony. For these reasons, definitions of the West Indies always remained provisional and amorphous in the period. But, in general, the term referred to a chain of colonial possessions extending (roughly) from Guiana and Surinam in the south, through the islands of the Greater and Lesser Antilles, to Louisiana, Florida, and South Carolina. A number of modern scholars have characterized this region as a "Greater Caribbean" or "extended Caribbean." Composed of what historians David Patrick Geggus and David Barry Gaspar call "basically similar worlds," the region was defined by shared tropical and semitropical ecosystems, a black majority demographic, and patterns of social and economic development centered on plantation slavery and the commercial export of a narrow range of cash crops. The region was stitched together, moreover, by patterns of commercial exchange and human mobility that routinely traversed imperial, national, and linguistic boundaries, often in blatant disregard of official mercantilist policies. It thus maintained considerable coherence through the early nineteenth century, even as factors including the territorial expansion of the United States, the political isolation of Haiti, and the gradual decline of the West Indian sugar economy brought increased fragmentation.[10]

10. For various definitions of the greater or extended Caribbean, see Immanuel Wallerstein, *The Modern World-System II: Mercantilism and the Consolidation of the European World-Economy, 1600–1750* (New York, 1980), 157, 166–167, 179; Wallerstein, *Modern World System III: The Second Era of Great Expansion of the Capitalist World-Economy, 1730–1840* (San Diego, Calif., 1989), 141, 236–237; Peter Hulme, *Colonial Encounters: Europe and the Native Caribbean, 1492–1797* (London, 1986); David Barry Gaspar and David Patrick Geggus, eds., *A Turbulent Time: The French Revolution in the Greater Caribbean* (Bloomington, Ind., 1997), viii–ix.

Through a series of sustained, close readings, Section 2 argues that the Greater Caribbean was central to the scientific and literary culture of late-colonial North America and the early Republic, during a period when representations of nature were key to the articulation of new social and political identities. Because natural history provided an indispensable medium of self and social transformation for Revolutionary-era and early republican authors (with the interest in empirical reportage from the New World remaining one of the more reliable means of provincial intellectual advancement), because slavery quickly became an ideological flash point within debates over the implications of the American Revolution, and because economic and political developments in the Greater Caribbean continued to present both possibilities and perils to the emergent nation, these authors were compelled to engage the textual tradition and representational techniques traced in Section 1 of this study in ambivalent ways. This is not a study of how Revolutionary and early republican authors represented what was perceived as an exotic and culturally retrograde region at the southern fringe of a new, enlightened nation. Rather, it argues that a long and durable tradition of natural history writing from the Greater Caribbean established the conditions of possibility for these authors' subsequent literary and scientific endeavors at a time when cosmopolitan intellectuals throughout the Atlantic world maintained a consuming interest in the natural history of the West Indies. Nature was only available to these authors as a medium of self-fashioning because of the previous history of Caribbean nature discourse, which had established important institutional structures, networks of patronage, and reading publics for colonial letters. This is why many of the most influential printed natural histories of the American Enlightenment have their origins in carefully planned collecting expeditions to the northern fringe of the Greater Caribbean (for example, John Bartram, William Bartram, and Audubon). As important, that history had also established certain ideological assumptions, discursive conventions, and representational techniques as fundamental to the genre. Natural history had long been among the most widely read and penetrating literary forms for understanding what David Brion Davis has called "the problem of slavery" in an age of putative moral, political, and intellectual progress. That problem is more deeply ingrained in the literature of American Enlightenment than we have yet realized. In order to stake their claim to equality and autonomy in the realms of manners, taste, and intellect, New World writers turned to a genre that had been formed by the long history of its confrontation with colonial slavery. Because of this history, representations of nature raised intractable questions about the situation of the early Republic within the transnational networks of the slave trade and the West India trade.[11]

The Routes of American Literature

Few methodological trends in early American literary studies over the last two decades have been more pronounced, and more remarked upon, than the shift from national "roots" to transnational "routes," with the latter term posed by cultural theorists such as Paul Gilroy as a challenge to forms of nationalist essentialism long entrenched in the disciplines of history and literary criticism. Seeking to move the study of modern cultural practice beyond the territorial boundaries of modern nation-states, Gilroy calls attention to "a new structure of cultural exchange . . . built up across the imperial networks which once played host to the triangular trade of sugar, slaves and capital." In keeping with this trend, this study reexamines a sequence of late-eighteenth-century texts that have long been considered in terms of their contribution to a foundational vision of national identity and purpose. Since the beginnings of American literary studies, scholars of American nature have been preoccupied with the problem of national origins, and texts such as Crèvecoeur's *Letters from an American Farmer* and Jefferson's *Notes on the State of Virginia* have been interpreted as crucial contributions to a particular myth of national origins. Such texts are better understood, however, as the products of a transnational intellectual culture that, until the very end of the eighteenth century, was concerned, not primarily with the rise of North America and the United States to material prosperity and cultural prestige, but rather with the "culture" of the West Indies as a means to planetary refinement. The authors under consideration here assumed that the routes of material and intellectual progress were "circum-Atlantic."[12]

First coined by literary scholar and performance theorist Joseph Roach in *Cities of the Dead: Circum-Atlantic Performance*, the term has been adapted by historian David Armitage in his widely read essay "Three Concepts of Atlantic History." Because the methodology and conceptual framework of

---

11. David Brion Davis, *The Problem of Slavery in the Age of Revolution, 1770–1823* (1975; rpt. New York, 1999); Davis, *The Problem of Slavery in Western Culture* (1967; rpt. Ithaca, N.Y., 1988).

12. Paul Gilroy, *"There Ain't No Black in the Union Jack": The Cultural Politics of Race and Nation* (Chicago, 1987), 157; Gilroy, *The Black Atlantic: Modernity and Double Consciousness* (Cambridge, Mass., 1993); Perry Miller, *Errand into the Wilderness* (Cambridge, Mass., 1956); Henry Nash Smith, *Virgin Land: The American West as Symbol and Myth* (New York, 1950); Leo Marx, *The Machine in the Garden: Technology and the Pastoral Ideal in America* (New York, 1964).

this study derive more directly from Roach's model and because Armitage's translation of that model has proved so influential within the growing field of Atlantic history, it is worth distinguishing between their uses of the term here. For Armitage, circumatlantic history is defined by its attention to patterns of transnational exchange between Europe, the Americas, and Africa and is therefore distinct both from transatlantic analyses focused on international comparisons between the Americas and Europe (most often in the north Atlantic) and cisatlantic studies centered on the history of a particular region or nation as it is influenced by wider developments in the Atlantic basin. Circumatlantic history is a history of circulation in general. It encompasses "the history of the people who crossed the Atlantic, who lived on its shores and who participated in the communities it made possible, of their commerce and their ideas, as well as the diseases they carried, the flora they transplanted and the fauna they transported."[13]

As employed by Roach, the term denotes a more precise regional geography. His study unfolds a map of the circumatlantic world with the Caribbean at its vital center: "The concept of a circum-Atlantic world (as opposed to a transatlantic one) insists on the centrality of the diasporic and genocidal histories of Africa and the Americas, North and South, in the creation of the culture of modernity. In this sense, a New World was not discovered in the Caribbean, but one was truly invented there." Roach repeatedly emphasizes the primacy of the Caribbean within this model, which he defines elsewhere as a "region-centered conception, which locates the peoples of the Caribbean rim at the heart of an oceanic interculture." Roach's concept of a circumatlantic world thus draws on some of the founding insights of Caribbean studies. In particular, it shares with C. L. R. James's *Black Jacobins* a desire not only to critique dominant accounts of the origins of Western modernity (focused too narrowly on the North Atlantic) but also to supplant them with an alternative narrative. As James was the first to argue, because the West Indian plantation was formed by the collision of peoples and materials from around the globe and was devoted almost exclusively to the production of cash crops for overseas export, Caribbean slaves "from the very start lived a life that was in its essence a modern life," far in advance of any European proletariat.[14]

13. David Armitage, "Three Concepts of Atlantic History," in Armitage and Michael J. Braddick, eds., *The British Atlantic World, 1500–1800* (New York, 2003), 11–27 (quotation on 16).

14. Joseph Roach, *Cities of the Dead: Circum-Atlantic Performance* (New York, 1996), 4, 5; C. L. R. James, *The Black Jacobins: Toussaint L'Ouverture and the San Domingo Revolution* (1938; rpt. New York, 1989), 392.

This region-centered conception of the circumatlantic world goes hand in hand with Roach's distinctive methodology. As James also knew, the importance of the Caribbean to the culture of modernity was obscured by a long history of conscious negation. This led not only to the reflexive national framework of much subsequent scholarship (including the assumption that the history of the French Revolution could be narrated separately from events in Haiti) but also severely limited the kinds of documentary and archival sources available for contesting such assumptions. In the context of this legacy of forgetting, and as exemplified by *Cities of the Dead,* a specifically literary approach to the history of the circumatlantic world holds considerable promise. Attending to the circulation of aesthetic and signifying practices between New Orleans and London, and proposing subtle connections between cultural forms as seemingly disparate as colonial vernacular performance (Mardi Gras), metropolitan theater (Thomas Southerne's version of *Oroonoko*), and canonical belles lettres (Alexander Pope's *Windsor-Forest*), his study sketches the contours of a circumatlantic interculture in ways that could never fully be registered by tracing the movement of goods, people, diseases, flora, fauna, or even ideas.[15]

Drawing on Roach's region-centered conception and focusing on the circulation of representational practices, this book argues that the genre of natural history played an indispensable role in the development of a new circumatlantic world of letters. This means, for one thing, that natural history established institutional channels and discursive conventions through which West Indian colonists began to take part in that world. But it also means that the genre of natural history infused the facts of circumatlantic exchange with legible meaning. Relying on sophisticated assumptions, lost to posterity, about the reading and writing of natural history books, the curious and learned developed a specific understanding of modern com-

15. This reconstituted formalist methodology is likely one reason that Roach's study has not been easily assimilated within recent overviews of Atlantic history. Armitage's essay is a notable exception. For some overviews, see Bernard Bailyn, *Atlantic History: Concept and Contours* (Cambridge, Mass., 2005); Jack P. Green and Philip D. Morgan, eds., *Atlantic History: A Critical Appraisal* (New York, 2008). For some examples of modern circumatlantic criticism, see Ian Baucom, *Specters of the Atlantic: Finance Capital, Slavery, and the Philosophy of History* (Durham, N.C., 2005); Christopher L. Miller, *The French Atlantic Triangle: Literature and Culture of the Slave Trade* (Durham, N.C., 2008); Laura Doyle, *Freedom's Empire: Race and the Rise of the Novel in Atlantic Modernity, 1640–1940* (Durham, N.C., 2008). For Caribbeanist and postcolonial scholarship that pursues the historiographic possibilities of literary form, see Sibylle Fischer, *Modernity Disavowed: Haiti and the Cultures of Slavery in the Age of Revolution* (Durham, N.C., 2004); David Scott, *Conscripts of Modernity: The Tragedy of Colonial Enlightenment* (Durham, N.C., 2004).

merce and colonialism, assessing the deep and necessary connections between the histories of slavery, commercial progress, and intellectual enlightenment.

The emphasis on printed books creates possibilities and limitations. As practiced on the ground in the Caribbean, natural history was an intercultural enterprise. Modern work in the history of science has established that nonelite women, native Americans, and enslaved Africans played vital roles as purveyors of natural knowledge, as elite naturalists acknowledged. In *Voyage to . . . Jamaica,* for instance, Sloane claims that his printed accounts of Jamaican flora and fauna derive from "the best Informations I could get from Books, and the Inhabitants, either *Europeans, Indians or Blacks."* Conventional in the archive of colonial natural history writing, Sloane's candid admission points to an important paradox. Though dependent on indigenous and enslaved African informants, and attributing considerable authority to their oral testimony, the print culture of natural history was exclusively the province of propertied white men. Almost none of the major black Atlantic intellectuals of the eighteenth century gained access to print publication through scientific networks, even as scores of enslaved people participated daily in the gathering of specimens and information. Rather, nearly all of the major black Atlantic writings of the period were published through the religious networks of evangelical Protestants as they began to challenge the moral and legal foundations of the slave trade. The culture of natural history was dominated by individuals with a direct material interest in the stability of colonial slavery and thus with good reason to limit access to print along strict racial lines.

The chapters that follow are necessarily focused on the published writings of a relatively narrow social elite, though they assess the impact of cross-racial collaboration on the form and content of these texts. As eighteenth-century literary genres go, natural history developed in close relationship to the triangle trade and the colonial plantation. Yet the representational strategies that emerged from this relationship also had considerable bearing on the development of more familiar genres such as the early novel. Indeed, one of the primary virtues of foregrounding printed books is that it creates a clearer picture of how the formal techniques of natural history reached a wider audience—beyond a circle of intimate correspondents—to eventually saturate the literary culture of the early Americas. By tracing the process through which the formal experiments of texts such as Sloane's *Voyage to . . . Jamaica* and Catesby's *Natural History of Carolina* influenced the writings of important naturalists in colonial and Revolutionary North America, this study casts new light on the relationship between West Indian slavery, empiricist science, and the history of genre.[16]

It also bears acknowledging that the emphasis in Section 2 on writers from within the eventual boundaries of the early Republic may seem to run counter to the intentions of circumatlantic method. As Roach puts it, one of the benefits of such a framework lies in its challenge to the self-evidence of "canons organized around the existence of national borders." Such canons are in one sense anything but representative of the kinds of routine trans-oceanic and transnational exchange that characterized eighteenth-century literary and performance culture. They are artifacts of "the deeply ingrained division within English studies between American literature, on the one hand, and English or British literature, on the other, [which] has foreclosed the exploration of certain historical relationships in a particularly invidious way." However salutary the claim, it risks minimizing the extent to which these historical relationships were also foreclosed within eighteenth-century literary culture itself, as various forms of literary nationalism took hold toward the end of the century, long before the modern institutional division of literary studies into national units.[17]

Considered in this context, this study's emphasis on canonical writings of American Enlightenment serves a double purpose. One of the main arguments, however counterintuitive it may seem, is that the writings of William Bartram, Crèvecoeur, Jefferson, and Audubon provide a sensitive register of the vitality and influence of Caribbean natural history as a literary enterprise. These authors had to engage this textual tradition to reach an international readership. But they did so in paradoxical ways. On the one hand, their writings drew consciously on the representational strategies of Sloane, Catesby, and others to depict an extended Caribbean region that encompassed the valuable and volatile colonies of Carolina, Florida, and Louisiana; this rendered the southern boundaries of the United States, when they finally emerged toward the end of the century, exceedingly porous—indeed, all but chimerical. On the other hand, their published writings also supplanted the place of the West Indies within the mercantile and cosmopolitan imagination, proposing a radical new vision of New World nature in

16. Hans Sloane, *A Voyage to the Islands Madera, Barbados, Nieves, S. Christophers, and Jamaica, with the Natural History of the Herbs and Trees, Four-Footed Beasts, Fishes, Birds, Insects, Reptiles, etc. of the Last of Those Islands* . . . , 2 vols. (London, 1707–1725), I, 1, preface (unpaginated).

17. Roach, *Cities of the Dead*, 183.

which the natural abundance of North America, as prospective material basis of the incipient nation, would fuel a planetary future of republican liberty. The emergence of this vision in their published writings was both conflicted and contingent. But it was also an intentional outcome of their confrontation with ideological problems associated with trade and empire that natural historians had been grappling with for decades. While employing circumatlantic theoretical and historical methods, Chapters 3 through 6 of this study account for the protonational formulations of these North American authors, who, long before the likes of Perry Miller and Henry Nash Smith, began to separate continental America from the extended West Indies.[18]

The Nature of Slavery

The story of the growth of the West Indian plantation is by now well known. Beginning with the sugar revolution of the mid-seventeenth century, as modern forms of labor organization, commercial agriculture, and economic botany took shape in the Caribbean and new consumer appetites for West Indian comestibles developed simultaneously in Europe, the islands emerged as valuable and volatile colonies. Their volatility owed to pervasive violence, for the cultivation and exchange of West Indian staples depended on the invention of another transoceanic "commodity"—the hereditary chattel slave. In black majority islands where planter rule could be maintained only through daily rituals of discipline, torture, and execution, insurrection was a constant threat.[19]

Even so, planters and merchants continued to reap spectacular profits. Over the course of the century, as the numbers of slaves shipped to the Caribbean and the tonnage of tropical staples shipped from them grew exponentially, the region served as primary engine of capital accumulation

18. As Myra Jehlen argues, although scholars such as Miller and Nash Smith sought to historicize and thus demystify the assumption that there was something unique about the origin of the United States, they confirmed the assumption that the United States was "objectively continental" and that its history was incarnated in the physical constitution of North America. She captures the effects of this assumption with a metaphor that any eighteenth-century naturalist would admire: "But though they pulled it up to examine its roots, somehow the myth went on flowering." See Myra Jehlen, *American Incarnation: The Individual, the Nation, and the Continent* (Cambridge, Mass., 1986), 27–29. Although Miller and Nash Smith reinforce a certain geographic perspective on early American literary history, the process of "forgetting" the West Indies begins within the literary culture of the early Republic itself.

19. Sidney Mintz, *Sweetness Is Power: The Place of Sugar in Modern History* (New York, 1985); Robin Blackburn, *The Making of New World Slavery: From the Baroque to the Modern, 1492–1800* (London, 1997); Eric Williams, *Capitalism and Slavery* (1944; rpt. Chapel Hill, N.C., 1994); James, *Black Jacobins*.

for the major European powers. By 1750, sugar would overtake grain as the most valuable commodity entering the global market. The total tonnage of sugar exports from the British islands would increase by nearly fivefold between 1700 and 1787, with the volume shipped from the French West Indies increasing twelvefold over the same period. By 1787, the French and British Caribbean provided 80 percent of the world's sugar. The commerce in human beings fueled the economic growth of the region. Between 1680 and 1790, the number of enslaved Africans increased from 64,000 to 480,000 in the British West Indies and from 11,000 to 675,000 in the French islands. By 1773, imports to Britain from Jamaica alone were nearly five times as valuable as imports from Britain's North American colonies combined. In Barbara Solow's concise summary, "What moved in the Atlantic in these centuries was predominantly slaves, the output of slaves, the inputs to slave societies, and the goods and services purchased with the earnings on slave products." What also moved were representations of West Indian slavery.[20]

These facts were widely appreciated by eighteenth-century chroniclers. Consider the following passage from Abbé Raynal's *Philosophical and Political History of the Settlements and Trade of the Europeans in the East and West Indies* (1776), near the end of its long examination of the Caribbean possessions of France, England, Spain, Holland, and Portugal:

> The labours of the people settled in those islands are the sole basis of the African trade: they extend the fisheries and the cultures of North America, afford a good market for the manufactures of Asia, and double, perhaps treble, the activity of all Europe. They may be considered as the principle cause of the rapid motion which now agitates the universe. This ferment must increase, in proportion as cultures, that are so capable of being extended, shall approach nearer to their highest degree of perfection.

For Raynal, the West India trades would continue to link the fates of five continents.[21]

---

20. Barbara Solow, *Slavery and the Rise of the Atlantic System* (Cambridge, 1993), 1. Statistics are from Blackburn, *Making of New World Slavery*, 403. See also Richard B. Sheridan, *Sugar and Slavery: An Economic History of the British West Indies, 1623–1775* (London, 1973); Richard S. Dunn, *Sugar and Slaves: The Rise of the Planter Class in the English West Indies, 1624–1713* (Chapel Hill, N.C., 1972); Richard Pares, *Yankees and Creoles: The Trade between North America and the West Indies before the American Revolution* (London, 1956); Lowell J. Ragatz, *The West Indian Approach to the Study of American Colonial History* (London, 1935).

21. Abbé [Guillaume-Thomas François] Raynal, *A Philosophical and Political History of the Settle-*

Natural history is among the most important structuring discourses of this influential treatise. At this key juncture in his argument, Raynal assumes an ideal reader who is conversant in the natural history of the Greater and Lesser Antilles, in part because he has himself labored to form that reader. The authority of his prediction depends on the accumulated weight of empirical detail in prior sections, which had discussed the flora, fauna, soil, climate, and geography of dozens of individual islands, drawing on firsthand reports from legions of colonial naturalists. In articulating his commercial vision, moreover, Raynal draws on the idiom of post-Newtonian natural philosophy, blending empirical precision with theoretical sweep as he describes the systematic unfolding of commercial and agricultural history.[22]

The importance of natural history to his treatise is anything but anomalous. Gaining a secure institutional footing with the chartering of the Royal Society and the Académie royale des sciences, the discourse rapidly attained new prestige and influence. By the early eighteenth century, as historian Richard Drayton describes it, natural history had "captured the attention of the upper and middle classes of imperial Britain." By the end of the century, it served as lingua franca of letters, art, and politics in Europe and the Americas. Within this broader milieu, Raynal's focus on the West Indies is hardly anomalous, either. Science traveled predominantly along trade routes in the eighteenth century, and with the growth of the triangle trade those routes invariably converged in the sugar islands, radiating outward to the ends of the globe. The archive of West Indian natural history is thus both deep and varied, as historians of science have begun to recognize. The region is at the core of "colonial bioprospecting," through which, as described by Londa Schiebinger, Europeans scoured the tropics for new sources of foods, drugs, dyes, and luxury goods. For Drayton, similarly, it is through its efforts in the Caribbean that the Royal Society "harnessed national commerce to the chariot of natural history," an effort imperative to the success of mercantilism as an economic philosophy and imperialism as a political ideal. Parrish further highlights the preeminent status of the Caribbean among early botanists, arguing, "In the late seventeenth century, the southern colonies and the Caribbean became especially key zones of

ments and Trade of the Europeans in the East and West Indies* (1798), 6 vols., trans. J. O. Justamond (New York, 1969), V, 107.

22. On the popularity of Raynal's treatise, see Robert Darnton, *The Forbidden Best-Sellers of Prerevolutionary France* (New York, 1995), 65.

nature inquiry and collection." The diverse writings of these botanists and explorers constitute a major colonial American literature.[23]

Correspondence was the lifeblood of natural history. By the 1680s, building on the encouraging response to earlier West Indian questionnaires, the Royal Society sought additional informants among Barbadian planters, even as it received numbers of letters from established sources in Jamaica. The society also sought contributions from the French West Indies, fostering routine cosmopolitan exchange. The Jesuit missionary Charles Plumier (who would publish his *Description des plantes de l'Amerique* in 1695) corresponded frequently. Nor was the society the only metropolitan institution devoted to cultivating correspondence. In 1689, upon his return from Jamaica, Sloane helped to establish the Temple Coffee House Botany Club. He thus helped to make Caribbean natural history a vital activity within one of the new voluntary associations and sites of sociability so significant to the development of the bourgeois "public sphere." During the first decades of the century, the Botany Club received even more correspondence on Caribbean nature than did the Royal Society itself. Individual collectors such as James Petiver, meanwhile, augmented the private initiative of the Botany Club. Of the eighty-four individuals listed as his colonial correspondents, a full fifty-four had resided in or traveled through the Caribbean and South Carolina (commonly referred to as "Carolina in the West Indies"). By comparison, New England and Pennsylvania were home to only four correspondents. By midcentury, a far-flung and tightly integrated epistolary network linked London to the West Indies, with dozens of informers representing every British West Indian island, whereas "Barbados and Jamaica tended to dominate the flow of correspondence and exchange of data" from British America.[24]

English authors depended intimately on these correspondents as they began to compile printed chronicles of the region. But they also relied on previous Spanish and French volumes. Composed during his tenure as overseer of the mines in Hispaniola and later governor of Santo Domingo, Gonzalo Fernández de Oviedo's *Historia general y natural de las Indias*

23. Richard Drayton, *Nature's Government: Science, Imperial Britain, and the "Improvement" of the World* (New Haven, Conn., 2000), 17 (quotation), 62–71; Londa Schiebinger, *Plants and Empire: Colonial Bioprospecting in the Atlantic World* (Cambridge, Mass., 2007), 75–82; Parrish, *American Curiosity*, 19.

24. Raymond Phineas Stearns, *Science in the British Colonies of America* (Chicago, 1970), 212–220, 260, 315, 337–397 (quotation on 337); Stearns, "James Petiver: Promoter of Natural Science, c. 1663–1718," American Antiquarian Society, *Proceedings*, LXII (1952), 243–365; Parrish, *American Curiosity*, 19. On coffeehouses and the public sphere, see Warner, *Letters of the Republic*, x; David S. Shields, *Civil Tongues and Polite Letters in British America* (Chapel Hill, N.C., 1997), xiii–xxxiii, 19–22, 52–63.

(1535) proved a durable and adaptable source, with long sections translated into English by Richard Eden in *Decades of the New World or West India* (1555) and subsequently republished in Samuel Purchas's *Hakluytus Posthumus* (1625). By the mid-seventeenth century, numerous French publications were also available to English readers, including Charles de Rochefort's *Histoire naturelle et morale des Iles Antilles de l'Amérique* (1658; translated into English by John Davies in 1666) and the works of Jean-Baptiste Du Tertre (1667–1671) and Charles Plumier (1693).[25]

Inspired by this precedent, a few English authors had begun to publish original books on the region by the late 1600s, including William Hughes's *American Physitian* (1672) and Sloane's *Catalogus plantarum quæ in insula Jamaica* (1696). The topic was also a prominent interest among travel writers. Richard Ligon's *True and Exact History of the Island of Barbadoes* (1657) included detailed descriptions and engravings of commercially valuable plants. The publication of Sloane's *Voyage to . . . Jamaica* (1707–1725), however, was followed by a deluge of English texts over the next century, even as French naturalists sustained their pace. Volumes appeared from Maria Sibylla Merian (1705), Jean-Baptiste Labat (1722), Catesby (1731–1743), Charles Leslie (1740), Pierre Barrère (1741), William Smith (1745), Griffith Hughes (1750), Patrick Browne (1756), Jean-Baptiste Thibault de Chanvalon (1763), Philippe Fermin (1765), Edward Bancroft (1769), M. Fusele Aublet (1775), and Père Nicolson (1776), to name only some. The Age of Revolutions did little to immediately alter this basic cultural landscape. Extensive treatises continued to appear, including multivolume works by Edward Long (1774), Bryan Edwards (1793), and Méderic Louis-Élie Moreau de Saint-Méry (1797). The publication, reprinting, and translation of these volumes played a substantial role in the business of enlightenment.[26]

25. Gonzalo Fernández de Oviedo y Valdés, *Historia general y natural de las Indias* (Seville, 1535); Richard Eden, *Decades of the New World or West India* (London, 1555); Charles de Rochefort, *Histoire naturelle et morale des Iles Antilles de l'Amérique* (Rotterdam, 1658); [Rochefort], *The History of the Caribby-Islands, viz, Barbados, St Christophers, St Vincents, Martinico, Dominico, Barbouthos, Montserrat, Mevis, Antego, Etc.*, trans. John Davies (London, 1666); Jean-Baptiste Du Tertre, *Histoire générale des Ant-Isles habitées par les Français*, 4 vols. (Paris, 1667–1671); Charles Plumier, *Description des plantes de l'Amérique avec leurs figures* (Paris, 1693); Samuel Purchas, *Hakluytus Posthumus; or, Purchas His Pilgrimes* (London, 1625).

26. William Hughes, *The American Physitian; or, A Treatise of the Roots, Plants, Trees, Shrubs, Fruit, Herbs, etc. Growing in the English Plantations in America* (London, 1672); Hans Sloane, *Catalogus plantarum quæ in insula Jamaica sponte proveniunt* (London, 1696); Richard Ligon, *A True and Exact History of the Island of Barbadoes . . .* (London, 1657); Charles Plumier, *Nova plantarum americanarum genera* (Paris, 1705); Maria Sibylla Merian, *Metamorphosis insectorum Surinamensium* (Amsterdam,

Such texts served instrumental purposes. Flora and fauna were valuable commodities, and their cultivation and survival in the Caribbean was threatened by formidable ecological problems. As David Watts argues, the introduction of sugar monoculture produced "severe biological responses, which changed the nature of many plant and animal communities within the region for ever." By the 1730s, Caribbean ecology had been transformed almost entirely, as settlers dedicated themselves to cultivating a few cash crops for overseas export. The consequences of such practices were difficult to anticipate and not always favorable to the commercial empires that set them in motion. Almost from the inception of the sugar revolution, signs of its seemingly inevitable collapse were already apparent. Problems with deforestation, soil erosion, soil exhaustion, and the invasion of pest species plagued a rising plantocracy, leading to declining agricultural yields and waves of species extinction. Such crises resulted from the fact that, like the vast majority of people and consumer products in the Caribbean, much of the flora and fauna was also transplanted. As Schiebinger puts it, "By the eighteenth century there were few unadulterated indigenous plants, humans, or knowledges to be collected in the West Indies: peoples and plants, languages and knowledges had churned, mingled, and melded for over two hundred years."[27]

1705); Jean-Baptiste Labat, *Nouveau voyage aux isles de l'Amerique: Contenant l'histoire naturelle de ces pays, l'origine, les moeurs, la religion, et le gouvernement des habitans anciens et modernes*, 6 vols. (Paris, 1722); [Charles Leslie], *A New History of Jamaica, from the Earliest Accounts to the Taking of Porto Bello by Vice-Admiral Vernon, in Thirteen Letters from a Gentleman to His Friend* (London, 1740); Pierre Barrère, *Essai sur l'histoire naturelle de la France equinoxiale* (Paris, 1741); William Smith, *A Natural History of Nevis, and the Rest of the English Leeward Charibee Islands in America* . . . (Cambridge, 1745); Griffith Hughes, *The Natural History of Barbados: In Ten Books* (London, 1750); Patrick Browne, *The Civil and Natural History of Jamaica* . . . (London, 1756); Jean-Baptiste Thibault de Chanvalon, *Voyage a la Martinique, contenant diverses observations sur la physique, l'histoire naturelle, l'agriculture, les mœurs, et les usages de cette isle* (Paris, 1763); Philippe Fermin, *Histoire naturelle de la Hollande équinoxiale; ou, Description des animaux, plantes, fruits, et autres curiosités naturelles, qui se trouvent dans la colonie de Surinam* (Amsterdam, 1765); Edward Bancroft, *An Essay on the Natural History of Guiana, in South America: Containing a Description of Many Curious Productions in the Animal and Vegetable Systems of That Country* . . . (London, 1769); M. Fusele Aublet, *Histoire des plantes de la Guiane françoise* (Paris, 1775); Père Nicholson, *Essai sur l'histoire naturelle de l'isle de Saint-Domingue, avec des figures en taille-douce* (Paris, 1776); [Edward Long], *The History of Jamaica; or, General Survey of the Antient and Modern State of That Island* . . . , 3 vols. (London, 1774); Bryan Edwards, *The History, Civil and Commercial, of the British Colonies in the West Indies*, 2 vols. (London, 1793); [Méderic Louis-Élie] Moreau de Saint-Méry, *Description topographique, physique, civile, politique, et historique de la partie française de l'isle Saint-Domingue* . . . , 3 vols. (Philadelphia, 1797).

27. David Watts, *The West Indies: Patterns of Development, Culture, and Environmental Change since 1492* (New York, 1990), 438; Schiebinger, *Plants and Empire*, 14. On ecological transformation, see also Richard H. Grove, *Green Imperialism: Colonial Expansion, Tropical Island Edens and the Origins of Environmentalism, 1600–1860* (New York, 1995), 63–72.

This contemporary scholarly analogy between plants and peoples in the West Indies is, perhaps surprisingly, one that the readers of eighteenth-century natural histories would have recognized. The West Indian specimen was regarded not only as a source of economic value and empiricist knowledge but also as a powerful heuristic lens for contemplating the modernity of the Caribbean plantation. The transformation of the West Indian environment was directly related to those radical processes of social and economic upheaval that were embodied by and centered on the tropical plantation. In consuming a seemingly endless series of printed texts from the region, learned readers engaged in a sustained and nuanced meditation on the implications of these transformations for the British Empire more broadly, not only because they were the acknowledged material basis of metropolitan refinement but also because they seemed like intensified versions of the kinds of social, cultural, and economic change that were simultaneously occurring at home and as a result of circumatlantic commerce.[28]

The Specimen-as-Emblem

This consciousness of the region is most clearly discerned when we attend to the formal properties of natural history as a literary genre. It should be emphasized here, however, that, in describing natural history as a genre, the intention is not to diminish or obscure its importance to the history of empiricist science. The aim is to shed light on the process through which the gradual diffusion of empiricist principles in the culture at large led to a new understanding of genres as particular kinds of epistemological instruments.

The revival of georgic verse provides a good illustration of this new conception. As Kevis Goodman demonstrates, by the early eighteenth century, commentators such as Joseph Addison had begun to theorize the representational capacities of georgic verse on the model of new "artifical organ[s]" (such as the microscope) that were the source of endless fascination for the virtuosi. Part of the appeal of georgic for these commentators derived from its apparent fidelity to "the paradoxical logic at work within the new science, whereby the demand for sense-immediacy was met by a multiplication of the techniques of mediation." Fascinated by the genre's distinctive combination of homely subject matter (the virtues of rural labor) and opu-

---

28. Mimi Sheller argues, "The Caribbean island is one of the first 'global icons' to encapsulate modernity, enfolding within itself a deep history of relations of consumption, luxury, and privilege for some." See *Consuming the Caribbean: From Arawaks to Zombies* (New York, 2003), 37.

lent diction (including obscure technical terms), and deeply engaged by the new science, Addison and others "explore[d] the specificity of poetry as one epistemological instrument among others." Much like the new ocular technology of the microscope, such commentators proposed, georgic provided a new verbal medium for the deliberate enhancement and extension of sensory perception, allowing for the influx of new kinds of empirical knowledge. As wielded by poets such as James Thomson and William Cowper, georgic verse functioned as a "microscopic eye" for perceiving troubling new social realities at the outer limits of empire, as in Thomson's account of summer in the tropics in *The Seasons* (1730).[29]

Although critics such as Addison sought to recast georgic on the model of the new science, the process of interaction between literary and scientific culture could as easily work the other way around. Natural history writers in turn drew on the model of georgic and other nascent genres. In exploring the specificity of that genre in this study, however, the emphasis will be, not on the relationship between natural history and georgic (surely a rich area for future research), but between natural history and the emergent novel. There is a venerable tradition of understanding the emergent novel as a product of the interaction between residual early modern genres such as chivalric romance and Christian pilgrimage and new empiricist techniques for the representation of physical places, individual characters, natural objects, and mental processes, with the Royal Society as one influential site for the development and dissemination of the latter. The reshaping of generic categories as a result of this interaction, furthermore, has long been understood as integral to the "rise" of the novel as a dominant cultural instrument, one capable of mediating new problems of epistemology and socio-ethical understanding associated with the rise of mercantile capitalism and liberal individualism.[30]

Thus the pages of early novels are filled with reconstituted emblems. The early novel is the product of a moment of transition in the late seventeenth century when, as Cynthia Sundberg Wall argues, "the Puritan habit of emblematization becomes absorbed into fictional techniques," simultaneous

29. Kevis Goodman, *Georgic Modernity and British Romanticism: Poetry and the Mediation of History* (New York, 2004), 12, 22, 56–66. On early American georgic, see Timothy Sweet, *American Georgics: Economy and Environment in Early American Literature* (Philadelphia, 2001); David S. Shields, *Oracles of Empire: Poetry, Politics, and Commerce in British America, 1690–1750* (Chicago, 1990).

30. On empiricism and the novel, see Ian Watt, *The Rise of the Novel: Studies in Defoe, Richardson, and Fielding* (Berkeley, Calif., 1957), 9–34; Michael McKeon, *The Origins of the English Novel, 1600–1740* (Baltimore, 1987), 65–89.

with the absorption of new protocols for empirical description. Representations of physical objects in works such as Daniel Defoe's *Life and Strange Surprising Adventures of Robinson Crusoe* (1719), to specify one canonical instance, possess more empirical substance and specificity than in early modern allegories such as John Bunyan's *Pilgrim's Progress* (1678) but frequently retain the basic function of the emblem as an orienting device for discerning providential patterns.[31]

In ways that both derive from and bear upon the development of the early novel, the genre of natural history was also informed by the interaction between empiricist technique and emblematic method, however starkly such a notion contradicts Michel Foucault's account of the rise of natural history. For Foucault, natural history emerges in the seventeenth century as the quintessential expression of a new "classical" episteme, marking a decisive break with prior assumptions structuring the representation of nature. Before the classical period, "to write the history of a plant or an animal was as much a matter of describing the resemblances that could be found in it, the virtues that it was thought to possess, the legends and stories with which it had been involved, its place in heraldry, the medicaments that were concocted from its substance, the foods it provided, what the ancients recorded of it, and what travellers might have said of it." These assumptions are most fully embodied by the book of emblems, a genre that includes massive serial works by Joachim Camerarius and Ulisse Aldrovandi. As William B. Ashworth, Jr., argues, these texts function emblematically in that they seek to capture "the entire web of associations that inextricably links human culture and the animal world." For Foucault, the age of the emblem gives way to a new cultural ideal of empirical objectivity that depends, in Thomas Sprat's classic formulation, on linguistic practices that are purely referential of things, stripped of metaphor and rhetorical ornamentation. Such practices seek to close the distance between things and words, "to bring language as close as possible to the observing gaze."[32]

31. Cynthia Sundberg Wall, *The Prose of Things: Transformations of Description in the Eighteenth Century* (Chicago, 2006), 108. Through close readings of Bunyan and Defoe, Wall argues, "Early fiction tends to use the detail emblematically, but it frequently invests those emblems with a rich ordinariness, a telling local concreteness, that seems to hold them more firmly to the here and now than the hereafter. The things in *The Pilgrim's Progress, Part II (1684)*, for example, paradoxically transcend their emblematic status and behave more like ordinary things-in-themselves" (3). Whereas Wall's analysis of reconstituted emblems emphasizes the progressive transformation of emblems into novelistic details, my own stresses the persistence of emblematic technique in prose narrative throughout the eighteenth century.

32. Michel Foucault, *The Order of Things: An Archaeology of the Human Sciences* (New York, 1970), 129, 132; Thomas Sprat, *History of the Royal Society*, ed. Jackson I. Cope and Harold Whitmore Jones

There can be little question that, over the long run, this modern ideal of "truth to nature" supplanted emblematic method. But emblematic techniques retained an important function within scientific discourse well into the eighteenth century. Printed natural histories continued to rely on a kind of reconstituted emblem that I call the "specimen-as-emblem."[33]

Since the early decades of the Royal Society, even committed empiricists such as Robert Boyle had envisioned the purpose of empirical description largely in emblematic terms. Boyle asserts,

> The Book of Nature is to an ordinary Gazer, and a Naturalist, like a rare Book of Hieroglyphicks to a Child, and a Philosopher: the one is sufficiently pleas'd with the Oddnesse and Variety of the Curious Pictures that adorne it; whereas the other is not only delighted with those outward objects that gratifie his sense, but receives a much higher satisfaction in admiring the knowledg of the Author, and in finding out and inriching himselfe with those abstruse and vailed Truths dexterously hinted in them.

Through sustained observation, Boyle advocates here, the natural specimen becomes a medium for the revelation of spiritual knowledge and providential meaning. Perhaps especially in the colonial Americas, such assumptions proved remarkably durable, enjoying a long and vibrant afterlife.[34]

Richard Ligon's *True and Exact History of the Island of Barbadoes* (1657, 1673) provides a clear example of the interplay between empiricist descrip-

---

(St. Louis, Mo., 1959), 113; William B. Ashworth, Jr., "Emblematic Natural History of the Renaissance," in N. Jardine, J. A. Secord, and E. C. Spary, eds., *The Cultures of Natural History* (Cambridge, 1996), 17–37, esp. 35.

33. On the transition from "truth to nature" to "objectivity," see Lorraine Daston and Peter Galison, *Objectivity* (New York, 2007), esp. 55–63.

34. [Robert Boyle], *Some Considerations Touching the Usefulnesse of Experimental Naturall Philosophy, Propos'd in Familiar Discourses to a Friend, by Way of Invitation to the Study of It* (Oxford, 1663), 3–4 (discussed in Wall, *Prose of Things*, 77–78). On visual emblems in early modern natural history, see Ashworth, "Emblematic Natural History of the Renaissance," in Jardine, Secord, and Spary, eds., *Cultures of Natural History*, 17–38; Ashworth, "Natural History and the Emblematic World View," in David C. Lindberg and Robert S. Westman, eds., *Reappraisals of the Scientific Revolution* (Cambridge, 1990), 303–332; Kay Dian Kriz, "Curiosities, Commodities, and Transplanted Bodies in Hans Sloane's 'Natural History of Jamaica,'" *William and Mary Quarterly*, 3d Ser., LVII (2000), 35–78. On linguistic emblems in early modern prose narrative and natural history, see Wall, *Prose of Things*, 96–114; J. Paul Hunter, *The Reluctant Pilgrim: Defoe's Emblematic Method and the Quest for Form in Robinson Crusoe* (Baltimore, 1966). An area for further research concerns the relationship between Anglo-Atlantic and Ibero-Atlantic genealogies of emblematic reading. The subject is addressed in Jorge Cañizares-Esguerra, *Puritan Conquistadors: Iberianizing the Atlantic, 1550–1700* (Stanford, Calif., 2006). Cañizares-Esguerra suggestively remarks, "It would seem that what scholars of early modern Catholicism have called the 'baroque,' scholars of Calvinism have called 'typology,' namely, exuberantly allegorical reading of the Book of Nature" (121).

tion and emblematic method. Describing the banana tree in one of the numerous specimen depictions that made the book a source of considerable interest among the virtuosi, Ligon argues the utility of the species on surprising grounds. Following his initial concession that the banana is less nourishing than the plantain, Ligon continues,

> Yet she has somewhat to delight the eyes, which the other wants, and that is the picture of Christ upon the Cross; so lively exprest, as no Limner can do it (with one colour) more exactly; and this is seen, when you cut the fruit just cross as you do the foot of Ferne, to find a spread Eagle: but this is much more perfect, the head hanging down, the armes extended to the full length, with some little elevation; and the feet cross one upon another.

The aesthetic delight provided by this "picture of Christ" goes hand in hand with its spiritual application. After commenting on the superiority of this natural crucifix to the most expert engraving, Ligon offers the following interpretation:

> Much may be said upon the subject by better wits, and abler souls then [sic] mine: My contemplation being only this, that since those men dwelling in that place professing the names of Christians, and denying to preach to those poor ignorant harmless souls the *Negroes*, the doctrine of Christ Crucified, which might convert many of them to his worship, he himself has set up his own Cross, to reproach these men, who rather then [sic] they will lose the hold they have of them as slaves, will deny them the benefit and blessing of being Christians. Otherwise, why is the figure set up for these to look on, that never heard of Christ, and God never made any thing useless, or in vain.

The passage pursues a literalized version of emblematic interpretation, disclosing concrete evidence of providential design within the keenly observed particulars of the narrator's natural surroundings. Because of such practices, the specimen-as-emblem provided a heuristic lens for contemplating the moral and ideological conundrum of colonial slavery. We find here a classic example of the tradition of thought that historian Christopher Leslie Brown names "antislavery without abolitionism."[35]

---

35. Richard Ligon, *A True and Exact History of the Island of Barbadoes: Illustrated with a Map of the Island, as Also the Principal Trees and Plants There, Set Forth in Their Due Proportions and Shapes, Drawn out by Their Several and Respective Scales* . . . (London, 1673), 82. Ligon's text remains under-

Chapter 1 traces the interconnected development of empiricist method and emblematic technique in Sloane's *Voyage to . . . Jamaica,* a text that played no small part in securing Sloane's reputation as a leading figure of the new science. Having arrived in London in the late 1670s as an aspiring physician and naturalist and been elected an FRS (Fellow of the Royal Society) in 1685 through his ties with Robert Boyle and John Ray, Sloane accepted an appointment in 1686 as physician to the duke of Albemarle during his term as governor of Jamaica, hoping to capitalize on the burgeoning interest in the natural history of the island among virtuosi, coffeehouse intellectuals, merchants, investors, and physicians. The venture was an unqualified success. Returning to London after fifteen months with some eight hundred dried specimens, along with income from his new wife's Jamaican plantations, Sloane established the Chelsea Physic Garden as an important center of experimental botany, going on to serve as secretary (1691–1713) and then president (1727–1741) of the Royal Society. Although Sloane's importance to the history of science in general and to the history of plant classification, in particular, has long been acknowledged, the significance of his published writings on Jamaica for the literary history of the British Atlantic world has remained almost entirely unexplored. Yet Sloane's experiments in the *Voyage to . . . Jamaica* are related to the major literary innovations of the period. In order to augment the appeal of his text to a diverse readership and to conform to new representational protocols of the Royal Society, Sloane pursued strategies for synthesizing empirical description, first-person narration, and emblematic method. *Voyage to . . . Jamaica* is the product of a transformative moment in British Atlantic literary history when the collision between empiricist and emblematic methods played an essential role in the evolution of the emergent novel, including circumatlantic narratives such as Aphra Behn's *Oroonoko; or, The Royal Slave. A True History* (1688) and Daniel Defoe's *Life and Strange Surprising Adventures of Robinson Crusoe.*[36]

Chapter 2 focuses on Mark Catesby's *Natural History of Carolina,* argu-

---

studied by literary critics. For two insightful interpretations, see Myra Jehlen, *Readings at the Edge of Literature* (Chicago, 2002), 179–191; Keith A. Sandiford, *The Cultural Politics of Sugar: Caribbean Slavery and Narratives of Colonialism* (Cambridge, 2000), 24–40. On "antislavery without abolitionism," see Christopher Leslie Brown, *Moral Capital: Foundations of British Abolitionism* (Chapel Hill, N.C., 2006), 33–101.

36. John F. M. Cannon, "Botanical Collections," in Arthur MacGregor, ed., *Sir Hans Sloane: Collector, Scientist, Antiquary, Founding Father of the British Museum* (London, 1994), 135–149. Cannon asserts, "It would be difficult to overstate the significance of the Sloane herbarium for the history of plant classification" (136).

ing that Catesby's descriptions and engravings extend Sloane's precedent in ways that have far-reaching consequences for the development of scientific and literary culture within the British Americas themselves. Orchestrating a dynamic interpretive movement between images and linguistic descriptions within printed volumes that were among the most expensive and technically ambitious of the eighteenth century, his book modifies the basic emblematic techniques at the heart of Sloane's text. Focusing the attention of learned readers on new environmental relationships in the Carolinas—relationships that have emerged as a direct consequence of plantation development—his text is designed to prompt reflection on the implications of the natural and human history of the colony for the future of British cultural refinement and intellectual progress. Because they chart the rapid expansion of the West Indian plantation into southern North America, Catesby's volumes were of special interest to early mainland naturalists such as John Bartram, William Byrd II, and Eliza Lucas Pinckney as they construed their own identities through study of the natural world.

Reaping the Early Republic

The longer section of this book traces an occluded history of American Enlightenment, arguing that British Atlantic natural histories such as *Voyage to . . . Jamaica* and the *Natural History of Carolina* exert a substantial influence on the literary culture of late-colonial North America and the early United States. The authors at the core of this section inhabited an intellectual culture still preoccupied with Caribbean slavery and commerce and a social world in which the wealth produced by Caribbean plantations was vital to colonial and (later) national survival. People, commodities, and cultural practices flowed unrelentingly across emergent political borders, with seemingly little resistance. Like their peers throughout the Atlantic world, early American elites consumed, reprinted, and translated natural historical volumes focused on the sugar islands, subscribed to expensive and technically innovative maps of the region, and read magazine and newspaper pieces on the region's weather and curiosities. They founded museum collections and botanical gardens in which West Indian specimens occupied a prominent position, maintained a vigorous correspondence with learned societies and individuals throughout the Caribbean, and organized collecting expeditions to the southern fringe of North America. They turned to signal texts by Sloane, Catesby, and dozens of others as representational models, intellectual inspirations, and authoritative references.

To register the impact of this forgotten intellectual and cultural history on early American literature, each chapter of this section pursues a historicized close reading of a single text, charting connections between the early careers of these authors and thinkers and key institutions, patrons, writings, and regions within a circumatlantic world of letters. Each chapter traces the effects of these interactions on the manuscript and epistolary sources from which the authors' best-known printed works would emerge, unearthing a series of unfinished, abandoned, or unpublished writings that engage the central ideological problems and representational strategies of prior West Indian natural histories in remarkably direct fashion.

Chapter 3 reinterprets the original published version of Crèvecoeur's *Letters* (1782) in light of his relatively obscure essay "Sketches of Jamaica and Bermudas and Other Subjects" (1773). Though it remained unpublished in Crèvecoeur's lifetime, the essay contains his earliest and most insightful meditation on Raynal's *History,* the book that, as described in the dedication of *Letters,* first awakened the author to the extended ramifications of West Indian slavery and trade. Translating Raynal's prophecy of imperial corruption and decline into quasifictional form, the sketch explores its implications for late-colonial North America. Through the novelistic fusion of empiricist description and incremental narration, the sketch refines and popularizes the narrative experiments of metropolitan naturalists such as Sloane. Describing the travels of an unseasoned colonial youth from Pennsylvania to Jamaica and back again in disillusionment, the themes and narrative pattern of the sketch would prove crucial to the organization of *Letters.*

Chapter 4 considers William Bartram's *Travels* (1791) in the context of an outpouring of texts on the natural history of colonial Florida after the Seven Years' War, when Britain moved aggressively to settle the region as a circum-Caribbean sugar colony and commercial hub and when the American Philosophical Society promoted scientific expeditions to the region. Though it remained unpublished until long after the American Revolution, *Travels* originates in a draft manuscript composed during the early 1770s. Organized around a narrative persona that blends the enlightened botanist with the Protestant pilgrim and making conscious use of emblematic techniques derived from his father's copy of the *Natural History of Carolina,* Bartram's manuscript reflects on his recent failure as a rice planter, presenting the pursuit of natural knowledge as penitence for some unspecified original sin.

Chapter 5 establishes Jefferson's *Notes on the State of Virginia* (1787) as one in a series of colonial responses to the comte de Buffon's thesis of creole degeneracy. Recovering important intertextual relationships between Jefferson's treatise and works including Edward Long's *History of Jamaica*, Bryan Edwards's *History, Civil and Commercial, of the British Colonies in the West Indies*, and Moreau de Saint-Méry's *Description topographique . . . de la partie française de l'isle Saint-Domingue*, the chapter argues that the problem of hemispheric slavery is of primary import in *Notes*. The problem would continue to weigh heavily on Jefferson's literary and political imagination throughout the 1790s, as he turned to the rhetoric of natural history to assess the Haitian Revolution. Through a sequence of personal letters, Jefferson recast his meditations on slavery from the original printed version of *Notes*, envisioning an expanded edition that would address the implications of Haiti for the future of American republicanism. In composing those letters, moreover, Jefferson entered a hemispheric ideological contest in which Saint-Dominguan exiles such as Baudry, on the one hand, and associates of Toussaint L'Ouverture, on the other, employed the discourse of natural history to divergent ends.

The final chapter uncovers the beginnings of Audubon's *Birds of America* in the artist's early career in lower Louisiana and New Orleans, a region routinely depicted both as a source of moral and physical corruption owing to Caribbean intercourse and as the key to national prosperity. Focusing on Audubon's unpublished journal of his early struggles in lower Louisiana, his published "ornithological biographies" from the region, and his later autobiographical sketch of his birth in and flight from revolutionary Saint-Domingue, the chapter casts new light on his visual aesthetics of extravagant violence. Throughout the 1820s and 1830s, Audubon planned to publish these linguistic descriptions side by side with his ornithological engravings, much in the same manner as Catesby's volumes. Recovering the allegorical dimensions of Audubon's writings, the chapter demonstrates that the appeal of the specimen-as-emblem persisted well into the nineteenth century. Through a coordinated movement between word and image, these writings dramatize Audubon's struggle to negotiate his personal history as a French West Indian creole and Saint-Dominguan exile. His earliest ornithological and artistic labors, the writings reveal, attempt to synthesize the ambitions of two contradictory efforts to chronicle the natural history of lower Louisiana at the turn of the nineteenth century. Even as Jeffersonian Republicans presented settlement of the region as essential to their vision of an expanding yeomanry, Saint-Dominguan exiles (including Baudry) argued that the development of sugar plantations in the Delta was vital to the defense of hemispheric slavery.

The Birds of America illustrates a paradox that becomes increasingly prominent in later chapters of this study, as literary nationalism begins to play a more central role. The authors under consideration in these pages fulfilled their literary ambitions through their recourse to a representational legacy that radiated outward from the West Indian plantation. As the archival record makes plain, at crucial junctures in their careers, each contemplated the publication of a natural history book that would have addressed the interrelated problems of West Indian commerce, "culture," and slavery in far more direct fashion than the printed volumes that would establish their reputations. As the record also makes plain, the nonpublication of these texts resulted less from conscious authorial intention than a variety of contingent factors, including the disruption of transatlantic networks of patronage during the American Revolution (Bartram), the shifting winds of literary fashion in the same period (Crèvecoeur), and the desire to avoid significant expenses associated with British copyright law (Audubon).

Such historical contingencies, however, cannot account entirely for the nonpublication of these books. This study also traces a number of ideological developments that bear on each author's decision to abandon or suppress his extended written meditations on West Indian affairs: the new prominence of slavery as a subject of moral and political dispute in the post-Revolutionary period, the outbreak of the Haitian Revolution, and the growth of protonationalist sentiment within the early Republic itself. Though their aesthetic practices and intellectual assumptions were shaped by their engagement with West Indian natural history, these authors also articulated a strange, new account of enlightened modernity, grounded in the material possibilities of New World nature, in which Caribbean slavery, trade, and knowledge seem present only as traces. Between the facts of planetary history as Raynal confidently proclaimed them and their reconstruction by scholars including C. L. R. James and Eric Williams lies a long history of conscious forgetting, exerting a profound impact on the development of modern culture and literature. This book is primarily about the place of the West Indies in the making of American Enlightenment. But it is also a meditation on the ways that the literature of the period effaces the West Indies from the history of modernity—though never completely.

Part I

The Nature of Slavery

Strange Things, Occult Relations

EMBLEM AND NARRATIVE IN HANS SLOANE'S

VOYAGE TO . . . JAMAICA

Hans Sloane's natural history of Jamaica begins with the fascination of things. Printed in two folio volumes in 1707 and 1725, the *Voyage to the Islands Madera, Barbados, Nieves, S. Christophers, and Jamaica* opens by recalling the childhood origins of Sloane's desire to travel to the sugar islands. Writing amid his collections of West Indian curiosities, some eighteen years after his tenure in Jamaica, the author reflects:

> I had from my Youth been very much pleas'd with the Study of Plants, and other Parts of Nature, and had seen most of those Kinds of Curiosities, which were to be found either in the Fields, or in the Gardens or Cabinets of the Curious in these Parts. The Accounts of these strange Things, which I met with in Collections, and, was inform'd, were common in the West-Indies, were not so satisfactory as I desired. I was Young, and could not be so easy, if I had not the pleasure to see what I had heard so much of, especially since it had been a great contentment to me, to see many things cultivated in *English* Gardens which I had seen grow wild in other Countries, whereof I conceived my self afterwards to be better appris'd, than I was of such as I had not seen common in the Fields, and in plenty. I thought by that means the *Ideas* of them would be better imprinted in my Mind, and that, upon occasion, both the knowledge of them and their Uses might be afterwards more familiar to me. These Inclinations remain'd with me some time after I had settled my self to practice Physic in *London,* and had had the Honour to be admitted a Fellow of the College of Physicians, as well as of the Royal Society. These unmerited Favours did not at all alter my mind, but rather incited me to do what I could to be no useless Member . . . and by that means endeavour to deserve a Place amongst so many Great and Worthy Persons.

On its surface, the passage presents Sloane's labors in Jamaica as the practical fulfillment of Lockean empiricism as a theoretical program and thus as an unquestioned public good. Dissatisfied with secondhand accounts of West Indian plants and curiosities and struck by their strangeness as displayed objects, the young Sloane is convinced that only firsthand perception of these things in their place of origin will yield an adequate understanding of them, imprinting them in his developing mind as simple ideas and rendering them available for future reflection. The passage thus suggests a clear narrative arc for the *Voyage to . . . Jamaica* that links the incremental improvement of the naturalist's intellect and character to the labor of observation and collection in the colonies.[1]

Even here at the staid opening of the text, however, there is something excessive about the intensity of Sloane's attraction to these particular "strange things." So overpowering is his youthful desire to visit the islands that the adult seizes the first opportunity to fulfill it, anxious that his new social position among the curious and learned is less than legitimate. But what if he had pursued that desire before reaching "settled" adulthood as physician and naturalist, an alternative intimated clearly by the passage? The danger of prodigality and dissipation, common enough fates for young Britons in the West Indies, shadows the text from its first pages. Moreover, the adult seems no more capable than the youth of maintaining his composure in the presence of West Indian things. There is a certain tension in Sloane's self-characterization as a "settled" adult still bound by youthful "inclinations," which seems to derive initially from some strange power in the curiosities themselves.

This opening narrative gesture points to a theme that will take on increasing importance in subsequent sections of the text. Though it helped to consolidate Sloane's reputation as a leading practitioner of the new science, the *Voyage to . . . Jamaica* is nonetheless beset by problems concerning the representation of things. Sloane was by no means alone in addressing such difficulties. As noted in the introduction of this study, since the late seventeenth century, institutions such as the Royal Society had proposed detailed guidelines for composing accurate and credible descriptions of natural objects and for integrating those descriptions into the chronological framework of a first-person travel narrative. The distinctive formal organization of *Voyage to . . . Jamaica,* as it experiments with numerous methods for synthesizing empiricist description and personal narrative, reflects Sloane's

1. Hans Sloane, *A Voyage to the Islands Madera, Barbados, Nieves, S. Christophers, and Jamaica, with the Natural History of the Herbs and Trees, Four-Footed Beasts, Fishes, Birds, Insects, Reptiles, etc. of the Last of Those Islands . . .*, 2 vols. (London, 1707–1725), I, preface (unpaginated).

close engagement with questions of epistemology and representation at the heart of scientific culture in early modern Britain. However, the self-conscious and improvisatory character of Sloane's formal experiments, and the conspicuous incoherence of the narrative structure that emerges from them, makes his text a revealing historical lens, suggesting that the problems posed by West Indian knowledge during the period were especially urgent and complex.

These problems only began with the rapid transformation of the Caribbean's natural environment, amid the almost daily introduction of new flora and fauna from around the globe and the ensuing, often severe, ecological consequences. Nor did they end with the fact that the "improvement" of natural knowledge in the region required a far-flung network of scientific correspondents, incorporating such potentially untrustworthy figures as the colonial planter and enslaved African. Rather, Sloane's most palpable difficulties with describing natural objects and phenomena and with narrating his firsthand experiences of them derive from two fundamental challenges. The first is that the value of the natural historical specimen by the early eighteenth century no longer derives exclusively, or perhaps even primarily, from its capacity to communicate natural knowledge, thus assisting in the conversion of botanical species such as sugarcane or insects such as the cochineal beetle into vendible commodities. With the emergence of a full-scale commercial society in the period, West Indian curiosities and printed natural histories had become commodities in their own right, among the myriad new consumer goods derived from the region. At the same time, the very conceptual category of the natural object had expanded to include new kinds of content, including the human inhabitants of the island as potential evidence of the effects of tropical climate on bodies, manners, and moral character. Perhaps most disturbingly, the category now encompassed that radically new "thing" that is the hereditary chattel slave—at once property and person, commodity and laborer, object of study and bearer of knowledge.

To address these challenges, Sloane turns to the representational device of the early modern emblem. For this basic understanding of *Voyage to . . . Jamaica,* I am indebted to the groundbreaking art historical scholarship of Kay Dian Kriz, the first study to approach Sloane's book not only as a valuable documentary source but also as a complex aesthetic artifact. Although it ranges widely across the text, Kriz's focus is on a sequence of four images positioned at a crucial juncture in volume I, where they provide a transitional visual essay between Sloane's lengthy introduction and a subsequent section entitled "Natural History of Jamaica," comprised of descriptions and illustrations of the island's flora and fauna. (These images are numbered separately from the 274 plates included in the "Natural History" proper.) Other than the map of Jamaica, which opens the sequence, all of these images combine natural specimens and human artifacts within the same pictorial field, in ways that distinguish them from most other illustrations in the text. The striking compositions of these images, furthermore, rely on a "heightened visual interplay between disparate objects." Their prominent structural position and distinctive form and content, Kriz argues, testify to their special importance. Her central insight is that the plates are structured according to traditional protocols of emblematic reading, inviting the reader to draw intricate and subtle connections between a visual image, its printed label, and relevant linguistic descriptions scattered throughout the two volumes (and collated in a detailed index). Her readings of the engravings have gone far toward clarifying the interpretive practices that early modern readers brought to bear on printed natural histories, and, in so doing, they have uncovered a broader intellectual culture in which "images of human artifacts, plants, and animals helped articulate the new and fraught relationships under construction in the Atlantic world," whether between investors, merchants, and consumers in Europe and the various inhabitants of the West Indies or between planters and enslaved Africans in the West Indies themselves.[2]

Building from this analysis, this chapter establishes the importance of *Voyage to . . . Jamaica* for British Atlantic literary history. Sloane's recourse to a version of the early modern emblem as a crucial organizing device within a text also deeply informed by emergent empiricist criteria for description and narration hardly occurred in a vacuum. It is the mark of his close engagement with a literary culture in which the complex interaction between emblematic method and empiricist technique was integral to the development of new kinds of prose narrative. We can gain additional insight into Sloane's text by comparing it to a series of contemporaneous prose narratives that were also preoccupied with West Indian "things"— Richard Ligon's *True and Exact History of the Island of Barbadoes* (1657, 1673), Aphra Behn's *Oroonoko; or, The Royal Slave. A True History* (1688),

2. Kay Dian Kriz, *Slavery, Sugar, and the Culture of Refinement: Picturing the British West Indies, 1700–1840* (New Haven, Conn., 2008), 11, 16. Kriz's specific argument concerns the kinds of repressed memory and consciousness that begin to surface in Sloane's text as a result of this reading practice. It is "in the strange disjunctions among particular images and between image and text that one can glimpse the traces of human conflict and resistance" (15), including forms of slaveholder violence and slave resistance that are all but banished from the field of direct visual representation.

and Daniel Defoe's *Life and Strange Surprising Adventures of Robinson Crusoe* (1719).

The sequence includes two signal works in the history of the emergent novel. As discussed in the introduction of this study, one effect of the attempt to synthesize empiricist description with traditional allegorical genres in early novels such as *Oroonoko* and *Robinson Crusoe* means that the pages of those narratives are filled with reconstituted emblems, with descriptions of physical objects that are imbued with more particularity and ordinariness than in John Bunyan's *Pilgrim's Progress*, for instance, but nevertheless retain the basic hermeneutic function of emblematic things. Considered from this vantage, we have also seen, the persistence of the emblem in the literary culture of the eighteenth century is best explained, not as a residue of Protestant allegory in a period of secularization that eventually will sweep it away, but rather as vital to the capacity of the early novel to mediate what Michael McKeon calls the "transition to modernity." It is in part through emblematic method rather than despite it that the genre addresses those new questions of truth and virtue posed by the rise of scientific empiricism, mercantile capitalism, and liberal individualism.[3]

In the texts under consideration here, the relevance of emblematic method derives in part from a desire to contemplate the moral implications of colonial slavery, as in Ligon's description of the cross-section of a banana with its seeds arrayed in a perfect icon of Christ crucified. The history of the circumatlantic novel, however, suggests another function of the reconstituted emblem. Drawing on J. G. A. Pocock's account of the rise of speculative finance after the financial revolution of the 1690s, critics such as Catherine Gallagher and Ian Baucom have argued that the early novel provided a crucial form of epistemological training for the subjects of a new transoceanic empire. By the 1710s, as Pocock states, the financial revolution had given rise to a situation in which "reality was seen as endangered by fiction and fantasy," as the worth of "imaginary" forms of paper (including stocks, government bonds, and bills of exchange) began to exceed the value of tangible property such as land and bullion. Issues of credibility and trust thus came to dominate the cultural landscape. A new system of finance capital required some program of reification to secure its legitimacy. The early realist novel, according to Gallagher and Baucom, contributed

3. Michael McKeon, *The Origins of the English Novel, 1600–1740* (1987; rpt. Baltimore, 2002), xxi; Cynthia Sundberg Wall, *The Prose of Things: Transformations of Description in the Eighteenth Century* (Chicago, 2006), 77, 108, 110.

to such a program not only by familiarizing readers with an array of new social types inhabiting the edges of empire but by training readers to invest suppositional characters with real passion and sympathy, to credit those fictional identities with real value. Readers of novels grew accustomed to performing a cognitive procedure that was fundamental to a new speculative economy. As Baucom notes, the novel provided the epistemological conditions of possibility for the extension of finance capital throughout the circumatlantic world.[4]

However insightful, the argument attributes far too much agency to a single literary genre, one that did not saturate the literary culture of the colonial Americas until the end of the eighteenth century (when colonial authors themselves began to publish novels). This chapter extends and challenges such accounts of the early novel by arguing that natural history is the eighteenth-century literary genre (or incipient genre) most directly engaged with the problem of slavery and finance in its full circumatlantic dimensions. This is why early novelists such as Behn and Defoe found natural history such a vital representational model.

Throughout *Voyage to . . . Jamaica*, Sloane's representations of natural specimens mediate the problem of finance in two related, if at times contradictory, ways. On one hand, by adhering to empiricist protocols for description, narration, and visual display, Sloane attempts to persuade readers that they are virtual witnesses of his firsthand inquiries, that they may credit his representations as real. Through his recourse to emblematic protocols, on the other hand, he also trains his readers to look through material objects for their underlying pattern or essence. As Defoe perhaps most clearly understood, this hermeneutic technique bore a close analogical relationship to new practices of financial speculation. Even as Sloane's emblematic specimens contribute to a form of epistemological training, however, they also allow the reader to reflect critically on the social and cultural effects of finance capital in the era of the triangle trade. The formal experiments of *Voyage to . . . Jamaica* reflect on the capacity of commerce and finance to transform material objects—including enslaved people—into a medium of exchange.

4. J. G. A. Pocock, *The Machiavellian Moment: Florentine Political Thought and the Atlantic Republican Tradition* (Princeton, N.J., 1975), 423–461 (quotation on 451); Pocock, *Virtue, Commerce, and History: Essays on Political Thought and History, Chiefly in the 18th Century* (Cambridge, 1985), 113; Ian Baucom, *Specters of the Atlantic: Finance Capital, Slavery, and the Philosophy of History* (Durham, N.C., 2005), 56–57, 65–72, 215–218, 277–281; Catherine Gallagher, *Nobody's Story: The Vanishing Acts of Women Writers in the Marketplace, 1670–1920* (Berkeley, Calif., 1994), xv–xvii, 194.

Harvesting Bones in Sloane's Jamaica:
Narration, Collection, Mass Death

The opening paragraph of *Voyage to . . . Jamaica* announces a set of difficult problems concerning the representation of natural objects, problems that only increase in importance and complexity during the remainder of the preface and the lengthy introduction of volume I. Indeed, Sloane's inclusion of a sequence of emblematic engravings between the introduction and the "Natural History" attempts to orient his reader toward a written text that is organized according to a variety of competing models.

Having begun the preface by recounting his lifelong fascination with West Indian curiosities, Sloane mounts a sustained defense of the utility of his book. That he found such a defense necessary is notable in itself. In an era when natural history had captured the imagination of imperial Britain and when West Indian nature was believed to possess untold economic potential, Sloane might well have assumed the utility of his endeavors. That defense becomes even more interesting when we attend to the contradictory understandings of West Indian nature at its troubled core. Sloane's first justification begins as a classic account of the enhanced stability and accuracy of knowledge gained directly through the senses and of the close affinity between natural history as a practical discipline and empiricism as a theoretical program. But it ends as something different:

> It may be ask'd me to what Purposes serve such Accounts, I answer, that the Knowlege of *Natural-History*, being Observation of Matters of Fact, is more certain than most Others. . . . These are things we are sure of, so far as our Senses are not fallible; and which, in probability, have been ever since the Creation, and will remain to the End of the World, in the same Condition we now find them: They afford great Matter of Admiring the Power, Wisdom and Providence of Almighty God, in Creating, and Preserving the things he has created. . . . And conclude them, very ignorant in the History of Nature, who say, they were the Productions of Chance.

Much as in Ligon's description of the banana, a rigorous commitment to empiricism works hand in hand with one form of emblematic interpretation. Scrutiny of the specimen yields evidence of hidden providential patterns. The new textual praxis of specimen description as delineated here thus seems to depend on an a priori assumption that Caribbean nature is fundamentally static, unchanged since divine creation. The specimen must be isolated from the contingencies of time and context so that its visible surface may be rendered in minute detail. The majority of Sloane's specimen descriptions in the "Natural History" adhere closely to this model.[5]

In Sloane's second justification, however, Caribbean nature resembles nothing so much as a "production of chance." Time and context reenter the scene:

> Another Use of this History may be, to teach the Inhabitants of the Parts where these Plants grow, their several Uses, which I have endeavour'd to do, by the best Informations I could get from Books, and the Inhabitants, either *Europeans, Indians* or *Blacks. Jamaica* had been, before it was taken by the *English,* in the possession of the *Spaniards,* almost from the time the *West-Indies* were discover'd: They had brought many *Fruit-Trees* from the *Main-Continent,* where they are Masters, and suffer no other *Europeans* to come; which throve wonderfully, and now grow as it were *Sponte:* These they made use of for Food, Physic, etc. And were forc'd to leave with their Habitations, to the *English,* and the Skill of Using them remain'd with the *Blacks* and *Indians,* many of whom came, upon a Proclamation that they should be Free, submitted peaceably, and liv'd with the *English* after the *Spaniards* had deserted it. There were among these, several which made small Plantations of their own, wherein they took care to preserve and propagate such Vegetables as grew in their own Countries, to use them as they saw occasion: I made search after these, and what I found, is related in this History.

The possession of fruit trees and other valuable plants by the English depends on an unlikely sequence of interconnected events. First cultivated by Spanish colonists who transplanted them from mainland South America, wild fruit trees are found thriving throughout the island. Sloane's phrase "as it were Sponte" points to the special difficulties posed to the naturalist by a locale shaped at all levels by such transplantations. Whereas the young Sloane longed to observe West Indian species in their natural setting, he realizes subsequently that the presence of many of these species in the West Indies—seemingly so natural—is dependent on a long history of successive dislocations. Integral to that history are the dislocations of human populations from West Africa and South America. For, amid the ruins of the Span-

---

5. Sloane, *Voyage to ... Jamaica,* I, preface.

ish colony, knowledge of these species survived only with certain "Blacks" and "Indians," who have now transmitted it to Sloane. Whereas Sloane previously had excluded oral testimony, or "hearsay," as a form of evidence, here it is fundamental to his method. To judge the veracity of that oral testimony, moreover, requires detailed knowledge of the character and life history of the informant. To sketch the character of one set of informants, the passage concludes with a description of their "plantations" (most likely their provision plots) as mirror images of the European botanical garden.[6]

Proper representation of nature understood on this second model requires narration. Things have a history that unfolds in time and that cannot be grasped through observation alone. Extracted from its local situation in the first passage, the specimen must now be reinserted into that setting and traced through the sequence of events that brought it there for the naturalist to observe in the first place. By the opposite token, the naturalist must provide a firsthand account of his progress toward and encounter with a specific informant and specimen.

Sloane maintained an unusually strong commitment to narration—first-person and otherwise—as a mode and vehicle of natural historical knowledge. By the time he began to arrange his notes from Jamaica for publication, it had long been standard in natural histories of the West Indies to examine the social and cultural life of the islands alongside their natural productions. Works as prominent as Gonzalo Fernández de Oviedo y Valdés's *De la natural hystoria de las Indias* (1526) and César de Rochefort's *Histoire naturelle et morale des Iles Antilles de l'Amérique* (1658), both familiar to the Royal Society, had established a firm precedent. Sloane's introduction to volume I includes an account of the discovery and initial settlement of Jamaica, a broad overview of the island's geography and climate (including its rivers, soil, and weather patterns), and a discussion of dietary customs among its varied inhabitants. Although this was standard to the genre, Sloane was the first author on the region to include a first-person travel narrative in a work that also contained lengthy specimen descriptions within a comprehensive catalog. More accurately, Sloane includes two separate travel narratives. Whereas a section of volume I entitled "Voyage to Jamaica" describes Sloane's circumatlantic itinerary, including his brief visits to colonies such as Barbados and Nevis, the introduction

6. Ibid. On "slave gardens" as a prominent feature of the plantation landscape and an important site of resistance, see, for instance, Jill H. Casid, *Sowing Empire: Landscape and Colonization* (Minneapolis, 2005), 206–215.

contains an account of his travels to the remote northern coast of Jamaica, where he visited the provision plots described above.[7]

Considered from the vantage of the Royal Society and its influential treatises on method, Sloane's simultaneous commitment to travel narration and specimen description was not inherently problematic. As part of its general effort to reform English prose style and to establish a scientific network encompassing the British Empire, the society had issued detailed directives for maintaining travel diaries that could later serve as the basis of first-person travel accounts. Narratives conforming to those directives appeared in the Royal Society's *Philosophical Transactions* in ever-increasing numbers throughout the Restoration. According to the issuers of these directives, narrative would enhance what McKeon calls the "documentary historicity" of the direct observations recorded in the journal, rendering the truths of the journal "more stylistically accessible and 'methodical.'" This is not to say that narrative was seen as free of epistemological complications, for the enjoinment that the author "forgo the moral judgments of an overarching narrative voice" points to the danger that the requirements of narrative might work against the Baconian injunction to collect facts indiscriminately, in the absence of any governing hypothesis. Yet there remains an implicit confidence that narrative will not alter the basic conception of the specimen, as initially observed and described in the journal, in any fundamental way.[8]

In Sloane's volumes, however, these disparate textual praxes produce a formal pattern that is anything but seamless. Although the inclusion of multiple travel narratives might in itself point to a degree of uncertainty about structure, that uncertainty is palpable in Sloane's regular musings about how and when to provide a proper description of an individual plant or animal—when first mentioned in one of his manners and customs sketches or geographic overviews, or when encountered in one of his travel narratives, or among the natural history catalogs that conclude volume I and begin volume II? As often as not, Sloane chooses to include detailed descriptions of an individual species in multiple locations in the text and to collate those accounts in his index, itself an unusual feature of his volumes.

One implication of the index is that comprehensive knowledge of a species may result from the cross-referencing of multiple depictions. Yet

---

7. Kriz, *Slavery, Sugar, and the Culture of Refinement*, 13.

8. McKeon, *Origins of the English Novel*, 103. See also Ralph Bauer, *The Cultural Geography of Colonial American Literatures: Empire, Travel, Modernity* (New York, 2003), 14–18.

Sloane's conspicuous difficulties with transitions, both between and within sections of his text, are one stylistic indication of his doubt as to the efficacy of such a process. To specify just one example, in the midst of his geographic overview of Jamaica, Sloane abruptly shifts into an extended travelogue, seemingly undecided in its opening paragraph about how to depict his physical surroundings:

> I was resolved to go to the North side of the Island, and visit the Mountains between it and the South side, to see what they brought forth. Wherefore I got some Gentlemen of the Country, one who drew in *Crayons*, a very good Guide, and a sure-footed Horse, and set out. Having passed Sixteen Miles Walk before-mentioned, where are some of the best and securest Plantations of the Island, I came to the *Magotty*, a large *Savanna* or Plain. I met here, growing in great plenty, a sort of small and low sensible Plant, not described by any person. If any one mov'd a Switch or Whip over it, as a Pen on Paper, the forms of the Letters remain'd legible for some time after: this is describ'd hereafter. I went on towards Mount *Diablo*, at the bottom of which, being benighted, I lay. . . . Our Sleep was very much interrupted by the Croaking of a sort of Tree Frogs, described hereafter, the singing of Grashoppers, and noise of night *Animals*.

Geographic writing is interrupted suddenly and without explanation by a travel narrative that all but advertises the clash between the diverse representational modes it draws from. For one thing, Sloane seems uncertain whether to treat the natural objects he encounters on the journey as bare details of physical setting (thus maintaining the momentum of his narrative) or to interrupt the narrative progression to provide specimen descriptions. The difficulty is in part resolved by referring the reader to full-scale specimen descriptions elsewhere in his volumes (to be located through the index). In the case of the "sensible Plant," however, Sloane embeds a brief account into the narrative. In so doing, he invites the reader to invest the plant with a providential significance. This is why he acknowledges (and undercuts) such allegorical modes of reading through his wry reference to his benighted condition at the foot of Mount Diablo.[9]

Such difficulties continue to bedevil the text. A mere ten pages later, travel narrative transforms into journal. Sloane abruptly announces, "For

9. Sloane, *Voyage to . . . Jamaica*, I, lxv.

the better understanding of several matters in the *West-Indies,* I think it proper to subjoin some accounts I received from several Credible Persons.... These follow without any other order than that of the time they were told me, and enter'd in my Journal which was generally when the Persons came upon their first arrival to wait on the Duke of *Albemarle* as Governour of the Island." Sequence is determined here by no other principle than when Sloane happened to hear some curious "account." The "curiosity" of these accounts is the only criterion linking them, for they touch on an eclectic range of topics—from a description of "King *Jeremy*" of the Mosquito Coast to the cochineal insect to sunken Spanish galleons. Sloane refers within these curious accounts to more learned and systematic discussions of these topics elsewhere in the text. In relaying a report on the "Cochineel-Tree" (or, more properly, the cochineal beetle, harvested from prickly pear cactus as the source of a valuable red dye), he remarks, "I shall have occasion to speak more of this hereafter." So he does in three different places in volume II— providing a standard specimen description, a discussion of the trade disputes and imperial controversies it has occasioned, and an engraving of a cochineal plantation reproduced from a Spanish natural history.[10]

Sloane's meditation on fruit trees goes far toward illuminating the kinds of formal difficulties we have just been tracing. At precisely the moment that the text announces the utility of narration, it also first confronts the difficult fact of slave agency. Sloane's initial perception of West Indian nature as a contingent outcome of human history is linked closely in the passage to the powerful agency of "things," as a result of enslaved Africans' complex social status both as objects of inquiry and purveyors of knowledge. Sloane relies on the testimony of certain "blacks," undoubtedly slaves, who, by cultivating and studying the trees, have played an active role in the history of nature.

The passage cues us to understand one of the more striking formal characteristics of Sloane's natural history in relation to a distinctive and pervasive feature of Jamaican social life. Enslaved informants played an indispensable role in the day-to-day conduct of colonial natural history. Informants ranged from field slaves familiar with the habits, traits, and location of unusual species to West African "magi" who combined, roughly, the roles of European physician and priest. Drawing on their deep knowledge of West African species transplanted to the West Indies while experimenting with new varieties they encountered daily, these "Negro Doctors" com-

10. Ibid., I, lxxvi, lxxviii. On the cochineal tree, see ibid., II, vi, 152–154, plate 9.

manded broad respect for their skilled application of herbal cures—this in an era when the authority of white male physicians remained highly disputed, both in Europe and the Americas. Sloane's putative scorn for "Negro Doctors" and their cures belies the careful attention he pays to their methods at numerous points in the text, perhaps owing to competitive jealousy. One of Sloane's most prestigious patients in Jamaica, Sir Henry Morgan, replaced him with a "Black doctor" when dissatisfied with the results of English physic.[11]

Whereas the "Negro Doctor" was a figure of considerable authority and esteem, the "obeah man" was his inverted double. Such individuals were deemed exceptionally dangerous by colonial authorities. Thought to be proficient in the use of plants as fetishes to control and manipulate their fellow slaves, obeah men were also suspected of poisoning a growing number of white colonists. By 1730—a mere five years after the publication of Sloane's second volume—slave medicine had been banned in the English sugar islands owing to fear of poisonings.[12]

That Sloane perceives the importance of narration more acutely than other naturalists of his day is linked in the text to the peculiar circumstances of West Indian social organization, which create special problems for the study of nature. One of the most pressing of these, as we have just seen, is that the boundary between specimen and naturalist, thing and agent, is neither clear nor stable. The figure of the indolent planter provides another example of this problem. The discussion of slave knowledge and agency in the meditation on Spanish fruit trees also highlights the disturbing absence of volition among English colonists. Ironically, Sloane must draw on the testimony of blacks and Indians to instruct white colonists on the uses of plants growing around them. The text in this way addresses a theory of tropical physical degeneracy and mental torpor that would surge into prominence in the following decades. Grounded in a humoral model of human physiology, this theory held that excessive heat and humidity in the West Indies would corrupt and enervate English minds, bodies, and moral sensibilities, to the point that, by the close of the eighteenth century,

11. On the role of enslaved Africans in the culture of natural history, see Susan Scott Parrish, *American Curiosity: Cultures of Natural History in the Colonial British Atlantic World* (Chapel Hill, N.C., 2006), 259–306; Londa Schiebinger, *Plants and Empire: Colonial Bioprospecting in the Atlantic World* (Cambridge, Mass., 2004), 82–90. For the detail about Henry Morgan, see G. R. de Beer, *Sir Hans Sloane and the British Museum* (1953; rpt. New York, 1975), 41–42.

12. J. S. Handler and K. M. Bilby, "On the Early Use and Origin of the Term 'Obeah' in Barbados and the Anglophone Caribbean," *Slavery and Abolition*, XXII (2001), 87–100 (discussed in Schiebinger, *Plants and Empire*, 88).

the creole, or American-born English colonist, could be considered in many ways as a distinct racial subcategory. As this view took shape earlier in the century, complaints about white colonists became a staple of natural history treatises and correspondence. In 1725, the virtuoso Thomas Hoy groused in a letter to William Sherard that planters were "so indolent and lazy that . . . Sugar and Indico are the only Curiositys of the Jamaica Philosophers." Although the unique importance of narration to Sloane's text can be seen to address a West Indian social world in which "things" perform important labor and possess valuable knowledge, it also contends with special problems of authority arising from the possibility of planter dissipation and degeneracy.[13]

Sloane takes up the emergent theory of degeneracy more directly in the introduction, if only to dismiss it. In discussing the prolific sexual appetites of male colonists, he proposes:

> The heat of the Air exhausting the Spirits, no wonder if some of the edge of Mankind to Venery be taken off; it is thought by some Men, that they are bewitch'd or charm'd by the Air; by others that that desire in Women by this heat is Augmented, but I believe neither; for what I could find by several People this Appetite is the same as in other places, neither are men more bewitch'd or charm'd here than in *Europe;* but I believe People being here more debauch'd than in *England,* the Consequences may be more taken notice of.

Despite the blithe confidence of the passage, the theory of degeneracy could not be dismissed so quickly. Sloane's detailed discussions of diet and drink and his inclusion of numerous medical case histories involving debauched colonists were intended to support his contention that high mortality and low fertility among white colonists are an effect of behavior rather than climatic influence. But this denial gives rise to precisely the possibility that found such sharp expression in English discourse on obeah—West Indian nature as charm or fetish, subjecting the passive observer to its uncanny agency. As specimens accumulate in Sloane's pages, through the steadiness and industry of Britons in their progressive march toward ever-greater

13. Thomas Hoy to William Sherard, Sept. 20, 1725, Sherard Letters, V, 601, Royal Society. On scientific theories of creole degeneracy, see Kathleen Wilson, *The Island Race: Englishness, Empire, and Gender in the Eighteenth Century* (New York, 2002), 129–168; Roxann Wheeler, *The Complexion of Race: Categories of Difference in Eighteenth Century British Culture* (Philadelphia, 2000), 66–72, 210–233; Jim Egan, "The 'Long'd-for Aera' of an 'Other Race': Climate, Identity, and James Grainger's *The Sugar-Cane,*" *Early American Literature,* XXXVIII (2003), 189–212; Parrish, *American Curiosity,* 77–102.

civility and power, so, too, does the counterimage of Caribbean nature as capable of arresting progress, whether through its degenerative effects on residents of the colonies or, later in the century, its corrupting influence on English consumers of tropical goods.[14]

Problems of temporality thus emerge in the text as an extension of its more direct confrontation with the special conditions of West Indian agency. This same conjunction can be seen in retrospect in the meditation on fruit trees, where Sloane describes the transmission of knowledge—via enslaved Africans—from prior Spanish colonists to their English successors. The "Black Legend" of Spanish barbarity and decadence held that Catholic superstition was antithetical to enlightened rationality. In Sloane's account, by contrast, one of the primary tasks of the English naturalist in Jamaica is to ensure that botanical knowledge accumulated by the Spanish and preserved by enslaved Africans is secured for English posterity. The danger of crop failure lends urgency to the task. Almost from the inception of the sugar revolution, islands such as Barbados and Jamaica were seen as vulnerable to imminent collapse.[15]

So pervasive is the problem of temporality in the text that it begins to seem like an effect of the natural environment:

> 'Tis a very strange thing to see in how short a time a Plantation formerly clear'd of Trees and Shrubs, will grow foul, which comes from two causes; the one the not stubbing up of the Roots, whence arise young Sprouts, and the other the Fertility of the Soil. The Settlements and Plantations of, not only the *Indians*, but even the *Spaniards*, being quite overgrown with tall Trees, so that there were no Footsteps of such a thing left, were it not for old Palisadoes, Buildings, Orange-Walks, *etc.* which shew plainly the formerly clear'd places where Plantations have been.

Without proper management, imperial history runs its course in the New World tropics with unnerving speed. Spanish plantations established only a few decades ago are now completely overgrown, producing a historical present that is deeply sedimented. Oddly, though almost "no Footsteps" re-

14. Sloane, *Voyage to . . . Jamaica*, I, xxxi; Charlotte Sussman, *Consuming Anxieties: Consumer Protest, Gender, and British Slavery, 1713–1833* (Stanford, Calif., 2000).

15. On fears of decline, see Richard Grove, *Green Imperialism: Colonial Expansion, Tropical Island Edens, and the Origins of Environmentalism, 1600–1860* (Cambridge, 1996), 62–72; David Watts, *The West Indies: Patterns of Development, Culture, and Environmental Change since 1492* (New York, 1990), 37, 77, 119, 157, 211, 221–223, 237.

main of Spanish plantations, Sloane encounters reminders of those plantations at every turn, both as material remains in the landscape and in the recollections of blacks and Indians. Jamaican nature is a living record of colonial epochs that are experienced less as successive than simultaneous. Sloane's dual commitment to narrative and description can be understood in this context as responding to a colonial situation in which the nontransmission of vital knowledge casts doubt on the possibility of a progressive national history.[16]

We have seen thus far that some of the unique formal properties of Sloane's written text derive from his confrontation with problems of agency and temporality in Jamaica, closely associated with the fact of slave knowledge and labor. The structural difficulties that pervade the written text provide one indication that these problems remain irresolvable for Sloane, that he fails to arrive at a settled understanding of how to tell the truth (or at least the whole truth) about West Indian specimens. But by addressing these problems, Sloane's text arrives at a sophisticated understanding of the relationship between the West Indian plantation as a new social and economic formation and the specimen-commodity as a new cultural form. The transformation of the natural curiosity into an exchangeable commodity, he begins to perceive, is linked by some occult logic to the redefinition of human beings as chattel property.

This perception is clearest in Sloane's extraordinary meditation on Jamaican burial and funerary practices. As historian Vincent Brown has established, the "morbid environment" of British Jamaica in the early eighteenth century made it a "demographic catastrophe" for slaves and colonists alike, with death rates for the British exceeding 10 percent a year and blacks dying at slightly lower rates owing to greater immunity to yellow fever but in much higher numbers owing to malnutrition, overwork, and violence. Brown argues, "By the mid eighteenth century, Jamaica was the vital hub of British America, far and away Britain's most significant American colony. It was also a death trap." As a result, "death was at the center of social experience for everyone on the island." It is for this reason that Sloane's observations on a new burial ground outside Port Royal, constructed in response to this ongoing demographic catastrophe, have far-reaching implications in the text.[17]

16. Sloane, *Voyage to . . . Jamaica*, I, xiv.
17. Vincent Brown, *The Reaper's Garden: Death and Power in the World of Atlantic Slavery* (Cambridge, Mass., 2008), 13. Mortality rates for the enslaved in Barbados during the same period were com-

In the midst of an extended discussion of the "inhabitants of Jamaica," Sloane shifts suddenly into a meditation on the dead:

> The Air here being so hot and brisk as to corrupt and spoil Meat in four hours after 'tis kill'd, no wonder if a diseased Body must be soon buried. They usually bury twelve hours after death at all times of the day and night.
>
> The burial place at *Port Royal* is a little way out of Town, in a sandy Soil, because in the Town or Church it is thought unhealthy for the living. Planters are very often buried in their Gardens, and have a small Monument erected over them, and yet I never heard of any of them who walk'd after their deaths for being buried out of Consecrated ground.
>
> An ampurated Member buried there, and dug up some days after, was found eaten by the Ants all but the Bones. In the Caves where the *Indians* used to bury, the Ants would eat the whole Flesh off of the Bodies, and would perforate the Bones, and eat up the Marrow, of which I have a proof, having brought with me from thence the Bone of the Arm of an *Indian* so perforated, and its Marrow eaten by them.
>
> The *Negroes* from some Countries think they return to their own Country when they die in *Jamaica,* and therefore regard death but little, imagining they shall change their condition, by that means from servile to free, and so for this reason often cut their own Throats. Whether they die thus, or naturally, their Country people make great lamentations, mournings, and howlings about them expiring, and at their Funeral throw in Rum and Victuals into their Graves, to serve them in the other world.

The passage extends Sloane's treatment of the problem of temporality. Just as colonial regimes rise and fall with startling rapidity, just as plantations begin to grow rank almost at the instant they are cleared, so human bodies decompose with terrifying speed. This state of affairs is powerfully evoked by the central dramatic action of the first paragraph, as Sloane buries "an ampurated Member" (or amputated human limb) in the soil of the graveyard to exhume the bones a few days later. This morbid experiment blurs the distinction between the present moment and the precolonial past, for the bones exhumed from the graveyard, as Sloane attests, bear a striking

parable at about 6 percent. See Richard Sheridan, *Sugar and Slavery: An Economic History of the British West Indies, 1623-1775* (Baltimore, 1974), 124–147.

resemblance to the native American bones he unearthed in a cave in northern Jamaica, which he counted among his most prized and valuable specimens.[18]

At the same time, the passage addresses two other defining features of the tropical plantation: the invention of the hereditary chattel slave as a legal and social entity and appalling rates of slave mortality. In Sloane's comparison of human corpses to freshly butchered meat, it is as if the moment of death and decomposition reveals or confirms the equivalence between livestock and persons that is encoded in British slave law. The effect of this comparison, however, is less to naturalize the equivalence than to capture something of its shocking novelty, an effect also achieved by Sloane's image of gravediggers working around the clock to inter the dead.

Sloane is not alone in attempting to make sense of this situation. In the final paragraph of the passage, he attends to the funerary rites of enslaved Africans. As Brown persuasively argues, funerals were among the most important sites for contests over power between slaveholders and the black majority of Jamaica. Because funerals were understood as a potential resource for rebellion (much like the practice of obeah), strict laws were implemented against the performance of certain kinds of rites. Nevertheless, funerals remained an important site for the exercise of agency. Specifically, in Brown's account, the retention of certain kinds of animistic thinking within African-evangelical Christianity, as embodied in practices such as listening to coffins and corpses during funeral processions, constituted a direct challenge to European materialism and in particular to the legal fiction that enslaved persons had been reduced to a form of brute matter, subject to the control of higher laws and powers.[19]

Despite his deeply ingrained cultural biases, Sloane seems capable of some limited understanding of funerary performance as a philosophical reflection on the institution of slavery. In order to comprehend the exuberance and extravagance of slave funerals, he maintains, one must first comprehend a belief system in which the transition from life to death is regarded as a passage from New World to West Africa and thus as a "change [of] condition" from servility to freedom. So desirable is death within this belief system (which Sloane refrains from calling a religion) that the enslaved often "cut their own Throats," initiating what he describes as a reverse Middle Passage, a release from enslavement as death in life. Through their puta-

18. Sloane, *Voyage to . . . Jamaica*, I, xlviii.
19. Brown, *Reaper's Garden*, esp. chaps. 2–4.

tive disregard for their own bodies (they "regard death but little"), the en-slaved Jamaicans in Sloane's account appropriate and transform the logic of a planter regime that treats chattel property as expendable, as evidenced by the numbers of corpses hauled daily to the new burial ground. Through the observation and description of funerary rites, Sloane conceives of slavery as a form of social death, a necessary condition for the "demographic catastrophe" afflicting the colony.[20]

Late-seventeenth-century political philosophers anticipated this twentieth-century concept. In the section on slavery in *Two Treatises of Government*, John Locke struggles to reconcile his belief in consent as the only legitimate basis of government with his intimate awareness of slavery as a form of civil organization in the colonies. (Locke attended numerous meetings of the Board of Trade and Plantations and might have helped to draft the constitution of Carolina.) Adamant that consenting to slavery is an illegitimate act, yet anxious to legitimize colonial slavery as an institution, Locke proposes an elaborate legal fantasy. The slave is, in effect, a prisoner of war, sentenced to death for some unspecified crime, committed at some unspecified time and place, whose punishment has been deferred indefinitely by the slaveholder. In the eyes of the law, for Locke, the slave is already dead.[21]

This peculiar legal status, however, only begins to explain the paradox of a society centered on the mass mortality of economically valuable laborers. In his history of Saint-Domingue, C. L. R. James comments on "the unusual spectacle of property-owners apparently careless of preserving their property." He explains that spectacle as part of "a régime of calculated brutality and terrorism" designed to subdue the black majority of the island. More recently, Joseph Roach has provided a related explanation of slaveholder violence as a form of conspicuous consumption or spending. In a new credit economy in which "products accumulate more rapidly than they can be consumed," violence against enslaved people functions as a "performance of waste." Whether in the form of public torture or execution or more routine spectacles of neglect and overwork, violence serves a ritual function. In particular, it is designed to relieve those powerful and persistent anxieties associated with the production of new forms of material excess in the

---

20. Orlando Patterson, *Slavery and Social Death: A Comparative Study* (Cambridge, Mass., 1982).

21. John Locke, *Two Treatises of Government* (1690), ed. Peter Laslett (New York, 1960), 283–285. For an analysis of Locke's *Two Treatises* in this context, see Sibylle Fischer, "Haiti: Fantasies of Bare Life," *Small Axe*, XI, no. 2 (2007), 1–15.

circumatlantic world, as they destabilize traditional social hierarchies and cultural values. As an example of profitless expenditure, the violent waste of human life is closely related to other forms of conspicuous spending, and in particular to the creation and consumption of an array of new luxury commodities. Violence and consumption both represent a form of "excess production and expenditure of social energy" beyond what is necessary to ensure survival but serving a social purpose as a public sacrifice.[22]

This connection between slaveholder violence and luxury consumption provides one way of understanding why Sloane's meditation on Jamaican burial practices yields a new understanding of the natural history specimen. As remarked above, the burial and retrieval of the human limb intimates an uncanny resemblance between the graveyard and the West Indian plantation as sites for planting flesh and harvesting bones. The cultivation of bones in the graveyard also provides a macabre mirror image of natural history collection. What Sloane reaps from the graveyard is a curiosity, one that occasions a recognition that the new commercial value of Jamaican specimens is linked to mass mortality.

This recognition lies at the thematic center of the *Voyage to . . . Jamaica.* The relationship between mass death and the commodification of specimens is a focus of Sloane's emblematic engravings, with the written description of the burial ground playing a key role in the hermeneutic process initiated by those images. The transformation of the curiosity into a luxury good and the violent waste of human property, the sequence reveals, are related expressions of a new cultural logic, a new way of assessing the value of "things" in a British Atlantic empire rooted in speculative finance and slave-driven commerce. Before examining those images in detail, we must first widen the frame of analysis beyond Sloane's text to include a series of contemporaneous prose narratives by Ligon, Behn, and Defoe. Sloane was by no means anomalous in turning to the West Indian specimen as a way of understanding and representing the nature of finance.

---

22. C. L. R. James, *The Black Jacobins: Toussaint L'Ouverture and the San Domingo Revolution* (1938; rpt. New York, 1989), 12; Joseph Roach, *Cities of the Dead: Circum-Atlantic Performance* (New York, 1996), 40–41. Roach's theory derives from Marcel Mauss, *The Gift: Forms and Functions of Exchange in Archaic Societies* (New York, 1967), and George Bataille, *The Accursed Share: An Essay on General Economy*, I, *Consumption*, trans. Robert Hurley (New York, 1967). For a counterargument that planters "coldly calculated" the economic benefits of driving enslaved laborers past the point of exhaustion and replacing the dead with new imports from West Africa, see Laurent Dubois, *Avengers of the New World: The Story of the Haitian Revolution* (Cambridge, Mass., 2004), 40.

The Natural History of the Circumatlantic Novel

Between the Glorious Revolution and the collapse of the South Sea Bubble, at least three other important prose narratives undertook the representation of West Indian things, within the rhetorical conventions of natural history, as one of their primary tasks. We have already observed that Ligon punctuated his travel narrative with detailed descriptions of flora and fauna. Appearing some fifteen years later, Behn employs the rhetoric of natural history in her account of Surinam. The long and detailed catalog of West Indian curiosities near the opening of *Oroonoko* provides an authenticating frame for the sensational narrative of enslavement, rebellion, and violent death that follows. By 1719, as Sloane worked diligently on his second volume, Defoe had reworked many of the conventions of travel narratives by Ligon and Behn into the fictional ordeals of *Robinson Crusoe,* a text that presents its readers with an array of Caribbean specimens and artifacts (including melons, limes, tobacco plants, and earthenware pots) as its narrator maintains a detailed journal in adherence to the Royal Society's instructions to travelers.[23]

Through their treatment of West Indian things, these texts address one of the dominant social conflicts and epistemological crises of the early eighteenth century. According to Pocock, the decades between the financial revolution of the 1690s and the first, spectacular crash of the financial system after the South Sea Bubble are marked by an ongoing contest between "real" and mobile property and thus between a traditional aristocracy whose authority and station are based in the tangible and inheritable value of land and bullion and a new moneyed class whose social identity and economic substance derive from trade and credit. What emerged from this conflict was a type of "new social person," one dependent upon, and indeed constituted by, the diffuse, colateral networks of promises and desires that are integral to credit and finance. At the same time, the gradual displacement or subversion of "real" by mobile property—as the value of land and bullion diminished in relation to stocks, bonds, and bills of exchange—unsettled prevailing epistemological assumptions. Because the value of these paper instruments depended on the passions and imaginative projections of an

---

23. On the authenticating function of the catalog in *Oroonoko,* see McKeon, *Origins of the English Novel,* 111–113; Laura Brown, *Ends of Empire: Women and Ideology in Early Eighteenth Century English Literature* (Ithaca, N.Y., 1993), 43–44. On Crusoe's journal as modeled on Royal Society directives, see McKeon, *Origins of the English Novel,* 316.

investing society, that society found itself in a situation in which the new object of its knowledge (namely, the medium of exchange) was not entirely real.[24]

Though Ligon composes his text well before the financial revolution, he anticipates some of its features and effects. As the travel narrative of a defeated Royalist, it is born of a social landscape thrown into disarray by the conflict between landed and moneyed interests. Though his dreams of planter prosperity remain unfulfilled, Ligon remains confident that natural history writing might help him to recover his lost standing. In a new social world of terrifying fluidity, that is, the natural history specimen might ground a renovated social identity. Through his painstaking descriptions of specimens, Ligon argues that he is among the men "of middle earth," inured to the hardships of labor, whom he proposes as ideal colonial settlers.[25]

At the same time, however, he acknowledges that land itself has transformed into an exchangeable commodity of fluctuating value, in ways that bear on his representation of nature. Noting that the price of land has exploded in the preceding five years and that Barbados soon will soon become "one of the richest Spots of earth under the Sun," Ligon recounts his diligent study of the sugarcane:

> When I first arrived upon the Iland, it was in my purpose, to observe their several manners of planting and husbandry there; and because this Plant was of greatest value and esteem, I desired first the knowledge of it. I saw by the growth, as well as by what I had been told, that it was a strong and lusty Plant, and so vigorous, as where it grew, to forbid all Weeds to grow very neer it; so thirstily it suck't the earth for nourishment, to maintain its own health and gallantry.

The West Indian thing again serves as an emblem. Through focused and trained observation of the plant, one may detect the hidden workings of a comprehensive design, the gradual unfolding of a collective destiny. Yet mercantile capitalism, rather than divine providence, now seems the appropriate name for that system.[26]

Behn's *Oroonoko* also confronts the transformation of West Indian land

24. Pocock, *Machiavellian Moment*, 423–461.

25. Richard Ligon, *A True and Exact History of the Island of Barbadoes: Illustrated with a Map of the Island as Also the Principal Trees and Plants There, Set Forth in Their Due Proportions and Shapes, Drawn out by Their Several and Respective Scales* . . . (London, 1673), 108.

26. Ibid., 87.

and nature into circulating commodities. As Laura Brown argues, Behn's narrative is structured around the collision between the residual early modern genre of chivalric romance and the new empiricist genre of "history," with the account of Oroonoko's experiences in Surinam drawing equally from both narrative models. That collision indicates Behn's ambivalence regarding the social transformations wrought by the rise of liberal individualism and mercantile capitalism. It results from the ideological contradiction between the text's veneration of aristocratic values and its fascination with imperialist acquisition. Behn attempts to bridge that contradiction through her use of the natural history curiosity as a narrative device. The catalog of curiosities from Surinam—including marmosets, parakeets, and feathered wreaths that the author-narrator procured during a visit to a native American village—is located at the juncture between aristocratic romance and mercantilist history. On the one hand, Behn traffics in these curiosities as a form of exotic tribute, as she attempts to demonstrate and bolster her status within an aristocratic social order. The metropolitan reader can observe some of these curiosities firsthand in London, both on stage as part of a costume in Dryden's *Indian Queen* and in the "King's reliquaries." Items such as the headdress emblematize the author-narrator's innate nobility, despite her loss of social standing due to the death of her father. On the other hand, the catalog also expresses the narrator's fascination with the new social order brought into being by mercantile capitalism. The curiosities function as a "sign and product of the expansion and commercialization of English economy and society in the eighteenth century." By describing those specimens according to empiricist protocols, Behn crafts a modern social identity as a credible author. The catalog lends authority to the narrator's claim to provide a "true history," however strange and romantic some of her truths might appear to those unfamiliar with the colonies.[27]

Building on Brown's analysis, Catherine Gallagher understands Behn's narrative as an attempt to negotiate the new social and epistemological landscape of finance capitalism. One of the most significant achievements of the early novel, in Gallagher's account, concerns its proliferation of fictional characters, or its "release into the culture of strongly marked overtly suppositional identities, belonging to nobody and hence temporarily appro-

27. Brown, *Ends of Empire*, 43–44. Natural historians continued to cite Behn's account of the electrical eel as authoritative throughout the eighteenth century. See, for instance, Henry Collins Flagg, "Observations on the Numb Fish, or Torporific Eel," American Philosophical Society, *Transactions*, II (1786), 170–173.

priate to anybody." By training English readers to invest their real passion and sympathy in this "social nobody," the novel helps to secure the legitimacy of Pocock's "new social person," who is also composed of the desires and imaginative projections of a broad public. The release into the culture of the "social nobody" does more than simply reflect the rise of a new financial epistemology at the level of form. Rather, it "should be seen as one among many modes of facilitating property exchange and investment in the period, of creating the speculative, commercial and sentimental subject." Significantly, Gallagher identifies the original "social nobody" in the titular hero of *Oroonoko*. The conscious artificiality of Behn's depiction, established through repeated insistence on Oroonoko's "inky blackness," signals his overt fictionality and infinite exchangeability.[28]

In *Robinson Crusoe*, West Indian specimens again play a key role in the text's broader meditation on British society and economy. For Defoe, Crusoe's exile on a tropical island should be understood as just retribution for his "original sin" when he rejected his father's advice to maintain "the middle Station of Life." Crusoe repeats that sin during his time as a tobacco planter in Brazil immediately before his shipwreck. On the verge of settling himself as a "rich and thriving Man on my new Plantation," Crusoe is overcome by his sudden desire for more immediate speculative gains. Specifically, he purchases a stake in an illegal shipment of African slaves, agreeing to oversee the voyage personally. The narrator recounts that moral error in intriguing terms. By making his own fortunes dependent on the success of a slaving venture, he has "pursue[d] a rash and immoderate Desire of rising farther than the *Nature of the Thing* admitted." By the logic of the passage, to cultivate a cash crop such as tobacco for overseas markets is in keeping with the nature of the thing, but to engage in the transoceanic purchase and shipment of West African people is not.[29]

This distinction has little to do with any moral reservations about slavery. Rather, through his oddly precise determination that only this last venture was out of scale with the nature of the thing, Crusoe alludes to the highly abstract, speculative, and financial character of the slave trade. Driven primarily by chartered corporations such as the Royal Africa Company and the South Sea Company as the value of their shares grew exponentially in

28. Gallagher, *Nobody's Story*, 194. My understanding of Gallagher's argument has been sharpened by Baucom, *Specters of the Atlantic*, 68–71.

29. McKeon, *Origins of the English Novel*, 320–323; Daniel Defoe, *The Life and Strange Surprising Adventures of Robinson Crusoe* . . . (1719), ed. J. Donald Crowley (London, 1972), 38 (emphasis mine).

the early decades of the eighteenth century, that trade established London as the unrivaled center of stock speculation. During the same period, the British imperial state accrued massive debts as it sought to establish military dominion over the Caribbean basin, fueling the expansion of the paper money supply and the proliferation of financial instruments. Individual slave-trading voyages depended on the extension and circulation of credit and debt between capital houses and traders in London and ostensibly reliable factors in the West Indies and North America.[30]

Brought to ruin by his insidious speculative desires, Crusoe employs his time on the island to reorient his values. Removed from the influence of exchange, he is able to cultivate a renewed understanding of use value as the proper measure of things and to experience the sheer pleasure of things independent of use. Running counter to both narrative movements, however, is Crusoe's newfound capacity to understand objects and events in emblematic terms as signs of God's providence. One threatening, though never articulated, implication of the novel concerns this close analogy between financial speculation (a variant of Crusoe's original sin) and emblematic reading (the instrument of his conversion) as hermeneutic practices. Seen from this vantage, Crusoe does not renounce speculation on the island but rather refines the basic mental faculties and cognitive techniques necessary to its successful practice once returned to civilization. This is why, upon his deliverance from the island, he can engage immediately in what McKeon describes as a "bewildering but completely characteristic barrage of financial and legal quantifications."[31]

This brief survey of prose narrative in the early eighteenth century demonstrates that the West Indian specimen occupies an important position in the history of the emergent novel, or, more precisely, in that particular strain of the novel that sought to map cognitively the new circumatlantic scale of British society and economy. Such "things" are integral to the process through which the novel emerges from the rubble of prior generic

30. Jacob M. Price, *Capital and Credit in British Overseas Trade: The View from the Chesapeake, 1700–1776* (Cambridge, Mass., 1980); James D. Tracy, ed., *The Rise of Merchant Empires: Long Distance Trade in the Early Modern World, 1350–1750* (New York, 1990).

31. McKeon, *Origins of the English Novel*, 335. On emblematic reading in *Robinson Crusoe*, see J. Paul Hunter, *The Reluctant Pilgrim: Defoe's Emblematic Method and Quest for Form in "Robinson Crusoe"* (Baltimore, 1966); Wall, *Prose of Things*, 108–114. Wall argues, "Crusoe's clusters of grapes and green limes and raisins . . . are emblematic in that they are signs of God's providence, as the beached canoe emblematizes to Crusoe his own improvidence, the goat in the cave his own fears" (112). On West Indian things as central to the action of the narrative, see Lydia H. Liu, "Robinson Crusoe's Earthenware Pot," *Critical Inquiry*, XXV (1999), 728–757.

categories as a cultural instrument capable of mediating new problems of epistemology and social organization, as new forces of trade and speculative finance destabilize older hierarchies, values, and concepts. By drawing so consistently from the reservoir of Caribbean natural history, these early prose narratives open a window onto a historical moment in which natural history was itself understood as a crucial cultural instrument. Authors such as Behn and Defoe turned intuitively to the natural history specimen as a key narrative device because they recognized it as the source of a rich conceptual vocabulary for grappling with some of the questions that most perplexed and concerned them. It is through the discourse of natural history, their texts suggest, that English readers confronted the relationship between the ascendancy of mobile property and the development of colonial slavery; between the transformation of metropolitan cities such as London and Liverpool into centers of finance and the new global circum-Caribbean scale of British empire; between financial investment and speculation as new social practices and cognitive procedures and the emergence of West Indian plantations as highly profitable spaces of social death and mass death. By consuming a seemingly endless array of West Indian specimens and texts, that is, the curious and the learned were also undergoing a form of epistemological training. Through these specimens, they realized that trust must flow within particular channels, that credit must be extended over a specific transoceanic geography, that their social identity was dependent on their connection to strange and distant places where the concepts of credibility and personhood had been stretched to their limit.

Consider the status of the botanical specimen. By the 1700s, the curious and the learned had long engaged in an informal exchange of botanical specimens within a genteel gift economy for conferring status and prestige. By the late 1600s, the most sought-after of these specimens were coming from the New World, with the overwhelming majority originating from plantation colonies. With this shift in the geographic distribution of specimens came a transformation in the underlying character of botanical exchange. By the time that Sloane set to work on his volumes (during the speculative fervor that would lead to the South Sea Bubble), the exchange of plants, seedlings, and seeds had developed the characteristics of an organized market. Botanical specimens served as "hard cash" in a new "stock exchange" of scientific goods, one in which the market price of a given species was subject to rapid fluctuation. The purchaser of a specimen had to judge the value of the species in general and determine whether the source of the specimen personally was credible. Steven Shapin has identified trust as a key element in the making of early modern scientific knowledge. In the workings of this virtual stock exchange, one perceives an overlap between the forms and practices of trusting that develop simultaneously within scientific culture and economic life.[32]

Consider, as well, the status of the printed natural history text. In his influential study of early modern print and science, Adrian Johns has uncovered a set of lost cultural assumptions about the meaning of printed objects, charting a cultural landscape in which modern assumptions about the relationship between printedness on the one hand and, on the other, the "enhanced fidelity, reliability, and truth" of a text had not yet been forged. Johns unearths a set of early modern assumptions in which "profound problems of credit . . . attended printed materials of all kinds," problems that were especially acute in relation to scientific texts. The Royal Society began working closely with printers to create and disseminate knowledge about the natural world in particular. They worked tirelessly, often with little success, to create the conviction that printed knowledge was authoritative, that the reader of a printed text was a virtual witness to whatever phenomenon or organic object was therein described. So pervasive were these efforts that, in Johns's concise summation, "Printers and booksellers were manufacturers of credit."[33]

This is one vital context in which to consider Sloane's innovative efforts to synthesize description and narration, word and image. For a reader to accept a printed natural history as authoritative in this period required an assessment of credibility not unlike that involved in the evaluation of a bank note or bill of exchange—those other ubiquitous and newly valuable works on paper—and every bit as tenuous. But Sloane's interest in the climate of speculative finance he worked within goes beyond the question of how to ensure the credibility of knowledge within a natural history network that must now span the entirety of the British Empire. Sloane also reflects on the pernicious social effects of a system in which paper achieves a seemingly autonomous and tangible existence, whereas things are reduced to a form of currency. He takes up this particular question most directly and insightfully through his emblematic engravings.

32. Steven Shapin, *A Social History of Truth: Civility and Science in Seventeenth-Century England* (Chicago, 1994). On the geographic distribution of colonial specimens, see Raymond Phineas Stearns, *Science in the British Colonies of America* (Chicago, 1970), 212–257, 337–397. On the emergence of a botanical "stock-exchange," see Sverker Sörlin, "Ordering the World for Europe: Science as Intelligence and Information as Seen from the Northern Periphery," *Osiris*, XV (2000), 51–69, esp. 64.

33. Adrian Johns, *The Nature of the Book: Print and Knowledge in the Making* (Chicago, 1998), 5, 31, 33.

Specimens of Finance

"Land Crab and Pot Shards Found in a Cave" (Fig. 1) is a striking engraving. First in the sequence of three engravings that follows the introduction of the *Voyage to . . . Jamaica,* the image announces its importance in a number of ways. Filling an entire double folio sheet, the plate serves as showcase for the expertise and sophistication of the illustrator, engraver, and printer. The land crabs pictured from above and below in the upper half of the sheet and the fragments of pottery also pictured from above and below in the lower half are imbued with a strong sense of three-dimensionality by the finely engraved parallel and cross-hatched lines that cover their surface. The objects are illuminated by a single light source, which appears to originate above and to the right of the plate and which produces some virtuosic visual effects, rare in natural history illustration of the day—creating highlighted areas that contrast dramatically with the deep chiaroscuro of the objects while also casting strong and intricate shadows on the stark white of the background. Particularly inspired are the shadows cast on the underside of the crab to the right by its extended and upheld claws, a posture that in itself lends a strangely lifelike quality to the dead specimen.[34]

By announcing the importance of the plate and by investing its contents with a heightened sense of presence and volume, these aesthetic features also place interpretive pressure on the juxtaposition of natural specimen and human artifact. How are we to understand the coexistence of these objects in the same pictorial field, especially considering that artifacts and natural objects are normally depicted separately in Sloane's engravings, as in most other printed natural histories? Through manipulations of scale and form, the objects are depicted as roughly equivalent in shape, size, and mass, an effect underscored by similarities in texture, shading, and positioning. It is as if some as-yet occult relation might link these objects, as if their proximity is determined by some indiscernible logic.

For a sophisticated reader, as Kriz demonstrates, this problem initiates a dynamic movement between image and word. The printed labels in the engraving are meant to enable this interpretive practice. Using Sloane's detailed index, the reader might turn to the catalog description of the land crab. A reader trained in Latin would learn that the fragments of pottery

34. I am indebted to Kriz's analysis of the image for my understanding of many of these compositional details. See Kriz, *Slavery, Sugar, and the Culture of Refinement,* 16–19.

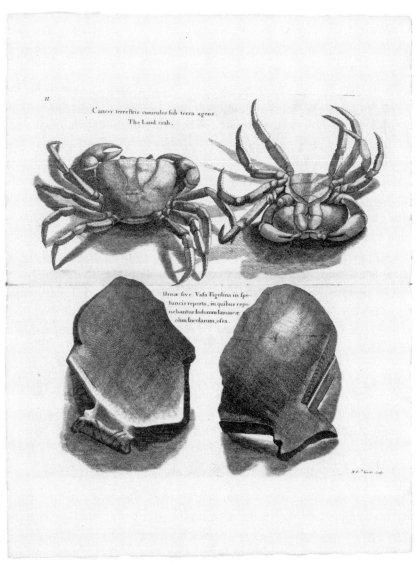

FIGURE 1. Michael van der Gucht, Land Crab and Pot Shards Found in a Cave. Hans Sloane, *Voyage to the Islands Madera, Barbados, Nieves, S. Christophers, and Jamaica*, 2 vols. (London, 1707–1725), I, pl. 2. Courtesy of the John Carter Brown Library at Brown University

pictured here are in fact "earthenware urns or pots, discovered in a cave containing the bones of an Indian who had previously lived in Jamaica" and likely would recall Sloane's intriguing discussion of these artifacts in his travel narrative on northern Jamaica.[35]

Turning to the catalog description of the land crab in volume II, the reader would discover that the inhabitants of Jamaica regularly consume the species, which is prized for its "Delicacy of Taste" by white colonists and provides an important source of nourishment to enslaved Africans. As Sloane's disciple Mark Catesby later observed, the crabs "are no small help to the Negro Slaves, who on many of the Islands would fare very hard without them." The species, however, must be prepared for human consumption with great caution and expertise, as it is poisonous under certain conditions.[36]

Locating the appropriate passage in the introduction, the reader would learn that the fragments of pottery were excavated from a burial site near the plantation of one Mr. Barnes. Ten years before Sloane's visit, Barnes had discovered "a Cave in which lay a human Body's Bones all in order, the Body having been eaten by the Ants." Sloane details his own observations upon reexamining the cave:

> The Ants Nests we found there, the rest of the Cave was fill'd with Pots or Urns, wherein were Bones of Men and Children, the Pots were Oval, large, of a redish dirty colour. . . . The *Negroes* had remov'd most these Pots to boil their Meat in. . . . The Ants had eat one Carcass to the Bones, and had made holes in their ends, whereat they enter'd, I suppose, to eat the Marrow.

Bringing these written texts to bear on the image, the viewer might surmise that crab and potsherd are proximate on the page because of their customary usage among Jamaican slaves. Slaves have removed most of the pottery from the Carib burial chamber to use as cookery, and they are known to scavenge the shore for edible land crabs. Slave custom, then, provides one possible link between these seemingly disparate objects, which turn out to be necessary components in the preparation of a meal. The knowledge and agency of the enslaved, which had been such a prominent concern in the

35. Ibid., 17.
36. Sloane, *Voyage to . . . Jamaica*, II, 269; Mark Catesby, *The Natural History of Carolina, Florida, and the Bahama Islands: Containing the Figures of Birds, Beasts, Fishes, Serpents, Insects, and Plants . . .*, 2 vols. (London, 1731–1743 [1729–1747]), II, 32.

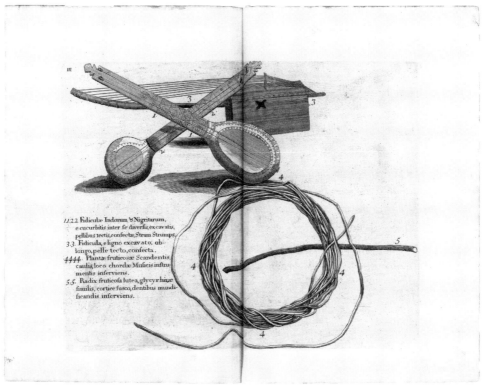

FIGURE 2. "Indian" and African Musical Instruments, Scandent Vine, and Jamaican *Luteus*. Sloane, *Voyage to . . . Jamaica*, I, pl. 3. Courtesy of the John Carter Brown Library at Brown University

introduction, turns out to be an integral theme in the first of Sloane's emblematic images.[37]

Such an understanding of the image would only be confirmed and strengthened after considering the next plate in the sequence, which at first appears to depict a cluster of slave instruments in the same pictorial field with some of the raw materials used to construct them (Fig. 2). Read in conjunction with the appropriate written passages and retrospectively in light of the subsequent plate, "Land Crab and Pot Shards Found in a Cave" is concerned in part with the use value of these objects to Jamaican slaves and, by extension, with their use value to English slaveholders, who are spared the expense of importing much of the food necessary to sustain their human property.

37. Sloane, *Voyage to . . . Jamaica*, I, lxx–lxxi.

Such an insight, however, does not foreclose an interpretive process that would also attend to metaphoric associations in the written text. In both passages discussed above, the reader is encouraged to view these objects as testaments to a long history of mass death. Much like cassava, the land crab is a source of vital nourishment that can also be fatal to those who depend on it. It is representative of environmental dangers that have contributed to high rates of mortality since the beginnings of colonization. The potsherds are also linked with these dangers. In the accompanying text, Sloane dwells on the swarms of carnivorous ants that have devoured all but the bones of the Carib corpses interred beside the urns. At several points in the preceding pages, moreover, Sloane comments on the pervasive threat these ants continue to pose to colonists on the north side of the island. The ants "are said to have killed the *Spanish* children by eating their Eyes when they were left in their Cradles in this part of the island; this is given as one Reason why the *Spaniards* left this part of the Country, where they first settled." More recently, they have consumed the wooden bed-frame of an English planter from beneath him as he slept. So voracious is the species that, "If you thrust an *Animals* Thigh Bone into one of their Nests, they will be all kill'd by the Wood-Ants for love of the Bone."[38]

Whereas both land crab and potsherd evoke the dangers of the West Indian environment as one source of mass death, they also occasion a disturbing recognition that this phenomenon is more properly understood as an outcome of colonial history, itself a process of violent human expenditure that began with Spanish settlement and has been perpetuated by the English. Carib pottery and bones are among the only material remains of a once-thriving civilization decimated by Spanish barbarism, a historical legacy evoked by Sloane's reference, elsewhere in the introduction, to the remains of numerous burial sites. He recounts, "I have seen in the Woods, many of their Bones in Caves, which some people thought were of such as had voluntarily inclos'd or immured themselves, in order to be starved to death, to avoid the Severities of their Masters." An alert reader will recall Sloane's allegation that enslaved Africans also commit suicide to avoid the severities of English masters. Indeed, Sloane's description of the burial ground is linked closely to his account of the Carib burial chamber, owing to the shared preoccupation in both passages with the rapid consumption of human bones by tropical ants. In the former passage, Sloane had buried an amputated limb in the ant infested soil of the graveyard in order to re-

38. Ibid., lxviii.

trieve the remaining bone just a few days later, an experiment that had led him to recall his visit to the Carib burial chamber and the "Bone of the Arm of an Indian" that he had brought back to London as a prized curiosity. The Caribbean island had been revealed in this moment as fertile soil for the cultivation of bones.[39]

I have argued that the burial ground is where Sloane comes closest to articulating what he suspects is a necessary, yet hidden, connection between the accumulation of valuable specimens on the one hand and the violent waste of human life on the other. The sequence of emblematic engravings allows the reader to more closely contemplate the nature of that link.

Verbal and visual puns are crucial to this interpretive labor. This impulse is perhaps strongest in the second plate, "'Indian' and African Musical Instruments, Scandent Vine, and Jamaican *Luteus*" (Fig. 2). Like the opening engraving in the sequence, this image presents human artifacts and natural specimens together on the page. Three stringed instruments, identified by the Latin label as African in origin, are grouped together in the upper left quadrant, whereas the lower right quadrant contains the coiled vines and straight stalk of a plant identified in the inscription as Jamaican *luteus*. The image underscores the importance of slave agency and mortality as themes in the sequence. These are the very instruments that Jamaican slaves play during festival dances that Sloane describes just after his accounts of the graveyard and African-evangelical funerary rites. The reader might have gone looking for the image upon first reading this passage, for the text alerts us, "The Figures of some of these Instruments are hereafter graved." Sloane seems well aware that these performances are a source of intense curiosity. He includes a transcription of one song performed when he attended a festival, the earliest known attempt to transcribe music of African origin into European notation. Sloane's description of the festival recalls his earlier, brief description of another form of ritual music, the "lamentations, mournings, and howlings" that filled the graveyard during slave funerals.[40]

This second image also complements the preceding one by proposing slave custom as one way to understand its particular assemblage of natural object (luteus vine) and human artifact (lute). In the introduction, Sloane had commented, "They have several sorts of Instruments in imitation of

39. Ibid., iv, xlviii.
40. Ibid., xlviii, xlix. On punning wordplay in the engraving, see Kriz, *Slavery, Sugar, and the Culture of Refinement*, 24–26. For an analysis of the song transcription included in Sloane's text, see Richard Cullen Rath, "African Music in Seventeenth-Century Jamaica: Cultural Transit and Transition," *William and Mary Quarterly*, 3d Ser., L (1993), 700–726, esp. 723.

Lutes . . . strung with Horse hairs, or the peeled stalks of climbing Plants or
Withs." Perhaps the image is meant to display a complex Afro-Caribbean
instrument alongside the local climbing plant from which it is ingeniously
fashioned. The Latin descriptor, however, undercuts such a reading by informing us that slaves use luteus vines as rudimentary toothbrushes. Plant
and vine both are used by slaves, but not together.[41]

By inviting and then undercutting an interpretation based on use, the
engraving suggests a logic of association based instead on verbal and visual
puns. Note the witty wordplay through which the plate connects these African instruments, consciously (mis)labeled by Sloane as types of *lute*, with
a botanical species identified as *luteus*. Note also that the forms of the two
long-necked instruments closest to the viewer are mirrored by the coiled
stalk and slender, straight root of the luteus plant. The implication of the
pun is clearly derogatory. The instruments are presented as nothing more
than sticks and vines, as primitive as the "bawdy" slave music Sloane hears
at the festival. The alleged primitivity of slave craftsmanship and musician-
ship is contrasted pointedly with the wit and refinement of naturalist and
viewer as they savor the wordplay and visual mimicry of the engraving.

Related implications arise from the subtler punning in "Land Crab and
Pot Shards." It is unlikely that the typical viewer, upon first scanning the
plate, would read the objects in its lower half as human artifacts at all. As
Kriz remarks, these objects are marked as human only by the "crudely in-
cised parallel lines that form a broken 'v' on the lower edge of the piece
on the left." Before decoding the Latin inscription, the viewer may identify
the objects as a broken husk or shell, perhaps the shell of that iconic West
Indian species the coconut. The viewer might misinterpret the plate as displaying two examples of West Indian shells, of natural specimens linked
only by their shared possession of a hard exterior. Although the labels and
linguistic cues yield a pleasurable corrective, the pun nonetheless initiates a
competing interpretation. Whereas one reading links the objects according
to their local use value, then, a second constructs a connection or equivalence between these things that is more formal and abstract. Although the
objects have been assembled by the wit and ingenuity of the naturalist, they
have been rendered seemingly equivalent through the virtuosity of engraver
and printer. By contriving an apparent (or fictitious) equivalence between
these disparate and potentially threatening objects, the engraving converts
them into an elegant and valuable work on paper. It does so in a cultural

41. Sloane, *Voyage to . . . Jamaica*, I, xlviii–xlix.

STRANGE THINGS, OCCULT RELATIONS 69

moment marked by widespread fascination with the sudden discovery of exchange value as the hidden essence of things, with its ability to transform things into commodities and render formally equivalent an unending array of seemingly dissimilar things.[42]

The final engraving in the sequence, "Spanish Coins, Fragment of a Ship's Timber, and Portuguese Man-of-War" (Fig. 3), draws an explicit connection between the propensity toward visual and linguistic puns in the plates and an emerging culture of commodity exchange and financial speculation. At first glance, the plate pictures a strange assemblage of mysterious objects, including a jellyfish, three coral-encrusted coins, and a piece of ship timber containing an iron bolt and also encrusted with coral.

The engraving confronts the viewer with another problem of emblematic interpretation. The coins and timber fragment are so overgrown with coral that, without deciphering the Latin label, the viewer might have trouble correctly identifying them. With the aid of the label, the viewer would learn that the objects were recovered from a Spanish galleon that sank off the coast of Hispaniola in 1659. Alternately, the viewer might have turned immediately to the engraving after reading Sloane's account of the wreck in the introduction, included in the sequence of diary entries that interrupt his travel narrative of northern Jamaica. (After describing the objects, Sloane alerts the reader, "These things I have caused, at least some of them, to be graved.") With the aid of the introduction, the reader would also learn that Sloane's patron the duke of Albemarle had been a shareholder in the venture to recover the wreck's contents (including silver ingots, gold plate, and pieces of eight) and that his initial investment of eight hundred pounds sterling had yielded a spectacular return of fifty thousand pounds.[43]

The context of speculation would be firmly in mind as the viewer contemplates a number of prominent visual and linguistic puns. In the same way that the coins and timber fragment at first appear to be natural objects, the viewer is also prompted to regard the jellyfish as an object of human contrivance. The label identifies the creature as a "man-of-war," and the form of its body mimics the hull and sail of a ship, perhaps the very ship from which the wood spar and coins have been taken. To commemorate the

42. Kriz, *Slavery, Sugar, and the Culture of Refinement*, 18. For a discussion of commodity fetishism in relation to eighteenth-century literary culture, see Lynn Festa, *Sentimental Figures of Empire in Eighteenth-Century Britain and France* (Baltimore, 2006), 114–118. For the classic analysis of commodity fetishism, see Karl Marx, *Capital: A Critical Analysis of Capitalist Production*, trans. Samuel Moore and Edward Aveling, 3 vols. (London, 1971), 142–156.

43. Sloane, *Voyage to . . . Jamaica*, I, lxxx.

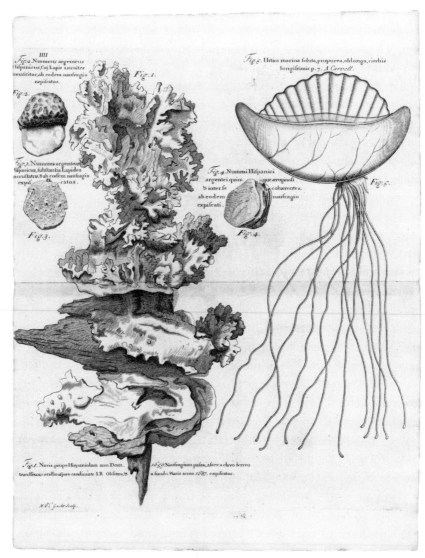

Fig. 2. Nummus argenteus Hispanicus, cui Lapis astroites innascitur, ab eodem naufragio expiscatus.

IIII

Fig. 1.

Fig. 2.

Fig. 3. Nummus argenteus Hispanicus, substantia Lapidea occrustatus, & ab eodem naufragio expiscatus.

Fig. 3.

Fig. 4. Nummi Hispanici argentei quinque æruginosi & inter se cohærentes, ab eodem naufragio expiscati.

Fig. 4.

Fig. 5. Urtica marina soluta, purpurea, oblonga, cirrhis longissimis p. 7. A Carvell.

Fig. 5.

Fig. 1. Navis, prope Hispaniolam ann. Dom. 1659. Naufragium passæ, aster a clavo ferreo transfixus corallio aspero candicante I.B. Oblitus, & a fundo Maris anno 1687. expiscatus.

M. Vd. Gucht Sculp.

FIGURE 3. Michael van der Gucht, Spanish Coins, Fragment of a Ship's Timber, and Portuguese Man-of-War. Sloane, *Voyage to . . . Jamaica,* I, pl. 4. Courtesy of the John Carter Brown Library at Brown University

success of the duke's venture, the engraving dwells on a cluster of objects that confuse the boundary between nature and manufacture—including timber and coins converted back into natural objects by the transformative power of the sea. The image revels in its ability to contrive purely linguistic or formal connections between disparate things. Considered in the context of the duke's investment and the vast economic fortunes to be amassed (or salvaged) in the West Indies, the engraving simultaneously personifies a natural species and naturalizes specie. It meditates on the transformation of Caribbean nature into a circulating commodity at a historical moment marked by the naturalization of the medium of exchange, by the new "fact" of its seemingly autonomous value.[44]

At the same time that the plate celebrates the duke's speculative savvy, however, it also attests to a long history of mass death. As in the engraving of pottery fragments (Fig. 1), these valuable things have been scavenged from the human graveyard that is the extended Caribbean region, encompassing Indians who perished in Spanish American mines, sailors who drowned in wrecked merchant ships, and, by implication, slaves cast overboard (alive or dead) during the Middle Passage. (Citing an account in Richard Hakluyt's *Principal Navigations* [1589], Sloane elsewhere refers to the jellyfish as a "ship of Guinea.") This history of demographic catastrophe, moreover, is linked in the introduction to the dangers of an emergent culture of rampant speculation. The duke's windfall inspired numerous other investors to organize similar ventures:

> It happened so not only to the first Patentees, but to many other people, who by the example of this Project . . . hoping for the same Success, took out Patents for Wrecks lying at the bottom of Seas in all places, especially the *West-Indies*, where any Traffick is used, not considering that though there have been lost divers Ships laden with Money, on many Shoals of the *West-Indies* . . . there is such a Vegetation of Coralline matter out of the Sea-water, as that the bottom of the Sea is incrustated with it, and the Wrecks hid by them.

The coral-encrusted objects in the engraving thus also serve as material reminders of the difficulties confronting such projects.[45]

Such ventures, Sloane goes on to suggest, amount to a dangerous form of mass delusion and folly:

---

44. On visual punning in this image, see Kriz, *Slavery, Sugar, and the Culture of Refinement*, 19–22.
45. Sloane, *Voyage to . . . Jamaica*, I, 7, lxxx.

Though the Money brought into *England* from the first Wreck was very considerable, yet much more was lost on Projects of the same nature. For every silly Story of a rich Ship lost, was credited, a Patent taken out, *Divers,* who are us'd to Pearl-fishing, *etc.* and can stay under Water some Minutes, bought or hir'd at great Rates, and a Ship set out for bringing home Silver. There was one Ship lost amongst the rest, said to be very rich, near *Bermudas,* which was divided into Shares and sold. It was said to be in the Possession of the Devil, and they told Stories how he kept it. I do not find the People, who spent their Money, on this, or any of these Projects, excepting the first, got any thing by them.

Investors have been "possessed" by a feverish desire for speculative returns that makes them all too eager to credit "silly" fictions as tangible facts and even to purchase shares in these fictions, resulting (after the duke's initial success) in a downward spiral of financial losses. This cautionary tale reflects back on the puns at the center of the emblematic engravings. The type of linguistic and visual equivalence manufactured by these puns might be purely formal, in some cases even specious. But, in contributing to the appeal of his expensive work on paper, they are also a potential source of real value.[46]

One effect of the engravings is to focus the reader's attentions on the lavish physical format of Sloane's volumes, inviting them to contemplate the book's format as an integral component of its meaning. The opulence of the book had, of course, been a considerable source of its initial appeal. Consisting of two folio volumes and containing some 274 detailed copperplate engravings, the *Voyage to . . . Jamaica* sold for the considerable sum of around five guineas. Elite readers paid such high sums for books such as Sloane's because they saw them, in Joyce E. Chaplin's view, as "material indications of their refinement," a term and concept that entered common usage at a moment when the refinement of sugar loomed large in the British imagination. Such readers understood printed natural histories as one among many new articles of trade and instruments of intellectual and moral improvement that had been derived from Caribbean nature. On one level, the format of Sloane's volumes paid tribute to the capacity of European technology—whether in the form of the sugar mill or the printing press—to

46. Ibid., I, lxxxi.

transform West Indian flora and fauna into a source of wealth, knowledge, and civility. But, as we have seen, the reflections on Jamaica set in motion by Sloane's text also have less consoling implications for the history of British commercial empire, challenging key notions of scientific, economic, and moral progress at the core of an emergent imperial identity.[47]

This final point about physical format will take on increased significance in the following chapter on Sloane's best-known disciple, Mark Catesby. A folio printed on heavy imperial paper, Catesby's *Natural History of Carolina, Florida, and the Bahama Islands* included some 220 engraved plates. The intensity and range of color in the plates depended on an intricate and labor-intensive process of engraving and hand-coloring, making the book "one of the most expensive publications of the eighteenth century," at a cost of twenty-two guineas for a complete set. Format was integral to the text's critical reception. Sounding a familiar note among contemporary reviewers, a later, unsigned article in *Gentleman's Magazine* extolled "a work which exceeds all others of the same kind for its beauty, accuracy, and splendor . . . coloured from nature with so much elegance as to emulate a painting." In ways intimated clearly by such reviews, the appearance of Catesby's book was one of the ways that it engaged the contradictory relationship between cultural refinement and the barbarism of slavery, as that relationship continued to play out in the history of South Carolina.[48]

Since Michel Foucault's influential work on the "classical" episteme, as elaborated by subsequent scholars including Mary Louise Pratt, natural history has been understood primarily in terms of its radical effacement of historical content, as a discourse in which plants and animals are extracted from the circumstances of their local use to be placed in the appropriate spot in the book of nature. In Sloane's *Voyage to . . . Jamaica,* almost the opposite is true. The emblematic specimen travels to the reader freighted with troubling knowledge, not only of local conditions within colonial plantation societies but also of the new cultural and economic practices that link the West Indies to developments in the wider circumatlantic world. This is

47. On the format and expense of natural histories by Sloane and Catesby, see Kriz, *Slavery, Sugar, and the Culture of Refinement*, 201–202 (note 13), 202–203 (note 25); David R. Brigham, "Mark Catesby and the Patronage of Natural History in the First Half of the Eighteenth Century," in Amy R. W. Meyers and Margaret Beck Pritchard, eds., *Empire's Nature: Mark Catesby's New World Vision* (Chapel Hill, N.C., 1998), 93; Joyce E. Chaplin, "Mark Catesby, a Skeptical Newtonian in America," ibid., 83.

48. *Gentleman's Magazine,* XXII (1752), 300. Botanist Richard Pulteney later judged the *Natural History of Carolina* "the most splendid of its kind that England . . . ever produced." See Richard Pulteney, *Historical and Biographical Sketches of the Progress of Botany in England, from Its Origin to the Introduction of the Linnean System* (London, 1790), 226.

a reason that *Voyage to . . . Jamaica* would become such an influential text for the authors examined in the remaining chapters of this study, not only as an authoritative reference guiding their inquiries into natural history but also as a formal model for contemplating the place of the West Indies in the history of modern commercial progress and intellectual enlightenment.[49]

49. Michel Foucault, *The Order of Things: An Archaeology of the Human Sciences* (New York, 1970); Mary Louise Pratt, *Imperial Eyes: Travel Writing and Transculturation* (New York, 1992). In keeping with Foucault's analysis, Pratt argues, "The eighteenth-century classificatory systems created the task of locating every species on the planet, extracting it from its particular, arbitrary surroundings (the chaos), and placing it in its appropriate spot in the system (the order—book, collection, or garden) with its new written, secular European name" (31).

2

Fatal Latitudes

THE POETICS OF WEST INDIAN "IMPROVEMENT" IN MARK CATESBY'S *NATURAL HISTORY OF CAROLINA, FLORIDA, AND THE BAHAMA ISLANDS*

Even an initial consideration of Mark Catesby's engraving of "Green Tree Frog and Arum Americanum" (Plate 1) makes plain that it is a dramatic departure from the conventions of natural history illustration as established in Sloane's *Voyage to . . . Jamaica*. The use of vivid color creates a distinctive visual impression, the crucial initial stage in a Lockean model for acquiring and transmitting knowledge. A life-sized rendering of a single green leaf fills the center background, providing a strong tonal complement for the purple flowers while framing and grounding the interaction between frog, insect, and plant.[1]

The accompanying description of the frog emphasizes that the accurate rendering of tonal relationships—achieved through a laborious process of hand-coloring the individual plates in each copy—serves epistemological as well as aesthetic aims. Only through the perception of color can the viewer develop a proper understanding of this scene of nature. The frog conceals itself from its numerous predators in Carolina and Virginia by clinging to the undersides of large, green leaves. The texture of the engraving also communicates this. Tree frogs can only perform this feat owing to the "extraordinary Structure of their Toes," "somewhat like the Mouth of a Leech." Although they can affix these toes to even the smoothest of surfaces, the structure of the arum leaf makes it especially adhesive. Care is taken to specify the position of the frog's eight front and ten back toes as they adhere to the leaf, an effect that could only be achieved by eschewing a more traditional "method of cross-Hatching," just as in Catesby's images of birds,

---

1. Mark Catesby, *The Natural History of Carolina, Florida, and the Bahama Islands: Containing the Figures of Birds, Beasts, Fishes, Serpents, Insects, and Plants . . .* , 2 vols. (London, 1731–1743), II, 71. The type of schematic line engraving employed in most illustrations in Sloane's *Voyage to . . . Jamaica* was refined later in the eighteenth century by George Ehret, who became the dominant scientific illustrator of the day through his work on Carolus Linnaeus's *Hortus Cliffortianus*. See Loraine Daston and Peter Galison, *Objectivity* (New York, 2007), 55.

where his stylus instead "follow[s] the humour of the Feathers, which is more laborious, and I hope has proved more to the purpose."[2]

Through its distinctive pictorial techniques, as made legible by the prose description, the image yields a new form of empirical knowledge, more attentive to relationships between organisms, traits, and behaviors as they play out in a particular place at a specific moment in time. In the transparent light of the natural history illustration (the tree frog normally hunts at night, Catesby tells us), this specimen prepares to consume the spider suspended above it by a single vertical filament, which intersects with the central vein of the arum leaf to create a precise yet fragile sense of compositional balance, as precarious as the spider's fate at this decisive moment.

Like many New World botanists before him, Catesby was fascinated by arum because numerous varieties had been introduced into the Americas by enslaved Africans, who cultivated them in provision gardens throughout the West Indies as a food source. Multiple images and descriptions from the *Natural History of Carolina* depict new organic relationships resulting from the introduction of arum into Carolina, along with increasing numbers of enslaved Africans, at a transformative moment in the colony's history.

Because of this attention to organic relationships, it is surprising to learn that this variety of arum was not among those that Catesby observed and documented in Carolina, where the "green frog" was indigenous. Catesby encountered it only after his return to England, in Peter Collinson's botanical garden: "The Introduction of this most curious Plant with innumerable others, is owing to the indefatigable Attachment of Mr. *Collinson,* who in the Year 1735, received it from *Pensilvania,* and in the Spring following it displayed itself in this Manner at *Peckham.*" Though his source remains unnamed here, Collinson had received the plant from John Bartram, whose botanical garden outside Philadelphia would emerge as an important source of colonial seeds and plants for an expanding network of English gardeners and botanical collectors. What first appeared to be a faithful representation of a scene of nature within Carolina turns out to be a collage of specimens collected in colonies throughout British America. Moreover, Catesby's engraving depicts multiple stages in the seasonal growth cycle of the plant as if they occur simultaneously, when, in fact, "the Leaves appear of the Size here exhibited" only after "the Decay of the Flowers." So recent is the introduction of the plant to England that Catesby has yet to observe

2. Catesby, *Natural History,* I, xi, II, 71.

this final stage. Rather, "As the Flowers of this Plant were engraven before I had an Opportunity of seeing the Leaves, I was obliged to introduce a Leaf in the Manner as in the Plate," most likely tracing it from an herbarium.[3]

We begin with this engraving because it evinces the sophistication and intricacy of Catesby's poetics in the *Natural History of Carolina*. As important, it also helps us to understand the structure and format of the book in relation to a pivotal moment in the history of the West Indian plantation. The organization of the text as an extended visual essay is highly innovative. The reader is presented with a sequence of engravings that combine plants and animals in the same pictorial field, with the linguistic descriptions of those specimens provided on the subsequent page (in English and French in adjacent columns). This facilitates the deft interpretive movement between image and word that had been essential to Sloane's emblematic engravings. At the same time, however, this structural pattern also meant that Catesby largely eschewed the kind of extended first-person narration—examining the social and cultural life of a plantation colony—that had been customary in previous natural histories. (Only a cursory travel narrative of the Bahamas, Florida, and Carolina is included near the beginning of volume I.) Relatedly, Catesby also chose not to include illustrations of human artifacts. This is by no means to say, however, that the text neglects human history altogether. Art historian Amy R. W. Meyers argues that Catesby's distinctive pictorial and linguistic techniques comprise a "visual system to express environmental relationships" and in particular for examining "the ways in which newly introduced organisms from around the globe were changing existing patterns of organic interaction." Through this juxtaposition of animals and plants within a single image, Catesby's engravings provide a lens for contemplating the "improvement" of British America.[4]

Through such aesthetic innovations, the *Natural History of Carolina* attempts to make legible for its readers a new and shifting geography of

3. Ibid., II, 71. On arum, see, for instance, Hans Sloane, *A Voyage to the Islands Madera, Barbados, Nieves, S. Christophers, and Jamaica, with the Natural History of the Herbs and Trees, Four-Footed Beasts, Fishes, Birds, Insects, Reptiles, etc. of the Last of Those Islands . . .* , 2 vols. (London, 1707–1725), I, xxv, 166–167. On Catesby's interest in organic relationships, see Amy R. W. Meyers, "Picturing a World in Flux: Mark Catesby's Response to Environmental Interchange and Colonial Expansion," in Meyers and Margaret Beck Pritchard, eds., *Empire's Nature: Mark Catesby's New World Vision* (Chapel Hill, N.C., 1998), 228–258 (quotations on 234, 240). Collinson's earliest surviving letter to John Bartram mentions that "the Warmth of the ship and Want of Air had Occasion'd the Skunk Weed to putt Forth Two fine Blossoms, very beautiful it is of the Arum Genus." See Dorothy Smith Berkeley and Edmund Berkeley, eds., *The Correspondence of John Bartram, 1734–1777* (Gainesville, Fla., 1992), 4.

4. Meyers, "Picturing a World in Flux," in Meyers and Pritchard, eds., *Empire's Nature*, 234, 240.

plantation slavery and tropical agriculture in the Americas. Catesby's itinerant path through British America—ranging from Jamaica, the Bahamas, Florida, Georgia, South Carolina, and Virginia—put him in an ideal position to document the geographic expansion of the West Indian plantation as a template for social and economic organization in the colonies. Not unlike cultural geographers today, Catesby traces the emergence of a new cultural landscape in a particular locale as it is reshaped by global patterns of commercial and financial exchange. By training his powers of observation on new organic interrelationships in Carolina during its rapid transition to plantation agriculture, Catesby charts the incorporation of the colony into the Greater Caribbean.

However exhilarating the prospect for Catesby's diverse subscribers (including virtuosi of the Royal Society, horticulturalists, gardeners, merchants, investors, imperial administrators, colonial governors, and planters), it was not without troubling implications for the future of the British Empire. At the level of physical format, publication strategy, visual poetics, and linguistic form, the *Natural History of Carolina* addresses anxieties that were of cardinal import for the readers of colonial natural histories. In particular, the volumes confront those interrelated problems of epistemology, environmental transformation, and finance capital that were examined in the previous chapter. With the continued expansion of plantation agriculture and the triangle trade, such problems had only intensified. As Catesby's readers well knew, recent interest in Carolina was motivated both by a seemingly inexhaustible appetite for new speculative ventures in the West Indies (fed by growing consumer demand for Caribbean comestibles and dyestuffs) and by a mounting conviction that the profitability of islands such as Barbados and Jamaica faced serious threats, owing in large part to environmental factors such as soil exhaustion, erosion, pest invasion, and epidemic disease. By shipping annually to his subscribers a set of twenty engravings with accompanying descriptions and by focusing in many cases on complex interconnections between recently introduced species, the *Natural History of Carolina* met the demands of a readership hungry for more timely intelligence from the colonies, concerned that environmental change in the Caribbean might outpace the ability of metropolitan elites to document, interpret, and improve them for financial gain and scientific progress.[5]

5. David R. Brigham, "Mark Catesby and the Patronage of Natural History in the First Half of the Eighteenth Century," in Meyers and Pritchard, eds., *Empire's Nature*, 91–146, esp. 92, 113–119.

The opulent physical format of the text, however, indicates that it served far more than instrumental purposes. Catesby began to circulate his engravings and descriptions during a moment when the consumption of luxury goods from the West Indies had begun to take on contradictory new meanings. By the early to mid-eighteenth century, West Indian commodities occupied a complex position within a cultural debate over the potential civilizing effect of commercial empire. Confidence that civility and refinement were the inevitable rewards of commercial empire was far from unshakable. As Philip Gould demonstrates, texts such as John Trenchard's *Cato's Letters* (1720–1723) and Montesquieu's *Spirit of Laws* (1748) expressed growing fears over the morally corrupting influence of mercantile and finance capitalism. Such fears were born of an emerging hypothesis, articulated most fully in the stadial theory of the Scottish Enlightenment, that "Commerce produces forms of cultural refinement that potentially become enervating 'Luxury,'" in particular when they are associated with the "barbaric traffic" of the slave trade. It was because of this long-standing debate that abolitionists later in the century would attack the consumption of sugar as a debilitating influence on English bodies and manners, as part of a broader effort to "demarcate the boundary between virtuous and vicious commerce."[6]

On one level, the physical format of the *Natural History of Carolina* is designed to extol the civilizing effects of West Indian commerce, demonstrating the capacity of European technology and expertise (combined with African labor) to transform Caribbean nature into a source of commercial progress, intellectual advancement, and the refinement of man-

6. Philip Gould, *Barbaric Traffic: Commerce and Antislavery in the Eighteenth-Century Atlantic World* (Cambridge, Mass., 2003), 21. On ideologies of "barbarity" and "civilization" in the context of commercial and consumer society, see, for instance, J. G. A. Pocock, *Virtue, Commerce, and History: Essays on Political Thought and History, Chiefly in the Eighteenth Century* (Cambridge, 1985), 37–50; Albert O. Hirschman, *The Passions and the Interests: Political Arguments for Capitalism before Its Triumph* (Princeton, N.J., 1977); Paul Langford, *A Polite and Commercial People: England, 1727–1783* (New York, 1994); Roy Porter, "Consumption: Disease of the Consumer Society?" in John Brewer and Roy Porter, eds., *Consumption and the World of Goods* (New York, 1993), 58–81; John Brewer, "'The Most Polite Age and the Most Vicious': Attitudes towards Culture as a Commodity, 1660–1800," in Brewer and Ann Bermingham, eds., *The Consumption of Culture, 1600–1800: Image, Object, Text* (London, 1995), 341–361; T. H. Breen, *The Marketplace of Revolution: How Consumer Politics Shaped American Independence* (New York, 2004). On the role of colonial and especially West Indian commodities in these debates, see Laura Brown, *Ends of Empire: Women and Ideology in the Early Eighteenth-Century English Literature* (Ithaca, N.Y., 1993), 23–63; Charlotte Sussman, *Consuming Anxieties: Consumer Protest, Gender, and British Slavery, 1713–1833* (Stanford, Calif., 2000); Kathleen Wilson, *The Island Race: Englishness, Empire, and Gender in the Eighteenth Century* (New York, 2002), 16, 129–168; James Walvin, *Fruits of Empire: Exotic Produce and British Taste, 1660–1800* (New York, 1997), 91–98.

ners. The poetics of individual images such as "Green Tree Frog and Arum Americanum," however, present a more ambiguous vision of colonial development. Though he avoids many of the strategies Sloane employed in his emblematic engravings, Catesby's text nonetheless shares with *Voyage to . . . Jamaica* a basic commitment to using illustrations of Caribbean nature as emblems or orienting devices for discerning otherwise inscrutable patterns of imperial history. Deeply engaged with post-Newtonian efforts to theorize the natural world as an integrated system rather than a set of discrete particulars, Catesby's reconstituted emblems present contradictory hypotheses about the trajectory of historical and environmental change in Carolina. The introduction of West Indian flora, fauna, and agricultural techniques may result in a providential global garden, fulfilling the ambition of early modern naturalists to reassemble Paradise in a single, ordered locale. But it may also result in a barbaric natural environment characterized by upheaval and violence, especially in the complex, semiaquatic landscape of the rice plantation.[7]

We also begin with "Green Tree Frog and Arum Americanum" to highlight the importance of Catesby's text for the literary and scientific endeavors of learned North Americans in the period. The serial publication of the *Natural History of Carolina* over nearly two decades created opportunities for mainland intellectuals to participate in the wider world of imperial science as collectors for, subscribers to, and even critics of Catesby's volumes. The previous chapter argued that printed natural histories of the Caribbean provided a form of epistemological training for metropolitan and colonial readers as subjects of a new commercial empire. Through examination of the correspondence of John Bartram, William Byrd II, and Eliza Lucas Pinckney, this chapter provides a more concrete sense of how this process played out on the ground in British America. As they turned their atten-

7. On Catesby's interest in new catastrophist views of nature, which in some ways anticipated modern chaos theory, see Joyce E. Chaplin, "Mark Catesby, a Skeptical Newtonian in America," in Meyers and Pritchard, eds., *Empire's Nature*, 34–90. In tracing the persistence of emblematic method in Catesby's text, I diverge from Kay Dian Kriz, who argues that Catesby's exclusion of human artifacts reflects a "narrowing of the field of enquiry [that] was closely associated with the professionalization of the life sciences, which relegated curiosities and emblematic images to the realm of popular culture and the domain of amateur pursuits." See Kay Dian Kriz, *Slavery, Sugar, and the Culture of Refinement: Picturing the British West Indies, 1740–1800* (New Haven, Conn., 2008), 35. As I will argue in Chapters 4 and 6 below, this professionalization occurred only slowly and intermittently. Later naturalists such as Bartram and Audubon retained a strong interest in emblematic method. For a suggestive consideration of Catesby's "iconographic" technique, see David S. Wilson, "The Iconography of Mark Catesby," *Eighteenth-Century Studies*, IV (1971), 169–183.

tion to natural history in the early to mid-eighteenth century, these provincial intellectuals simultaneously learned to conceive of "local" experience in necessary relation to the West Indies. The circum-Caribbean geography of Catesby's volumes was fundamental to their developing sense of imperial belonging and thus to a range of epistolary self-representations designed to negotiate its terms.[8]

"Carolina in the West Indies"

Though Catesby resided in British America for a total of twelve years during two separate visits, two years at most were spent in the islands of the Antilles. As recounted in the preface to the *Natural History of Carolina*, Catesby traveled to Virginia for an extended stay between 1712 and 1719, leaving the colony only for a brief tour of Jamaica and possibly Hispaniola in 1714. With the encouragement of the botanist and Fellow of the Royal Society (FRS) William Sherard, Catesby returned to the Americas in 1722 with a more focused promotional and scientific agenda. On Sherard's advice, he embarked for South Carolina, "which Country, tho' inhabited by *English* above an Age past, and a Country inferior to none in Fertility, and abounding in Variety of the Blessings of Nature; yet it's Productions [are] very little known except what barely related to Commerce, such as Rice, Pitch and Tar." Once settled in Carolina, Catesby traveled widely and systematically. From his base of operations around Charleston (then the third largest port city on the mainland and the hub of a commercial network linking Britain's mainland and island colonies), Catesby organized expeditions to Georgia and East Florida (1723), the Carolina backcountry (1724), and the Bahamas (1725).[9]

Though Carolina was the avowed regional focus of his second expedition, and though his visits to the Bahamas and the sugar islands were relatively brief, specimens and narratives from these latter locales comprise a dispro-

---

8. On colonial criticism of Catesby's engravings as inaccurate and excessively theatrical, see David Scofield Wilson, *In the Presence of Nature* (Amherst, Mass., 1978), 139–140; George Frederick Frick and Raymond Phineas Stearns, *Mark Catesby: The Colonial Audubon* (Urbana, Ill., 1961); Alan Feduccia, ed., *Catesby's Birds of Colonial America* (Chapel Hill, N.C., 1985); Susan Scott Parrish, *American Curiosity: Cultures of Natural History in the Colonial British Atlantic World* (Chapel Hill, N.C., 2006), 130–133. For a representative example, see Alexander Garden to Carolus Linnaeus, Jan. 2, 1760, in James Edward Smith, ed., *A Selection of the Correspondence of Linnaeus and Other Naturalists from the Original Manuscripts* (London, 1821), 300–301.

9. Catesby, *Natural History*, I, v, vi. For Catesby's biography, see Frick and Stearns, *Colonial Audubon*.

portionate number of his engravings and descriptions. Of the one hundred engravings in volume I (devoted to birds and associated flora), twenty-six portray a species either observed by Catesby himself in the Bahamas and West Indies or known to be common there. Significant in its own right, that number only begins to account for the prominence of the region within the first volume. Catesby remarks at numerous points that birds observed in Carolina likely winter in the Caribbean, a conjecture that would lead to his groundbreaking theory of avian migration. This is just one reason for his increasing interest in the islands. Of the one hundred engravings in volume II (covering fish, crustaceans, reptiles, birds, and mammals, with associated flora), fully fifty-seven are from the Bahamas and West Indies.[10]

This uneven emphasis is partly explained by the simple fact that the Caribbean remained central to the mercantilist and scientific imagination in the period. As they had in the 1680s when Sloane traveled to Jamaica, natural historians still followed established trade routes to the Americas, this in a period when the volume of goods shipped annually from the sugar islands continued to grow exponentially. (The total tonnage of sugar exports from the British islands increased by nearly fivefold between 1700 to 1787, whereas the volume of sugar shipped from the French West Indies increased twelvefold over the same period.) By the 1740s, publication of a second generation of Anglophone books on West Indian natural history had begun, with Charles Leslie's *New History of Jamaica* (1740) followed in quick succession by William Smith's *Natural History of Nevis* (1745), Griffith Hughes's *Natural History of Barbados* (1750), and Patrick Browne's *Civil and Natural History of Jamaica* (1756). In compiling these books, the authors continued to rely on an extensive network of informants, collectors, and correspondents in the islands. As a result, eighteen West Indian correspondents were elected Fellows of the Royal Society between 1661 and 1778, ten from Jamaica alone. As Patrick Browne reminded his readers, islands such as Jamaica "supply us with a necessary appendage to our present refined manner of living. These are well known circumstances; and that the wealth of many, the subsistence of multitudes, the extent of our Navigation, the Revenues of the Crown, and in short the Emolument of the whole Nation, are deeply interested and augmented by the perpetual intercourse

---

10. Chaplin, "A Skeptical Newtonian in America," in Meyers and Pritchard, eds., *Empire's Nature*, 60–64; Mark Catesby, "Of Birds of Passage," Royal Society, *Philosophical Transactions*, XLIV (1747), 435–444.

with this distant Island." Catesby's prior volumes on the Americas, in this context, constituted one important indication of British refinement.[11]

But the Bahamas were not Jamaica. When Catesby visited the islands in 1725 and judged them an unpromising site for agricultural development, they were home to an estimated six hundred whites and two hundred blacks. The majority of the southern islands (near the southeastern tip of Cuba) were small, barren, and "not worth settling," whereas larger islands to the north (Nassau and Grand Bahamas) supported only scrub vegetation. The Bahamas were not a "necessary appendage" to British refinement in the same sense as Browne's Jamaica. Nor were they a potential "emolument" of the nation in the same sense as Carolina and Virginia, where planters were enjoying success with rice and tobacco respectively.[12]

Catesby's brief travel narrative of the Bahamas argues that their importance owes to their geographic position, extending "from the Gulph of *Florida* in a South East Direction almost the whole Length of *Cuba*." Though located within the tropics, islands such as Nassau are cooled by westerly winds:

> The North side of *Cuba* also enjoys the Benefit of these refreshing Winds, particularly that Part of the Island on which the *Havana* stands, to this, no doubt, is owing the Healthiness of the Air and good Character of that proud *Emporium;* the Conquest of which, by *British* Arms, would put us in Possession of a Country much more agreeable to *British* Constitutions, than any of the Islands between the *Tropicks,* and under God, enable them to multiply, and stand their Ground, without the Necessity of such numerous Recruits from their Mother-

---

11. Economic statistics are from Robin Blackburn, *The Making of New World Slavery: From the Baroque to the Modern, 1492–1800* (London, 1997), 403. Prominent West Indian natural histories after Sloane include [Charles Leslie], *A New History of Jamaica, from the Earliest Accounts to the Taking of Porto Bello by Vice-Admiral Vernon in Thirteen Letters from a Gentleman to His Friend* (London, 1740); William Smith, *A Natural History of Nevis, and the Rest of the English Leeward Charibee Islands in America . . .* (Cambridge, 1745); Griffith Hughes, *The Natural History of Barbados: In Ten Books* (London, 1750); Patrick Browne, *The Civil and Natural History of Jamaica . . .* (London, 1756), v. On colonial FRS, see Raymond Phineas Stearns, "Colonial Fellows of the Royal Society of London, 1661–1778," *Osiris*, VIII (1948), 73–121. West Indian FRS included Thomas Hoy (Jamaica), Walter Douglass (Leeward Islands), Henry Barham (Jamaica), Colin Campbell (Jamaica), John Gray (Cartagena), Rose Fuller, MD (Jamaica), William Houston (West Indies), Alexander MacFarlane (Jamaica), Griffith Hughes (Barbados), David Riz (Jamaica), John Martin Butt, MD (Jamaica), Thomas Lashley, MD (Barbados), Tesser Samuel Kukhan (Jamaica), John Greg (Dominica), John Coakley Lettson, MD (Tortola), John Taylor (Jamaica), William Wright, MD (Jamaica), Gilbert Blane, MD (West Indies).

12. Catesby, *Natural History*, II, xxxviii.

country, as has been always found necessary to prevent a total Extinction of the inhabitants of our unhealthy Sugar Islands.

The natural history of the Bahamas plays a unique role in securing the fragile future of the British Empire, for it provides a revealing vantage on a colony that was regarded as a potential jewel but had remained closed to British inquiry owing to the notorious insularity of Spanish colonial administration. Observation, description, and collection in the Bahamas will contribute to a more authoritative and detailed picture of Cuba as a physical place. The sense of urgency is palpable. The West Indies are an ornament to British wealth that is destructive of English health, which depends on a carefully calibrated relation between the physical constitution of Britons and a climate approximating the home nation. The human costs of residence in the British West Indies are measured precisely yet coolly. Possession of Cuba would eliminate "the Necessity of such numerous Recruits from their Mother-country," many of whom will perish in the morbid environment of Barbados and Jamaica, death traps for Britons and Africans alike. Questions about the relationship between civility and barbarism cast a deep shadow over Catesby's efforts.[13]

The author's posture as imperial projector here illuminates his interest in specimens from the Spanish Caribbean. Near the beginning of the first volume, Catesby describes the plumage of the "Parrot of Paradise of Cuba" in detail, from "the upper-part of the Head, Neck, Back and Wings, of a bright yellow, except the Quill-feathers of the Wing, which are white" to the reddish bands across the yellow tail feathers. Strangely, the description follows an image of the species on the previous page (Plate 2). Why the redundancy of a linguistic text that tells what has just been shown so effectively? Perhaps Catesby wanted to call attention to the range and intensity of color in his engravings. His facility with color was a valuable asset. Upon the publication of volume I, Catesby was elected to the Royal Society on the strength of numerous positive reviews (quoted at the end of Chapter 1) that characterized the reproduction of New World colors in the *Natural History of Carolina* as a momentous event in the history of print technology. For the bourgeois readers of such reviews, the intense coloring of Catesby's volumes made them valuable indicators of refinement. As David S. Shields remarks, the conspicuous public display of one's person through brightly colored clothing provided one of "the principal means of 'cutting a figure'

13. Ibid., i, xxxviii.

in society." New World commodities including logwood, indigo, and cochineal thus were "valued extravagantly" as the source of durable and dramatic dyes.[14]

Engravings such as "Parrot of Paradise of Cuba" function as the crudest of Catesby's emblematic specimens, using vibrant color to envision the spoils of Cuban conquest. Catesby's preoccupation with the natural history of the Bahamas is motivated by related speculative desires. Empirical scrutiny of the islands will provide the basis for authoritative conjectures on Cuban nature, as imperial projectors seek a more rational and stable balance between tropical wealth and English health. In this broader context, Catesby develops a scientific theory that Joyce E. Chaplin identifies as his boldest. He proposes that "a north-south continuum through the Americas . . . rather than latitudinal bands that looped around the globe, explained nearly all differences among American climates," challenging metropolitan assumptions that "the globe could . . . be divided into vertical bands in which the climate on one side of the globe was similar to that of its geographic opposite" and in which the same commodities could predictably be derived from each locale. In developing his theory of American climatic variation, Catesby arrived at a far less consoling and confident vision of the natural order and humans' ability to discern and control it, especially in the New World tropics. That vision is embodied in a series of specimens from the Bahamas and South Carolina.[15]

According to Chaplin, Catesby is best understood as a "skeptical Newtonian," part of a first generation of post-Newtonian naturalists who sought "to theorize nature as a set of *functions* (rather than as discrete objects) and thereby identify systemic qualities of the material world." Although the Royal Society continued to emphasize empirical studies including botany and natural history, the emergence of probability theory contributed to the rising prestige of mechanical and mathematical sciences devoted to the establishment of universal laws. This inspired a similar approach to studying organic nature. Catesby's text takes shape in a period when naturalists

14. Ibid., I, 10; David S. Shields, *Oracles of Empire: Poetry, Politics, and Commerce in British America, 1690–1750* (Chicago, 1990), 68. Catesby directly addresses the subject of dye products as valuable commodities in his engraving and description of "The Green Lizard of *Jamaica*" and "Logwood." Referring to the "bloody Disputes which this useful Tree has occasioned between the *Spaniards* and *English*," Catesby considers whether "the Inhabitants of our Southern Plantations could be induced to propagate it." See Catesby, *Natural History*, II, 66.

15. Chaplin, "A Skeptical Newtonian in America," in Meyers and Pritchard, eds., *Empire's Nature*, 47, 49. On latitudinal understandings of climate, see Richard H. Grove, *Green Imperialism: Colonial Expansion, Tropical Island Edens and the Origins of Environmentalism, 1600–1860* (Cambridge, 1996), 46–47.

were newly inclined to posit universal laws for organic nature but worked in the absence of any established theoretical model. (The rise of Carolus Linnaeus and the comte de Buffon would change matters later in the century.) As a result, post-Newtonian naturalists expressed new laws of nature in diffident, suggestive, and fragmentary terms. Many remained skeptical of the "human capacity to predict natural events," if predictable universal patterns even existed.[16]

Catesby's experiences in the Bahamas are integral to his theory of climate; there, he perceives the inadequacy of latitudinal understandings. In the travel narrative, Catesby insists that the islands "are blessed with a most serene Air . . . more healthy than most other Countries in the same Latitude." Indeed, they are even healthier than some more northerly colonies, to the point that "many of the sickly Inhabitants of *Carolina* . . . retire to them for the Recovery of their Health." Catesby locates the Bahamas in relation to the Torrid Zone in precise and technical terms: "The Northernmost of these Islands lie as much without the Northern *Tropick,* as the Southernmost do within it, their Extent of *Latitude* being about five Degrees; yet that Distance, so near the *Tropick,* causes little Difference in their Temperature." The character of a given colony as either temperate or tropical, it emerges, depends on numerous factors other than latitude:

> But those Islands that lye West, and nearest the Coast of *Florida,* are affected with cold Winds, blowing from the North-west over a vast Tract of Continent, to those which lye East, the Winds have a larger Tract of Sea to pass, which blunts the frigid Particles, and allays the sharpness of them. At the Island of *Providence* in *December* 1725, it was two Days so cold, that we were necessitated to make a Fire in the Governors Kitchen to warm us, yet no Frost nor Snow ever appears there, nor even on *Grand Bahama,* which lies not twenty Leagues

---

16. Chaplin, "A Skeptical Newtonian in America," in Meyers and Pritchard, eds., *Empire's Nature,* 35–37. On the impact of the Newtonian revolution more generally, see John Gascoigne, *Cambridge in the Age of the Enlightenment: Science, Religion, and Politics from the Restoration to the French Revolution* (New York, 1989); Peter Gay, *The Enlightenment: An Interpretation,* II, *The Science of Freedom* (New York, 1966), 128–141. On Newtonian principles as applicable to natural science, see Richard Drayton, *Nature's Government: Science, Imperial Britain, and the "Improvement" of the World* (New Haven, Conn., 2000), 68; Roger Hahn, *The Anatomy of a Scientific Institution: The Paris Academy of Sciences, 1666–1803* (Berkeley, Calif., 1971). For the geopolitical implications of Newtonian natural philosophy, especially in the colonies, see Mary Louise Pratt, *Imperial Eyes: Travel Writing and Transculturation* (New York, 1993), 1–36; Ralph Bauer, *The Cultural Geography of Colonial American Literatures: Empire, Travel, Modernity* (New York, 2003), 179–180.

from the Coast of *Florida*, yet there the Winters are attended with
Frost and Snow.

This depiction of the governor's hearth on two particular winter days lends
authority to Catesby's theory. The evidence of his own sensations tells him
that, along the latitudinal line running through Florida and the northern
Bahamas, temperature varies by longitude, growing warmer as one moves
east, away from the "vast Tract" of North America.[17]

As concerns other important questions of natural history, however, latitude is decisive. Describing coral and tropical fish in the Bahamas, Catesby
posits a sweeping mathematical and probabilistic theory of the relation between latitude and biodiversity:

> Frequent Opportunities has confirmed to me, that as the Productions
> of Nature in general are very scanty near the *Arctic Circle*, there is a
> Gradation of Increase at every Degree of Latitude approaching the
> Tropick, and tho' the Distance of one Degree may not be sufficient to
> perceive it, yet four or five Degrees makes it evidently appear, not only
> by the greater Number of Species of terrestrial Animals, but of Fish
> and Vegetables, which by how much nearer the torrid Zone, so much
> the more numerous they are. And I think it is not improbable that the
> numerous Species of Creatures that inhabit between the Tropicks, far
> exceed in Number all the rest of the Terrestrial World.

The authority of the claim depends on the reader's knowledge, at this late
date in the serial publication of the text, that Catesby's travels have covered
a nearly continuous range of latitudes. His experiences in Virginia, Carolina, Georgia, Florida, the Bahamas, and Jamaica have been documented in
prior specimen descriptions. (Catesby would appeal to this same itinerary,
in similar terms, in his published paper on avian migration.) Theoretical
speculations rooted in his colonial career unsettle assumptions about the
character and limits of the Torrid Zone. Stated in general terms, organic
plenitude increases incrementally along a north-south continuum as one
approaches the tropics, and temperature increases according to the same
principle. But interconnected factors create pockets of local variation. Carolina is less healthy (because more noxious and humid) than the Bahamas,
which shares a similar climate to Cuba, which is, in turn, healthier than
other islands within the tropics. Similarly, even the largest of the Bahamas

17. Catesby, *Natural History*, II, xxxix.

supports less botanical diversity than colonies to the north. Catesby's route through the plantation colonies of British America yields a malleable conception of tropical geography. Temperate conditions exist between the tropics, just as tropical conditions exist outside them.[18]

Catesby's keen interest in remapping the American tropics illuminates his visual poetics. As Meyers has argued, a number of illustrations employ an innovative formal strategy—"a visual language of reflected form"— to describe organic relationships between plants and animals in a shared locale. Such images focus on what we would call habitat, for by the mid-eighteenth century, as Chaplin notes, "a concept of the interconnectedness of nature was acquiring both richness and precision." Catesby's depiction of two "Natives of many of the *Bahama* Islands" provides one rudimentary example of this attention to local relationships. A bird identified as "Purple Gross-Beak" is pictured with its characteristic food, a plant called "Poison Wood" (Plate 3). Rotating its head so that its breast and profile can be observed simultaneously, the bird clutches a stem in its beak while its feet cling to the branch beneath. The shape and positioning of the bird's wing mirrors the surrounding leaves, just as the form and color of its body is reflected in miniature by the berries ("shaped like a Pear, of a purple Colour"). By foregrounding a detailed knowledge that depends on firsthand experience in the islands, Catesby lends authority to his broader speculations on American biodiversity and climate. His engraving of "Green Tree Frog and Arum Americanum" holds similar implications for his portrayal of Carolina as "a Country inferior to none in Fertility." In a period when speculative knowledge of less familiar regions in the Americas was increasingly vital (owing both to the rising prestige of Newtonian science and the inexhaustible consumer demand for West Indian products and profits), Catesby's language of reflected form achieves epistemological work, suggesting the stable basis of theoretical conjecture in direct perception.[19]

In numerous other images, however, Catesby labors to create a fictitious appearance of local organic relationships, in ways that rely on the aggressive visual punning we have seen in Sloane's emblematic engravings. "The Flamingo" (Fig. 4) appears to portray a West Indian landscape. Positioned

---

18. Ibid., xlii. For a more extensive consideration of Catesby's theory of biodiversity and latitude, see Chaplin, "A Skeptical Newtonian in America," in Meyers and Pritchard, eds., *Empire's Nature*, 49–50.

19. Meyers, "Picturing a World in Flux," in Meyers and Pritchard, eds., *Empire's Nature*, 230. Meyers argues, "Compositional associations describe a set of physical and behavioral relationships that seem to bind these organisms to one another within a shared habitat" (ibid.). See also Catesby, *Natural History*, I, 40; Chaplin, "A Skeptical Newtonian in America," in Meyers and Pritchard, eds., *Empire's Nature*, 51.

on a rocky shoreline characteristic of the Bahamas, the flamingo stands erect in front of a specimen of local flora identified as "Keratophyton dichotomum fuscum." Bird and plant are nearly identical in height. Two small islands (one containing palm trees) are visible in the background. Gestures toward verisimilitude, however, are undercut by the text. The type of coral pictured here grows not on dry land but rather "at the Bottom of the shallow Seas and Channels of the *Bahama* Islands." And whereas it typically reaches a height of "about two Feet," the flamingo, "when it stands erect, is five Feet high." Through this deconstruction of a seemingly faithful landscape, Catesby highlights his ingenuity in dislocating specimens and manipulating perspective and scale. The visual effect is striking, with the texture of the flamingo's plumage offset by the coral and its lurid pink complemented by the pale blue of the surrounding sea. In the context of Catesby's promotional agenda, the engraving celebrates the sophistication of European print technology. Performing this figurative transformation of the environment, Catesby's expensive volumes also advocate its literal improvement, promoting the transplantation of numerous species (such as logwood) into the British West Indies for profitable cultivation.[20]

Although reflecting venerable georgic ideals, Catesby's visual language as often conveys more ominous forms of knowledge, especially in illustrations that combine his focus on actual organic relationships (as in "Purple Gross-Beak") with his interest in manipulating scale and uprooting specimens for heightened aesthetic impact (as in "The Flamingo"). The dislocation of organic matter is understood in these images less as the result of human agency than as an inherent characteristic of the tropics, a natural "order" that verges on chaotic violence. In a republic of science concerned with the cultural toxicity of the West Indies, such images possessed special resonance.

Catesby's engraving of "Alligator and Mangrove Tree" is the most sophisticated of these images, and one that explicitly relates to his theoretical speculations on American climate (Plate 4). The image presents us with difficult problems of perspective and scale, initiating a recursive movement between illustration and text. Multiple formal associations link the alligator lying horizontally in the bottom third of the picture to what appears to be a large mangrove tree extending vertically from the alligator's midsection to bisect the page. Curling downward from the center of the flowers, three long, green appendages (later identified as seeds) echo the form of the alli-

20. Catesby, *Natural History*, I, 73.

FIGURE 4. *The Flamingo and Keratophyton Dichotomum Fuscum.* Mark Catesby, *The Natural History of Carolina, Florida, and the Bahama Islands: Containing the Figures of Birds, Beasts, Fishes, Serpents, Insects, and Plants . . .* , 2 vols. (London, 1731–1743), I, pl. 73. The Colonial Williamsburg Foundation

gator's body, which tapers gradually from its bulbous head to the point of its upraised and curled tail. The detached sprig of mangrove in the left foreground also mirrors the alligator's form. The scene is carefully located in time and space. A single light source emanates from the top left of the frame to cast a strong shadow beneath the alligator (in a swath of rich, brown mud) while highlighting a large egg in the right foreground. It is here, however, that conventions of perspective and scale begin to break down, and not only because the egg is wildly disproportionate to the alligator. Though the egg is lower on the page and thus should be "closer" to the viewer, the alligator's tail crosses in front of it to impede our line of vision. Conversely, two hanging seeds pass behind the alligator's body but curl in front of the egg.

Turning to the accompanying text, the reader receives new information on the alligator's geographic range. Because the species is so well known among Europeans, Catesby limits his observations to "some Things which have been omitted by others." His travels from southern North America through the sugar islands are again crucial to his ability to augment existing knowledge:

> Tho' the largest and greatest Numbers inhabit the *Torrid Zone,* the Continent abounds with them ten Degrees more North, particularly as far as the River *Neus* in *North Carolina,* in the Latitude of about 33, beyond which I have never heard of any, which Latitude nearly answers to the Northermost Parts of *Africa,* where they are likewise found.

The passage proposes a flexible analogy between African and New World climates in order to present an extended archipelago of island and coastal colonies—from North Carolina through the Torrid Zone—as an integrated environmental unit. This region can be demarcated by precise coordinates in part because the geographic range of the alligator in both Africa and the New World makes its boundaries visible while confirming its basic coherence. Catesby returns to this theme to conclude his description of the species. Though alligators are numerous in South Carolina, "the Northern Situation of that Country, occasions their being of a smaller Size than those nearer the *Line*" and causes them to "lie torpid from about *October* to *March.*" That the species is abundant throughout this region but becomes smaller and less numerous approaching its northern limit provides evidence of shared environmental conditions within a new, extended map of the Caribbean, including the colony that imperial officials were beginning to refer to as "Carolina in the West Indies." (It is telling that the heading of the French description reads "Crocodile des Indes Occidentales.")[21]

Having established the geographic range of the species, Catesby devotes the next two paragraphs to its predatory and reproductive behaviors respectively, described in ways that at once resolve the problem of scale in the engraving and provide a tableau of the West Indies as a space of predatory violence. Travelers in the West Indies must be on constant alert, for alligators "frequent not only salt Rivers near the Sea, but Streams of fresh Water in the Upper Parts of the Country, and in Lakes of salt and fresh Water, on the Banks of which they lye lurking among Reeds." The survival of numerous species preyed upon by the alligator, including human beings, depends in large part on divine Providence, which, "to prevent the Extinction, of defenceless Creatures, hath in many Instances restrain'd the devouring Appetites of voracious Animals, by some Impediment." In this case, a rigid spine limits the alligator's range of motion. However, the species itself benefits from this providential interposition, for the "devouring Appetites" of the adult alligators also pose a threat to their successful reproduction. Because the adults abandon their "young ones so soon as they are disengaged from their Shells [to] . . . shift for themselves" in the water, the hatchlings frequently "serve as a Prey, not only to ravenous Fish, but to their own Species."[22]

The disruptions of perspective and scale in the engraving focus attention on the outsized egg and thus on the mysteries of alligator reproduction. The text highlights the providential design embodied in the life cycle of the species: "It is to be admired that so vast an Animal should at first be contained to an Egg, no bigger than that of a Turkey." The engraving initially appears to reverse the terms of this contrast, with the egg exaggeratedly large in relation to what appears to be an adult alligator. But egg and reptile are, in fact, life-sized: "The Figure here exhibited, represents the Size and Figure of an Alligator, soon after the breaking out of the Shell."[23]

The description of the mangrove illuminates the problem of scale and perspective in related ways, as Catesby continues to dwell on the mysteries of tropical reproduction amid pervasive violence. Catesby begins by stressing the size of the mature trees, which grow "in some Places twenty, in others above thirty Feet." After describing the bark, branches, and leaves, he turns

21. Ibid., II, 63.
22. Ibid.
23. Ibid.

next to the flowers and seeds. The blossoms are "suceeded by green succulent Substances, in Form not unlike a Pear, at the small End of which hang a single Seed, about six Inches in Length, in Form of a Bobin, with which Lace is made. These Seeds when they fall, are carried floating on the Water, and lodged on muddy Banks, where their larger Ends settle in the Mud, and take Root, the smaller Ends sprouting, as in the Figure." Identified here are those strange but beautiful appendages that at first seemed drastically out of scale in the engraving (equal in length to the alligator) but are instead, we now discover, depicted at their actual size of "about six Inches." Reinterpreted in this context, the language of reflected form linking the hatchling with the bobbin-like seeds cues the reader to contemplate the inscrutable connections between reproductive behaviors of animal and plant. She or he would next reconsider the branch of mangrove in the center of the image, which turns out to document another unusual method of reproduction: "These Trees propagate not only by their Seeds in this Manner, but the smaller Branches falling into the Mud strike Root, and in a few Years become Trees, which increase in like Manner, and extend their Progress some Miles." The branch is also rendered at life size, as if it has taken root in the muddy earth. (Catesby notes previously that smaller branches "are jointed at the Distance of every Inch.")[24]

Having disclosed that all of the objects in the engraving are depicted in their exact dimensions, Catesby concludes his description by specifying the nature of the interconnection between mangrove and alligator. The description proceeds inside a mangrove forest, conceived as an integrated habitat. Especially along the seacoast, "these impenetrable Woods of Mangroves, are frequented by great Numbers of Alligators, which being too big to enter the closest Recesses of these Thickets, the smaller ones find a secure Retreat from the Jaws of their voracious Parents." The engraving details the process through which plant and reptile reproduce in tandem, even as the language of the description simultaneously evokes both divine providence and primordial chaos. The fallen mangrove branches create a miniature forest, in which the alligator hatchlings find a "secure Retreat" from their "voracious Parents." This ensures both the propagation of the species and the continuity of the mangrove forest as a site of natural violence: "These watery Woods are also plentifully stored with ravenous Fish, Turtles, and other Animals, which prey continually one upon the other, and the Alligators on them all, so that in no Place have I ever seen such remarkable

24. Ibid.

Scenes of Devastation as amongst these Mangroves, in *Andros,* one of the *Bahama* Islands, where the Fragments of half devoured Carcasses were usually floating on the Water." Amid this scene of devastation, the next generation of dominant predators finds refuge in tangled thickets sprouted from dismembered branches and floating seeds. Through multiple misperceptions of scale, subsequently emended by the text, the viewer traces the interconnected life cycles of the two specimens from long seed and diminutive hatchling to mature tree and reptile (and back again). In so doing, she or he develops an accurate understanding of the West Indies—extending as far north as the Carolinas—as a space of cyclical, creative destruction where the conceptual boundary between competing models of natural history, as providential telos and chaotic contingency, has been rendered inscrutable.[25]

This characterization of the West Indies had significant implications for the natural history of South Carolina. The question of how the colony might continue to transform as a physical place preoccupied imperial strategists. Prior natural historians, including Ligon and Sloane, had gravitated toward colonies undergoing the transition to plantation monoculture. So, too, did Catesby. After the introduction of rice culture, the colony quickly adopted the West Indian model of producing a single commercial crop for the world market through reliance on slave labor. Within a few decades, rice became the colony's primary source of income. A relatively small group of whites became immensely rich, leisured, and politically powerful by exploiting a large and growing population of enslaved Africans. When Catesby visited the colony in the 1720s, it was already home to roughly 20,000 slaves, more than half imported directly from Africa. This marked a rapid increase from the 2,400 slaves present in the colony at the turn of the eighteenth century. Like Jamaica before it, South Carolina had transformed rapidly into a black majority colony. By the time a second edition of Catesby's text was published in the mid–1750s, the slave population of the colony stood near 50,000.[26]

This socioeconomic transformation depended on the "improvement" of low-lying West Indian swamps, well known to Catesby's readers as tumul-

25. Ibid.

26. Population figures are estimated from tables in Philip D. Morgan, *Slave Counterpoint: Black Culture in the Eighteenth-Century Chesapeake and Lowcountry* (Chapel Hill, N.C., 1998), 61. On the transformative impact of rice on Carolina, see Daniel C. Littlefield, *Rice and Slaves: Ethnicity and the Slave Trade in Colonial South Carolina* (Baton Rouge, La., 1981); Peter H. Wood, *Black Majority: Negroes in Colonial South Carolina from 1670 to the Stono Rebellion* (New York, 1974); Judith A. Carney, *Black Rice: The African Origins of Rice Cultivation in the Americas* (Cambridge, Mass., 2001).

tuous sites of natural violence. For this reason, Catesby conveys detailed knowledge about the vagaries of the transition to rice cultivation as it intensified the demand for enslaved African workers and necessitated a radical reshaping of the physical environment. In his travel narrative of Carolina, he describes rice cultivation in considerable detail, from constant weeding ("not only with a Hough, but with the Assistance of Fingers") to cutting, threshing, stacking, and beating "by *Negro* Slaves, which is very laborious and tedious." In a prior discussion of topography, moreover, Catesby narrates the metamorphosis of the lowcountry from pestilential swamp to productive plantation in related terms. The passage elides any explicit reference to slave labor while evoking its grueling conditions. Though possessed of rich soil, the lowcountry is difficult to improve:

> *Rice Land* is most valuable, though only productive of that Grain, it being too wet for any thing else. The Scituation of this Land is various, but always low, and usually at the Head of Creeks and Rivers, and before they are cleared of Wood are called *Swamps,* which being impregnated by the Washings from the higher Lands, in a Series of Years are become vastly rich, and deep of Soyl, consisting of a sandy Loam of a dark brown Colour. These Swamps, before they are prepared for Rice, are thick, over-grown with Underwood and lofty Trees of mighty Bulk, which by excluding the Sun's Beams, and preventing the Exhalation of these stagnating Waters, occasions the Land to be always wet, but by cutting down the Wood is partly evaporated, and the Earth better adapted to the Culture of Rice.

Deforestation yields health and wealth. Through some vague yet formidable agency, the swamp alters before the reader's eyes, becoming "better adapted to the Culture" of a nourishing and valuable grain. The founding of a rice plantation is depicted here as the land's providential self-adaptation.[27]

Even as the passage naturalizes the transition to slave-driven commercial agriculture, it also registers the limits of planter industry and knowledge. Like sugar manufacture, rice cultivation demanded precise timing and coordination from skilled slaves working in onerous and variable environmental conditions, both in clearing and draining the swamps initially and in sowing and harvesting rice subsequently. The precariousness of rice culture is registered by Catesby's strangely indeterminate account of the trajectory and causes of recent colonial history. The established plantation

27. Catesby, *Natural History,* II, iii–iv, xvii.

FIGURE 5. *Rice-Bird* (male and female). Catesby, *Natural History,* I, pl. 14.
The Colonial Williamsburg Foundation

retains certain swampy qualities owing to Carolina's seasonal rains, "Yet great Rains, which usually fall at the latter Part of the Summer, raises the Water two or three Feet, and frequently cover the Rice wholly, which nevertheless, though it usually remains in that State for some weeks, receives no Detriment." For reasons unexplained here, the mature plants remain submerged in water for several weeks before harvest, remarkably without injury. Initiated by mysterious forces, the transition from swamp to plantation seems incomplete, almost stalled.[28]

This is not the only place where Catesby registers the tenuousness of this transitional moment. In his portrayal of "Rice-Bird" (Fig. 5), he again employs a visual language of reflected form to highlight the organic relationship between bird and plant, described as an artifact of recent commercial

28. Ibid., iv; Morgan, *Slave Counterpoint,* 147–159.

history. The female bird holds a seed in its mouth while perching atop a rice stalk, which bends under its weight. Whereas the golden tones of the bird's body reflect the color of the rice stalk, its posture echoes the plant's arc. Similarly, the large leaf sweeping downward from the stalk echoes the form of the male bird scanning the ground for fallen seeds.[29]

The text specifies the links between bird and plant. Catesby again insists on the value of firsthand natural historical inquiry across a range of latitudes, from the Bahamas through Carolina:

> In *September* 1725, lying upon the deck of a Sloop in a Bay at *Andros* Island, I and the Company with me heard, three nights successively, Flights of these Birds (their Note being plainly distinguishable from others) passing over our heads northerly, which is their direct way from *Cuba* to *Carolina;* from which I conceive, after partaking of the earlier crop of Rice at *Cuba*, they travel over sea to *Carolina*, for the same intent, the Rice there being at that time fit for them.

Appealing to the authority of itinerant experience, Catesby hypothesizes that the introduction of rice into Carolina has caused the ricebird to alter its migratory habits.[30]

This new pattern could have disastrous consequences: "In the beginning of *September,* while the Grain of Rice is yet soft and milky, innumerable Flights of these Birds arrive from some remote Parts, to the great detriment of the inhabitants. *Anno* 1724 an Inhabitant near *Ashley* river had forty acres of Rice so devoured by them, that he was in doubt, whether what they had left, was worth the expense of gathering in." In Catesby's nuanced conception, the introduction of rice has set in motion a chain of environmental events—integrating the Carolinas and Cuba—that are beyond the control of planters and can run counter to their interests. Evoking a biblical plague, the anecdote emphasizes the contingency and fragility of colonial development. The future of the Carolina rice plantation is hard to forecast.[31]

To envision this future, Catesby focuses on arum. A genus of low-lying tuberous plant found thriving in coastal marshes and lowcountry swamps, arum had long been of interest as nourishment for enslaved Africans. For naturalists including Sloane, moreover, the species was emblematic of West

29. My understanding of compositional details in the plate is indebted to Meyers, "Picturing a World in Flux," in Meyers and Pritchard, eds., *Empire's Nature,* 242–247.

30. Catesby, *Natural History,* I, 14.

31. Ibid.

Indian history, determined by a strange blend of chance and Providence. In a discussion of another edible plant, Sloane dwells on the fact that men would die in Jamaica

> were it not for Providence, and the due use of their Reason. It was some Matter of wonder to me, to think how so many People, perhaps one fourth Part of the Inhabitants of the whole Earth, should come to venture to eat Bread, made only by baking the Root of *Cassada*, which is one of the rankest Poisons in the World, both to Man and Beast, when Raw. . . . There is an Instance also of this in the Roots or Leaves of *Arum*, of which many kinds, uncommon to *Europe*, are eaten, when dry'd and prepar'd, as *Colocasia, etc.*

So potent is colocasia that unless "three or four days macerated in water, being slic'd to wash off its Mucilage . . . [it] kills by bringing the Dysentery." The accumulation and dissemination of botanical knowledge (to convert this potentially lethal plant into a vital source of human sustenance) is necessary to the fulfillment of providential design in the West Indies and the British Empire more broadly.[32]

Catesby's scrutiny of colocasia is inspired by Sloane. The introduction of arum into Carolina, he perceived, was one way that the recent history of the colony repeated the early settlement of Jamaica and Barbados, exhaustively documented by previous naturalists. Catesby's verbal description registers the plant's long-standing importance to plantation management in the West Indies and the accelerated pace of botanical and social transformation in Carolina:

> Sir *Hans Sloane,* has so amply treated of this useful Plant, that I shall ask Leave only to add a few Remarks more. It is Tropick Plant, not caring to encrease much in *Carolina,* and will grow no where North of that Colony; yet the Negro's there (who are very fond of them) by annually taking up the Roots to prevent rotting, get a small Encrease: They are of so acrimonious a Quality, that there is a Necessity of boiling them eight or ten Hours before they are eatable. A little before I left *Carolina,* there was introduced a new Kind, wholly without that bad Quality, and requiring no more than common Time to boil them, and may be eat raw, without offending the Throat or Palate; this was a welcome Improvement among the Negro's, and was esteemed a Bless-

32. Sloane, *Voyage to . . . Jamaica,* I, xxv, 167.

ing; they being delighted with all their *African* Food, particularly this, which a great Part of *Africa* subsists much on.

In paying homage to Sloane, Catesby once again specifies the complicated position of Carolina. That colocasia is not easily cultivated in Carolina appears to indicate the temperate character of its climate, for the plant survives in the colony only through the concerted efforts of enslaved people. But so rapid is the pace of botanical transformation and human settlement that the question of climate is by no means definite. Near the end of Catesby's stay, the introduction of a new variety reduces the labor necessary to prepare this African plant for consumption. The successful introduction of colocasia confirms the analogy between West Africa and an extended West Indies—now encompassing Carolina—that Catesby first proposed in his description of the alligator.[33]

Other images of arum also locate the swamps, savannas, and marshes of Carolina in direct relation to the volatile human and natural history of the West Indies. A sequence of two engravings from volume I employs the language of reflected form to picture environmental relationships linking certain varieties of arum to the migratory waterfowl of Carolina. The first depicts a bird identified as "Brown Curlew" and a plant labeled "Arum Sagitarie" (Fig. 6). The curlew stands in profile in its characteristic coastal habitat in Carolina, where the species "come[s] annually about the middle of *September,* and frequent[s] the watery *Savannas* in numerous Flights, continuing about Six Weeks." Its brief residence in Carolina once again indicates the temperate features of the colony's climate. Upon dissecting some female birds, Catesby discovers "Clusters of Eggs; from which I imagine they retire somewhere South to breed; *Carolina* at that time of the Year would probably be too cold for that Work of Nature." Other tropical denizens, however, successfully reproduce in the savannas. The roundish head and long, curved bill of the curlew mirrors the ovular seed vessel and curved stalk of the arum sagitarie, which also "frequent[s] the colony's shallow waters." The description emphasizes the plant's fertility, detailing the moment in its seasonal growth cycle that is pictured in the engraving. Large, arrow-headed leaves are supported by "long succulent Stalks springing from a tuberous Root, from which also shoot forth large round Stalks, at the End of each of which grows in a hanging posture a large roundish green Seed Vessel or Capsula. . . . This Seed Vessel (which is about the Size of a Hen's Egg) when

33. Catesby, *Natural History,* II, 45.

FIGURE 6. *Brown Curlew and Arum Sagitarie.* Catesby, *Natural History,* I, pl. 83. The Colonial Williamsburg Foundation

mature opens on both Sides, and discloses the Seeds." Drawing an obvious verbal and visual parallel between the eggs carried inside the female cur-lews during their brief residence in Carolina and the "hatching" seed ves-sels of the plant, the engraving offers another meditation on the mysteries of West Indian reproduction, this time in relation to a botanical genus asso-ciated with plantation agriculture.[34]

The curlew is also linked to plantation development. Rather than retire to the West Indies for the breeding season, some varieties of curlew instead find refuge in the fecund *"Bay-Swamps"* of Carolina, identified by Catesby as a kind of tropical microhabitat:

> The Swamps so filled with a Profusion of fragrant and beautiful Plants give a most pleasing Entertainment to the Senses, therein excelling other Parts of the Country, and by their Closeness and Warmth in Winter are a Recess to many of the Wading and Water-Fowls. This Soil is composed of a blackish sandy Loam, and proves good Rice-Land, but the Trouble of grubbing up and clearing it of the Trees and Underwood has been hitherto a Discouragement to the Culture of it.

Such difficulties could only be addressed—as Catesby well knew—through a substantial increase in the slave population of the colony.[35]

Catesby's engraving of "White Curlew and Arum Aquaticum Minus" (Fig. 7) on the previous plate contemplates another momentary seasonal association between waterfowl and aquatic plant. The description notes, "When the great Rains fall, which is usual at the latter End of Summer, these Birds arrive in *Carolina* in great Numbers, and frequent the low Watery Lands" where the variety of arum pictured is also common. The central visual pun in the engraving is particularly aggressive. Catesby ar-ranges the long stalk of the plant (topped with a cluster of hard berries) in relation to the large, ovular arum leaf to mimic the form of the curlew, fore-grounding the connection between bird and plant. The composition implies that transplanted "strangers" now constitute an encompassing habitat. The curlew is contained within the outline of the leaf, much as the large leaf in "Green Tree Frog and Arum Americanum" framed the interaction between reptile and insect.[36]

These depictions of arum illustrate differences between representations

34. Ibid., I, 83.
35. Ibid., II, iv.
36. Ibid., I, 82.

FIGURE 7. *White Curlew and Arum Aquaticum Minus.* Catesby, *Natural History,* I, pl. 82.
The Colonial Williamsburg Foundation

of slave agency by Catesby and Sloane. Descriptions of rice plantations and provision gardens scattered throughout the *Natural History of Carolina* indicate that slave agency continued to pose a problem of representation. Because his text devotes relatively scant attention to the manners and customs of enslaved people, however, Catesby's engagement with the problem of agency is less explicit than in *Voyage to . . . Jamaica*. But Catesby's text also implies that the botanical knowledge and horticultural practices of enslaved people have far-reaching effects. In ways that will influence later natural historians such as William Bartram and John Audubon, the problem of agency is subsumed within Catesby's representations of new organic interrelationships. Although this in part effaces the importance of slave knowledge and labor as historical realities, it also makes their environmental effects central to and more pervasive in the text, even as the natural environment itself is understood as a primary agent of historical change.

The problems of slave knowledge and agency thus haunt Catesby's most dramatic portrayals of environmental change and regional interconnection in Carolina. As noted above, the "great rains" of late summer marked a precarious juncture in a process of rice cultivation that was still imperfectly understood, with the maturing rice plants remaining submerged by swamp water for several weeks, in most cases without harm. As Catesby took care to document, however, the effects of these rains could be disastrous when they coincided with seasonal hurricanes from the Caribbean: "Usually once in about Seven Years these Rains are attended with violent Storms and Inundations, which commonly happen about the time of the Hurricanes that rage so fatally amongst the Sugar Islands, between the *Tropicks*, and seem to be agitated by them or from the same Cause." If the natural history of "Carolina in the West Indies" tended toward divergent outcomes as global garden or primordial chaos, then these seasonal "Inundations" comprised a decisive moment. The colony's vulnerability to such phenomena was only increasing. By the late 1730s and 1740s, planters had begun to establish large tidewater plantations in swamps nearer the coast, relying on the tidal flow of estuarial rivers to periodically inundate their fields.[37]

Meditating on the potentially catastrophic effects of seasonal flooding, Catesby's "Brown Viper and Arum Maximum Ægyptiacum" (Plate 5) takes one such moment as its subject, commemorating the inland flooding of the Savannah River after a coastal hurricane in 1722. As Meyers observes, the

37. Ibid., II, ii; Morgan, *Slave Counterpoint*, 156; Joyce E. Chaplin, *An Anxious Pursuit: Agricultural Innovation and Modernity in the Lower South, 1730–1815* (Chapel Hill, N.C., 1993), 243–247, 272–275.

language of reflected form is particularly intricate in this image. ("Alligator and Mangrove Tree" is its only rival.) The curve of the newt's body to the left and the curling form of the large leaf to the right echo the body of the snake as it coils back on itself, with the association between its slender tail and the body of the newt especially strong. The swollen form of the arum blossom (uprooted and lying sideways on the ground) corresponds to a bulge in the lower segment of the snake's body, which may contain some recently devoured prey, whereas the long stamen correlates in color and shape to the snake's tongue. A footnote beneath the description provides an important hermeneutic key for this turbulent scene: "The Subject of this Plate is as it appeared to me at a great Inundation, where by the Violence of the Current, Fish, Reptiles, with other Animals and Insects, were dislodged from their Holes, etc. floating upon Heaps of Vegetable Refuse, where the voracious and larger Serpents were continually preying upon the smaller, as well those of their own Kind, as others, which in that Confusion were more easily surprized." Catesby recounts the sudden degeneration of the plantation landscape (evoked by the prominence of the colocasia plant amid the "Vegetable Refuse") in terms resembling his description of mangrove swamps. Both semiaquatic habitats host spectacular violence. Voracious reptiles prey indiscriminately, even on their own species. The image implies not only that plantation management has failed to mitigate the unruly tropical characteristics of lowcountry swamps but also that conditions conducive to violence have been manufactured in Carolina, however inadvertently. The historical trajectory of the plantation appears at this moment to have run, not forward toward refinement, but backward toward primordial chaos.[38]

It is tempting to interpret "Brown Viper" as a moral commentary on plantation development, an allegorical representation of slavery as a serpent introduced into an Edenic New World. Since Thomas Tryon and Richard Ligon, of course, West Indian specimens had been interpreted typologically within a conventional Christian temporality of Fall, Redemption, and Revelation. Questions concerning the nature of the anxieties underlying "Brown Viper," however, lead us away from Catesby's poetics toward the question of his American reception, a process that begins with the correspondence of colonial naturalists such as John Bartram, William Byrd II, and Eliza Lucas Pinckney and extends through printed natural histories by Thomas Jefferson, William Bartram, and John Audubon. As they drew on the conceptual

38. Catesby, *Natural History*, II, 45; Chaplin, "A Skeptical Newtonian in America," in Meyers and Pritchard, eds., *Empire's Nature*, 74–75.

and aesthetic resource of the *Natural History of Carolina*, Catesby's most influential colonial successors would also reinterpret his text through their own emblematic representations of the nature of slavery.

The Traffic in Letters

Probing the characteristics and limits of the New World tropics as a site of organic diversity and plenitude on the one hand and natural catastrophe on the other, Catesby took up a question of considerable relevance to his British American correspondents and subscribers, perhaps especially to those on the mainland. North American elites were painfully aware of the political and economic consequences of prevailing mercantilist theory, which held that colonies were of greater value to the imperial state insofar as their climates differed from the home nation, and new articles of exchange derived from the flora and fauna of those colonies would not compete with domestic products. With the passage of increasingly restrictive Navigation Acts by Parliament, as they sought to appease the West Indian lobby, mainland colonists began to contest their subordinate status within this broader imperial vision, albeit in contradictory ways, arguing the greater economic utility of "temperate" colonies to the empire and the suitability of southern colonies to the cultivation of new tropical staples.[39]

Beyond this, Catesby's work appeared during a period when events in the Caribbean had captured the public imagination. In a growing number of periodicals and newspapers (published increasingly in colonial port cities), provincial readers consumed reports of global military conflicts with the Caribbean basin at their epicenter, including the War of Jenkins' Ear (1739–1742) and the War of the Austrian Succession (1740–1748). The implications of these ongoing crises varied by region. For the planters of Carolina and Virginia, the disruption of West Indian trade routes created new opportunities for speculative agriculture. With British consumers cut off from their customary suppliers of indigo, planters devoted their energy and capital to developing a strain of the crop in South Carolina, as we will see in more detail below. For every North American colony, however, the volatility of West Indian affairs also presented challenges. Since the seventeenth

---

39. Richard B. Sheridan, *Sugar and Slavery: An Economic History of the British West Indies, 1623–1775* (Baltimore, 1973), 40–43; Andrew Jackson O'Shaughnessy, *An Empire Divided: The American Revolution and the British Caribbean* (Philadelphia, 2000), 58–66; Michael Kammen, *Empire and Interest: The American Colonies and the Politics of Mercantilism* (Philadelphia, 1970); John J. McCusker and Russell R. Menard, *The Economy of British America, 1607–1789* (Chapel Hill, N.C., 1985), 35–50.

century, mainland merchants and planters had established vital trading relationships with the Antilles, often defying restrictions against trading with
French and Spanish colonies. Economic historians John J. McCusker and
Russell R. Menard are unequivocal about the significance of these connections:

> The demands of the sugar planters proved central to the economic
> development of the mainland colonies. Traders were able to operate
> independently of the major metropolitan merchants (although some-
> times on London capital); farmers had customers for their surplus;
> the credits earned—"returns via the West Indies"—helped settle un-
> favorable trade balances with England; and the elaborate linkages
> generated made the mainland economies more diverse, more flexible,
> and less "colonial." By 1770 all the continental colonies, but notably
> those in the North, depended on West Indian markets to a greater or
> lesser degree.

Implicit in this account is that the administration of West Indian trade was
emerging as a shared political grievance in British North America, indeed,
as one of the only shared interests in what might be described as a loose
archipelago of mainland societies, each more tightly integrated with London (and with the West Indies in many cases) than with adjacent colonies.[40]

Such was the geopolitical and geoeconomic situation when Catesby's
American subscribers began to receive their earliest bound installments of
the *Natural History of Carolina*. By turning to the correspondence of three
prominent mainland authors—John Bartram of Pennsylvania, William
Byrd II of Virginia, and Eliza Lucas Pinckney of South Carolina—we gain
a more concrete sense of how this state of affairs conditioned the practice
of natural history. The extensive reach of the cultural discourse and geographic vision we have been tracing will become clearer if we begin far from
the Caribbean, in the rural outskirts of Philadelphia.[41]

By 1740, with Catesby's second volume nearly completed, John Bartram
was also beginning to reap the fruits of his scientific efforts over the prior

40. McCusker and Menard, *Economy of British America*, 155.
41. Prominent colonial subscribers included James Oglethorpe (founder of Georgia), Woodes Rogers
(governor of the Bahamas), Sir Francis Nicholson (governor of South Carolina), Thomas Penn (proprietor
of Pennsylvania), and William Byrd II (the prominent Virginian planter). The subscriber list in the copy of
Catesby's *Natural History* at the John Carter Brown Library, Brown University, Providence, Rhode Island,
is reprinted in Brigham, "Patronage of Natural History," in Meyers and Pritchard, eds., *Empire's Nature*,
141–145.

two decades. Through the patronage of Peter Collinson, Bartram's garden had become a vital source for North American rarities. With the increasing popularity of gardening as a scientific and aesthetic practice—a material performance of knowledge and taste—new plants from Pennsylvania and surrounding colonies were now in greater demand. Through trial and error, horticulturalists had come to realize that seeds and live specimens shipped from temperate colonies were often more successful as transplants than tropical imports. Such specimens also held greater novelty for collectors already familiar with West Indian species. Moreover, the aesthetic, scientific, and spiritual ideal to which many of these gardeners aspired involved the reassembling of God's original creation—encompassing the Torrid, Temperate, and Frigid Zones—as an ordered totality in a single locale.[42]

Catesby's own efforts in British America helped to initiate this shift in geographic orientation. Catesby shipped numerous plants to Collinson while on his expedition to the Carolina backcountry and was later rewarded with a substantial, interest-free loan to support publication of his findings. It was through Collinson's intervention that Catesby was nominated as an FRS in 1732/3 after publication of the first volume and through Collinson's mediation that Catesby's varied cargo from America found its way to menageries, cabinets of curiosity, libraries, and gardens throughout England and America. It is hardly surprising, in this context, that Catesby himself turned to horticulture upon his return to England, maintaining a garden on the grounds of Christopher Gray's nursery. Collinson again lent his assistance, putting Catesby in direct contact with his most skilled North American correspondent, John Bartram.

Catesby first appears in Bartram's extant correspondence in 1737/8. With Collinson's encouragement and letters of recommendation, Bartram had undertaken a botanical expedition through Maryland and Virginia. Writing to Bartram in Maryland, Collinson makes a request on Catesby's behalf:

Dear friend I must beg the Favour of thee to remember what I have formerly Requested In behalf of a Curious Naturalist—who to Ingage thy memory sends thee a Specimen of his prformance [sic]—He neglected when in Virginia to Draw the Papaw, and as this is a Curious plant, In Flower and Fruite and not Figur'd by any Body. Now there

---

42. Douglas Chambers, *The Planters of the English Landscape Garden: Botany, Trees, and the Georgics* (New Haven, Conn., 1993); Therese O'Malley, "Mark Catesby and the Culture of Gardens," in Meyers and Pritchard, eds., *Empire's Nature*, 147–183; Drayton, *Nature's Government*, 3–25.

is no Ways to Convey to us perfect Ideas of this plant but by gathering the Blossoms and Leaves and drying them between paper, but as the Colour and figure of the Flower is Liable to Change, then he begs a short Discription of its Colour.

The letter underscores the value of live plants and on-the-spot descriptions for a scientific artist devoted to the eighteenth-century ideal of "truth-to-nature," of conveying what Collinson refers to, within the prevailing Lockean vocabulary of the age, as "perfect Ideas of this plant." Collinson spells out a request that seems to have been neglected previously. His "Ingenious Friend" requires a description of the color of papaw, carefully preserved specimens of the flower and fruit (both "Full Ripe" and "half Ripe"), and information on the "Height of Its Growth, and the Size of its Stem and what soil and place is most natural to It."[43]

Collinson's appeal highlights the modicum of power and authority that this state of affairs conferred on the colonial naturalist. Whereas Catesby accompanies his request with a number of valuable original drawings (which Bartram later describes as "fine draughts"), Bartram appears to chide the highly regarded virtuoso in a subsequent letter to Collinson. Complying with Catesby's request, Bartram complains to Collinson, "I much [illegible] that the ingenious Mr Catesby omited drawing this remarkable snake in that glorious performance which our Proprietor lent me last winter but that I suppose he was never subject to that hard fortune which I am to be so often grabing in the earth and amongst the rocks for these snakes are seldom seen abroad." Bartram's admiration for a book that has earned the esteem of the powerful and wealthy (including Thomas Penn) is coupled with a tart reminder of the arduous nature of fieldwork in the colonies, where Bartram's "hard fortune" brings him in contact with the materials and information the well-born Englishman requires to complete his "glorious performance." Despite this implicit challenge to Catesby's authority, however, Bartram's initial usefulness depends on his itinerary through Virginia, northern limit of a plant from the tropics that is especially desirable because it is as yet undocumented.[44]

43. Peter Collinson to John Bartram, Jan. 27, 1737/8, *CJB*, 81; Daston and Galison, *Objectivity*, 55–63. For some modern considerations of John Bartram's correspondence, see Christoph Irmscher, *The Poetics of Natural History: From John Bartram to William James* (Piscataway, N.J., 1999), 13–55; Parrish, *American Curiosity*, 132–134, 136–173; Thomas P. Slaughter, *The Natures of John and William Bartram* (New York, 1997).

44. Bartram to Collinson, [summer 1738?], *CJB*, 95.

Catesby plainly set a high value on this service. After receiving the requested cargo, he wrote to Bartram with an attractive proposal. In exchange
for regular shipments of interesting seeds and plants, Bartram would receive a copy of the *Natural History of Carolina*. Catesby is at pains to establish the book's worth:

> It will be first necessary to give you some account of it. The whole
> book, when finished, will be in two folio volumes, each volume con-
> sisting of an hundred plates of Animals and Vegetables.
>
> This laborious work has been some years in agitation; and as the
> whole, when finished, amounts to twenty guineas, a sum too great,
> probably, to dispose of many, I chose to publish it in parts: viz., twenty
> plates with their descriptions, at a time, at two guineas. By this easy
> method, I disposed of many more than I otherwise should. Though
> I shall set a due value on your labours, the whole book would be too
> considerable to send you at once; Therefore, I propose to send you,
> annually, a Part (i.e. twenty plates with their descriptions), for what
> you send me.

Catesby relies on a practiced sales pitch, honed during two decades spent
soliciting subscribers. Serial publication normally began with the printing
and circulation of a detailed prospectus. Employing some of the basic terms
of his prospectus, Catesby feels his way toward a proper assessment and
framing of a new kind of social and commercial relationship.[45] As Catesby
knows from reading Bartram's correspondence to Collinson, this is a new
kind of field man, less a purveyor of raw material than a learned interlocutor
of considerable taste. Conceptions of social hierarchy and economic value
are thus complex and unstable in the letter. Trading on the production value
of his opulent book, Catesby addresses Bartram in the manner of a subscriber, even as he drafts an informal contract for a kind of manual labor.
He specifies the current market value of his printed text while also proposing an exchange based on the equivalent value of Catesby's artisanal labor
with Bartram's daily work "grabing in the earth and amongst the rocks." The
vigor with which Catesby promotes his volumes to Bartram and the precision of his attempt to establish the relative value of their efforts are striking,
and they provide a sensitive register of Bartram's rising yet still subordinate

45. Mark Catesby to Bartram, May 20, 1740, *CJB*, 132–133; Brigham, "Patronage of Natural History,"
in Meyers and Pritchard, eds., *Empire's Nature*, 110–119.

status within the hierarchy of imperial science, enacted daily through the social practice of correspondence.[46]

The basic terms of the correspondence as negotiated here depend on a distinct cognitive geography. Bartram will assist Catesby in completing his work by providing descriptions and specimens of plants and animals that Catesby neglected to document while traveling in more valuable colonies to the south of Pennsylvania. Bartram can also contribute unknown species from his immediate environs, where natural historical interest has belatedly turned. For this, Bartram will appear as a subscriber to the *Natural History of Carolina,* eventually receiving the volumes themselves, sign and token of his growing transatlantic reputation.

As the correspondence evolved, it became even more evident that special value was attached to the transplantation of southern plants. Collinson's letter of 1741/2 is flush with excitement over recent horticultural successes: "It can hardly be imagined in the Agreement of American plants with our Climate." Seeking to build on his success, Collinson requests a plant that he has often received from more southerly correspondents: "A few plants of Sassafras and Laurel [will be] acceptable as coming from a colder country than Carolina they will agree better with our Climate." Letters such as these show that Bartram operated in a cultural terrain established by previous printed volumes on the West Indies, including the *Natural History of Carolina.*[47]

For this reason, Bartram accepted the post of King's Botanist in East Florida after Britain acquired the colony from Spain in 1764. Hosted by botanist Alexander Garden during his return from Florida via South Carolina, Bartram left numbers of live specimens from Florida for safekeeping, to be shipped to Bartram's Pennsylvania garden when weather permitted. It is also for this reason that, almost the moment he began corresponding with Catesby, Bartram also cultivated a trading relationship with one J. Slingsby Cressy, a physician and botanist in Antigua. In acknowledging a gift of specimens and seeds in 1740, Bartram displays his enthusiasm and ambition:

> I am exceedingly pleased to have A Correspondent of such A curious tast in your southward Islands for botany which is my darling study

46. Catesby to Bartram, May 20, 1740, *CJB,* 95.

47. Collinson to Bartram, [Mar. 1741/2], *CJB,* 183. Similarly, the earliest surviving letter from Collinson to Bartram contains a request for "shrub Honesuckles . . . which I have had formerly from So Caroliny flower very fine but in Two or Three years went off, neither our soil or Climate agreed with It but yours phaps from the Northward may do better" (4).

altho I am very much hindered in the pursuite of it having to labour for the maintenance of my family but whenever I can steal A little time I miss no opertunity of making all the observations and discoveries . . . tho often my domestick affairs sufers for no institution of our province alows heavy support for any Curious enquiries; yet notwithstanding this confinement I have travailed several hundreds of miles in Searching the woods for plants with the success of having discovered many Hundreds of remarkable vegitables many of which was never before I sent them seen in europ nor mentioned in any bookes of botany.

Anticipating a long and beneficial correspondence, Bartram takes care to establish his sociability and credibility, unfolding an elaborate persona of a temperate and industrious yeoman, as attentive to domestic cares as to his prodigious scientific labors. Developed first in his earliest surviving letters with Collinson, this literary persona would make its most visible public appearance in Letter X of J. Hector St. John de Crèvecoeur's *Letters from an American Farmer* (1782) (see Chapter 3, below).[48]

Bartram's cultivation of this image is best understood in the context of the transoceanic system of knowledge production that Ralph Bauer terms "epistemic mercantilism." Originating as a central feature of the Baconian reform of Natural Philosophy in the early modern Atlantic world, this idealized model sought to establish a definitive "division of intellectual labor within the 'new' sciences," specifically between colonial "miners" of information and its metropolitan "refiners." Creole naturalists were to provide objective eyewitness reports to metropolitan institutions such as the Royal Society, where luminaries such as Sloane would process this raw material into an encompassing theory of nature. The rise of Newtonian natural philosophy led to new permutations of this basic model, including the emergence of what Bauer calls "the Natural History of historiographic [and scientific] authorship" in the eighteenth century. Rooted in climate-humoral theory, this theory of authorship held that the influence of a degenerative New World climate had transformed the physical constitution of creole colonists, damaging the intellectual faculties necessary to discern natural laws and principles and leaving the creole fit only for a circumscribed role within imperial science as diligent collector of minutiae. Bartram's epistolary persona conforms to metropolitan expectations by emphasizing his

48. Bartram to J. Slingsby Cressy, [March / April 1740?], *CJB*, 130–131.

physical capacity for the labor of collection. In so doing, however, he simultaneously advertises the beneficial effects of colonial residence on his constitution, both corporeal and mental. The only limit on his full participation in the republic of science—as the intellectual peer of correspondents such as Collinson—is the lack of adequate colonial institutions.[49]

First articulated as a response to metropolitan authority, this provincial persona became the template for describing an emerging intercolonial relationship between the "northern governments" and "the Southward islands." West Indian planters had long been the primary targets of the "Natural History of historiographic authorship," which had taken shape as a theory in large part because of the demand for information from the tropics. Bartram's location at the temperate periphery of colonial America thus created rhetorical opportunities for negotiating a distinct position within the intellectual culture of the circumatlantic world. Implicit in the opening letter to Cressy is a distinction between the industrious yeoman of Pennsylvania and the opulent planter of Antigua, dependent for his leisure on the labors of slaves (or on greater numbers than Bartram owned).

The emphasis in this initial letter, however, is on the prospect of intercolonial commerce between botanical enthusiasts in Pennsylvania and Antigua. Bartram regards Antiguan planters both as a potential market for plants and seeds native to Pennsylvania and a source of new tropical transplants for his own garden, which may then be reexported to Collinson and Catesby. Surveying the West Indian species already in his garden ("the ricinus Gold I have growing in my garden four foot high the Papaver spinosum or Orgemone grows with us to perfection"), Bartram instructs Cressy about the kinds of plants that would be "acceptable" by him. He stresses that if an Antiguan plant "will not produce flowers or seed in 5 or 6 months from the planting it will not signify any thing to us," in part because the seeds and plants cannot be packaged for transshipment to English gardeners.[50]

Bartram's initial letter to Cressy also indicates that he saw West Indian patronage as possibly vital to another cherished prospect—the founding of a scientific society in Philadelphia. Following up on his earlier complaint that "no institution of our province alows heavy support for any Curious

49. Bauer, *Cultural Geography of Colonial American Literatures*, 14–29, 191–193.

50. Bartram to Cressy, n.d., *CJB*, 131. On the reexport of southern plants, see also Bartram to Cressy, Mar. 29, 1741, ibid., 153. Bartram inquires of Cressy: "Pray lett me know what success thee hath with ye seds that I sent the ——— by that I shall be informed what kinds to send that will be most like to prosper in your climate for if thee or any of thy friends desired varieties of seeds or specimens of different natures I can furnish you with large Colections of Curiosities."

enquiries," Bartram solicited a donation from Cressy in a subsequent letter. A related letter to naturalist Cadwallader Colden (who had traveled extensively in the West Indies as a commercial factor in his youth) holds out similar hopes that the supply of FRS and cash in the West Indies will help found a new "Philosophick Society." After describing his collaboration with Benjamin Franklin, Bartram remarks that the Edinburgh physician and itinerant lecturer Dr. Archibald Spencer "approves of our desighn: offers to take our proposals with him to the west indies with A favourable acount of our proceedings."[51]

Despite these ambitions, Bartram's correspondence with Cressy quickly deteriorated. Responding to Bartram's proposal to ship "large Collections of Curiosities" to Antigua, Cressy instead sketched the terms of a far more pedestrian commercial venture. If Bartram would supply large quantities of common garden seeds (for plantation kitchen gardens), Cressy "could sell them . . . at a good Price." Bartram's answer in his final letter to Cressy is pointed, invoking his rising esteem in a cosmopolitan scientific community:

> I very much admire what can be the reason that so few of the seed that I send thee grows I am sure thay was ripe and carefuly packed up which is as far as I can assist being unacquainted with the nature of your climate and soil it difering so much from europe and ours . . . at present my circumstances will not alow me time to raise any quantity of kitchen garden seeds I am so often abroad upon long Journeys in making discoveries of animals and vegitables and fosils and insects to oblige my corespondents in England holand france and sweden.

The cultivation of new and useful knowledge from the Middle Colonies is opposed to the more crass form of extraction envisioned in Cressy's proposal. Moreover, Bartram's insistence that his shared intellectual interests with learned Europeans leave him no time for base commercial ventures in the West Indies is linked to his assertion that Europe and the "northern governments" of British America share a similar climate. Cressy's residence in the Torrid Zone has marred his capacity for enlightened botanizing. Bartram can leave this connection implicit precisely because it is so commonplace. As we shall see in subsequent chapters, this distinction would take

51. Bartram to Cressy, n.d., Bartram to Cadwallader Colden, Apr. 29, 1744, *CJB*, 131, 238. In the same letter to Cressy, Bartram also invited him to subscribe to his published natural history of the Middle Colonies. Having witnessed firsthand the value of a printed book to Catesby and Sloane (who would send Bartram a copy of his *Voyage to . . . Jamaica* in exchange for specimens), Bartram presents Cressy with an informal prospectus.

sharper form over the next four decades, as North American resentments against the West Indian lobby intensified after the Seven Years' War with the concomitant rise of Buffon's thesis of New World degeneracy. It would find sharp expression in John Bartram's correspondence with his son William, who had remained in East Florida in the hopes of founding a rice plantation after traveling with his father during John's appointment as King's Botanist (see Chapter 4, below).[52]

In Bartram's correspondence, we detect the early stirrings of a paradoxical North American discourse on West Indian abundance and corruption that was pervasive throughout the mainland colonies, even in those that were neither characterized as tropical nor primarily supported by slave-driven plantation exports. Among southern naturalists such as William Byrd II of Virginia, however, the discourse took more explicit, contradictory, and self-implicating forms.

In Ralph Bauer's analysis, Byrd stands as colonial satirist par excellence of the natural history of scientific authorship, a creole author whose "attempts at Natural History frequently [turn] into hybrid meta-historical satires of the imperial production of knowledge and division of intellectual labor." Byrd's empirical scrutiny of his creole humors—as manifested in an unrestrained temperament and carnal appetite that should make objectivity impossible—exposes the underlying contradictions and, indeed, absurdities of metropolitan theory. Byrd's embittered relation to metropolitan theory and authority was born of his social position as a member of Virginia's planter oligarchy, heir of a family estate (Westover) established during the transformation of Virginia into a tobacco-producing colony in the late seventeenth century. Dependent on the labors of a growing population of enslaved Africans, Virginia was also increasingly subject to the volatile cycles of circumatlantic mercantile capitalism. Natural history thus provided a forum for creole planters to forge a more stable social identity within the empire, but, in so doing, they confronted the suspicion of the English gentry.[53]

52. Cressy to Bartram, Aug. 20, 1741, Bartram to Cressy, [October 1741], *CJB*, 166, 173. On Bartram's thinking regarding the appointment in Florida, see Bartram to Collinson, July 19, 1761, Garden to Bartram, Feb. 23, June 17, 1761, and Martha Logan to Bartram, [summer 1761?], all in *CJB*, 507, 522–523, 529.

53. Bauer, *Cultural Geography of Colonial American Literatures*, 198. For Byrd's biography, see Pierre Marambaud, *William Byrd of Westover, 1674–1744* (Charlottesville, Va., 1971); Kevin Berland, Jan Kirsten Gilliam, and Kenneth A. Lockridge, eds., *The Commonplace Book of William Byrd II of Westover* (Chapel Hill, N.C., 2001), 1–115. On the transformation of Virginia during Byrd's lifetime, see Edmund Morgan, *American Slavery, American Freedom: The Ordeal of Colonial Virginia* (New York, 1975); Rhys Isaac, *The Transformation of Virginia, 1740–1790* (Chapel Hill, N.C., 1982); Anthony S. Parent, Jr., *Foul Means: The*

Byrd's satirical impulses are displayed in his earliest letter to Hans Sloane, as he seeks improved rhetorical footing within an extended republic of science. The letter demonstrates that the intensity of Byrd's attack on the natural history of scientific authorship results from his ambiguous position within the circum-Caribbean geography of Catesby's *Natural History of Carolina*, to which he had contributed as informant and subscriber. Like John Bartram, Byrd found himself on the margins of colonial science, a denizen of British America's relatively unprofitable northern periphery. Yet, as a slaveholding creole from a colony known for its sweltering climate, he was also a more direct target of the emergent discourse of West Indian degeneracy, with more limited opportunities to wield it against Caribbean planters to define a personal and regional identity.

In his opening address to Sloane, Byrd laments the belatedness of Virginia as an object of natural historical interest. Writing to an individual whose acclaim as a naturalist owes to his brief experience in Jamaica—shrewdly leveraged through publication and display of his collections in London—Byrd offers his services as informant: "The country where fortune hast cast my lot, is a large field for natural inquirys, and tis much to be lamented, that we have not some people of skil and curiosity amongst us. I know no body here capable of makeing very great discoverys, so that nature has thrown away a vast deal of her bounty upon us to no purpose." Byrd's satirical intent is made explicit in the letter's postscript, where he flaunts his own "skil and curiosity" by announcing his most recent discovery: "P.S. Since I writ the other side I have discovered the true hypoquecuana, of which I send you a sample. Both the fashion of the root and the similitude of the operation leave me no doubt that tis the same with that sent from the Spanish West Indies. However pray try it, and give me yours and the societys opinion of it." On one level, Byrd's deference to Sloane and the Royal Society is merely rhetorical here. While soliciting Sloane's opinion, Byrd also expresses confidence in his own judgment. But, in selecting this particular root as a specimen of his abilities, Byrd adheres to a hierarchy of colonial value. To establish his intellectual bona fides, he must negotiate a botanical marketplace long dominated by West Indian things, demonstrating his knowledge of a Caribbean species prized as a powerful emetic. For

Formation of a Slave Society in Virginia, 1660–1740 (Chapel Hill, N.C., 2003); T. H. Breen, *Tobacco Culture: The Mentality of the Great Tidewater Planters on the Eve of Revolution* (Princeton, N.J., 1985); Allan Kulikoff, *Tobacco and Slaves: The Development of Southern Cultures in the Chesapeake, 1680–1880* (Chapel Hill, N.C., 1986).

this reason, Byrd's correspondence with Sloane is punctuated by regular requests for a copy of *Voyage to . . . Jamaica.*[54]

Byrd's location in Virginia thus makes his authority as informant doubly tenuous, as revealed in Sloane's subsequent letters. Sloane appeals to his greater firsthand knowledge of the West Indies to refute Byrd's account of the "true hypoquecuana," identifying the specimen he has received from Byrd as a far less efficacious and valuable variety than the one exported from the Spanish Caribbean. This appeal to the authority of West Indian experience is habitual in Sloane's letter as a whole. A single paragraph contains two pointed corrections regarding other plants received in the same shipment from Byrd: "The root you call poke is not jalap but the root of the solanum racemosum americanum of Mr. Ray in his history of plants. This plant I mett with in the Caribe Islands and Jamaica and have given some account of it in my history of that island. A spoonfull or two of juice of the root when green will purge but when dryed the root has not that effect. . . . The James town weed is a stramonium which I have likewise mett with in Jamaica and the Caribes and is without question a great poyson."[55]

At the same time, Sloane insists that he possesses greater knowledge of colonies—such as Virginia—where he has never set foot. Given the universal laws of plant distribution as contrived by "the Author of nature" and confidently calculated in London as a center of Newtonian science, Sloane feels certain that Byrd could locate sufficient quantities of the "true hypoquecuana" in the vicinity of Westover, if he would only take the trouble to "look about."[56]

This cultural politics of location would continue to structure Byrd's struggles for due recognition by Sloane and the Royal Society. When Byrd promoted the medicinal properties of ginseng, Sloane stood in his way, denying that the plant possessed significant virtues. (Having promoted the virtues of chocolate since his return from Jamaica, Sloane had a stake in fending off competition from alternative New World aliments.) The dispute over the plant illuminates two developments for the practice of natural history in British North America. The first is the emergence of Catesby's *Natural History of Carolina* as a potential resource in cultivating transatlantic esteem. Increasingly frustrated with Sloane's resistance to ginseng, Byrd

54. William Byrd II to Hans Sloane, Apr. 20, 1706, in Marion Tinling, ed., *The Correspondence of the Three William Byrds of Westover, Virginia*, 2 vols. (Charlottesville, Va., 1977), I, 259–261.

55. Sloane to Byrd, Dec. 7, 1709, ibid., 272.

56. Ibid.

challenged his account of the plant in a 1737 letter to Catesby: "As to our ginseng, I must beg leave to differ from my learned friend Sir Hans Sloane, who thinks it is not the true sort." Catesby's attention to colonies such as Virginia and the success of his volumes had begun to create an alternative court of appeal for creoles like Byrd.[57]

The second development concerns Byrd's increasingly refined efforts to invent Virginia as a "distinct geocultural entity," one that could henceforth be known in distinction not only to North Carolina—an imperative of *History of the Dividing Line betwixt Virginia and North Carolina*, as Bauer demonstrates—but also to the West Indies. In a letter to Sloane of 1738, Byrd advances this effort through a charged, satirical reference to the bedrock of Sloane's authority, his firsthand experience in Jamaica: "I fancy you have been nibbleing of ginseng ever since you receivd that box from my good Lord Pembroke, by the vertue of which you have mended all the flaws which Jamaica had made in your constitution." From the creole's peculiar vantage, the joke insists, Sloane also inhabits a paradoxical position within the natural history of scientific authorship. By the late 1730s, Sloane's habitual claim that the natural history of Jamaica had been imprinted on his mind and body via direct experience of the island had multiple implications. If he continues to insist that his temporary residence in Jamaica makes him the authority for nearly all matters of New World natural history, then he also renders himself an object of climatological inquiry. By the opposite token, to admit the absurdity of Byrd's proposition leaves the question of authority more open-ended. Byrd's opening salvo in the 1737 letter lends a new resonance to his familiar concluding request: "I wish I were better acquainted with Jamaica, and shoud be glad of your history." Though he acknowledges Sloane's authority (by requesting his book), he also transforms his ignorance of Jamaica into a virtue. Yet the limited efficacy of such attacks is indicated by the fact that Byrd never received Sloane's book.[58]

Owing to his continued frustration, Byrd joined thirty-two other Virginians in subscribing to Griffith Hughes's *Natural History of Barbados* (1750). Though Sloane had denied him the gift of his printed book—as a medium and token of scientific learning—Byrd supported the publication of alter-

57. Byrd to Catesby, June 27, 1737, ibid., II, 518–519. On the "geopolitics of ginseng," see Bauer, *Cultural Geography of Colonial American Literatures*, 191–193.

58. Byrd to Sloane, Aug. 20, 1738, in Tinling, ed., *Correspondence of the Three William Byrds*, II, 528–529. On the *History of the Dividing Line*, see Bauer, *Cultural Geography of Colonial American Literatures*, 188.

native sources. In so doing, however, Byrd also confirmed his ambivalent geopolitical and geocultural position. To proclaim one's role in supporting Hughes's venture (through display in the subscriber's list) was to acknowledge the preeminence of West Indian productions in an imperial economy of knowledge. At the same time, it was also to remind Hughes's readership that Virginia and Barbados shared defining and disturbing traits.

Byrd was aware of the difficulty of negotiating planter identity in this hemispheric context. His oft-quoted letter to the earl of Egmont indicates that by 1736—around the time that Catesby shipped "Brown Viper" to subscribers—the "Africanization" of the southern mainland brought fears of West Indian–style rebellion and violence. Complaining that "they import so many Negros hither, that I fear this colony will some time or other be confirmd by the name of New Guinea," Byrd notes ominously, "We have mountains in Virginia too, to which they may retire as safely, and do as much mischief as they do in Jamaica." The letter also demonstrates that the disavowal of affinities between Virginia and the West Indies had become fundamental to the self-definition of the Virginia planter elite: "Another unhappy effect of many Negros, is, the necessity of being severe. Numbers make them insolent, and then foul means must do, what fair will not. We have however nothing like the inhumanity here, that is practiced in the islands, and God forbid we ever shoud." Similar denials would remain central to the public image of the Virginia plantocracy through the publication of *Notes on the State of Virginia* (1787).[59]

The question of disavowal returns us to South Carolina, where the contradictions we have been tracing were felt with greatest intensity. Although Eliza Lucas (later Pinckney) was never Catesby's direct correspondent, her letters of the 1740s navigate a cultural landscape shaped by the *Natural History of Carolina*. In 1740—at roughly the same time that Bartram received his first letters from Cressy and Byrd penned his final epistle to Sloane—Lucas reported some important botanical news to her father in Antigua, recently recalled from South Carolina to his post as lieutenant colonel in the British army: "Wrote my Father a very long letter on his plantation affairs . . . On the Augustine Expedition; On the pains I had taken to bring the Indigo, Ginger, Cotton and Lucerne and Casada to perfection, and had greater hopes from the Indigo (if I could have the seed earlier next year from the West India's) than any of the rest of the things I had tryd."

59. Byrd to John Perceval, earl of Egmont, July 12, 1736, in Tinling, ed., *Correspondence of the Three William Byrds*, II, 487–488.

The memorandum moves quickly from an account of James Oglethorpe's expedition to destroy the Spanish fort at Saint Augustine during the War of Jenkins' Ear (securing the dangerous borderland to the south of Georgia) to a discussion of her efforts to cultivate a variety of West Indian seeds sent by her father. The two events were indeed connected. As planter Henry Laurens insisted in 1755, "'Twas intirely owing to the last War that we became an Indigo Country." With Carolina rice planters cut off from their customary markets in Europe, the colony was in desperate need of a supplementary export, and because English drapers and dyers were themselves cut off from their normal suppliers of indigo in the French West Indies, a ready market for the commodity already existed.[60]

Having emigrated to South Carolina from Antigua in the 1730s, the Lucases were well positioned to experiment with indigo. The family had deep roots in Antigua, where Eliza's grandfather and father had been assemblyman and counselor of the colony, respectively, and George Lucas would be appointed governor soon after his return. He could thus rely on his social connections as he sought information from the island's leading botanists. The family also possessed extensive properties in Carolina. By 1739, with her father abroad, Eliza was managing not only the plantation on the family home at Wappoo near the Stono River (comprising six hundred acres and maintained by approximately twenty slaves), but also the pitch, salt pork, and tar plantation on the Combachee River (fifteen thousand acres) and a total of three thousand acres of rice pasture along Waccamaw River. In total, the three plantations were home to between eighty-six and two hundred slaves.[61]

60. Elise Pinckney, ed., *The Letterbook of Eliza Lucas Pinckney, 1739–1762* (Chapel Hill, N.C., 1972), 8 (for some recent critical assessments of the *Letterbook*, see Emily Bowles, "'You Would Think Me Far Gone in Romance': Eliza Lucas Pinckney and Fictions of Female Identity in the Colonial South," *Southern Quarterly*, XLII [2004], 35–51; and Parrish, *American Curiosity*, 201–208); David R. Chesnutt, Philip May Hamer, and George C. Rogers, eds., *The Papers of Henry Laurens*, 14 vols. (Columbia, S.C., 1968), I, 309; Joyce E. Chaplin, *An Anxious Pursuit: Agricultural Innovation and Modernity in the Lower South, 1730–1815* (Chapel Hill, N.C., 1996), 190–192. Chaplin explains: "The British West Indies produced some indigo (it had been a crop on some islands since the 1650s), but Caribbean planters' focus on sugar usually distracted them from secondary commodities. British drapers and dyers relied on imports of indigo from French or Spanish colonies in the Caribbean and Latin America, though this dependence gave the lie to mercantilistic assumptions of colonial trade. When war cut off supplies of French and Spanish indigo in 1739, imperial authorities could demonstrate how trust in foreign powers had, yet again, weakened the nation" (192).

61. On the Pinckney plantations, see Constance B. Schulz, "Eliza Lucas Pinckney," in G. J. Barker-Benfield and Catherine Clinton, eds., *Portraits of American Women from Settlement to the Present* (New York, 1991), 65–82, esp. 70; Ted Morgan, *Wilderness at Dawn: The Settling of the North American Continent* (New York, 1994), 262. Other biographical details are from Harriott Horry Ravenel, *Eliza Pinckney* (New York, 1896).

Attempts to transplant West Indian species had been undertaken with limited success since the establishment of the colony by Barbadian planters in the 1670s. Trade and migration between the colonies encouraged exchanges among naturalists even before the 1730s, when the founding of Georgia provided fresh impetus. The trustees of Georgia "hired botanists to tour the West Indies in search of plants for the experimental garden near Savannah—the trust's incubator of potential staple crops." Imperial war in the Caribbean brought an increased sense of urgency. Having received a single cochineal insect from Alexander Garden, the Society of Arts in London offered a £600 premium for its culture in South Carolina, Bermuda, Jamaica, and Sumatra, desperate to break the Spanish monopoly on the article, which was used to manufacture an intense, crimson dye. Indigo was by far the most successful of these new West Indian transplants. Commended by growing numbers of promotional writers in Carolina, the colony exported some one hundred thousand pounds of indigo by 1747, with output expanding to more than one million pounds by 1775.[62]

Concurrent events clarified the risks of transplanting the West Indian model. In 1739, around twenty whites were killed in a major slave insurrection along the Stono River in Carolina, five miles from the Lucas plantation at Wappoo. In 1741, the South Carolina Assembly described the Stono Rebellion as an awakening to the terror of plantation life: "Every one that had a Life to lose were in the most sensible Manner shocked at such Danger daily hanging over their Heads. With Regret we bewailed our peculiar Case, that we could not enjoy the Benefits of peace like the rest of Mankind and that our own Industry should be the Means of taking from us all the Sweets of Life and of rendering us liable to the Loss of our Lives and Fortunes." New restrictions on slave mobility did little to stem the flow of fugitives south to St. Augustine, as Lucas well knew. Horrific conditions on indigo plantations created new incentives for flight. Amid the stench of fermenting plants—which attracted swarms of disease-carrying insects— skilled workers stirred and beat the leaves according to a precise schedule, during just one phase of a labor-intensive process stretching from April to October.[63]

62. On indigo and other West Indian transplants in Carolina, see Chaplin, *An Anxious Pursuit*, 152–153 (quotation), 192–193. For the detail about cochineal, see Shields, *Oracles of Empire*, 68. For estimates of annual indigo exports, see Morgan, *Slave Counterpoint*, 159.

63. *Journal of the Commons House of Assembly*, July 1, 1741, 84, quoted in Robert Olwell, *Masters, Slaves, and Subjects: The Culture of Power in the South Carolina Low Country, 1740–1790* (Ithaca, N.Y.,

The character of southern planters was also under attack. Having completed his sensational tour through British North America, the itinerant Methodist preacher George Whitefield published a sharp moral rebuke of colonial slaveholders in 1740. The publicizing of Whitefield's tour in newspapers throughout the Eastern Seaboard shaped a new intercolonial sensibility. A moral geography sequestering southern planters was among its first and fundamental facts.[64]

The cultivation of indigo occasioned questions about the status of Carolinians in the empire at large. Concerning the purported physical degeneration and sexual impropriety of planters, such questions were especially challenging for an unmarried female planter of evident curiosity. Lucas's correspondence is structured by her navigation of these questions, both practically through the exchange of information about indigo (as preserved in the relatively cursory memoranda of her letters to her father) and rhetorically through her construction of an epistolary persona (in her fully transcribed letters to female correspondents). Her cultural coordinates in this endeavor are Virgil's *Georgics* and Samuel Richardson's novel *Pamela; or, Virtue Rewarded* (1741).

In a 1742 letter to Mary Bartlett (a niece visiting Charleston from England), Lucas thanks her for "the last volume of Pamela," commenting, "She is a good girl and as such I love her dearly." What follows, however, is a detailed critique of Pamela's moral failing and a defense of Richardson for publishing this flawed character. Pamela's "defect," as Lucas sees it, concerns her transgressions against feminine modesty in repeating the good character that her associates often give of her. Such praise was intended only as an encouragement to more virtuous action, just as Richardson's depiction of Pamela now serves as an example to the reader. Yet, despite this criticism, Lucas anticipates a defense of Pamela in terms that suggest close identification: "But then you answer she was a young Country Girl, had seen nothing of life." Before the events of the novel, the untutored Pamela was as ignorant of propriety as the colonial reader herself.[65]

Lucas identifies with Virgil's *Georgics* on similar grounds. A letter to Bartlett later the same year opens with the news "I have got no further than

1998), 25. For Pinckney's remarks on fugitives to St. Augustine, see Pinckney, ed., *Letterbook*, 57. On working conditions on indigo plantations, see Morgan, *Slave Counterpoint*, 160–161.

64. George Whitefield, "A Letter to the Inhabitants of Maryland, Virginia, North and South Carolina, concerning Their Negroes," in *Three Letters from George Whitefield* (Philadelphia, 1740).

65. Pinckney, ed., *Letterbook*, 47.

the first volume of Virgil but was most agreeably disappointed to find my self instructed in agriculture as well as entertained by his charming penn; for I am persuaded tho' he wrote in and for Italy, it will in many instances suit Carolina." Though the tone is wry and self-effacing (Lucas mocks her ignorance of the classical canon), she nonetheless discerns the importance attached to colonial learning and farming within the worldview of the *Georgics*. Carolina is a place where the ethos of the poem might be enacted literally. In this, Lucas is much like Charles Woodmason, who published a proposal for a book-length georgic poem on indigo in 1757. As Shields argues, Woodmason learns from Virgil that colonial farming is the "quint-essential imperial act, for the imposition of control upon nature, upon the newly conquered or colonized lands, was the justification of Roman power." Colonial planters recognized themselves in the *Georgics* as *"de novo* cre-ators, witnessing the imposition of design upon a seemingly chaotic natural profusion." So, too, did Lucas. Though she lacks the eloquence to compose her own poem on rural industry and virtue (or so she modestly claims), she can apply the insights of the *Georgics* to her father's "farm."[66]

In another letter to Bartlett, Lucas details her conduct at Wappoo, graft-ing the Virgilian planter to the Richardsonian heroine to evince the diffi-culties of her situation, both locally and within the wider empire. Lucas be-gins: "In general then I rise at five o'Clock in the morning, read till Seven, then take a walk in the garden or field, see that the Servants are at their re-spective business, then to breakfast." Though the account is idealized, the violent realities of plantation management seethe beneath the surface, not only in her early morning visit to the fields—as much to supervise her en-slaved "servants" as for exercise and contemplation—but also in devoting daily attention to "Polly and two black girls who I teach to read." This is part of her avowed commitment to educating slaves: "And if I have my paps's ap-probation (my Mamas I have got) I intend [them] for school mistres's for the rest of the Negroe children—another scheme you see."[67]

The stakes of such a project were high, and not only because signs of dis-contentment among the growing population of enslaved blacks were evi-dent all around her. Whitefield's indictment of planter morality had also put Carolina on the defensive (responding to Whitefield's rebuke in 1740, Rev-erend Alexander Garden had announced a similar plan to educate enslaved

66. Ibid., 35; Shields, *Oracles of Empire*, 69, 71. For Woodmason's proposal, see *South Carolina Gazette*, Aug. 25, 1757.
67. Pinckney, ed., *Letterbook*, 34.

Africans). The cultivation of indigo, moreover, required a skilled and knowl-edgeable labor force. According to Lucas's biographer, Harriott Ravenel, after the first unsuccessful efforts with indigo in 1741 and 1742, Eliza's father "sent out a negro from one of the French islands, and soon the battle was won."[68]

Tensions in Lucas's epistolary persona become prominent in the remain-der of the letter. Never mentioning indigo, she instead discusses another venture:

> I have planted a large figg orchard with design to dry and export them. I have reckoned my expence and the prophets to arise from these figgs, but was I to tell you how great an Estate I am to make this way, and how 'tis to be laid out you would think me far gone in romance. Your good Uncle I know has long thought I have a fertile brain at scheme-ing. I only confirm him in his opinion; but I own I love the vegitable world extremly. I think it an innocent and useful amusement. Pray tell him, if he laughs much at my project, I never intend to have my hand in a silver mine and he will understand as well as you what I mean.

The passage contains a series of odd reversals. Recounting her bold plan for improving the plantation in terms that emphasize her capacity for rational projection, Lucas anticipates her friend's rebuke. Rather than transgress-ing feminine virtue through pursuit of commercial success, Lucas has (she fears) committed the more conventionally feminine error of mistaking Ro-mance for reality. This only initiates Lucas's disavowal of commerce as a feature of plantation management. She has fallen prey to Romance not pri-marily through the heedless pursuit of fictitious profits (like Crusoe before her) but rather from her enthusiasm for botany: "I own I love the vegitable world extremly." Drawing a firm distinction between commercial agricul-ture (redefined as disinterested learning) and more base forms of extracting value from the earth (particularly mining), Lucas nonetheless obliquely ac-knowledges the speculative character of the Carolina plantation.[69]

These tensions play out in subsequent letters through an ambivalent rela-tion to the discourse of West Indian domesticity, as one aspect of the larger problem of creole corruption. At times, Lucas imagines the relationship be-tween Carolina and the British Caribbean (specifically Antigua) in terms of

68. Alexander Garden, *Six Letters to the Rev. Mr. George Whitefield.* . . . (Boston, 1740); Ravenel, *Eliza Pinckney*, 105.

69. Pinckney, ed., *Letterbook*, 35.

an extended household economy. Among numerous projecting visions, she includes her designs to supply daily necessities to the island in its time of trouble: "My scheme is to supply my fathers refineing house in Antigua with Eggs from Carolina." She seeks just as earnestly to secure provisions from the island, requesting "west India concumber seed" and cassada from her father. In envisioning these reciprocal relations, Lucas adopts a language of sentimental community: "I simpathize most sincerely with the Inhabitance of Antigua in so great a Calamity as the scarcity of provisions and the want of the Necessarys of life to the poorer sort." It is not clear at such moments whether Lucas, who migrated to Carolina only at age fifteen, considers Antigua and Carolina as distinct regions at all.[70]

At other moments, however, Lucas lays claim to the standard of propriety by using the discourse of domestic corruption against West Indians. In a letter to her father describing the recent departure of a British naval regiment from Charleston, she remarks, "They were very desirous to stay longer. . . . They are quite enamoured with Carolina; nor is it to be wondered at after coming from Jamaica, a place of which they give a most horrible character. The character they give of the women there must, I think, be exaggerated and therefore I wont enlarge on that head." Lucas displays her own decorum by refusing to repeat slanders about Jamaican women—which surely would have involved such standard fare as their indolence, violent temperament, yellow complexion, and sexual promiscuity—even as she intimates that the details would be scandalous. Apparent here are other implicit, because negative, literary coordinates in her navigation of colonial identity: the titular character of Aphra Behn's *Prologue and Epilogue to the History of Bacon in Virginia* (1689) and her theatrical descendant the Widow Lackit in Thomas Southerne's theatrical adaptation of Behn's *Oroonoko* (1696).[71]

Upon Lucas's success with indigo, the problem of negotiating planter identity only became more important, both personally and to the colony as a whole. Having married Charles Pinckney in 1744 and given birth to a daughter, Harriott, Lucas traveled to England in 1753, accompanying her husband during his appointment as commissioner on the Board of Trade. The family paid a social call to the Princess of Wales (Augusta) and her son the future George III, bearing a gift of live birds from Carolina. Fearing that only their daughter would be admitted, the parents prepared a card

70. Ibid., 16, 56, 58.
71. Ibid., 56–57.

for the seven-year-old girl to present to Augusta: "Miss Harriott Pinckney, daughter of Charles Pinckney Esqr, one of His Majesty's Council of South Carolina, pays her duty to her Highness and humbly begs leave to present her with an Indigo bird, a Nonpareil, and a yellow bird, wch she has brought from Carolina for her Highness."[72]

As Susan Scott Parrish argues, by selecting these live specimens as royal gifts—these "precious distillates of color"—the Pinckneys were, in effect, "staging their colony" as a vital semitropical source of metropolitan refinement, with the indigo bunting as a surrogate for the valuable luxury commodity that Lucas had transplanted to Carolina. In choreographing the presentation of the birds, the Pinckneys sought to demonstrate their role in the culture of refinement that had produced the colored engravings of Catesby's *Natural History of Carolina*. The episode reveals their confidence that Augusta would "read" the specimen and its diminutive female bearer as a moral emblem of colonial improvement, drawing on a long hermeneutic tradition that, as we have seen, had been carried forward by the *Natural History of Carolina*, a text dedicated to the Princess of Wales. The performance addressed widespread fears regarding colonial barbarism due to slavery and trade—the same fears that glossed the aesthetics of violence in Catesby's engravings. As the Pinckneys understood, the manners and appearance of their daughter would be scrutinized for evidence of Carolina's moral, cultural, and physical degeneracy.[73]

Circum-Caribbean Prospects

Despite their reputation within the republic of science and letters in the eighteenth century, texts such as Sloane's *Voyage to . . . Jamaica* and Catesby's *Natural History of Carolina* have faded from the literary history of the early Americas and the Atlantic world. Their fate owes to a number of powerful intellectual and scholarly trends, including the eventual separation of literary and scientific epistemologies within a modern division of knowledge, the division of literary study itself for much of the twentieth century along national lines, and the relative neglect in both literary studies and art history of hermeneutic practices linking the textual and the visual. But the letters of colonial North American intellectuals such as

72. Ravenel, *Eliza Pinckney*, 146.

73. Catesby, *Natural History*, II, dedication (unpaginated); Parrish, *American Curiosity*, 207; Chaplin, *An Anxious Pursuit*, 135.

Lucas, William Byrd II, and John Bartram demonstrate how much is to be gained from critical analysis of such texts, in particular for understanding the regional geography of early American literary and intellectual culture. *Natural History of Carolina* maps the expansion of the West Indian plantation into the southern colonies of North America in historical real time, refining a dominant cultural understanding of the Caribbean as the hub of transoceanic empire. Catesby's engravings and descriptions of rice plantations, lowcountry swamps, and mangrove forests in Carolina and the Bahamas are organized around contradictory hypotheses regarding the likely future of "Carolina in the West Indies" as a source of commercial progress and intellectual enlightenment on the one hand and, on the other, as a site of primeval violence. This ambivalent vision resonates with Sloane's meditations on the specters of mass death, epistemological crisis, and financial ruin in Jamaica. As they began to participate more fully in the republic of science and letters, individuals such as Byrd, Bartram, and Lucas negotiated this cultural and cognitive geography. Their efforts to fashion themselves as enlightened authors required that they cultivate extensive knowledge of Caribbean natural history. The style and content of their letters reveals that, in so doing, they also began to develop what Michael Warner calls a "practical sense of belonging to an imperium," of inhabiting a specific location within the temporal and spatial hierarchies that comprise colonial culture.[74]

Only by recuperating these earlier writings can we fully assess the landscape of cultural exchange between the early Republic and the colonial Caribbean in the late eighteenth century. Authors such as William Bartram, Crèvecoeur, and Jefferson conceived of the Greater Caribbean not only as a source both of economic value and of potential cultural corruption but also as a center of colonial science and letters, in part because the writings of Sloane, Catesby, and others continued to shape their intellectual outlook.

The influence of this textual tradition is most clearly evident in the career of William Bartram. The young naturalist studied his father's copies of *Voyage to . . . Jamaica* and the *Natural History of Carolina* before accompanying him during his travels to colonial Florida, then being transformed on a Caribbean model through a coordinated effort to found a sugar, indigo, and rice economy in the region. As we will see in Chapter 4, Bartram's *Travels through North and South Carolina, Georgia, East and West Florida* (1791)

74. Michael Warner, "What's Colonial about Colonial America," in Robert Blair St. George, ed., *Possible Pasts: Becoming Colonial in Early America* (Ithaca, N.Y., 2000), 49–70.

refines both Sloane's experiments with fusing empiricist description, emblematic technique, and novelistic narrative and Catesby's research into the relationship between plantation agriculture and new organic interconnections in the Greater Caribbean. Concerns about the impact of slavery are more central to the text than scholars have thought.

Before attending to Bartram, however, we must first examine Crèvecoeur's *Letters from an American Farmer* for two main reasons. The first is suggested by the physical format of Catesby's prose descriptions, arranged in parallel columns in English and French. Writers and thinkers in the early Republic, as elsewhere in the circumatlantic world, inhabited an intellectual culture formed through routine exchange across linguistic boundaries. This is perhaps nowhere so plain as in Crèvecoeur's consideration of Abbé Raynal's *Philosophical and Political History of the Settlements and Trade of the Europeans in the East and West Indies* (1776), among the "forbidden best-sellers of pre-revolutionary France."[75]

The writings of Crèvecoeur and Raynal also demonstrate that, by the late eighteenth century, the representational techniques of natural history had begun to saturate the literary culture of early America and the Atlantic world in general. Though not strictly a natural history writer, Crèvecoeur drew extensively on such techniques as he charted the emerging cultural geography of British America in the Revolutionary era, narrating the path of Farmer James through Nantucket, Martha's Vineyard, Pennsylvania, South Carolina, and (in sketches that remained unpublished in English) Bermuda and Jamaica. The discourses and representational strategies of natural history proved crucial to his efforts to contemplate the fact of colonial slavery in a period when it began to pose a more profound challenge to the ideals of the Enlightenment.

---

75. Grantland S. Rice, *The Transformation of Authorship in America* (Chicago, 1997), 102; Robert Darnton, *The Forbidden Best-Sellers of Pre-revolutionary France* (New York, 1995).

T. 71.

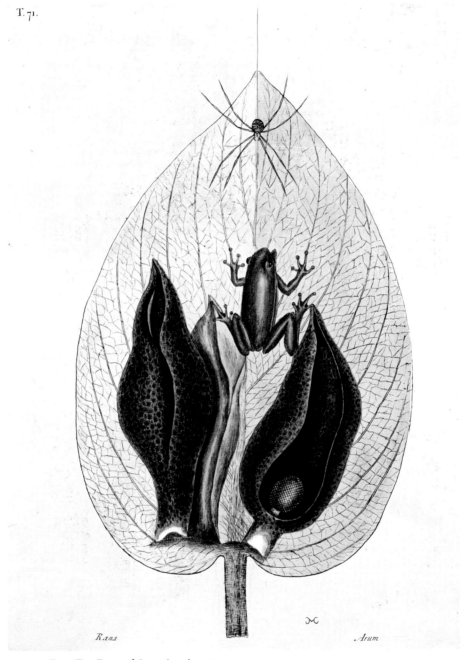

Rana

Arum

PLATE 1. *Green Tree Frog and Arum Americanum.*
Mark Catesby, *The Natural History of Carolina, Florida, and the
Bahama Islands: Containing the Figures of Birds, Beasts, Fishes,
Serpents, Insects, and Plants . . . ,* 2 vols. (London, 1731–1743),
II, pl. 71. The Colonial Williamsburg Foundation

PLATE 2. *Parrot of Paradise of Cuba.* Catesby, *Natural History*, I, pl. 10.
The Colonial Williamsburg Foundation

(*opposite*) PLATE 3. *Purple Gross-Beak and Poison Wood.*
Catesby, *Natural History*, I, pl. 40. Special Collections, John D. Rockefeller, Jr.
Library, The Colonial Williamsburg Foundation

Lacertus.

PLATE 5. *Brown Viper and Arum Maximum Ægyptiacum*, Catesby, *Natural History*, II, pl. 45. The Colonial Williamsburg Foundation

(*opposite*) PLATE 4. *Alligator and Mangrove Tree*. Catesby, *Natural History*, II, pl. 63. The Colonial Williamsburg Foundation

PLATE CCCCXXXI.

Drawn from Nature by J. J. Audubon, F.R.S. F.L.S.

Engraved, Printed and Coloured by R. Havell, 1838.

1. Profile view of Bill at its greatest extension.
2. Superior front view of upper Mandible.
3. Interior front view of upper Mandible.
4. Inferior front view of lower Mandible.
5. Interior front view of lower Mandible with the Tongue in.

American Flamingo.
PHOENICOPTERUS RUBER. Linn.
Old Male.

6. Profile view of Tongue.
7. Superior front view of Tongue.
8. Interior front view of Tongue.
9. Perpendicular front view of the foot fully expanded.

PLATE 7. *Great-Footed Hawk and Green-Winged Teal and Gadwal.*
Engraved by Robert Havell in Audubon, *The Birds of America*, pl. 16.
Special Collections, University Library System, University of Pittsburgh

(*opposite*) PLATE 6. *American Flamingo.*
Engraved by Robert Havell in John James Audubon,
The Birds of America, 4 vols. (London, 1827–38), pl. 431.
Special Collections, University Library System,
University of Pittsburgh

PLATE 8. *Black Vulture or Carrion Crow and American Deer.*
Engraved by Robert Havell in Audubon, *The Birds of America*, pl. 106.
Special Collections, University Library System, University of Pittsburgh

Part II

Reaping the Early Republic

"The Itinerant Man"

CRÈVECOEUR'S CARIBBEAN,

RAYNAL'S REVOLUTION,

AND THE FATE OF ATLANTIC

COSMOPOLITANISM

In 1782, two propitious events signaled the post-Revolutionary transformation of American culture and literature, each promising to crystallize a new sense of self-consciousness and tenuous interdependence in the former British colonies along the mainland. When a London publisher announced the availability of *Letters from an American Farmer* by J. Hector St. John de Crèvecoeur in October, recent developments on the mainland were still poorly understood by readers throughout Europe and the colonial Americas as they assessed the potential impact of an independent United States on the future of New World settlement and commerce, including the circumatlantic exchange of knowledge and moral opinion. The form and content of the published *Letters* were well suited to addressing such questions. The book contained detailed information on the social and physical constitutions of a range of North American colonies (from Massachusetts to South Carolina), conveyed in a compelling narrative voice that swung wildly from the near euphoria of the opening chapters to the despondency of its concluding meditation on the violence of revolution. Moreover, the narrator, Farmer James, addressed his learned European interlocutor in the familiar terms of the colonial naturalist. A number of modern interpretations have established the importance of natural history to Crèvecoeur's literary creation, whether in its use of standard rhetorical models such as specimen description and sketch of manners and customs, its analogy between the improvement of nature and the cultivation of personal character, or its metacritical commentary on the natural history of scientific and philosophical authorship. These analyses have illuminated the status of *Letters* as a text that is comfortably defined neither as a natural history nor a novel but rather incorporates the representational strategies of natural history into a more overtly fictionalized narrative pattern than in texts considered previously in this study. Thomas Philbrick describes this pattern as a "novel in embryo." Much like Behn's *Oroonoko* and Defoe's *Robinson Crusoe*, Crèvecoeur's *Letters* attests to a long history of cross-fertilization between natural history and the emergent novel, a history extended by colonial authors in the late eighteenth century as they began to experiment more systematically with fictional techniques.[1]

These stylistic traits were the result of the author's lifelong interest in empiricist science. Having made careful study of botany on his farm in Orange County, New York (including extensive reading and conversation at Cadwallader Colden's nearby estate), Crèvecoeur was elected to the American Philosophical Society in 1789. Some twenty years earlier, Pierre Eugene Du Simitière had also been elected on the strength of five productive years studying the natural history of Jamaica, Saint-Domingue, Cuba, St. Eustatius, and Curaçao, among other Antillean islands. (Nearly a dozen West Indians had been elected Fellows by 1771.) Best known to posterity as designer of the official seal of the United States and proposer of E Pluribus Unum as new national motto, Du Simitière drew on his social connections among the Fellows to gather funds and logistical support for a return to Jamaica and Saint-Domingue, where he collected additional material from 1772 to 1774. The French-speaking Swiss émigré was rewarded once more by the society upon his return to Philadelphia. Serving as curator of the society's growing collections from 1776 to 1781, Du Simitière worked diligently toward publication of a natural and civil history of North America and the West Indies. His notes and sketches for the book would sprawl to fill two thick folio volumes, during a period when he was also laying the groundwork for a second venture. In May of 1782, residents and visitors of Philadelphia could have attended the opening of Du Simitière's new American Museum on Arch Street. The museum contained an eclectic array of natural history specimens and human artifacts shaped in conscious emulation of Sir Hans Sloane's earlier collection in London. As noted in the printed advertisement, Du Simitière's cabinet was stocked primarily from his extensive travels in the West Indies. In the same year that Farmer James made his public debut as the representative American, Du Simitière requested financial contributions from enthusiasts of learning throughout the

1. Thomas Philbrick, *St. John de Crèvecoeur* (New York, 1970), 88. On *Letters* as a novel, see also Grantland S. Rice, "Crèvecoeur and the Politics of Authorship in Republican America," *Early American Literature*, XXVIII (1993), 91–119; Ed White, "Crèvecoeur in Wyoming," ibid., XLIII (2008), 379–407. On the role of natural history in *Letters*, see Pamela Regis, *Describing Early America: Bartram, Jefferson, Crèvecoeur, and the Rhetoric of Natural History* (1992; rpt. Philadelphia, 1999), 106–134; Thomas Hallock, *From the Fallen Tree: Frontier Narratives, Environmental Politics, and the Roots of a National Pastoral, 1749–1826* (Chapel Hill, N.C., 2003), 77–95; Ralph Bauer, *The Cultural Geography of Colonial American Literatures: Empire, Travel, Modernity* (New York, 2003), 200–240.

Continent, in the hopes that his West Indian collection might become "the foundation of the first American Museum."[2]

Within just a few years, *Letters* acquired a formidable transatlantic reputation, whereas Du Simitière had died in poverty, the result of physical ailments brought on after the failure of his museum in 1784. It is tempting to interpret these divergent outcomes as a consequence of the distinct cultural geographies embodied in the published *Letters* and the American Museum. Whereas Crèvecoeur answered the demands of a readership newly disposed to conceive of British North America as a discrete political and social unit, albeit of indeterminate cultural character, Du Simitière's museum relied on an older and now-superseded conception of circumatlantic imperial belonging, modeled on Sloane's museum and the informal coffeehouse exhibitions it had inspired throughout London since early in the century. However, the divergent careers of the American Museum and the American Farmer are determined by far more complex and contingent forces and in fact demonstrate the persistence of the cognitive geography of the Americas traced in the first section of this study.

The textual history of *Letters* indicates that it might have been a radically different book than the one Crèvecoeur published. When he was taken into custody by the New York City police department in July 1779 for alleged possession of rebel maps of New York Harbor, Crèvecoeur had thirty-two manuscript essays in his possession, only a limited selection of which would be included in *Letters*. Though no maps were found, suspicion intensified upon discovery of the curious trunk he had secreted through British lines outside the seaport. The magistrate's report records that, "when he came into this City, from among the Rebels, he brought with him Some Boxes in which he had curious Botanical plants and at the Bottom of those Boxes under the Earth in which these plants were, he had private Drawers or Cases

2. Unless noted otherwise, all biographical information is derived from Gay Wilson Allen and Roger Asselineau, *St. John de Crèvecoeur: The Life of an American Farmer* (New York, 1987). On West Indian inductees to the American Philosophical Society, see American Philosophical Society, *Transactions*, I (1769–1771). The *Transactions* note the election of the following: Paul Bedford, Esq., of Barbados; Joseph Hutchins, AB, of Barbados; Christian Frederick Post of the Mosquito Shore; Dr. Sandiford of Barbados; Pierre Eugene Du Simitière; Hon. Ashton Warner, Esq., physician; Hon. Thomas Warner, Esq.; Samuel Warner, Esq.; Samuel Felsted, of Jamaica; Dr. Archibald Gloster, of Antigua; Dr. Morton, of Jamaica. Details of this biographical sketch are from Paul G. Sifton, *Pierre Eugene Du Simitière (1737–1784): Collector in Revolutionary America* (Ph.D. diss., University of Pennsylvania, 1960); Sifton, ed., *Historiographer to the United States: The Revolutionary Letterbook of Pierre Eugene Du Simitière* (New York, 1987). For materials related to his interest in West Indian natural history, see Pierre Eugene Du Simitière, Papers Relating to Natural History (vol. I), and Papers Relating to the West Indies (vol. VI), LCP. For the advertisement, see Broadside 962.F.166, LCP.

in which he had his papers." Even after a reading of the papers revealed his loyalist sentiments, Crèvecoeur was held in prison for three months before finally receiving permission to sail for England and then France.[3]

The incident suggests that the production of *Letters* demanded painstaking negotiation of an Atlantic world troubled by a succession of imperial disputes. So, too, did the career of the author himself, who transformed from a French lieutenant during the Seven Years' War to a loyalist British subject and farmer in rural New York during the 1770s, to a British prisoner, to French trade consul to the United States in 1784. Throughout his life, Crèvecoeur treated identities and allegiances as provisional strategies designed to ensure his continued mobility and prosperity. In keeping with those biographical circumstances, Crèvecoeur's consuming artistic and philosophical interest—from the travel sketches of the early 1770s to the English *Letters,* through the expanded French editions of *Lettres d'un cultivateur americain* of 1784 and 1787—lay, not in the delineation of any one parochial identity, but in the fate of a particular form of enlightened cosmopolitanism. At the same time, the shifting political contours of the republic of letters informed his decisions about which sketches to publish and where. A number of the essays omitted from the 1782 edition are included in the subsequent French editions.

The recovery of this transnational dimension of Crèvecoeur's art and thought has marked a welcome development within the transformation of scholarship on the author. Grantland S. Rice argues that the shifts of tone and narrative perspective within *Letters* "elide potentially dangerous political affiliations in a rapidly nationalizing world . . . address the plurality of rising national audiences and . . . mediate the changes in attitudes within and between these audiences." Christine Holbo argues in similar terms that the formal tensions within *Letters* express Crèvecoeur's plight "as an international wanderer, both immigrant and émigré; as an individual with intellectual and personal affiliations in many nations, but without a basis for his sense of identity in any one national tradition." With his multinational audience and his restless migrations across a variety of shifting political borders, Crèvecoeur emerges in such readings as an author whose concerns were continually refashioned by his itinerancy in the eighteenth-century Atlantic.[4]

3. Peter Dubois, quoted in Bernard Chevignard, "St. John de Crèvecoeur in the Looking Glass: 'Letters from an American Farmer' and the Making of a Man of Letters," *Early American Literature,* XIX (1984), 173–190 (quotation on 175).

4. Rice, "Crèvecoeur and the Politics of Authorship," *Early American Literature,* XXVIII (1993), 108; Christine Holbo, "Imagination, Commerce, and the Politics of Associationism in Crèvecoeur's *Letters from*

Crèvecoeur's writings are deeply implicated not only in a larger Atlantic world but in a particular vision of that world that depended on the Caribbean. That vision first emerges in his 1773 "Sketches of Jamaica and Bermudas and Other Subjects." Though concealed at the bottom of the author's crate and included in revised and translated form in the 1787 *Lettres,* this fascinating text remained unpublished in English until 1995. "Sketches of Jamaica" insists that the very notion of stable and discrete cultural identities is untenable in an interconnected and volatile Atlantic. The insight would have significant implications for Crèvecoeur's literary development. "Sketches of Jamaica" grapples with a new maritime reality through its experiments with a narrative structure that would be crucial to the organization of *Letters*—involving the journey of a naïve colonial youth from a northern agrarian utopia to a decadent plantation society and back again in disillusionment.[5]

The sketch thus addressed an essential component of the intellectual world in which Crèvecoeur lived and wrote. In describing the voluminous flow of persons, commodities, and cultural forms between the mainland and the West Indies, "Sketches of Jamaica" marks Crèvecoeur's earliest and most intense effort to come to terms with the theories of Abbé Raynal—the man to whom *Letters* would be dedicated. In his *Philosophical and Political History of the Settlements and Trade of the Europeans in the East and West Indies,* Raynal propounded a theory of global development and decline cen-

---

an American Farmer," ibid., XXXII (1997), 20–65 (quotation on 57). Before the 1960s, readings of *Letters* tended to stress the idyllic aspects of the text and to privilege the earlier letters. Since the 1960s, most critics have complicated that vision, either by arguing that the narrator undergoes a profound shift in consciousness or by establishing a distinction between a naïve Farmer James and his sophisticated author, or both. For some representative examples of the later criticism, see A. W. Plumstead, "Hector St. John de Crèvecoeur," in Everett Emerson, ed., *American Literature, 1764–1789: The Revolutionary Years* (Madison, Wis., 1977), 213–231; Doreen Alvarez Saar, "Crèvecoeur's 'Thoughts on Slavery': *Letters from an American Farmer* and Whig Rhetoric," *Early American Literature,* XXII (1987), 192–203; Nathaniel Philbrick, "The Nantucket Sequence in Crèvecoeur's *Letters from an American Farmer," New England Quarterly,* LXIV (1991), 414–432; Norman Grabo, "Crèvecoeur's American: Beginning the World Anew," *William and Mary Quarterly,* 3d Ser., XLVIII (1991), 159–172; Larzer Ziff, *Writing in the New Nation: Prose, Print, and Politics in the Early United States* (New Haven, Conn., 1991), 18–33.

5. [J. Hector St. John de Crèvecoeur], "Sketches of Jamaica and Bermudas and Other Subjects," in Dennis D. Moore, ed., *More Letters from the American Farmer: An Edition of the Essays in English Left Unpublished by Crèvecoeur* (Athens, Ga., 1995), 106–113. Crèvecoeur also wrote a substantially revised French version of the sketch, entitled "Voyage à la Jamaïque et aux Isles Bermudes," which he included in *Lettres d'un cultivateur américain,* 2 vols. (Paris, 1784), I, 229–240. While the neglect of "Sketches of Jamaica" may in part be attributed to its brevity, and its fragmentary syntax, it is also likely owing to the North American focus of many Crèvecoeur critics. The two other manuscripts collected for the first time in Moore's *More Letters from the American Farmer* also chronicle societies beyond the mainland. Like "Rock of Lisbon" and "Sketch of a Contrast between the Spanish and the English Colonies," "Sketches of Jamaica" has been overlooked for its seemingly anomalous and peripheral subject matter.

tered on the Caribbean sugar revolution and the attendant growth of the Atlantic slave trade. Crèvecoeur's writings demonstrate a persistent awareness, extrapolated from the work of the philosophe, that relations between the West Indies and the mainland British colonies were of sweeping consequence. Given the importance of the Caribbean to Atlantic mercantilism, both men came to believe that the fate of enlightened cosmopolitanism—and the vision of global republicanism it cherished—would be decided in the sugar islands.[6]

Tracing the origins of that realization in "Sketches of Jamaica" and its subsequent influence on the form and content of *Letters*, this chapter provides an account both of the West Indian routes of Crèvecoeur's transnational oeuvre and of the convergence of those routes with the author's lifelong interest in the discourse and practice of natural history. Examination of Du Simitière's collections and museum establishes a context for interpreting Crèvecoeur's writings, revealing that, in late-Enlightenment Philadelphia, the natural history specimen still served as a lens for contemplating West Indian slavery. Conversely, close reading of "Sketches" and *Letters* uncovers a cultural moment of keen cosmopolitan interest in the natural and commercial history of the West Indies, a broader intellectual climate in which the American Museum was likely to have succeeded. The connection between *Letters* and prior fictional experiments by Defoe and Behn is more direct than it first appears. Much like Behn and Defoe, Crèvecoeur draws on the narrative and descriptive strategies of natural history for a specific purpose—namely, to dramatize his confrontation with problems of epistemology, social organization, and economic practice in a circumatlantic world centered on colonial slavery.

Letter from an American Commercial Factor in Jamaica

Among the manuscripts concealed in Crèvecoeur's crate, the earliest were composed in the early 1770s on the author's New York farm at Pine Hill. As Thomas Philbrick describes those years, they were a time of prolific and varied literary output, consisting "chiefly of impressionistic travel sketches that center on such varied locales as Lisbon, the islands of Jamaica, Ber-

6. Abbé [Guillaume-Thomas François] Raynal, *A Philosophical and Political History of the Settlements and Trade of the Europeans in the East and West Indies* (1798), trans. J. O. Justamond, 6 vols. (New York, 1969). For recent critical assessments of Raynal's *History*, see Srinivas Aravamudan, *Tropicopolitans: Colonialism and Agency, 1688–1804* (Durham, N.C., 1999), 289–325; Lynn Festa, *Sentimental Figures of Empire in Eighteenth-Century Britain and France* (Baltimore, 2006), 205–232.

muda, Nantucket, and Martha's Vineyard, and the colonies of Virginia and South Carolina." The pieces on Nantucket, Martha's Vineyard, and South Carolina would of course evolve into Letters IV through IX of Crèvecoeur's 1782 masterpiece. The core of *Letters* was extracted from a larger body of work spanning the Atlantic and the hemisphere, possibly by Crèvecoeur's editor in London. This textual history provides one way of understanding the narrative instability remarked by so many modern critics of *Letters*. The text may be viewed as a complex palimpsest in which the transnational concerns of the earlier versions of the sketches remain visible beneath the mainland narrative that is written over them.[7]

These comparative and transnational sketches constituted Crèvecoeur's attempt to engage with the emergent cosmopolitan culture of the late Enlightenment. Thomas J. Schlereth provides a valuable description of the republic of letters that connected intellectuals and learned societies throughout the Atlantic: "Within the eighteenth-century scientific societies, the philosophes came to realize that, although they belonged to a variety of countries, they were also a nation unto themselves; it was an elitist republic whose citizens of the world united in an effort . . . to promote 'all useful Knowledge of Benefit to Mankind in General.'" Essential to that effort was the new encyclopedic project of cultural geography, or "the study of the earth as a universal habitat for man." Cultural geographies were characterized by their focus on two related questions: the "physiographic conditions of the terrestrial globe and its origins" and "the vicarious, yet worldwide, anthropological study of man." Whereas Crèvecoeur's interest in physiographic questions—including the transatlantic debates that raged around the Buffon thesis—is well documented, his immersion in a kind of global anthropology emerges when one focuses on his writings of the early 1770s.[8]

7. Philbrick, *St. John de Crèvecoeur*, 20. For a survey of some critical questions related to the composition and publication of *Letters*, see Plumstead, "Hector St. John de Crèvecoeur," in Emerson, ed., *American Literature*, 213–231. Responding to speculation that Crèvecoeur's London publisher might have arranged the earlier manuscripts into the 1782 *Letters*, Plumstead argues from internal evidence that Crèvecoeur himself revised and arranged the earlier sketches. This argument is pursued in Chevignard, "St. John de Crèvecoeur in the Looking Glass," *Early American Literature*, XIX (1984), 173–190. Chevignard suggests that the bulk of the revisions were made during Crèvecoeur's detainment in New York City. My own belief is that the early sketches underwent significant revision during the late 1770s and early 1780s. Someone transformed a transnational body of work into an exclusively mainland narrative. Crèvecoeur's own experiences with his North American neighbors and British authorities may well have inspired him to conceal a form of cosmopolitan identity to which the Revolutionary Atlantic had grown increasingly hostile. His London publishers might have selected only the mainland sketches to satisfy the growing vogue for accounts of North America.

8. Thomas J. Schlereth, *The Cosmopolitan Ideal in Enlightenment Thought: Its Form and Function in*

This was the period when his Pine Hill neighbor, the well-known naturalist Cadwallader Colden, first introduced him to Raynal's *History*. In many ways, the *History* provided a cultural geography extraordinaire. First published in 1770, it would be released in fifty-five editions in five languages over the next thirty years. Its six volumes assay a comprehensive history and analysis of the major European colonialisms, and the societies they conquered and enslaved, from the first voyages of discovery through the revolutionary ferment of the late eighteenth century. Raynal and his many collaborators compiled histories of nearly every locality subject to European encroachment. Whereas volumes I and II are devoted primarily to the East Indies, volume III closes with a survey of the settlement of "the great Archipelago of America." The *History* then segues to a scathing indictment of the pillage of Africa to fuel to the Caribbean slave trade. It returns, in volumes IV and V, to detail the Spanish, Dutch, French, and English efforts to establish dominion over various West Indian islands. Volume VI covers North America, closing with a celebratory testament of the republican character of the northern British colonies.[9]

In the travel sketches of the early 1770s, Crèvecoeur sought to incorporate Raynal's cultural geographic ambitions within his own quasi-fictional project by experimenting with cosmopolitan narratives and narrators. "Sketch of a Contrast" is the most rudimentary experiment, involving methodical comparisons between Peru and Pennsylvania. "Rock of Lisbon" is more elaborate, relying on an extended flashback. Surveying colonial New York from a peak in the Adirondacks, an urbane narrator remembers a journey to a mountaintop convent near the Portuguese seaport and capital, where he observed the ruins of a slave-trading empire. "Sketches of Jamaica" marks Crèvecoeur's deepest engagement with Raynal, both for the critical implications of its narrative structure and its geographic location. The journey of Crèvecoeur's young narrator to Jamaica undermines comparisons between agrarian New York and the plantation culture of the British West Indies by stressing the involvement of both regions in the wider commercial culture of the Atlantic rim.[10]

Crèvecoeur was an astute interpreter of Raynal's treatise, attentive to the

---

the Ideas of Franklin, Hume, and Voltaire, 1694–1790 (Notre Dame, Ind., 1977), 32, 33, 41, 42. For more on Buffon's thesis, see Chapter 5, below.

9. Raynal, *History*, III, 384. The "Raynal" to whom I refer throughout this chapter is, in many ways, a term of convenience. Though Raynal compiled and edited the volumes, he did so with the help of a large editorial staff. Prominent intellectuals (including Denis Diderot) contributed many of the sections.

10. [Crèvecoeur], "Sketches of Jamaica," in Moore, ed., *More Letters*, 71.

prominence of the Caribbean within its volumes. As discussed in the introduction to this study, a crucial passage in the treatise surveys the vital role
of the Caribbean in the development of world commerce:

> The labours of the people settled in those islands are the sole basis of
> the African trade: they extend the fisheries and the cultures of North
> America, afford a good market for the manufactures of Asia, and
> double, perhaps treble, the activity of all Europe. They may be con-
> sidered as the principle cause of the rapid motion which now agitates
> the universe. This ferment must increase, in proportion as cultures,
> that are so capable of being extended, shall approach nearer to their
> highest degree of perfection.

Raynal articulates his global commercial vision in the influential idiom
of post-Newtonian natural philosophy, blending empirical precision with
theoretical sweep as he presents tangible evidence of universal natural
laws. The sugar revolution is described as a fatal fermentation, agitating
the farthest reaches of the known physical universe. Driven by burgeoning
European demand and the accompanying lure of spectacular profits, West
Indian planters will develop increasingly sophisticated knowledge of tropical "cultures," approaching the perfect fusion of agriculture with technology.
As a result, the range of valuable West Indian plants will continue to extend
geographically.[11]

In "Sketches of Jamaica," Crèvecoeur developed a narrator and narrative
structure—both rooted in the rhetorical conventions of natural history—
that allowed him to trace the ramifications of Raynal's theory of world
commerce for the culture and society of his adopted home in the Middle
Colonies. Depicting the voyage of a pre-Revolutionary American youth to
Jamaica, the sketch is narrated by the youth himself after his return to his
father's thriving farm and mill. He addresses a letter to a close friend—
another young gentleman—whom he imagines to be somewhere in Pennsylvania. "Are you still the Itinerant Man?" the narrator asks his confidant.
His friend's movements are of considerable import. The West Indian travel
sketch at the core of the letter is framed by two urgent appeals. Unless his
friend returns to their farming community in rural New York, the narrator's
faith in humanity is in danger of being permanently lost. "Every motive I
can possibly present you with ought to Induce you to repair here," the young

11. Raynal, *History*, V, 107.

protagonist writes his friend, "even a conscientious one, that of preventing an honnest Man from taking any Errative Paths."[12]

His problems began when his father, anxious to initiate his eldest son into the family business, sent him to serve as agent for his "great consignement of Flour" to Jamaica. From his arrival, the decadence of white settler society and the barbaric violence of the slave code shock the impressionable youth, who quickly flees back to the mainland via an excursion through Bermuda.[13]

The trajectory of "Sketches of Jamaica" will feel familiar to readers of *Letters*. In a similar manner to "Description of Charles-Town," the essay establishes a seemingly stark contrast between the plantation culture of the extended Caribbean and communities of smaller, more subsistence-oriented farmers in the northern colonies. The moral crisis initiated by the narrator's experience in Jamaica, however, is only accelerated after his return to the Middle Colonies. Shortly after his return, his father unexpectedly dies without a will, leaving his son to resolve a series of transactions before he can claim his patrimony. Troubles increase when the narrator gives his brothers and sisters their share of the father's estate, "reserving to myself no other Priviledge of Primogeniture than that of Posessing the old paternal Roof." The narrator must settle his father's affairs or face financial ruin. Comforted by his belief that trade in his native colony is conducted on more virtuous principles than in Jamaica, the youth sets out to emulate the forthright business practices he learned from his father. He declares, "The First Principle I fixed upon was to think no Man a Rogue untill I had Experienced the Contrary, this Principle I had not Imbibed in Jamaica." That policy, however, results in his near bankruptcy. The youth is subjected to repeated "Evasions subterfuges, positive denials," eventually losing "above £400 by the absurdity of my first Principles." It is then that the social and moral distinction between life in Jamaica and New York, between the virtue nurtured by a sedentary life in a northern farming community and the vice produced by a life of travel and trade, breaks down. "My Journal through this laborious Carrier wou'd in Point of difficulties, soundings observations etc. by far Exceed those of the boldest Navigators who have Ventured in quest of the North West Passage and all these dangers came from the Native Keeness of an appearantly simple and Ignorant people who had not / as I had lived in Jamaica and Bermudas."[14]

12. [Crèvecoeur], "Sketches of Jamaica," in Moore, ed., *More Letters*, 106, 113.
13. Ibid., 107.
14. Ibid., 109–111.

The basic narrative pattern of "Sketches of Jamaica" advances a penetrating argument regarding trade between the mainland and island colonies of British America. The distinction between commercial practices in Jamaica and rural New York proves untenable because the two societies had been economically integrated for more than a century. Since the mid-seventeenth century, merchants in the rapidly expanding port cities of North America had traded extensively with their fellow colonists in the West Indies. Trade with the islands of the French and Spanish Caribbean, though formally outlawed by British Parliament in the Navigation Acts and strictly policed after the Sugar Act of 1764, was also intense. As the Caribbean colonies transformed into a virtual sugar monoculture, devoting their scarce land resources to production of that increasingly profitable commodity, North American merchants quickly moved to supply the planters with the foodstuffs, lumber, and livestock necessary to daily survival.[15]

In Georgia and the Carolinas, goods shipped to the British West Indies (primarily rice and lumber) accounted for more than one-fifth of the region's total exports between 1768 and 1772, the period just before the composition of "Sketches of Jamaica." In the narrator's own Middle Colonies, sale of grain and grain products to the West Indies comprised the single largest export from 1768 to 1772. Total exports to the Caribbean accounted for just less than half of the total annual average value of exports from the region during the same period. At £223,610, the value of exports to the West Indies more than tripled that of sales to Great Britain. In New England, including the islands depicted in sections 4 through 8 of Letters, this imbalance was even greater. Exports of fish, livestock, wood, and whale products to the British West Indies accounted for more than half the total exports of the region. Estimated at £278,000, the average annual value of New England's trade with the Caribbean nearly quadrupled that of its exports to Great Britain. Significant in their own right, official figures fail to account for the thriving clandestine trade with French and Spanish islands.[16]

By specifying that the patriarch in his sketch is both a flour merchant and mill owner, Crèvecoeur demonstrates an acute sense of the social and cultural impact of the West India trade. By the early eighteenth century, the

15. On the transformative effects of this trade on both North America and the British Caribbean, see Andrew Jackson O'Shaughnessy, *An Empire Divided: The American Revolution and the British Caribbean* (Philadelphia, 2000), 69–76; John J. McCusker and Russell R. Menard, *The Economy of British America, 1607–1789* (Chapel Hill, N.C., 1985), 144–146.

16. These figures are adapted from tables in McCusker and Menard, *Economy of British America*, 115, 130, 174, 199.

miller-storekeeper was a common figure in British North America, found in nearly every rural community where grain was grown. Through their inter-actions with seaport merchants, they were able to provide local farmers with information on and access to wider and more profitable markets for their surpluses, often buying them to sell on consignment. By the 1740s, a broad shift had occurred. Large numbers of mill owners began to trade overseas directly, in order to eliminate the costs exacted by port city middle-men. They became "country merchants," to use Crèvecoeur's term, draw-ing rural farm communities deeper into the Atlantic market. According to John J. McCusker and Russell R. Menard, the miller-storekeeper become "the most immediate link for colonial farmers in a commercial chain that stretched all the way to Great Britain or the West Indies and back again."[17]

By invoking this transformative figure, Crèvecoeur's sketch dramatizes the question of whether the virtues of an "Eminent Farmer" are compatible with the market values necessary to success in his "multiplied business" as merchant and mill owner. In doing so, the essay addresses paradoxical fears of the material abundance resulting from the West India trade. For the crisis of agrarian virtue within the narrative is decisively linked to the Caribbean transit of its youthful American narrator. Just after his first ap-peal to his "Itinerant" friend, the narrator nostalgically recalls the details of his moral training and development:

> I was born with a natural Inclination to do humane actions, there is a *something* in obliging which allways appeared to Exceed any other Pleasure— . . . this disposition I believe I have Imbibed from my Father who never dismissed a man even when he refused what was asked, without sending him away Tolerably satisfyed— . . . he had Talents he had a disposition to e*ffect this* which I have not—I was too young to think and Inquire of him by what means he preserved the good will of all yet cou'd watch very carefully over his Interests;—what a ressource this Knowledge wou'd be to me in the scituation in which I am; he did not think that he shou'd have quitted us so soon—from him I had re-ceived what Ideas of Right and wrong I have cultivated since, as well as those principles of Relligion which have since directed the opera-tions of my Mind— . . . no sooner had I pursued this Carrier than he

---

17. Ibid., 321–325 (quotation on 322); [Crèvecoeur], "Sketches of Jamaica," in Moore, ed., *More Letters*, 109.

thought proper to send me to *Jamaica* where his great consignment
of Flour had often made him wish to have a Faithfull Correspondent.

The father, it seems, had little trouble accommodating the pursuit of private interests in overseas trade to his underlying agrarian values of public virtue, benevolence, and faithfulness. But the true drama of the sketch
turns on the question of whether the son will inherit that ability. The paragraph intimates that the narrator's journey to Jamaica might have disrupted the smooth transmission of knowledge and values from generation
to generation by removing the narrator from the resource of his father's example. "Wou'd to God," the narrator elsewhere pines, that "I had never seen
Jamaica and had spent that Time with my Father." Crèvecoeur finds an apt
correlative for this disrupted transmission in his narrator's crisis of primogeniture. His father's agrarian virtues are the moral equivalent of the narrator's financial inheritance, the security of which has also been threatened
by the penetration of the maritime market.[18]

The broader implications of that crisis extend far beyond a particular
colonial family. Crèvecoeur employs a variety of subtle strategies to suggest
that at stake in the youth's struggles and the wave of commercialization that
impelled him toward Jamaica is the fate of enlightened republicanism. The
only direct reference to republicanism occurs in some remarks on a visit
to the Treaty Maroons of Jamaica. Although in general the island seems "a
Chaos of Men Negroes and things which made my Young American head
Giddy," the narrator finds Maroon society uncannily familiar. "I observed
the singular Contrast of a Republick of Blacks in the middle of that Island."
"Surrounded on all sides with Slavery," he continues, "this object Pleased
me much." The narrator's use of the term "Republick"—the ideal system for
Montesquieu and other political theorists of the day—to refer to an Afro-
Caribbean society is integral to his critique of the planters. The luxury of
the slaveholder society that surrounds the Maroons is presented as incompatible with republican values.[19]

When, after his narrator's return home, Crèvecoeur begins to link the
corrupt business practices of settlers in Jamaica and New York, he also begins to undermine the basis of the mainland colony's self-image as an exemplary New World republic. Such implications are particularly strong, given

18. [Crèvecoeur], "Sketches of Jamaica," in Moore, ed., *More Letters*, 107, 109, 111.
19. Ibid., 108.

Crèvecoeur's focus on a farming family with newly "Multiplied business." The sketch opens an ambiguous space between two figures—yeoman and merchant—who were located at opposite ends of the social spectrum in conventional republican thought. By the late eighteenth century, the independent farmer had long occupied a privileged position within republican ideology. Strongly influenced by the French physiocrats, Thomas Jefferson would declare in 1787, "Those who labour in the earth are the chosen people of God, if ever he had a chosen people, whose breasts he has made his peculiar deposit for substantial and genuine virtue." "Corruption of morals in the mass of cultivators," Jefferson continued, "is a phaenomenon of which no age nor nation has furnished an example."[20]

Crèvecoeur's rural New York threatens to furnish something like this example. His imperiled narrator, heir of a newly commercialized agrarian world, makes frequent recourse to a language of male sympathy that was deeply embedded in republican notions of civic virtue. Near the beginning of the sketch, the narrator pointedly claims that he "was born with a natural Inclination to do humane actions," which makes the assistance of his fellow man "Exceed any other Pleasure." Later, he similarly insists that his virtuous division of his father's estate among his siblings was guided by "the secret calls of Equity the powerfull wisper, of an Inward sentiment." Gordon Wood argues that late-eighteenth-century theorists envisioned a republican polity held together by the collective exercise of a "natural social disposition, a moral instinct, a sense of sympathy, in each human being." When, near the end of the sketch, Crèvecoeur's narrator threatens that he "shall repell those swellings of the heart from whence comes Kindness Good will etc.," he warns of the imminent corruption of the moral instinct in a descendant of the very social group that was to provide its mainstay.[21]

20. Ibid., 109; Thomas Jefferson, *Notes on the State of Virginia*, ed. William Peden (1982; rpt., Chapel Hill, N.C., 1995), 164–165. Jeffersonian notions of agrarian virtue, and their relation to classical republicanism, were central to the development of a "republican synthesis" thirty years ago. For the classic statements of that synthesis, see J. G. A. Pocock, *The Machiavellian Moment: Florentine Political Thought and the Atlantic Republican Tradition* (Princeton, N.J., 1975); Bernard Bailyn, *The Ideological Origins of the American Revolution* (Cambridge, Mass., 1967); and Gordon S. Wood, *The Creation of the American Republic, 1776–1787* (Chapel Hill, N.C., 1969). These seminal works were challenged by a liberal counterthesis, which questioned the characterization of republicanism as an inherently anticommercial and anticapitalist ideology. For summaries of this position, see Joyce Appleby, *Liberalism and Republicanism in the Historical Imagination* (Cambridge, Mass., 1992); Isaac Kramnick, *Republicanism and Bourgeois Radicalism: Political Ideology in Late Eighteenth-Century England and America* (Ithaca, N.Y., 1990). More recent scholars generally argue for the tense coexistence of liberalism and republicanism as competing and overlapping ideologies. See, for instance, Bruce Burgett, *Sentimental Bodies: Sex, Gender, and Citizenship in the Early Republic* (Princeton, N.J., 1998).

21. [Crèvecoeur], "Sketches of Jamaica," in Moore, ed., *More Letters*, 107–109, 111; Gordon S. Wood,

The sketch attempts to balance the threat of moral decline against the addition of a cosmopolitan dimension to the narrator's classical education. Comparing himself to his provincial neighbors, the narrator boasts that he has "read Cicero ovid sallust etc. and . . . seen great Plantations." Yet, while broadening his horizons, the youth's experience in plantation America has challenged both his affective and rational capacities. Mary E. Rucker argues that *Letters* raises profound questions regarding the efficacy of Enlightenment rationality. Overwhelmed by his journey to the plantation South, its narrator is rendered "incapable of penetrating phenomena to discover either scientific or spiritual laws." The narrator of "Sketches of Jamaica" suffers from a similar inability, one that Crèvecoeur dates from his residence in the decadent and polyglot space of the British sugar islands. On a stylistic level, the collapse of rationality is represented through syntax. In the central paragraphs on island society, the narrator shifts from subject to subject in a disjointed, loosely associative manner that belies his intermittent gestures toward systematic analysis. Individual sentences cover a dizzying array of subjects, ranging from climate to the sexual exploitation of female slaves, to the contraband trade with neighboring French and Spanish colonies, to the island's vulnerability to natural disasters.[22]

Enlightenment rationality is questioned more deeply through the narrator's sporadic attempts to implement a range of scientific and philosophical theories. As exemplified by texts including Montesquieu's *Spirit of Laws*, the new science of cultural geography sought to determine the effects of the physical environment upon societies and the political systems produced by them. Crèvecoeur's narrator engages in a related attempt to link the climate of a region to the character of its society. Upon arriving in Jamaica, he notes, "It appeared to me an horrid Climate, I was shocked at that perpetual

The Radicalism of the American Revolution (New York, 1991), 239. It should be noted that Wood relies in part on Garry Wills's understanding of the importance of Scottish Common Sense philosophy to late-eighteenth-century America in *Inventing America: Jefferson's Declaration of Independence* (Garden City, N.J., 1978). Wills's argument has been severely questioned by Ronald Hamowy in "Jefferson and the Scottish Enlightenment: A Critique of Gary Wills's *Inventing America: Jefferson's Declaration of Independence*," *WMQ*, 3d Ser., XXXVI (1979), 502–523. For a nuanced examination of the combined influence of Common Sense philosophy and Lockean sensationalism on notions of civic virtue that incorporates key aspects of Hamowy's critique, see Jay Fliegelman, *Prodigals and Pilgrims: The American Revolution against Patriarchal Authority, 1750–1800* (New York, 1982), 23–26. For some attempts to link republicanism with a broader discourse of masculine sentiment, see Burgett, *Sentimental Bodies*, 112–134; Julie K. Ellison, *Cato's Tears and the Making of Anglo-American Emotion* (Chicago, 1999).

22. [Crèvecoeur], "Sketches of Jamaica," in Moore, ed., *More Letters*, 111; Mary E. Rucker, "Crèvecoeur's *Letters* and Enlightenment Doctrine," *Early American Literature*, XIII (1978), 193–212 (quotation on 196). All of the topics mentioned above are covered in the one-sentence paragraph that begins the narrator's account of Jamaica.

Collision and Combination of Crimes and Prophligacy which I observed there." His thesis is reiterated a few lines later: "Life ressembled a Delirium Inspired by the warmth of the sun urging every Passion and desire to some prémature Extreme." Almost immediately, however, cracks begin to appear in this model. In his discussion of Jamaican religion, the narrator wonders at the conspicuous lack of connection between climate and culture. The frequent hurricanes and earthquakes that afflict Jamaica should have produced equally intense forms of worship: "This is the Climate which ought to produce the most sincere Devotees and the greatest Saints—.... For the lease which Nature and her Elements hath given them for the Period of their Existence is but at will 'tis prècarious Indeed." Throughout the island, however, the narrator "cou'd perceive no Traces whatever of Relligion save few Temples." The attempt to link Jamaican social ills to climate is further undercut after the narrator's return to a profligate New York. By the time an acquaintance states that "vices and virtues are often Local and Geographical," the authority of such Enlightenment wisdom has been challenged by the narrator's experiences with a commercial culture that subsumes the Middle Colonies and the West Indies.[23]

The West Indian Routes of the First American Museum

Like "Sketches of Jamaica," Du Simitière's American Museum also transports the uninitiated American to a terrifying yet strangely familiar locale, one understood to have an important influence on the Middle Colonies. As noted above, Du Simitière's advertisement reveals that, although his cabinets contain items from across the planet, including "most parts of America, the West-Indies, Africa, the East-Indies and Europe," all regions are not equally represented. Much as in Raynal's natural law of commercial circulation, the Caribbean is central to his collections. Du Simitière's "Land Productions" consist of "Rare birds, and parts of Birds and Nests; a variety of Snakes, Lizzards, bats, Insects, and Worms, the most of them from different parts of the West-Indies." The catalog of botanical items foregrounds "a very considerable Collection of the most curious Plants of the West-Indies, together with the several productions of those Plants; such as their Wood,

---

23. [Crèvecoeur], "Sketches of Jamaica," in Moore, ed., *More Letters*, 107, 108, 112; Charles L. de Secondat, baron de Montesquieu, *The Spirit of the Laws*, trans. Thomas Nugent (New York, 1949). On Montesquieu's relation to cultural and political geography, see Karl Marcus Kriesel, "Montesquieu: Possibilistic Political Geographer," *Annals of the Association of American Geographers*, LVIII (1968), 557–574.

Bark, Fruits, Pods, Kernels, and Seeds." Likewise, the "Artificial Curiosities" on display include "Antiquities of the Indians of the West-Indies" as well as "Various Weapons, Musical Instruments and Utensils of the Negroes, from the coast of Guinea, and the West-Indies."[24]

We can only speculate as to how these objects were displayed. The typographic division between natural and artificial curiosities in the advertisement might suggest that separate displays were devoted to each category of object, perhaps in different rooms. Yet, as we have seen, the deliberate juxtaposition of natural and manmade objects was also fundamental to the visual culture and reading epistemology of natural history. Just as Richard Ligon's description of the banana had conflated nature and manufacture when it described a perfectly executed representation of Christ in the cross-section of the fruit, Sloane's engraving celebrating the duke of Albermarle's investment in a sunken galleon had relied on a series of puns confusing the conceptual boundary between coins and creatures, specie and species.

Du Simitière's museum followed this pattern. Among his surviving manuscript plans for the museum is a detailed roster entitled "Subjects of Natural History Collected in the Island of Hispaniola (by the French Call'd Saint Domingue) in 1773–1774 and Preserved in Vials with Spirit." Another extensive list, similarly titled, records items collected in Jamaica during the same period. Under numerous items in both lists, Du Simitière provides draft copy for display labels in his future museum. Of one curious reptile from Saint-Domingue, he notes: "This lizard which is the largest of the two in this vial, I found under a great rotten beam which formed the floor of a Sugarmill in Leogane. The negroes [————] it venomous. Perhaps it is a species of galliwasp of Jamaica or what Dr. Browne in his nat. hist. of Jamaica p.463 calls the *Wood Slave* and others the *croaking lizzard*." Just a few entries later, he includes a similar notation on a specimen identified as "Lezard par les negres d'habitations a St. Domingue," informing the reader, "This species the negroes of Hispaniola distinguish from all the other sorts whom they call by the general name of snails whereas they give this the name above [e.g. Lizard] whether on account of his beautifull skin or for some other reasons I have not learnd. They live in the cane pieces, and are difficult to be catch'd." Both notations query taxonomic divisions between natural categories, dwelling on a Saint-Dominguan reptile punningly labeled a "Wood Slave" by Patrick Browne and on a snail misidentified as

24. For Du Simitière's advertisement, see Broadside 962.F.166, LCP.

a lizard by the enslaved inhabitants of Jamaica because of its uncanny appearance. Whereas the first label explicitly refers the reader to the contents of an adjacent vial, the second assumes an ability to observe the specimen firsthand, perceiving physical details ("his beautiful skin") that are alluded to but never described.[25]

The notes also assume a reader who is familiar with a by-now canonical series of printed Caribbean natural histories, stretching in the papers as a whole to include such notable figures as Sloane, Père Labat, Jean-Baptiste Du Tertre, Catesby, Patrick Browne, Griffith Hughes, Edward Long, and dozens of others. The notes further depend on the viewer's knowledge of West Indian social organization and cultural practice, inviting them to contemplate the displayed objects in their "original" context, including their various colloquial names, what is known about them by enslaved Africans, and their location within a plantation landscape painted in precise, if cursory, strokes (the descriptions refer without further explanation to "cane pieces" and the "floor of a sugar mill" as well as particular towns and islands). In evoking these contexts of collection, both entries are consistent with Du Simitière's handwritten notation beneath an especially valuable artifact from Saint-Domingue, a scrap of paper containing a line of Arabic script written in a courtly hand (Fig. 8). Du Simitière explains, "The above was written in my presence by a negro Mondinga at Leoganne in January 1773." The handsome presentation of this West-African gris-gris suggests that it was carefully prepared for public display.[26]

Du Simitière relies on the viewer's familiarity with the region to cultivate a more vivid and concrete sense of daily life, a virtual experience of the tropical plantation. In one note for a preserved specimen from Jamaica, he writes:

> This is the largest of all the Spiders known. It has its French name from the resemblance it bears to the crabs in burrowing and living under ground. It comes out at night especially when the moon shines at which time this was catch'd, it comes into the houses to seize its prey which are cockroaches and other insects. It is found in the mountains as in the plains and in hoeing the ground you are almost sure to meet with some, its bite is said to be dangerous. It is not described by Sir Hans Sloane in his natural hist. of Jamaica.

25. Du Simitière, Papers Relating to Natural History, 963.F.14.

26. Ibid., 968.F.22–25. I am grateful to Phil Lapsansky at the LCP for alerting me to this West African gris-gris and sharing the translation by Emine Evered.

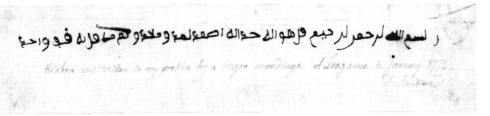

FIGURE 8. Pierre Eugene Du Simitière, West African Gris-Gris, Leogane, Saint-Domingue, 1773. The Library Company of Philadelphia

The description moves deftly from the local name of the species as written on the display note to the visual form of the specimen, creating an association between the spider and a local species of burrowing crab. Through this felicitous movement between word and object, emphasizing linguistic and morphological resemblances, the note conveys a visceral sense of the specimen's appearance and behavior at the moment of collection. The homely details of farming life—familiar to a Pennsylvania audience—take on a sense of danger. So common is this bizarre nocturnal creature—which obeys lunar rhythms, is as large as a crab, and secretes dangerous venom—that "you are almost sure to meet with some" when performing an act as routine as "hoeing the ground." Yet the species remains poorly understood by science, undocumented in Sloane's magisterial survey.[27]

Further evidence from Du Simitière's papers suggests that he derived these visual and linguistic techniques from study of Sloane's volumes. The book was undoubtedly a constant reference. Among other painstaking uses of *Voyage to . . . Jamaica,* Du Simitière compiled a detailed and visually arresting chart correlating birds he had observed in Saint-Domingue to Sloane's descriptions of identical species under different names in Jamaica. As he collected interpretive materials for his West Indian antiquities, moreover, Du Simitière transcribed numerous passages from Sloane on the archaeology of precolonial Jamaica. Under a rough sketch of a native American figurine excavated from a possible burial ground near Legoane in Saint-Domingue and identified as "une Idole des Indiens de St. domingue," Du Simitière includes a handwritten transcription of Sloane's account of a subterranean burial chamber in northern Jamaica, where he discovered pottery fragments and human bones. As argued in Chapter 1, the passage plays a role in the emblematic reading initiated by Sloane's engraving

27. Ibid., 963.F.22e.

of "Land Crab and Pot Shards" (Fig. 1). Instructed by Sloane's example, Du Simitière also relied on linguistic and visual resemblances between displayed objects to create occult associations and quasi-gothic effects.[28]

Because Sloane's descriptions and engravings were a valuable precedent for Du Simitière and because his own notes on preserved specimens make frequent reference to slave custom, it seems probable that organic objects and human artifacts were displayed side by side in the American Museum. However they were displayed, a visitor to the rooms on Arch Street would have surveyed not only a substantial collection of preserved flora and fauna from the Caribbean but also a range of material objects related to West Indian slavery, including the gris-gris, a mahogany sword allegedly used during Tacky's Rebellion in Jamaica (see below), creole vocabularies and proverbs, and satirical sketches of West Indian manners and customs. As was conventional for natural history museums in the eighteenth century, Du Simitière's displays made visible both the material spoils of West Indian nature and its necessary connection to an alien colonial society. But it did so in a cultural climate reshaped by events including the political independence of North America and the rise of newly vociferous forms of abolitionist complaint against colonial planters, most commonly directed at the sugar islands.

Du Simitière's understanding of this new state of affairs was mediated by his reading of the newest generation of imperial treatises on the Americas, including Long's *History of Jamaica* and Raynal's *History*. Sometime between 1776 and 1782, Du Simitière compiled lists of passages from Long, Raynal, and numerous other recent treatments of the Caribbean to include in a proposed published volume of extracts. As we have examined above, by the opening of the American Museum in 1782, Raynal's treatise had proposed a sweeping and influential new theory of the relation between West Indian natural history, global commercial progress, and cosmopolitan refinement. As we have also begun to see in our analysis of Crèvecoeur's "Sketches of Jamaica," this was a theory with troubling implications for the Middle Colonies. The form and content of the sketch points to Crèvecoeur's assumption that Raynal's theory was familiar to his potential readership, which included the learned provincials who would have patronized Du Simitière's cabinet. In order to comprehend the scope and character of those anxieties, however, we must examine Raynal's *History* itself.[29]

---

28. Ibid., 963.F.4g, 963.F.4m.

29. Ibid., 968.F.17. Commenting on Long's description of a mineral spring in Jamaica, for instance,

Raynal's Revolution

In Holbo's reading of the *History,* republican virtue and Enlightenment rationality occupy central positions in its analysis of New World colonialism and commerce. Holbo writes:

> On the one hand, Raynal saw commerce as the source of the global, humanitarian sympathies which ground his critique of slavery, and help to hold together the diverse histories presented in his book. Economically and socially, commerce gave rise to the discoveries of science, to the expansion of sentiment, and to the possibility of universal or philosophical reflection. . . . On the other hand, Raynal recognized that commerce caused the enslavement of Africans and native Americans, and transformed their owners into unfeeling monsters, slaves to passion and to limitless appetite.

This paradoxical thesis plays out in two opposing narratives: "A narrative of Enlightenment, of progress toward a world united by sympathetic knowledge; and a narrative of disintegration, of an entropic worldwide slide toward slavery and anarchy." Raynal's central examples of these movements were "the establishment of new, republican, and virtuous settlements in North America, and the spread of multiple forms of slavery."[30]

Raynal's imagination of slavery, however, was also centered in a specific region. Whereas the Middle Colonies of North America (and especially Pennsylvania) were his exemplary republics, the Caribbean plantation formed the epicenter of Atlantic slavery. This geographic vision has significant implications for interpretation of the *History.* With the West Indies at its center, the *History* offers a far less ambivalent and far more despairing account of the effects of international commerce. Raynal believed that the West India trade would continue to propagate the vices of chattel slavery and decadent luxury along its triangular routes and would thus destroy the bonds of sociability necessary to his redemptive project. That belief emerges with particular clarity in his analysis of a variety of anticolonial movements.

Du Simitière notes: "The history and description of the town of Bath its buildings, the roads, the rivers, the mountains and the adjacent country, as also the account of the company that resorted there and their amusement are all very curious and well written, but not quite calculated for my plan of extracts and besides of too great a length" (ibid.).

30. Holbo, "Imagination, Commerce, and the Politics of Associationism," *Early American Literature,* XXXII (1997), 31, 32.

Crèvecoeur's own West Indian narrative displays his grasp of the darker implications of Raynal's New World geography. He was, it seems, a more careful reader of the *History* than his Anglo-American contemporaries. In pre-Revolutionary America, Raynal was customarily understood as prophesying the birth of a New World republican power. The thirteen North American colonies, in such a reading, would inspire a series of Old World revolutions against feudalism and tyranny. To read Raynal as expecting global redemption to result from American Independence, however, readers had to elide the staggering pessimism of his conclusions. In the lengthy recapitulation at the close of volume VI, Raynal attempted to conclusively determine "the influence which the intercourse established with the New World has had upon the opinions, government, industry, arts, manners and happiness of the Old." Balancing advances in intellectual and political culture against genocide and slavery, Raynal's judgment on the Age of Discovery is unflinching:

> Let us stop here, and consider ourselves as existing at the time when America and India were unknown. Let me suppose that I address myself to the most cruel of the Europeans in the following terms: There exist regions which will furnish thee with rich metals, agreeable clothing, and delicious food; but read this history, and behold at what price the discovery is promised to thee. Dost thou wish or not that it should be made? Is it to be imagined that there exists a being infernal enough to answer this question in the affirmative?

Looking back on three centuries of European settlement of and commerce with the New World and Asia, Raynal judges them a colossal mistake.[31]

The despair of the *History*'s conclusions is linked to its Caribbean-centric commercial theory. The fate of enlightened republicanism, for Raynal, turned on the empirical question of whether events in North America or the West Indies would have greater effect on world history. A dark corollary to his belief that ideas and sentiments (whether virtuous or decadent) circulated along the same international routes as commodities was that the

---

31. Raymond J. Moras, "Abbé Raynal and the America Independence Movement," in John W. Rooney, ed., *Consortium on Revolutionary Europe, 1750–1850: Proceedings*, XXI (Tallahassee, Fla., 1992), 284–293; Raynal, *History*, V, 215, VI, 491. Explicit discussions of the American Revolution are, of course, to be found solely in post-Revolutionary editions of the *History*. It should be noted, however, that the threat of colonial rebellion also stalks the earliest edition. Internal evidence from the 1782 *Letters* suggests that Crèvecoeur continued to consult later editions of the *History*.

magnitude of a region's influence on world history depended on the volume of its trade. Like Eric Williams and C. L. R. James after him, Raynal viewed the colonial Caribbean as the main mover of world commerce, "primary cause of the rapid motion which now agitates the universe." An American War of Independence would be of limited global impact, given the poverty of British North America in relation to the Caribbean and the relative paucity of its commerce with Europe. In 1773, as noted in the introduction of this study, imports to Britain from Jamaica alone were nearly five times as valuable as imports from the mainland colonies combined.[32]

Concluding his analysis of the British Caribbean, Raynal notes the detrimental effect on the British Empire of "the revolution which hath detached North America." His interest immediately turns to the impact that revolution might have on the West Indies: "Is the possession of the islands, which are become very wealthy, and have been placed by nature in the vicinity of that great continent, which is still in a state of poverty, better secured to the nations that have cultivated them? It is in the position, in the interests, in the spirit of the new republics that we must endeavour to explore the secret of our future destiny." Raynal's entire analysis of North American society is framed as an extension of his attempt to determine whether conditions in the island colonies might foster revolutionary movements that would be truly shattering to the European world-system.[33]

Raynal's answer to that question was deeply informed by his location in metropolitan France. Although he claims to offer a synthesis of planter attitudes in the Spanish, French, and British islands, his account of growing West Indian unrest reflects the particular situation of French Caribbean colonists. Since the 1720s, sugar cultivation in Saint-Domingue had enjoyed such explosive growth that the island had quickly become the most productive colony in the Caribbean. At the start of the American Revolution, it produced more sugar than all the British islands combined. Owing to their importance to a rising French maritime bourgeoisie, the Caribbean colonies "constituted a major cornerstone of France's prerevolutionary political economy." With their newfound prosperity, French West Indian planters and merchants had grown to resent mercantile restrictions—whether in the form of the French *exclusif* or the British Navigation Acts—on commerce across imperial boundaries. It was solely because of those restric-

32. Raynal, *History*, V, 107.
33. Ibid., 112.

tions that French Caribbean colonists still struggled to compete with planters in Jamaica and Barbados despite producing cheaper and higher quality sugar.[34]

Attentive to the interests of an important sector of the metropolitan economy, Raynal predicted that easing mercantile restrictions and allowing the colonists a limited form of political autonomy might address their grievances. The prospect of West Indian rebellion marks the sensational climax of this antimercantile argument. Warning of the eventual loss of Caribbean revenues, Raynal frames a paradoxical argument whereby allowing colonial trade to transgress national boundaries will strengthen the bonds between the center and periphery of each European empire. In a more prosperous and cosmopolitan future, such bonds would be based on mutual gratitude rather than edict and force. Generalizing from the plight of French Caribbean colonists, Raynal argues that the national attachments of all West Indian settlers had been weakened by resentments over imperial trade policies. This was, however, far from the case in the British West Indies, where planters were in full support of mercantile restrictions that protected them from fierce French competition. Indeed, the British colonists lobbied passionately for the tightened restrictions in the 1764 Sugar Act. That act limited the clandestine trade between British North America and the French West Indies through stiffer inspections and higher duties.

The French Caribbean bias of Raynal's cosmopolitan vision was one source of his popularity in the mainland British colonies. Elite North Americans largely shared the abbé's opposition to British mercantile policy regarding Caribbean trade. Like Raynal, they kept a keen eye on the lucrative arena of the French West Indies and were increasingly frustrated by the influence of the British planters. Such frustrations fueled revolutionary sentiments. Crèvecoeur composed his bitter portrait of Jamaican colonists in the midst of the continued aftershocks from the 1764 Sugar Act and its reinforcement in the Townshend Revenue Act of 1767. Throughout the 1770s, the link between the Sugar Act and the movement toward rebellion was relatively clear. Looking back on the Sugar Act protests, John Adams would later proclaim, "I know not why we should blush to confess that molasses was an essential ingredient in American Independence, many great

---

34. Carolyn E. Fick, "The French Revolution in Saint Domingue: A Triumph or a Failure?" in David Barry Gaspar and David Patrick Geggus, eds., *A Turbulent Time: The French Revolution and the Greater Caribbean* (Bloomington, Ind., 1997), 52–61 (quotation on 52); O'Shaughnessy, *Empire Divided*, 58–62.

events have proceeded from smaller causes." In *Capitalism and Slavery*, Eric Williams offers an even stronger assessment. The Sugar Act was a "greater blow to rising colonial consciousness than the Stamp Act. . . . The attempt to render the Act effective and stamp out smuggling led directly to the American Revolution."[35]

A more nuanced interpreter of the *History* than many of his contemporaries, Crèvecoeur perceived (much like Paine) that Raynal's antimercantilism in no way sanctioned colonial revolt. Although Raynal's cosmopolitan viewpoint was opposed to mercantile restrictions, it was even more hostile to the amoral and insatiable desire for profit that lay at the root of his imagined West Indian rebellion. Crèvecoeur transposed aspects of this portrait of profligate Caribbean colonists to his depiction of the social transformations that would lead to the American Revolution. In 1773, mere months before militias would begin drilling throughout the northern colonies, his "Sketches of Jamaica" linked the incipient breakdown of moral and social order in colonial New York to the penetration of a maritime market that stretched to Jamaica. Extending that insight, the 1782 *Letters* would adopt a highly ambivalent stance toward the Revolution itself.

In order to grasp the full influence of Raynal's Caribbean on *Letters*, we must first attend to the most sensational aspect of Raynal's West Indian revolt. When, amid the predictions of volume VI, Raynal asks, "If a revolution should take place in [the islands], by what means will it be brought about, and what people will reap the advantage of it?" his question resonates with some haunting passages from the beginning of his Caribbean analysis in volume IV. In perhaps the best-known passage from the *History*, Raynal prophesied that Caribbean revolution would erupt, not in white-settler rebellion, but in a slave-led insurrection:

> If then, ye nations of Europe, interest alone can exert its influence over you, listen to me once more. Your slaves stand in no need either of your generosity or your counsels, in order to break the sacrilegious yoke of their oppression. Nature speaks a more powerful language than philosophy or interest. Already have two colonies of fugitive Negroes been established, to whom treaties and power give a perfect security from your attempts. These are so many indications of the im-

---

35. O'Shaughnessy, *Empire Divided*, 62–69 (quotation on 68–69); Eric Williams, *Capitalism and Slavery* (1944; rpt., Chapel Hill, N.C., 1994), 120.

pending storm, and the Negroes only want a chief, sufficiently coura-
geous, to lead them on to vengeance and slaughter.

The passages were likely composed by Jean de Péchmèja, whom Robin
Blackburn identifies as "an early utopian socialist of colonial extraction."
Such passages made the *History* "one of the most remarkable, radical,
and widely disseminated attacks on slavery to be published in the pre-
revolutionary epoch."[36]

Whatever we make of its politics, however, the intensity of the passage is
remarkable in itself:

> They will rush on with more impetuosity than torrents; they will leave
> behind them, in all parts, indelible traces of their just resentment.
> Spaniards, Portuguese, English, French, Dutch, all their tyrants will
> become the victims of fire and sword. The plains of America will suck
> up with transport the blood which they have so long expected, and
> the bones of so many wretches, heaped upon one another, during the
> course of so many centuries, will bound for joy. The Old World will
> join its plaudits to those of the New. In all parts the name of the hero,
> who shall have restored the rights of the human species, will be blest.

Raynal's vision of slave revolution points to the limits of his vision of cosmopolitan fellowship in a future era of international free trade. Even if national
restrictions on West Indian enterprise were eliminated, Raynal recognized,
there was no guarantee that the abuses of slavery would be diminished.
By creating new opportunities for profit, such a system might intensify
the brutalities of the Middle Passage and the sugar plantation, sparking a
more explosive form of Caribbean discontent. Fearing that Euro-American
elites, corrupted by the decadence of the West India trade, could not re-
deem the Age of Empire from its violent excess, Raynal here espouses a
form of radical antislavery well beyond the norms of cosmopolitanism, with
its belief in the saving function of elite humanism. Incorporating the politics of Péchmèja, Raynal attributes the virtues of cosmopolitanism to the
future rebels. Black revolutionaries would become the true defenders of the

---

36. Raynal, *History*, V, 109; Robin Blackburn, *The Overthrow of Colonial Slavery, 1776–1848* (London,
1988), 53, 54. Although Blackburn elsewhere writes, "The tenor of French writing on slavery," including
statements by Condorcet, Montesquieu, and Rousseau, "had often been more radical, if also more rhetorical, than that to be found in Britain or the United States" (170), Raynal's statements nonetheless remained
anomalous. For a comparison of British and French antislavery, see Seymour Drescher, *From Slavery to
Freedom: Comparative Studies in the Rise and Fall of Atlantic Slavery* (New York, 1999), 35–52.

universal rights articulated by the Enlightenment. Their broad-scale movement would transgress the boundaries of nation and language between the
Caribbean colonies of the various empires.[37]

Raynal's reference to "two colonies of fugitive Negroes" establishes
Jamaica as a center of the "impending storm." Those fugitives were the
Treaty Maroons of Jamaica, an island that, according to Blackburn, "was
notable for the frequency of revolts and the stubbornness of maroon resistance." Throughout the early eighteenth century, the Treaty Maroons
waged continual war on British plantations, until a series of settlements
in the 1770s officially recognized their sovereignty. Raynal's description
of Jamaica devotes six pages to the Treaty Maroons, detailing how those
former slaves will instigate a broad-based revolution. They will, he pre-
dicts, join England's great imperial rival France in a coordinated attack on
Jamaica from within and without. Such an attack will cause nothing less
than the fall of the British Empire. France's treachery, however, will lead to
its own demise, for "the revolt of the Blacks in one colony would probably
occasion it in all the rest," including Saint-Domingue.[38]

Crèvecoeur's portrayal of Jamaican slavery is far removed from the more
apocalyptic moments in the *History*. His depiction of slaveholder violence
is limited to a curiously detached account of the daily whippings adminis-
tered by his British-born landlady, whereas his depiction of slave resistance
is limited to a comment, before his narrator's departure, on "the perpetual
struggle subsisting between the 2 great Factions which Inhabit this Island."
As noted above, however, Crèvecoeur does devote at least one sentence to
the Treaty Maroons, in a paragraph filled with revulsion for white settler society. Its reference to republicanism suggests that, like Raynal, Crèvecoeur
was capable of momentary rhetorical identification with the political aims
of maroonage. Whatever his attitude toward the Maroons and the prospect of a broad insurrection, Raynal's prophecy exerted a strong impact on
Crèvecoeur. To register that impact, we must look beyond Jamaica to *Letters*, where New World slavery and slave resistance play a pivotal role in the

37. Raynal, *History*, IV, 128–129. Raynal's advocacy, elsewhere in the *History*, for gradual emancipation of slaves over twenty-five years, with training and education, is more consistent with the cosmopolitan
viewpoint of most antislavery philosophes. See Blackburn, *Overthrow of Colonial Slavery*, 170. Blackburn
argues, "Pechmeja's extreme anti-slavery passages were retained as a warning of what might happen if a
moderate reform was not adopted."

38. Blackburn, *Overthrow of Colonial Slavery*, 55; Raynal, *History*, V, 61. On the Treaty Maroons, see
Michael Mullin, *Africa in America: Slave Acculturation and Resistance in the American South and the
British Caribbean, 1736–1831* (Urbana, Ill., 1992), 45–61.

text's broader meditation on the fate of enlightened cosmopolitanism in an age of accelerated maritime commerce.[39]

Consciousness in Charleston

In his dedication of *Letters* to Raynal, Crèvecoeur describes the transforming experience of reading the *History* on his New York farm:

> For the first time in my life, I reflected on the relative state of nations; I traced the extended ramifications of a commerce which ought to unite, but now convulses, the world; I admired that universal benevolence, that diffusive goodwill, which is not confined to the narrow limits of your own country, but, on the contrary, extends to the whole human race. As an eloquent and powerful advocate, you have pleaded the cause of humanity, in espousing that of the poor Africans.

The dedication insists that the depiction of North American society in *Letters* must be understood in a broader comparative framework, one that, like the *History* itself and Crèvecoeur's own writings of the early 1770s, encompasses the territories of and relations between a variety of nations and their New World colonies. The "convulsions" with which the text will concern itself—including the growth of the plantation economy of the Carolinas in Letter IX and the outbreak of the American Revolution in Letter XII—are to be interpreted in relation to the development of maritime trade. By adopting that commercial worldview, the author-narrator of *Letters* attempts to emulate a form of cosmopolitanism exemplified by Raynal. With his "diffusive goodwill," Crèvecoeur's Raynal embodies the enlightened cosmopolitan, the "true philosophe," who, as Robert A. Ferguson writes, "thinks in terms of a universal language, identifying less with nations than with the republic of letters. . . . As Enlightenment thinkers, they believe in the global sphere of connections and the promise of republicanism throughout the world." From nearly the first words of *Letters*, Crèvecoeur announces that his interest in elite transnational fellowship subsumes his meditations on American identity. A passionate antislavery stance, he further declares, is integral to the cosmopolitanism he encountered in Raynal's treatise.[40]

Such a reading provokes the question of why cosmopolitanism plays a

---

39. [Crèvecoeur], "Sketches of Jamaica," in Moore, ed., *More Letters,* 108.

40. J. Hector St. John de Crèvecoeur, *Letters from an American Farmer,* ed. Susan Manning (New York, 1997), 7; Robert A. Ferguson, *The American Enlightenment, 1750–1820* (Cambridge, Mass., 1997), 34.

seemingly limited role in the narrative, with its exclusively North American setting and its reliance on a narrator (Farmer James) with little experience of the world beyond the mainland. Near the end of the dedication, the author-narrator provides an oblique answer. "There is, no doubt," he writes, "a secret communion among good men throughout the world; a mental affinity, connecting them by a similitude of sentiments. Then why, though an American, should not I be permitted to share in that extensive intellectual consanguity?" Crèvecoeur neglects to specify the forces that prohibit alliances between residents of late-colonial America and the members of a wider intellectual community. Fresh from his experiences with antiloyalist violence in rural New York and the suspicion of British colonial officials in New York City, however, Crèvecoeur was well aware that, with the advent of the Anglo-American conflict, his identity as an Atlantic cosmopolitan had become difficult to maintain.[41]

Crèvecoeur's complaint points to the new limitations on mobility and allegiance in a "rapidly nationalizing" Atlantic. Negotiating that new reality, the narrative of *Letters* appears to limit itself to the subject of mainland identity. Yet Crèvecoeur produces the core of that text by reworking a series of sketches rooted in a cosmopolitan outlook that situated North America within a range of overlapping comparative frameworks. The alternative geographical perspectives of the earlier travel sketches, encompassing Lisbon, Lima, and the British Caribbean, haunt the 1782 narrative. In the complex palimpsest of *Letters*, that is, the broader concerns of the original body of work are never effaced by the more geographically circumscribed narrative that is written over them. They enjoy a prominent textual afterlife, disrupting the published narrative with their insistent yet spectral presence. By bringing *Letters* into conjunction with the *History*, the dedication helps to raise those residual cosmopolitan perspectives, and the interpretive possibilities that adhere to them, to the very surface of Crèvecoeur's later text. The perspective carried over from "Sketches of Jamaica" is of particular importance. Crèvecoeur draws on his sketch of the West India trade both for the basic narrative structure of *Letters* and for a dystopic account of Atlantic society that was centered in the Caribbean.[42]

That alternative geography surfaces most notably in Letters IV through VIII on Nantucket and Martha's Vineyard, the first of the revised travel sketches that we encounter in the 1782 narrative. Though comprising the

---

41. Crèvecoeur, *Letters from an American Farmer*, ed. Manning, 7–8.
42. Rice, "Crèvecoeur and the Politics of Authorship," *Early American Literature*, XXVIII (1993), 108.

central five sections of *Letters,* the depiction of those islands is neglected by most critics. For Nathaniel Philbrick, however, the island letters provide a crucial, if subtle, transition from the utopianism of "What is an American?" to the despair of "Description of Charles-Town." Similarly, for Holbo, those spatially central letters ponder the central thematic question of the text as a whole. They offer "an extended meditation on the effects of commerce upon manners." At first, commerce appears to have a salutary effect. Because the sterility of their soil obliges the islanders to "seek abroad for the means of subsistence," the development of a decadent, landed elite is forestalled. Later, however, James worries about the use of opium among the islanders and warns, "Could the manners of luxuriant countries be imported here, like an epidemical disorder they would destroy every thing." Read in the context of "Sketches of Jamaica" and the plight of its narrator, such contamination is all but inevitable, given the extent of the islands' overseas trade.[43]

The West Indian voyages of the New England islanders have a powerful impact on their overall behavior. James writes, "They employ also several vessels in transporting lumber to the West-Indian Islands, from whence they procure in return the various productions of the country, which they afterwards exchange wherever they can hear of an advantageous market." Tellingly, it is in this West Indian allusion that the association between seafaring and market values is made most explicit.[44]

This is not the Caribbean's only appearance in the Massachusetts *Letters.* Letter VIII, entitled "Peculiar Customs at Nantucket," concludes with a description of a Nantucket home built at the extreme eastern point of the island. The home is representative of the industry, moderation, and sociability James purports to find in Nantucket society. Crèvecoeur's description, however, also stresses the unpredictable and invasive quality of the surrounding ocean. Whereas the dedication to Raynal referred to a commercial network that "ought to unite, but now convulses, the world," Farmer James describes an Atlantic that "seems to be the destroyer of this poor planet, yet, at particular times, accumulates the scattered fragments, and produces islands and continents fit for men to dwell on." The Atlantic convulsions both narrators observe have their source in the Caribbean. The imagery of

43. Holbo, "Imagination, Commerce, and the Politics of Associationism," *Early American Literature,* XXXII (1997), 44; Crèvecoeur, *Letters from an American Farmer,* ed. Manning, 87, 106; Philbrick, "Nantucket Sequence," *New England Quarterly,* LXIV (1991), 414–432.

44. Crèvecoeur, *Letters from an American Farmer,* ed. Manning, 112.

the Nantucket passage is derived from a similar moment in "Sketches of Jamaica," in which, just before leaving Bermuda, Crèvecoeur's young narrator witnesses a tropical hurricane. As does James in Nantucket, the youth describes the local custom of gathering plunder from shipwrecked vessels and stresses the visual contrast between small, isolated societies and "the great Circumjacent ocean." "How diminutive," James asserts, "does a man appear to himself when filled with these thoughts, and standing, as I did, on the verge of the ocean." The young narrator in Bermuda similarly exclaims, "How diminutive did this little spot appear when I compared it to the Vast Extent of the watery mass whose percussion seems to shake the very Foundation of the Island."[45]

Holbo argues that the sublime imagery of the Nantucket passage literalizes Crèvecoeur's troubled realization that, "if societies are no longer concretely defined by their land, people, and history, but are extended around the globe by commercial and intellectual relations, then no society can ultimately be defined." Crèvecoeur first arrived at that realization, and that literary technique, in his essay on the West India trade. In "Sketches of Jamaica," the hurricane passage blurs distinctions between Jamaica, Bermuda, and the mainland. After the storm, the simple virtue of Bermudan society, based, as that of Nantucket would later be, on the poverty of its soil, no longer seems stable. Nor is the contrast with decadent, soil-rich Jamaica sustainable. His Bermuda idyll shattered, the narrator flees "for a securer habitation, on a large Continent." But that distinction also breaks down. Back in New York, the young man exclaims, "But where was I? if not in the Midst of the Great Storm at Bermudas, I found myself full as Exposed." Like its companion text in "Sketches of Jamaica," the ocean passage in *Letters* also blurs the distinction between an island and mainland society, this time between the New England fisheries and slaving Charleston. The transition from Nantucket to Charleston in *Letters* provides a mirror image of the transition from the Caribbean to rural New York in "Sketches of Jamaica."[46]

In Crèvecoeur's depiction of Charleston and the surrounding lowcountry, another of the pre-1774 writings revised for inclusion in his later work, the alternative geographies of the early travel sketches attain their greatest prominence within *Letters*. The first sentence of Letter IX establishes a hemispheric frame uncharacteristic for the narrative voice of the first sec-

45. Ibid., 148; [Crèvecoeur], "Sketches of Jamaica," in Moore, ed., *More Letters*, 109.
46. Holbo, "Imagination, Commerce, and the Politics of Associationism," *Early American Literature*, XXXII (1997), 45; [Crèvecoeur], "Sketches of Jamaica," in Moore, ed., *More Letters*, 109, 110.

tions. Echoing similar statements from "Sketch of a Contrast between the Spanish and the English Colonies," James declares, "Charles-Town is in the north what Lima is in the south; both are capitals of the richest provinces of their respective hemispheres." A few pages later, James again surprises by situating southern slavery in a global frame worthy of his author's mentor. Speaking of Carolina traders, James says, "With gold, dug from Peruvian mountains, they order vessels to the coasts of Guinea; by virtue of that gold, wars, murders, and devastations, are committed in some harmless, peaceable, African neighbourhood." As the passage indicates, the Atlantic and hemispheric perspectives of Letter IX derive from its imperative to portray the violence and exploitation of slavery in its full dimensions. That imperative also explains the specific presence of the Caribbean within the letter. While Crèvecoeur's Nantucket and Martha's Vineyard are in part written over his earlier representation of the Bermudas, the Charleston of 1782 is written over the Jamaica of 1773. Both texts stress the litigiousness, physical debility, moral decadence, and brutal slave regime common to the societies they chronicle.[47]

Nor is the West Indian connection merely implicit. In a long passage near the opening of Letter IX, Crèvecoeur begins to write of Charleston high society:

> The inhabitants are the gayest in America; it is called the center of our beau monde, and is always filled with the richest planters in the province, who resort hither in quest of health and pleasure. Here is always to be seen a great number of valetudinarians from the West-Indies, seeking for the renovation of health, exhausted by the debilitating nature of their sun, air, and modes of living. Many of these West-Indians have I seen, at thirty, loaded with the infirmities of old age; for, nothing is more common, in those countries of wealth, than for persons to lose the abilities of enjoying the comforts of life at a time when we northern men just begin to taste the fruits of our labour and prudence. The round of pleasure, and the expences of those citizens tables, are much superior to what you would imagine: indeed the growth of this town and province have been astonishingly rapid.

The passage contains a series of unmarked transitions between discussions of residents of the West Indies and Carolinas. Whereas the first sen-

---

47. Crèvecoeur, *Letters from an American Farmer*, ed. Manning, 151, 153.

tence speaks of Charleston planters who visit the city to restore their health, the second speaks of valetudinarians from the West Indies who come to Charleston for the same purpose, as if to include them among the "richest planters in the province." Similarly, when the end of that sentence distinguishes between the poor health of West Indians and that of northern men, it leaves open the question of whether residents of Charleston are numbered among northern men or among West Indians "loaded with the infirmities." The syntax remains ambiguous throughout the passage. When, at the beginning of the final sentence, Crèvecoeur refers to "those citizens tables," he appears to mean the visiting West Indian gentlemen. The end of the same sentence, however, concerns the growth of "this town," meaning Charleston. It is uncertain whether, at any moment in the passage, James is speaking of Charleston or a Caribbean seaport. In Crèvecoeur's palimpsest, such a distinction is largely without a difference.[48]

Farmer James's only direct reference to Caribbean slavery holds similar implications. While deploring the inhumane treatment of lowcountry slaves, James pauses to rehearse a familiar defense of their southern masters: "It is said, I know, that [slaves] are much happier here than in the West-Indies; because, land being cheaper upon this continent than in those islands, the fields, allowed them to raise their subsistence from, are in general more extensive." The next sentence disrupts his comparison. "The only possible chance of any alleviation depends on the humour of the planters, who, bred in the midst of slaves, learn, from the example of their parents, to despise them; and seldom conceive, either from religion or philosophy, any ideas that tend to make their fate less calamitous." By failing to note whether it here refers to planters in the West Indies or Carolinas, the text again leaves its reader in a telling state of confusion.[49]

References such as these implicitly map South Carolina as the periphery of an extended Caribbean and thus as a region implicated in the commercial revolution, radiating out along the networks of Atlantic slavery, that grounded Raynal's global analysis. Recovering that broader perspective illuminates the dramatic impact of Letter IX on the overall narrative. Caribbean slavery, however, exerts its most profound influence on Letter IX, not directly, but through a largely unremarked aspect of James's infamous encounter with a tortured slave near Charleston. From a cage suspended in

48. Ibid., 151–152.
49. Ibid., 155–156.

the branches of a tree, a man, left to starve to death, begs James for a fatal dose of poison. Birds of prey have plucked out his eyes and picked the flesh from his cheeks and arms. The incident has long been acknowledged as a turning point within *Letters*, the moment when the relatively coherent narrative voice of the early sections suffers an irrevocable collapse. By James's own admission, the encounter provides the immediate impetus for the series of bleak global meditations that pervade his account of Charleston. Those meditations do, indeed, mark a shocking departure from the tone of earlier letters. "The history of the earth!" James declares at one sweeping moment of his invective against slaveholder violence; "doth it present any thing but crimes of the most heinous nature, committed from one end of the world to the other?" James's belief in republicanism is but one casualty of this new worldview: "Republics, kingdoms, monarchies, founded either on fraud or successful violence, increase by pursuing the steps of the same policy, until they are destroyed, in their turn, either by the influence of their own crimes or by more successful but equally criminal enemies."[50]

Such declarations amount to a grotesque parody of the cosmopolitan viewpoint. Filled with the international and transhistorical knowledge that characterized the texts of the philosophes, they remain void of nearly all belief in the redemptive possibility of humanist sympathy. Cosmopolitan optimism suffers an acute crisis in *Letters* at almost the precise moment that the characteristic global scale of cosmopolitan awareness fully surfaces.

This is, of course, the very paradox we have traced within "Sketches of Jamaica." Yet that James's crisis of faith is linked to the dramatic expression of antislavery sentiment suggests that Letter IX is shaped by an even deeper engagement with the lessons of Raynal's West Indies than marked that earlier manuscript. Cosmopolitan optimism is initially undermined through an antislavery perspective that stresses the susceptibility of the Carolinas to the degenerative influence of West Indian intercourse. As in Raynal's Caribbean analysis, where the loss of cosmopolitan faith was expressed through

---

50. Ibid., 159, 162. For some examples of critics who locate the turn in the ninth letter and James's encounter with the tortured man, see Saar, "Crèvecoeur's 'Thoughts on Slavery,'" *Early American Literature*, XXII (1987), 192–203; Rucker, "Crèvecoeur's *Letters* and Enlightenment Doctrine," *Early American Literature*, XIII (1978), 91–119; Grabo, "Crèvecoeur's American," *WMQ*, 3d Ser., XLVIII (1991), 159–172; Stephen Carl Arch, "The 'Progressive Steps' of the Narrator in Crèvecoeur's *Letters from an American Farmer*," *Studies in American Fiction*, XVIII (1990), 144–158. For an astute reading of the episode, see Elizabeth Heckendorn Cook, *Epistolary Bodies: Gender and Genre in the Eighteenth-Century Republic of Letters* (Stanford, Calif., 1996), 160–167. Cook argues that Crèvecoeur's belief in the cosmopolitan ideals of the Enlightenment is finally undermined by the paradoxical status of the slave's body as both subject and object, agent of labor and article of property, within a market economy.

a radical and apocalyptic vision of hemispheric insurrection, the specter of slave revolt also plays a pivotal role in the final disillusionment of *Letters*. The episode both obscures and evokes the revolutionary agency of enslaved people as depicted in the *History*. Whereas James's initial encounter with the slave stresses his passive status as victim, his later conversation with some planters stresses the individual's active resistance. "The reason for this slave's being thus punished," the planters inform him, "was on account of his having killed the overseer of the plantation. They told me that the laws of self-preservation rendered such executions necessary." The planters' recourse to a rhetoric of "self-preservation" intimates that they viewed the man's resistance, not as a random and isolated act, but as symptomatic of the genuine threat that wider revolt posed to the plantation order.[51]

Other references to slave revolt within the letter also evoke the possibility of insurrection. The plantation order is only partly maintained, James had earlier insisted, by a system of corporal discipline. Lowcountry slaves are "perpetually awed by the terrible cracks of whips, or by the fear of capital punishments, while even those punishments often fail of their purpose." More pointedly, after documenting a variety of forms of exploitation, James wonders, "Is there any thing in this treatment but what must kindle all the passions, sow the seeds of inveterate resentment, and nourish a wish of perpetual revenge? They are left to the irresistible effects of those strong and natural propensities." In James's view, the growth of insurrectionary sentiments within the entire slave population is all but inevitable. I am suggesting neither that Crèvecoeur invokes the threat of broad-scale slave revolt with anything like the directness and intensity of Raynal nor that he shared the radical politics of a Juan de Péchmèja. Rather, I am arguing that one way to understand the disruptive effect of the episode, and the notorious narrative discontinuity of *Letters* in general, is to recall the fiery rhetoric of Raynal's revelation. In order to fully account for the radical shift within Letter IX, we might attend both to the hemispheric and circumatlantic dimensions of plantation slavery in the letter itself and the global significance of West Indian insurrection within the *History*. Crèvecoeur's dystopic vision of Charleston and the lowlands is haunted by his own earlier account of

---

51. Crèvecoeur, *Letters from an American Farmer*, ed. Manning, 165. According to Peter Linebaugh and Marcus Rediker in *The Many-Headed Hydra: Sailors, Slaves, Commoners, and the Hidden History of the Revolutionary Atlantic* (Boston, 2000), the 1770s saw an intense cycle of revolts in the Caribbean. In 1775 alone, moreover, plots and insurrections were reported in New York, Maryland, Virginia, and Charleston, South Carolina (224).

Jamaican corruption and by the sensational prophecy at the heart of Raynal's Caribbean.[52]

The Natural History of Cosmopolitan Despair

Crèvecoeur grounds and substantiates his narrative of the incident and accounts for its effect on the narrator's psychology through his rhetoric and topos of natural history. At the moment that the world-historical perspective of Raynal's treatise becomes evident in *Letters*, the text depicts the narrator as one of the legions of colonial collectors who provided accurate reportage to the metropole. The narrator happens upon the scene while engaged in careful study of lowcountry fauna. In the midst of "attentively examining some peculiar plants which [he] had collected," he is alarmed by a sudden transformation of the local atmosphere:

> All at once I felt the air strongly agitated, though the day was perfectly calm and sultry. I immediately cast my eyes toward the cleared ground, from which I was but a small distance, in order to see whether it was not occasioned by a sudden shower; when at that instant a sound, resembling a deep rough voice, uttered, as I thought, a few inarticulate monosyllables.

Looking up from his southern specimens, the narrator at first misinterprets these phenomena, instinctively scanning the horizon for indications of rain (perhaps fearing one of the sudden tropical storms for which the colony was well known). At this instant, he also hears another initially unintelligible sign, which the reader and narrator might assume was thunder (the sound *resembles* a deep, rough voice) but instead turns out to be an actual voice, probably human. Perplexed by these inscrutable signs, the observer enters a state of nonvolition and enhanced perception.[53]

A subsequent passage describes the victim's situation and the narrator's psychology in empirical detail:

> I perceived, at about six rods distance, something resembling a cage, suspended to the limbs of a tree, all the branches of which appeared covered with large birds of prey, fluttering about, and anxiously endeavouring to perch on the cage. Actuated by an involuntary motion

52. Crèvecoeur, *Letters from an American Farmer*, ed. Manning, 157, 158.
53. Ibid., 163.

of my hands, more than by any design of my mind, I fired at them; they all flew to a short distance, with a most hideous noise: when, horrid to think and painful to repeat, I perceived a negro, suspended in the cage, and left there to expire! I shudder when I recollect that the birds had already picked out his eyes.

The passage as a whole moves from the beauty and plenitude of botanical creation to the violence of the plantation, as the object of the narrator's attention shifts from curious southern plants to scavenging birds, to the bleeding eye sockets of an individual human being.[54]

In so doing, the passage enacts an oddly literalized version of the hermeneutic process we have examined in prior natural histories by Sloane and Catesby. The emblematic structure of these texts meant that images and descriptions of natural history specimens yielded unstable and multivalent meanings. Whereas West Indian specimens were normally presented as indications of refinement through the opulent physical format of such texts, the interpretive movement between image, textual label, and accompanying written descriptions as often resulted in more disturbing forms of knowledge regarding the barbarity, instability, and toxicity of the colonial plantation, whether through meditations on mass human death in Sloane's *Voyage to . . . Jamaica* or depictions of environmental chaos due to colonial "improvement" in Catesby's *Natural History of Carolina.* In Crèvecoeur's rendering of this episode in South Carolina, the narrator's empirical examination of the natural landscape reveals the human violence underlying the plantation landscape. In one sense, the passage resembles Ligon's much earlier description of the banana. But, in another, the episode transforms this hermeneutic tradition, particularly regarding the representation of agency. For one thing, the narrator is preoccupied not primarily with the botanical knowledge and skilled agricultural labor of enslaved people (as were Sloane and Catesby) but with the possibility of coordinated insurrection. In part, this reflects the increased threat of insurrection in the late eighteenth century, as made plain by a cycle of revolts throughout the Greater Caribbean. But it also reflects an increased sense of powerlessness and despair among cosmopolitan intellectuals regarding their necessary complicity in a triangular system of slave-driven commerce that they regarded as both the material foundation of intellectual progress and a contradiction to the professed moral and political ideals of the Enlightenment.

54. Ibid., 163–164.

Crèvecoeur captures this sense of powerlessness through his description of the narrator's psychology. So acute are the narrator's sensations of pity and terror, as he continues to observe and graphically describe the man's wounds, that they produce a condition of involuntary moral as well as physical action:

> From the edges of the hollow sockets, and from the lacerations with which he was disfigured, the blood slowly dropped, and tinged the ground beneath. No sooner were the birds flown, than swarms of insects covered the whole body of this unfortunate wretch, eager to feed on his mangled flesh and to drink his blood. I found myself suddenly arrested by the power of affright and terror; my nerves were convulsed; I trembled, I stood motionless, involuntarily contemplating the fate of this negro in all its dismal latitude.

Unable or unwilling to relieve the man's suffering, the narrator proceeds on his way to dinner with some local planters, possessing newly concrete and comprehensive knowledge of slavery in "all its dismal latitude," including his own complicity.[55]

Crèvecoeur's use of the geographic term "latitude"—crucial to theorists of New World climate such as Catesby—crystallizes the importance of natural history in explaining and rendering the transition from local phenomenon to planetary pattern, from a particular incident in South Carolina to a sweeping theory of the nature of man and the brutality of nature. It is hardly coincidental that the narrator's expansion of historical consciousness depends on a new understanding of the regional environment. Organic relationships are described in terms that recall Catesby's renderings of mangrove swamps and seasonal inundations in Carolina. No sooner are scavenging birds frightened away from the tortured man by the narrator's gunshot than swarms of hungry insects begin to feast on his wounds, as his blood stains and nourishes the landscape. The episode provides a tableau of Carolina as a natural and social system—seemingly tropical in character— in which violence and human blood generate overabundance. In depicting his narrator's dramatic shift in consciousness, Crèvecoeur depends upon a reader for whom Caribbean nature and slavery are familiar and interconnected subjects and for whom the interpretive movement from an empirical description of a natural history specimen to a moral examination of colonial slavery is potentially legible.

55. Ibid., 164.

Specimens of Insurrection

A brief return to Du Simitière's museum demonstrates that, within this hermeneutic tradition, reflections on the possibility of slave rebellion were by this time conventional. We have already speculated that Du Simitière displayed West Indian specimens, slave artifacts, and manners and customs sketches side by side according to long-established conventions. Within this basic format, it should now be emphasized, Du Simitière also exhibited items related to insurrection. The West African gris-gris from Saint-Domingue discussed previously is only one indication of this broader interest (Fig. 8). Neither collector nor viewer might have known that the Arabic script transcribes a Koranic verse that protests slaveholder violence while pleading for divine retribution. But an informed viewer would have known that creolized West African religions were habitually linked to conspiracy and insurrection in the imperial imagination, as in the discourse on obeah and poisoning discussed in Chapter 1, above. They might even have known, like Du Simitière himself, that the link between Voudun and insurrection had been widely discussed in relation to the island from which the gris-gris derives. Du Simitière arrived on Saint-Domingue amid the panic induced by the fugitive slave Makandal in 1757. Knowledgeable in botany, Makandal concocted poisons from harvested plants, which he used to kill livestock, enemy slaves, and planters. According to Méderic Louis-Élie Moreau de Saint-Méry, the creole historian of Saint-Domingue, after Makandal's execution by public immolation in January 1758, enslaved Africans began to use his name to refer to ritual talismans such as the gris-gris and the priests who devised them. Du Simitière maintained a special interest in this episode as he later compiled a dossier of newspaper clippings, periodical accounts, and eyewitness correspondence under the heading of "Negroes Conspiracies in Several Parts of the West Indies and of No America." One item records an herbal antidote for a local poison allegedly related by Makandal during his interrogation.[56]

Further evidence of Du Simitière's interest in insurrection is provided by the "Various Weapons . . . of the Negroes" mentioned in the broadside advertisement for his museum. Among the most prominent and memo-

---

56. On Makandal, see Laurent Dubois, *Avengers of the New World: The Story of the Haitian Revolution* (Cambridge, Mass., 2004), 51–52; Méderic Louis Élie Moreau de Saint-Méry, *Description topographique, physique, civile, politique, et historique de la partie française de l'isle Saint-Domingue . . .*, 3 vols. (Philadelphia, 1797), I, 631; Du Simitière, Papers Relating to the West Indies, 968.F.22–25, 968.F.11.

rable of these would have been a curious sword—elaborately carved from mahogany and painted in bright colors—obtained under notable circumstances in Jamaica. In his dossier on "Negroes Conspiracies," Du Simitière alleges that the sword played a key role in the organization of Tacky's Rebellion on Jamaica in August 1761, soon after the naturalist's arrival. Perhaps for inclusion in his published natural history, Du Simitière annotated his copy of a letter from St. Mary, Jamaica, that contained firsthand observations on the uprising and its aftermath. The letter describes "a sword of an extraordinary size and weight, the hilt covered with Black Velvet, and studded with brass nails, and under the Velvet a Parrot's red feathers which it seems is with the Coromantees the Banner of war. This sword we are assured has been seen at Spring-path the three Sundays last past." In a footnote, Du Simitière includes transcribed references to the sword from Long's *History of Jamaica,* along with his own eyewitness narrative of Tacky's Rebellion. This includes his account of the trial and execution of the sword's owner (where it was "proved that this sword was a token of war and of Rebellion amongst the Coromantees"). After the trial, Du Simitière claims, he received the sword as a gift from Arthur Chavet, a prominent Jamaican physician who performed autopsies on two leaders of the revolt following their public torture and execution. Declaring that the sword "remains in my possession," Du Simitière refers the reader to a "drawing in my collection of designs." The care with which he establishes the sword's provenance, social function, and physical appearance indicates its value to the collector.[57]

Du Simitière's pen-and-ink drawing of a public execution during Tacky's Rebellion suggests his disposition toward the artifact (Fig. 9). The sketch is possibly meant as a study for one of the "curious paintings" mentioned in the museum advertisement. In the center, a coach driver pauses to take in the spectacle of two dying men hung in iron cages, casually surveying the victims as his long whip rests on his shoulder. The market woman kneeling beneath the metal cages, with her wares spread on her apron, creates an incongruous sense of normalcy, almost literally in the shadow of this ritual exhibition of violence. A church steeple in the left background, framed between the center post of the garret and the body of the slave to the left, provides a possible moral commentary. So, too, do the caricatures included in the right margin of the sheet, perhaps as studies for the faces of individual spectators.[58]

57. Du Simitière, Papers Relating to the West Indies, 968.F.7, 968.F.20a–21.
58. Ibid., 968.F.19h.

FIGURE 9. Pierre Eugene Du Simitière, *Slaves Hanging from Gallows in Street.*
The Library Company of Philadelphia

These satirical and moralizing gestures coexist with a heightened sense
of immediacy and realism in the sketch, as underscored by the verbal description in French at the bottom of the sheet. Du Simitière informs the
viewer that these are the two leaders of Tacky's upon whom Chavet performed autopsies. In an English translation of this passage elsewhere in
his papers, Du Simitière depicts their death and autopsy in detail. After
describing the construction of the cages and gallows, the physical position
of the two prisoners within them, and their slow and painful death over a
period of eight to nine days, he relates that they were "carried to Dr. Chavet
in order to make some anatomical observations upon so strange a death,
which having done he sewed them up." In a transcribed passage from Long's
History of Jamaica in the margin of the same page, the incident is described
with a further degree of anatomical precision and psychological complexity:

> The morning before the latter expired, he appeared to be convulsed
> from head to foot; and upon being opened, after his decease, his lungs
> found adhering to the back so tightly, that it required some force to
> disengage them. The murders and outrages they had committed were
> thought to justify this cruel punishment inflicted upon them *in ter-*

rorem to others; but they appeared to be very little affected by it them-selves; behaving all the time with a degree of hardened insolence, and brutal insensibility.

By documenting the physiological effects of suffocation, the passage raises a moral question about planter brutality, even as it defends slaveholder prac-tice through its hypothesis of African insensibility. Based on observations of the dying prisoners, this claim derives its authority from the same type of empiricist rhetoric as the description of the autopsy. In a period marked by the emergence of racist pseudoscience, the observational techniques of the physician provide the basis for an argument questioning African humanity. In related ways, though to seemingly different ideological ends, the tech-niques of botanist and climatologist had provided the basis for Crèvecoeur's examination of the same question in "Description of Charles-Town."[59]

Du Simitière probably displayed the mahogany sword from Jamaica with some of the material discussed above. The sketch and letter from Tacky's are driven by the same imperative to authenticate and contextualize the object as the display labels for Du Simitière's natural history specimens. Relying on related verbal and visual techniques, they attempt to provide a virtual ex-perience of West Indian life, conveying sensations of fear and wonder along with scientific knowledge. The eye of the museumgoer on Arch Street would have traveled in the course of a visit, and perhaps in a single glance, from Du Simitière's natural history specimens to the token of a large and porten-tous slave rebellion, one that provoked a brutal display of planter violence.

The convergence of these subjects in Du Simitière's museum and manu-script owes to his engagement with the cosmopolitan intellectual culture, to which we must now return, that shaped both "Sketches of Jamaica" and the encounter with the tortured slave in Letter IX. Consideration of the Ameri-can Museum suggests a close relationship, within late-Enlightenment cul-ture, between natural history and slave rebellion as objects of knowledge. In so doing, it helps us to further understand the repercussions of the episode within the overarching formal structure of *Letters*.

59. [Edward Long], *The History of Jamaica; or, General Survey of the Antient and Modern State of That Island* . . . , 3 vols. (London, 1774), II, 458. Du Simitière translates the French passage beneath the drawing in another footnote in his annotated copy of "Extract of a Letter from a Gentleman at St. Mary Jamaica April 14, 1760," in Papers Relating to the West Indies, 968.F.11.

"Extended Ramifications"

Although the residual West Indian narrative within *Letters* reaches its climax in Charleston, the crisis of cosmopolitan faith that it occasions persists through later sections. As in "Sketches of Jamaica," a disillusioned narrator returns from a decadent plantation society to view a northern colony through altered eyes. Upon his return to Pennsylvania in Letter X, for instance, James depicts a volatile and predatory natural environment that is at odds with the celebratory early letters. The section ends with a dramatic account of a battle between a white water snake and its black challenger (perhaps containing a subtle echo of Raynal's Caribbean revolt). On its surface, Letter XI appears to counter the sweeping pessimism of the previous two sections. A Russian visitor to John Bartram's home and garden praises his host's participation in a natural historical network that spans the Atlantic. The knowledge gleaned from Bartram's cosmopolitan activities is presented as invaluable to the developing colony. By introducing an entirely new narrator, however, Crèvecoeur distances a now-worldly James from such humanist dreams, which do little to alter the trajectory of the narrative.[60]

In the most dramatic reversal of his earlier idyll, James's vision of universal violence and exploitation in Letter IX finds its echo in the anti-Revolutionary sentiments of Letter XII. James interprets the outbreak of hostilities within the dystopic account of world history and human nature first advanced in his portrait of New World slavery. "Why has the Master of the world," he asks, "permitted so much indiscriminate evil throughout every part of this poor planet, at all times, and among all kinds of people?" Within Letter XII, Crèvecoeur remains nearly silent as to how he interpreted the origins of the American Revolution and why he might have applied the rhetoric of his critique of plantation slavery to his lament on the violence of the Anglo-American conflict. The dedication to Raynal, however, reveals that Crèvecoeur viewed both phenomena as products of the development of Atlantic mercantilism, cueing the reader to understand events in the British North American colonies within the framework of the *History*. It is extensive commerce, the author-narrator insists, that "now convulses the world." For the Raynal of the *History* and the Crèvecoeur of "Sketches

60. On the snake battle as an echo of plantation violence, see Jennifer Rae Greeson, "The Figure of the South and the Nationalizing Imperatives of Early United States Literature," *Yale Journal of Criticism*, XII (1999), 209–248 (215, n. 19).

of Jamaica," the volatile and corrupting effect of Atlantic commerce could always be traced to its origin in West Indian sugar and slavery. Recognizing "Sketches of Jamaica" as an important shadow text within *Letters* and recalling Adams's comments on the link between sugar and Independence, we might speculate that Crèvecoeur's earlier lament over the degenerative influence of Caribbean trade (and the wider maritime system it made possible) plays a role in his later refusal to endorse the American Revolution as the advent of universal republicanism. Whatever the source of Crèvecoeur's anti-Revolutionary position in 1782, it remains clear that, with the outbreak of war, James desperately seeks a society beyond the reach of the Atlantic commercial network. The narrator hopes to flee North American hostilities, not, as his author did, through a return to Europe, but by moving his family inland to join an unnamed indigenous tribe. Disillusioned by his experiences in a range of port cities, James turns his back on the Atlantic world that formed the natural habitat of enlightened cosmopolitans, including his author and his author's mentor.[61]

Or so we might reasonably conclude, had the career of Crèvecoeur's best-known work ended in 1782. In 1783, however, Crèvecoeur quickly compiled the two volumes of *Lettres d'un cultivateur americain* while preparing to depart from Paris for his new post as trade consul to New York, New Jersey, and Connecticut. According to Rice, the 1784 *Lettres* "reinvented Crèvecoeur as the French champion of American democratic idealism." In nearly all instances, Crèvecoeur revised material from the English edition so as to qualify its anti-Revolutionary and pessimistic aspects and augment its idyllic traits. Among the new writings were the portraits of Franklin and the marquis de Lafayette that Thomas Philbrick calls "sops to the French enthusiasm for the celebrities of the American Revolution." Concessions to contemporary French taste made *Lettres* an immediate success.[62]

It is odd, then, that Crèvecoeur would include "Voyage à la Jamaïque"—a significantly revised version of the most critical of his early travel sketches—in the French editions of *Lettres*. This inclusion, however, was essential to the author's attempt to reinvent himself as the champion of cosmopolitan idealism. The encyclopedic form of *Lettres* pays tribute to the project of the philosophes, as its two dense and varied volumes strive to fulfill the cultural geographic ambitions of the early 1770s. In the more comprehensive

61. Crèvecoeur, *Letters from an American Farmer*, ed. Manning, 197.
62. Rice, "Crèvecoeur and the Politics of Authorship," *Early American Literature*, XXVIII (1993), 112; Philbrick, *St. John de Crèvecoeur*, 140.

1784 text, the face of America extends south beyond the mainland, into the sugar islands.

The major revisions of the earlier sketch soften the critique of West Indian trade as morally corrupt and corrupting and underscore the possibility that its dangers may be offset by the civic virtue of a scattered, yet enlightened, elite. In the most significant revision, Crèvecoeur reflects on the enslaved blacks who often manned and piloted Bermuda's merchant fleets:

> The majority of these vessels are commanded by Negroes; a race of men completely regenerated, no less by their long stay on this island, than by the education they receive from their Masters. They assist in the construction, and sail afterwards to the other islands, where they are preferred over all others for coastal trade and smuggling. Their skill as Mariners and Carpenters, their fidelity as supercargoes, the punctuality with which they carry out the business of their Masters, and bring back their vessels, is a truly edifying spectacle. I have seen several of these black Skippers at the tables of the rich planters of Jamaica, treated with all the respect their intelligence and faithfulness deserve.

The new passage is addressed to the root of Raynal's anxieties regarding cosmopolitanism. His vision of a general insurrection expressed his fear that free trade might expand an inherently violent and exploitative slave system. In "Voyage à la Jamaique," Crèvecoeur accommodates the development of international capitalism to a far more conservative form of antislavery than prevails in either Letter IX or the *History*. Through their central role in a transcolonial contraband trade—an illicit precursor to a system of free trade—the black pilots of Bermuda gain their gradual emancipation. In Crèvecoeur's view, their travels provide them broad training and education and allow them to achieve a social status unimaginable in his earlier depiction of Jamaica. The pilots are presented as an elite class of black cosmopolitans whose prospects for social mobility, economic prosperity, and cultural refinement increase as the maritime enterprises of their colonial masters expand.[63]

Of course, few passages in Crèvecoeur's writings may be taken at face

63. Crèvecoeur, *Lettres d'un cultivateur américain*, I, 236 (translation mine). On the role of black mariners from Bermuda in the contraband trade, see Michael J. Jarvis, "Maritime Masters and Seafaring Slaves in Bermuda, 1680–1783," *WMQ*, 3d Ser., LXIX (2002), 585–622. Jarvis argues that the owners of Bermuda ships preferred to use crews of slaves on smuggling trips in part because British law made it impossible for slaves to offer testimony (602).

value. Just as the form and content of the English *Letters* reflect its author's attempt to negotiate the volatile context of Anglo-American hostilities, *Lettres* is shaped by his efforts to negotiate the conflicting demands of the French public sphere. The question of precisely how awaits future study. I point to the inclusion of a revised French version of "Sketches of Jamaica" in *Lettres* only to insist that the exclusion of Caribbean natural history and slavery as explicit topics in the English *Letters* is highly contingent.

Yet the narrative pattern of the English edition—with the itinerary of the narrator limited to the mainland colonies—would shape assumptions about the coherence of North America as a geographic and cultural unit distinct from the West Indies. In retrospect, that is, the form and content of *Letters* would contribute to the formation of a protonationalist sensibility in which the omission of the travel sketch seemed as inevitable (and indeed "natural") as the failure of Du Simitière's cabinet of West Indian wonders in post-Revolutionary America. As we shall see, however, such outcomes were only made to seem inevitable through long and complicated ideological struggle, and never completely so.

The publication of Thomas Jefferson's *Notes on the State of Virginia* (1787) is a crucial episode in that struggle. The text argues that the prosperity of the early Republic depends, not on the circumatlantic system chronicled by Sloane, Raynal, and Crèvecoeur, but rather on the industry and virtue of yeoman farmers. As Jefferson realized, the published *Letters* provided a valuable resource for promoting that agrarian ideal, however ironic this would have seemed to the author of "Sketches of Jamaica." Indeed, the fact is doubly ironic. *Notes on the State of Virginia* remains haunted by the problems of West Indian commerce and empire addressed in Crèvecoeur's unpublished manuscripts. Before turning to Jefferson's text, however, we must first attend to William Bartram's *Travels through North and South Carolina, Georgia, East and West Florida* (1791). Much like Crèvecoeur's *Letters*, Bartram's *Travels* is also a palimpsest. The published text evolves from a manuscript begun during Bartram's travels in colonial Florida during the 1760s and 1770s, when the settlement of the region on a Caribbean model was a subject of passionate debate as a potential key to the refinement of the Americas.

4

"All the West-Indian Weeds"

WILLIAM BARTRAM'S *TRAVELS* AND THE
NATURAL HISTORY OF THE FLORIDAS

In 1766, having just returned from two productive years collecting specimens in East and West Florida, John Bartram penned a complaint to Peter Collinson: "I have left my son Billy in florida. nothing will do with him now but he will be A planter upon St. Johns river about 24 mile from Augustine and 6 from the fort of Picolata this frolic of his hath and our maintenance drove me to great straits." Though exasperated by his son's decision to establish a rice plantation in this dangerous region, which he had first visited with his father in 1765, the elder Bartram nevertheless provided financial and logistical support, securing investors and advisors from among his natural history connections in South Carolina and Georgia. By the early 1770s, with his son continuing to flounder after abandoning his plantation, John Bartram turned to these connections once more, negotiating an attractive position for the young man as collector and informant for the English botanist John Fothergill, who would sponsor his further travels in the Floridas.[1]

Sometime in 1788, approximately a decade after his final departure from East Florida in 1777, William Bartram sent naturalist Joseph Banks a portfolio of fifty-nine drawings originally intended for Fothergill, who had died just before their completion. Included among them was a striking depiction of a plant identified in a handwritten notation on the back of the drawing as "Colocasia" (the colloquial name of the plant Catesby identifies as "Arum Maximum Ægyptiacum") (Fig. 10). As discussed in Chapter 2, English botanical collectors had long been fascinated by the species not only for its aesthetic beauty but also for its curious history as a botanical stranger from West Africa, cultivated in provision gardens throughout the Greater Caribbean. Bartram's drawing is indebted to Catesby's images of

---

1. John Bartram to Peter Collinson, June 30, 1766, *CJB*, 668. Unless noted otherwise, all biographical information is from Thomas P. Slaughter, *The Natures of John and William Bartram* (New York, 1996).

FIGURE 10. William Bartram, *Colocasia.* © Natural History Museum, London

the species, even as it extends his formal experiments to convey a new form of empirical knowledge. Bartram manipulates scale and perspective to create a strong visual impression, a concrete Lockean idea of the specimen and its environs. The flowers of five outsized colocasia plants are depicted in various stages of flowering to provide a comprehensive understanding of morphology as it unfolds through time. The large, circular leaf floating on the surface of the lake also conforms to empiricist protocols. Resembling a dried specimen in an herbarium, the leaf is tilted toward the viewer along a vertical axis for accurate scrutiny and convenient reference, much like the leaf in the background of Catesby's engraving of "Green Tree Frog and Arum Americanum." By adhering to certain conventions of landscape perspective, the overall composition underscores this sense of epistemological stability and transparency. Objects generally become smaller in size and less sharply detailed as the viewer's eye moves from the "Dionaea muscipula" (Venus flytrap) at the extreme left foreground to the aquatic flowers in the right background, along the faint horizon between water and sky. The viewer is located firmly in space and time. Standing at the near shore, he perceives the sensuous beauty of the colocasia plant at a moment of heightened serenity (note the calm surface of the lake) and atmospheric clarity (the flowers are bathed in light).

This fusion between botanical illustration and landscape painting points to what is distinctive about the form of empirical knowledge conveyed here, namely, its emphasis on sensibility. In a period when Scottish Common Sense philosophers had begun to construe sensibility as an important epistemological faculty—an innate moral sense—Bartram's drawing reveals his conviction that proper understanding of a botanical specimen demands the sensuous apprehension of its total situation. However, this new emphasis on the role of individual subjectivity and sensibility in Bartram's writings and drawings brings with it a preoccupation with the possibility of perceptual error and delusion. Such dangers are given tangible form in his drawing of "Colocasia." The two-dimensional treatment of the large, floating leaf disrupts the spatial organization of the composition as a whole. It is as if the viewer has lurched forward to look down over the leaf, or the lake's surface has risen up to meet him. To similar effect, the outsized flowers appear to loom over the comparatively miniature heron, as it prepares to strike a small fish near the shore of the lake. Related themes of misperception and sensibility are evoked by the natural historical drama enacted in the left foreground, where the Venus flytrap prepares to consume the next insect attracted to its jawlike leaf lobes, perhaps the dragonfly perched on a small flower above, itself disguised as a leaf. Bartram recounted this particular plant behavior in the introduction to *Travels through North and South Carolina, Georgia, East and West Florida:* "See the incarnate lobes expanding, how gay and ludicrous they appear! ready on the spring to intrap incautious deluded insects, what artifice! there behold one of the leaves just closed upon a struggling fly, another has got a worm, its hold is sure, its prey can never escape—carnivorous vegetable!" Viewer and naturalist are incorporated into a total scene of nature in which expectations of hierarchy and categorical integrity are subtly unsettled.[2]

The drawing reveals the underlying character of William Bartram's *Travels*—published some fourteen years after Bartram's diverse experiences in the region—as a text originally crafted during the settlement of East Florida as a West Indian colony. Bartram's earliest travels in the region, during his father's appointment as King's Botanist, were undertaken in the context of broad imperial enthusiasm for the colony as a lucrative new source of West Indian staples, including rice, indigo, and even sugar. Finding precedent in prior debates over the environmental character of South Carolina, such visions of the region inspired an outpouring of promotional and natural historical writing. Moreover, these ambitions for improving East Florida on a West Indian model received significant financial support from the Board of Trade in London, which placed public advertisements requesting applications for subsidized land grants in newspapers throughout the colonies. As a result, the settlement of East Florida grew rapidly to "dwarf all other contemporaneous plantation schemes in the number of acres granted." Because enthusiasm for settlement was so high, Bartram's immediate failure as planter held important social and cultural implications, both for the mainland colonies and the British Empire at large. Responding to criticisms leveled against him in his father's correspondence, Bartram took up these implications when he began drafting key sections of the published *Travels* during his return to East Florida as botanist between 1773 and 1777. In so doing, he drew on the formal and conceptual re-

2. The phrase "sensuous apprehension" is of course adapted from Perry Miller, "Jonathan Edwards on the Sense of the Heart," *Harvard Theological Review,* XLI (1948), 123–145. Miller argues: "In Edwards' 'sense of the heart' there is nothing transcendental; it is rather a sensuous apprehension of the total situation. And what makes an idea in the total situation important for man, as the idea taken alone can never be, what makes it in that context something more than an inert impression on passive clay, is man's apprehension that for him it augurs good or evil. It is, in short, something to be saluted by the emotions as well as the intellect" (127). On the influence of Edwards's aesthetics and epistemology on American nature writing, see Joan Richardson, *A Natural History of Pragmatism: The Fact of Feeling from Jonathan Edwards to Gertrude Stein* (New York, 2007), 1–23, 24–61. On the culture of sensibility, see G. J. Barker-Benfield, *The Culture of Sensibility: Sex and Society in Eighteenth-Century Britain* (Chicago, 1992); Julie Ellison, *Cato's Tears and the Making of Anglo-American Emotion* (Chicago, 1999). On the rich interplay between the cultures of sensibility and natural history in the period, consider that members of the Friendly Club in New York City published an American edition of Erasmus Darwin's poem *The Botanic Garden* in the late 1790s as a demonstration of their sensibility. See Bryan Waterman, *Republic of Intellect: The Friendly Club of New York City and the Making of American Literature* (Baltimore, 2007), 46. All quotations from the published *Travels* come from the standard edition, Francis Harper, ed., *The Travels of William Bartram: Naturalist's Edition* (Athens, Ga., 1998), liv. On the Bartrams' interest in the Venus flytrap, see Slaughter, *Natures of John and William Bartram,* 29–30, 34, 231.

source of Catesby's *Natural History of Carolina, Florida, and the Bahama Islands*.[3]

Bartram was fascinated by species such as colocasia in large part because he was intimately familiar with the contingencies of social and environmental change during the transition to plantation agriculture. Like Catesby before him, he understood the potential impact of these changes in sweeping terms, both world-historical and eschatological. As a creole naturalist engaged in the day-to-day details of plantation management, however, Bartram also understood these changes in terms of their effects on the mental, moral, and physiological constitution of the transplanted self. This new conception is reflected in his generic synthesis of natural history, travel writing, and spiritual autobiography in the draft manuscript of section 2 of *Travels*, in ways that hearken back to the novelistic experiments of Hans Sloane and Richard Ligon. The draft manuscript is structured around the narrative persona of the Philosophical Pilgrim, an ardent and pious inquirer into the mysteries of botanical creation. The practice of natural history is framed in the pilgrimage narrative as penance for some indeterminate original sin involving ambition and avarice. Specimens serve as stages or trials in the pilgrim's progress, promising either to restore his faith in the underlying providential order of tropical nature or to seduce him into spiritual and epistemological error. Bartram's sensuous apprehension of tropical specimens includes the all-important question of whether they augur good or evil for the observer. Specimens become literal agents in the narrative, transforming both the landscape of East Florida and the mind and body of the naturalist in ways that are increasingly difficult to predict and manage. Though excised from the manuscript as Bartram revised it in the 1780s—during a period when the fragile political constitution of the United States was still being debated in Philadelphia—this West Indian pilgrimage narrative haunts the structural and thematic center of the published *Travels*.[4]

3. David Hancock, *Citizens of the World: London Merchants and the Integration of the British Atlantic Community, 1735–1785* (New York, 1995), 155.

4. Scholars of the draft manuscript are indebted to Nancy Everill Hoffmann, "The Construction of William Bartram's Narrative Natural History: A Genetic Text of the Draft Manuscript for *Travels through North and South Carolina, Georgia, East and West Florida*" (Ph.D. diss., University of Pennsylvania, 1996). See also William Bartram, *The Search for Nature's Design: Selected Art, Letters, and Unpublished Writings*, ed. Thomas Hallock and Nancy E. Hoffmann (Athens, Ga., 2010). Consisting of three journals in William Bartram's hand, the draft manuscript is housed at HSP (Bartram Papers, Small Miscellaneous Manuscripts box). For important critical assesments of *Travels*, see, for example, William Hedges, "Toward a National Literature," in Emory Elliott, ed., *Columbia Literary History of the United States* (New York, 1988), 187; Christopher Looby, "The Constitution of Nature: Taxonomy as Politics in Jefferson, Peale, and Bartram," *Early American Literature*, XXII (1987), 252–273; Douglas Anderson, "Bartram's *Travels* and

Promoting Florida, Founding Science

Scholars of William Bartram have characterized his Florida plantation as the misguided venture of an eccentric colonial youth, described by one historian as a "Failure in Xanadu." In the context of the mid-1760s, however, such a scheme was anything but quixotic. Upon obtaining the Floridas from Spain in the negotiations following the Seven Years' War (in exchange for the return of Cuba), Parliament began awarding substantial land grants to individuals with the means and desire to initiate large-scale, slave-driven agricultural development. Such initiatives were further supported by the rapid infusion of Caribbean knowledge and capital. By 1764, the new governor, James Grant, arrived in the colonial capital of St. Augustine fresh from a tour of the sugar islands, where he had received instruction in the intricacies of plantation management. Intending to lead by example, Grant organized his own venture with the London merchant Richard Oswald, owner of prospering plantations in South Carolina, Georgia, and Jamaica. British attempts to settle East Florida also involved many of the same actors who had transplanted Caribbean models of economy and society into South Carolina earlier in the century, with dazzling results. Florida planters expected to prosper on a similar scale. The Bartrams' ambition is suggested by their selection of Henry Laurens, the mainland's biggest slave trader, as their main adviser. By the time John Bartram conveyed his disapproval to Collinson over his son's chosen path, the fortunes of his family were bound to the improvement of East Florida as a West Indian slave society.[5]

This had been the case since John Bartram's appointment as King's Botanist. The robust market for natural histories of East and West Florida made his researches possible. Published in 1766, John Bartram's *Diary of a Journey through the Carolinas, Georgia, and Florida* joined a large body of promotional and scientific writing, including such prominent contri-

the Politics of Nature," ibid., XXV (1990), 3–17; Larzer Ziff, *Writing in the New Nation: Prose, Print, and Politics in the Early United States* (New Haven, Conn., 1991), 39–53; Christoph Irmscher, *The Poetics of Natural History: From John Bartram to William James* (Piscataway, N.J., 1999), 13–55; Thomas Hallock, *From the Fallen Tree: Frontier Narratives, Environmental Politics, and the Roots of a National Pastoral, 1749–1826* (Chapel Hill, N.C., 2003), 149–176; Hallock, "Male Pleasure and the Genders of Eighteenth-Century Botanic Exchange: A Garden Tour," *William and Mary Quarterly*, 3d Ser., LXII (2005), 697–718. For important art historical scholarship on Bartram's drawings, see Amy R. Weinstein Meyers, "Sketches from the Wilderness: Changing Conceptions of Nature in American Natural History Illustration, 1680–1880" (Ph.D. diss., Yale University, 1985); Michael Gaudio, "Swallowing the Evidence: William Bartram and the Limits of Enlightenment," *Winterthur Portfolio*, XXXVI (2001), 1–17.

5. Bernard Bailyn, *Voyagers to the West: A Passage in the Peopling of America on the Eve of the Revolution* (New York, 1986), 430–474; Hancock, *Citizens of the World*, 143–171.

butions as Thomas Jeffery's *Description of the Spanish Islands and Settlements on the Coast of the West Indies* (1762), William Roberts's *Account of the First Discovery, and Natural History of Florida* (1763), William Stork's *Account of East-Florida, with Remarks on Its Future Importance to Trade and Commerce* (1766), and William Gerard De Brahm's "Report on the General Survey in the Southern District of North America" (1773). Colonial North Americans were enthusiastic participants. Naturalists including John Lorimer, George Gauld, Bernard Romans, Thomas Hutchins, John Ellis, André Michaux, and Alexander Garden filed reports on Florida with the American Philosophical Society and were inducted as members partly because of these labors.

Informed by a strain of mercantilist thinking that regarded West Indian cultivation and trade as the key to British prosperity, natural historians of the Floridas shared a fascination with the region's geographic location and semitropical climate. Published in multiple editions in the 1760s, William Stork's volume extols the possibilities of the peninsular climate with particular intensity. An official proclamation included in the 1769 edition asserts, "From the great luxuriancy of all the West-Indian weeds, found in the southern part of this province, it is not to be doubted, but that all the fruits and productions of the West-Indies may be raised here." Such predictions included the West Indian staple foremost in the minds of readers and investors. In the abstract of a letter included in the 1769 edition, a "gentleman in St. Augustine" informs his friend in London, "Some gentleman are gone to the southwards, to a place called Musquito, to take up land, as there is great expectation of sugar; as in that part they never have any frost, and the soil naturally produces the West-Indian plants." Stork misses no opportunity to underscore such claims. Commenting on a fertile stretch of the St. Johns River, near the eventual site of William Bartram's plantation, Stork argues, "The tropical fruits and plants are found in great abundance, and afford the strongest evidence that both the soil and climate are fit for sugar, cotton, indigo, and other West-India productions." Circum-Caribbean prospects formed a staple of the growing natural historical literature on the Floridas.[6]

The efforts of enthusiasts such as Stork conditioned the reception of John Bartram's writings on the region. A reprinted version of Bartram's

6. William Stork, *A Description of East-Florida, with a Journal Kept by John Bartram of Philadelphia* . . . (London, 1769), viii, 6, 35. For similar remarks, see [William Gerard De Brahm], *De Brahm's Report of the General Survey in the Southern District of North America*, ed. Louis De Vorsey, Jr. (Columbia, S.C., 1971), 218–219.

Diary of a Journey through the Carolinas, Georgia, and Florida, appended to the 1769 edition of Stork's *Account of East-Florida,* includes Stork's intrusive editorial commentary. In numerous footnotes, Stork projects his own vision of Florida's commercial future onto a journal that emphasizes the temperate character of the peninsular climate. When John Bartram notes the presence of a common species of palm tree, Stork refers the reader to a description in Sloane's *Voyage to . . . Jamaica:* "It appears from this Palm growing here, (which is a native of the West-Indies,) that many others of the West-India productions may also be cultivated." When Bartram recounts eating a breakfast of boiled tanniers, Stork again refers the reader to Sloane, identifying the plant as a "species of Eddos . . . [or] Arum." Such passages present East Florida as suitable ground for the forms of slave-driven crop production that had made the sugar islands indispensable to the imperial economy.[7]

In the eyes of promoters, the strategic geographic location of Florida was every bit as important as its semitropical climate. Naturalists understood the colonies within the same mercantilist map of the Americas that had shaped Catesby's earlier commentary on Cuban conquest. They believed that possession of East Florida would prove decisive in the ongoing struggle with France and Spain over the control of West Indian trade routes. De Brahm echoes similar passages by William Roberts and Stork: "All the East India Treasures collected at the Manillas, all the Riches of Mexico, New Spain, Peru and Cili [Chile] are hived in the Havannah on Cuba Island; and from thence under the Auspice of a Spanish Admiral escorted to Old Spain, by the Way of the New Bahama Channel." Presenting the Straits of Florida as the great highway of New World trade, naturalists proclaimed that continued maritime dominance turned on development of East Florida's strategic coastline.[8]

North American attitudes toward these southerly developments were ambivalent and at times contradictory. On one hand, mainland colonists saw possession and settlement of the Floridas as a means of challenging the political and economic power of British West Indian planters. Bitterness toward the West Indian lobby is palpable in the pamphlet war over the terms of the 1763 Treaty of Paris and in mainland responses to the Sugar Act of 1764. Negotiations leading to the Treaty of Paris sparked a heated debate over whether to retain Guadeloupe, Martinique, and Cuba (captured late in

7. Stork, *Description of East-Florida,* 10, 32.
8. [De Brahm], *General Survey,* ed. De Vorsey, 229.

the war) or return them to Spain in exchange for Florida and Canada. Individuals as prominent as William Fitzmaurice Petty, second earl of Shelburne and president of the Board of Trade, supported an exchange for Canada and Florida, claiming, "The total exclusion of the French from Canada and the Spaniards from Florida gives Great Britain the universal empire of that extended coast." Other pamphleteers, grounded in older mercantile conceptions, recoiled at the thought of exchanging lucrative sugar islands for the supposed wastelands of Canada and Florida.[9]

Indeed, many promoters of Florida took pains to accommodate this older and still-influential map of the Americas. Comparing the value of St. Christopher to Rhode Island, Stork maintains that any colony located within the same latitudinal range as Europe could provide little in the way of profitable exports: "The conveniences of life are to be had in Rhode-Island, but if we are in search of articles of commerce, we must approach nearer to the West-Indies." Carrying his eye southward along the Eastern Seaboard, from Hudson Bay to Cuba, Stork concludes, "It is not only in sugar and indigo, that Cuba surpasses all the English settlements, lying to the north, but in every other production, that depends upon the powers of the sun. And in this respect, as well as in the salubrity of the air, East Florida hath the advantage of Carolina and Georgia, as much as Cuba hath the advantage of East-Florida."[10]

The most important North American opinion came from Benjamin Franklin, who radically shifted the terms of debate over the relative value of colonial possessions. Whereas prior mercantilist thinkers had emphasized the ability of British colonies to produce profitable exports (which favored the West Indies), Franklin called attention to the consumption of English manufactures (which had exploded in North America). In so doing, he echoed Shelburne's claim that the exclusion of France and Spain from an ascendant North America outweighed the benefits of adding new Caribbean territories to an empire already possessing "sugar-land." Franklin's stance against retaining the islands, however, was by no means representative of mainland opinion, nor was the decision to obtain Canada and Florida necessarily a sign of his pamphlet's success. For Eric Williams, England's decision to give up the more lucrative sugar islands can only be explained as

9. Robert L. Gold, *Borderland Empires in Transition: The Triple-Nation Transfer of Florida* (Carbondale, Ill., 1969), 20–23 (quotation on 23). For a discussion of the pamphlet war from a Caribbean perspective, see Laurent Dubois, *A Colony of Citizens: Revolution and Slave Emancipation in the French Caribbean, 1787–1804* (Chapel Hill, N.C., 2004), 34–35.

10. Stork, *Description of East-Florida*, iv, v.

the result of political pressure from British West Indian planters, wary of incorporating new and more dynamic sugar colonies into the empire's system of generous trade protections and subsidies. Many North American merchants could not have welcomed the loss of official commercial ties to Guadeloupe and Martinique, which had grown substantially in the brief period of British possession. They protested vociferously when the Sugar Act cut off their thriving clandestine trade with the French islands the next year. Though the prosperity of the sugar islands had been essential to North American development, the political power of the Anglo-American planter lobby was now an obstacle to continued growth.[11]

Similar tensions shaped the emerging institutional structure of American natural history. Historians of colonial science have long understood the founding of the first learned societies in North America, including the American Philosophical Society, as expressions of cultural autonomy and resistance in response to imperial legislation of the 1760s. The Sugar Act provided one key impetus. Anticipating the expiration of the 1733 Molasses Act in 1764, merchants in Boston and Philadelphia organized committees to lobby Parliament for trade policies more advantageous to the mainland. When such efforts failed, these same merchants, concerned by a postwar depression that coincided with and was popularly blamed on enforcement of the Sugar Act, continued to meet regularly. In New York, related anxieties led to the formation of the Society for the Promotion of Arts, Agriculture, and Œconomy, in the Province of New York, in North America.[12]

West Indian concerns are also prominent in the first volume of the American Philosophical Society's *Transactions* (1771), though in ways that complicate the link between the establishment of colonial scientific institutions and the emergence of protonationalist sentiments. The preface to the earliest number envisions the future organization of England's commercial empire. By lending crucial support to the study of experimental botany in the colonies through their patronage of the American Philosophical Society, imperial administrators will usher in a new era of stability and prosperity:

11. Benjamin Franklin, "The Interest of Great Britain Considered, with regard to Her Colonies and the Acquisitions of Canada and Guadaloupe," in Jared Sparks, ed., *The Works of Benjamin Franklin* (Boston, 1837), IV, 49; Eric Williams, *Capitalism and Slavery* (1944; rpt. Chapel Hill, N.C., 1994), 114–115. On Franklin's contribution to the pamphlet wars, see Sean X. Goudie, *Creole America: The West Indies and the Formation of Literature and Culture in the New Republic* (Philadelphia, 2006), 25–63.

12. Brooke Hindle, *The Pursuit of Science in Revolutionary America, 1735–1789* (Chapel Hill, N.C., 1956), 106–107; Raymond Phineas Stearns, *Science in the British Colonies of America* (Chicago, 1970), 670–672.

For if, by these means, the continental colonies can supply her with the rarities of *China,* and her islands can furnish the rich spices of the *East-Indies,* her merchants will no longer be obliged, in order to obtain these, to traverse three quarters of the globe, encounter the difficulties of so tedious a voyage, and, after all, submit to the insolence, or exorbitant demands of foreigners.

On one hand, the sugar islands are explicitly and prominently included in this vision of creole science as the practical fulfillment of mercantilist ideals. On the other, the preface simultaneously positions Philadelphia as a potential New World metropole, challenging the preeminence of the West Indies within the imperial worldview. The city "hath, by its central situation, not only a ready communication by land, with our Continental-Colonies; but likewise with our Islands, by vessels employed in carrying on our trade." Despite this implicit conflict, creole associations between continent and islands are presented as mutually beneficial throughout the *Transactions.* Volume I notes the induction of at least eleven West Indian members in the earliest years of the society, eight alone on January 18, 1771, as tensions between mainland and islands were building. In similar fashion, John Ellis's *Directions for Bringing over Seeds and Plants from the East-Indies and Other Distant Countries in a State of Vegetation* (1770) suggests the continued dominance of a long-standing mercantilist cognitive geography. The frontispiece to Ellis's original pamphlet testifies that the desires of metropolitan collectors remained fixated on the tropics (Fig. 11). Each of the four boxes is engineered for transporting a particular kind of delicate specimen, including "East India seeds," "West India and West Florida plants," "cut moss from the southern colonies and the West Indies," and "the roots of West Florida and West India plants surrounded with earth."[13]

The society's role in supporting the natural history of the Floridas must be understood in the context of this contradictory effort to dispute the prestige of the West Indies while cultivating hemispheric associations. The career of Bernard Romans, one of the Florida naturalists supported by the Ameri-

13. "Preface," American Philosophical Society, *Transactions,* I (1771), xiii–xiv, xvi; John Ellis, *Directions for Bringing over Seeds and Plants from the East-Indies and Other Distant Countries in a State of Vegetation* (London, 1770), frontispiece; Raymond Phineas Stearns, "Colonial Fellows of the Royal Society of London, 1661–1788," *Osiris,* VIII (1948), 73–121. Members resident in the West Indies include Paul Bedford, Esq., of Barbados; Joseph Hutchins, AB, of Barbados; Christian Frederick Post of the Mosquito Shore; Dr. Sandiford of Barbados; Pierre Eugene Du Simitière; Hon. Ashton Warner, Esq.; Hon. Thomas Warner, Esq.; Samuel Warner, Esq.; Samuel Felsted of Jamaica; Dr. Archibald Gloster of Antigua; Dr. Morton of Jamaica.

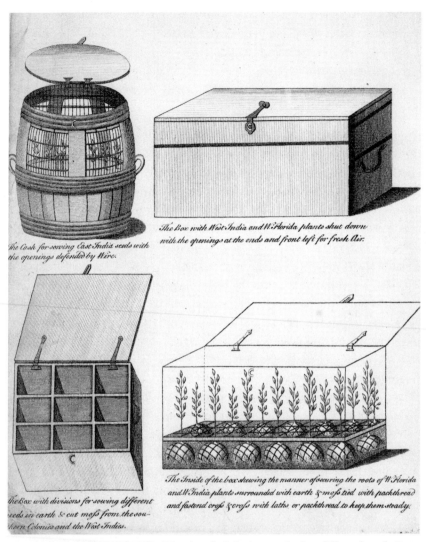

The Cask for sowing East India seeds with the openings defended by Wire.

The Box with West India and W. Florida plants shut down with the openings at the ends and front left for fresh Air.

The Box with divisions for sowing different seeds in earth & cut moss from the southern Colonies and the West Indies.

The Inside of the box shewing the manner of securing the roots of W. Florida and W. India plants surrounded with earth & moss tied with packthread and fastend cross & cross with laths or packthread to keep them steady.

FIGURE 11. Frontispiece. John Ellis, *Directions for Bringing over Seeds and Plants from the East-Indies and Other Distant Countries in a State of Vegetation* (London, 1770). Courtesy of the John Carter Brown Library at Brown University

can Philosophical Society, embodies these contradictions. Romans's *Concise Natural History of East and West Florida* (1775) draws on his experience as trader and surveyor in the Floridas to advance a commercial prospect as far-reaching as Stork:

> When we survey the harbours, *Charlotte, Tampe, St. Joseph, Pensacola,* all proper for the admission of ships of rank, besides others we

know not yet; what a field is open here! what a prospect of power and grandeur seems to be already welcoming us! no country had ever such inexhaustible resources; no empire had ever half so many advantages combining in its behalf: methinks I see already the *American* fleets inhabiting the ocean, like cities in vicinity!

Just as the preface to the first volume of the *Transactions* had located Philadelphia at the hub of hemispheric commerce and science, Romans fantasizes thriving port cities in the present-day backwater of the Floridas, where trade and cultivation will unlock the economic potential latent in its situation and topography.[14]

Romans's inclusion of North America within an advancing empire seems untroubled here. In the years before publishing his natural history, however, he had pursued several initiatives shaped by emerging tensions between London, North America, and the West Indies. In 1772, Romans provided English naturalist John Ellis with plans for a botanical garden in Pensacola, where "curious plants from the Floridas, as well as the West Indies, might be transplanted, tended, and systematically studied." Like John Bartram before him, Romans sought a foothold in the market for Caribbean curiosities. Similarly, while raising subscriptions for his natural history in Boston in 1774, Romans advised local farmers to raise indigo domestically rather than rely on costly imports. At the same time, Romans's career depended on cosmopolitan connections between the mainland and the sugar islands. In the printed prospectus for *A Concise Natural History,* he anticipated a readership for his book among "Trader[s] from North-America, especially the Merchants who trade to Jamaica, Hispaniola, and to the two Floridas." His cartographic career suggests that he also anticipated a substantial audience among the sugar planters themselves. His sumptuous *Map of East and West Florida* (1781) (Fig. 12) places clear visual emphasis on the spatial relationships between the coastlines of southern Florida and northern Cuba. In a cartouche along the left border, Romans dedicates his effort "to the Honble the Planters in Jamaica and all Merchants Concerned in the trade of that Island."[15]

Affiliations of this kind were problematic for reasons that went beyond mainland resentment of West Indian wealth in the years leading up to political independence. Though promotional tracts on Florida normally paid

14. Bernard Romans, *A Concise Natural History of East and West Florida,* ed. Kathryn E. Holland Braund (Tuscaloosa, Ala., 1999), 197.
15. Ibid., 12, 16.

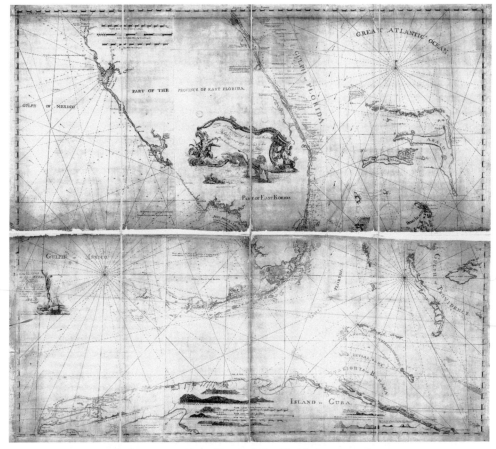

FIGURE 12. Bernard Romans, *A Map of East and West Florida*, Boston, 1781.
Courtesy, The Library of Congress, Washington, D.C.

limited attention to the subject of slavery, their attention to natural history
ensured that anxieties related to the expansion and influence of slavery remained close to the surface. As we have glimpsed in prior chapters, Caribbean nature had long been endowed with the revolutionary capacity to
alter bodies and corrupt sensibilities, producing a degenerate variant of
Englishness among those born in the region, or even temporarily residing
there. By the 1770s, this discourse on the West Indian climate was clearly
articulated and widely circulated. Following the lead of naturalists including Griffith Hughes and Charles Leslie, Edward Long's *History of Jamaica*
(1774) attributed traits such as irritability to the influence of a hot climate.
Among other physical features distinguishing the creole, "their cheeks are

remarkably high-boned, and the sockets of their eyes deeper than is commonly observed among the natives of England; by this conformation, they are guarded from those ill effects which an almost continual strong glare of sunshine might otherwise produce." Kathleen Wilson summarizes the prevailing view: "English observers [spoke] of Creoles as exemplifying a 'national character,'" and sometimes a racial identity, "of their own, one that was litigious, extravagant, generous, sensual, promiscuous and so on." British Caribbean colonists served as "performers in the spectacle of degeneracy produced by tropical torpor and the mimetic effects of cultural hybridity and difference."[16]

West Indian naturalists were not exempt from the charge of degeneracy. Patrick Browne, metropolitan author of the highly regarded *Civil and Natural History of Jamaica* (1756) complained that, among learned creoles,

> the means of acquiring Wealth and Power, have generally occupied their thoughts; or the love of ease and pleasure, to which the Climate but too much disposes even the most determined minds, have dissipated the best established Resolutions; and in consequence, scarcely any thing has been attempted towards exhibiting a just idea of this Island, considered both in a Civil and Natural Light; except what bears the evident marks of Imbecility, Inattention, or erroneous Information.

The creole planter-naturalist became an object of study for metropolitan theorists of tropical degeneracy such as the comte de Buffon.[17]

So, too, did the Floridas as a region. Concern over the degenerate "national character" developing in black majority sugar islands fed anxieties regarding the "Africanization" of colonial Florida. During the eleven years of British possession, slave traders as prominent as Richard Oswald and Henry Laurens imported thousands of slaves, most of them "new Negroes." One contemporary chronicler estimated that one thousand slaves were intro-

16. [Edward Long], *The History of Jamaica: or, General Survey of the Antient and Modern State of That Island . . .*, 3 vols. (London, 1774), II, 261, 267; Kathleen Wilson, *The Island Race: Englishness, Empire, and Gender in the Eighteenth Century* (New York, 2002), 154. On the discourse of the degeneracy, see also Roxann Wheeler, *The Complexion of Race: Categories of Difference in Eighteenth-Century British Culture* (Philadelphia, 2000), 65–73, 210–233; Jim Egan, "The 'Long'd-for Aera' of an 'Other Race': Climate, Identity, and James Grainger's *The Sugar-Cane*," *Early American Literature*, XXXVIII (2003), 189–212.

17. Patrick Browne, *The Civil and Natural History of Jamaica. . . .* (London, 1756), v–vi; George Louis Leclerc, comte de Buffon, *Natural History, General and Particular*, trans. William Smellie, 8 vols. (London, 1781), III, 164–165.

duced in 1771 alone. Continued Spanish influence in the region—across the porous border with Cuba—also contributed to fears of contamination.[18]

Though Romans systematically refutes the theory of degeneracy in *A Concise Natural History,* his text reveals that British settlers in the Floridas served as important specimens. Like Sloane before him, Romans maintains that alarming mortality rates result from manners rather than climate. While pausing to "enquire a little into the universally dreaded, though chimerical unhealthiness of this climate," Romans insists that yellow fever is not endemic to the Floridas but rather is imported from Jamaica and Cuba. But his defense highlights the perils of Florida's location in other ways, as does Romans's account of a group of British settlers at Mobile in West Florida. Lamenting their tragic fate, Romans emphasizes the prodigal lifestyle of these young emigrants: "Our sons of incontinence, who upon their arrival, and after their first taking possession of this country, lived there so fast, that their race was too soon scampered over; midnight carouzals, and the converting day into night, and night into day was all the study of those gay, those thoughtless men." Weakened by excess, the young men succumbed to a contagious fever imported by an "intemperate" regiment from Jamaica.[19]

In the decade before William Bartram set out to establish a plantation in East Florida, "incontinent sons" such as these had become central to the debate over British settlement. Their success or failure had important consequences for British America and required careful examination.

*From Prodigal Planter to Philosophical Pilgrim
in the Draft Manuscript of* Travels

In his father's correspondence, William Bartram bears a strong resemblance to the "incontinent sons" haunting Romans's natural history. John Bartram draws on the discourse of West Indian degeneracy to present his son's decision to "turn planter" as evidence of an unrestrained and possibly disordered imagination. But William's failure is just as disturbing. Reply-

18. Jane Landers, *Black Society in Spanish Florida* (Urbana, Ill., 1999), 158–159; Hancock, *Citizens of the World,* 203–204; Daniel L. Schafer, "'Yellow Silk Ferret Tied Round Their Wrists': African Americans in British East Florida, 1763–1784," in David R. Colburn and Jane L. Landers, eds., *The African American Heritage of Florida* (Gainesville, Fla., 1995), 71–103. Romans noted the illegal presence of Cuban fishermen along the coast and their thriving clandestine trade with the Seminoles (*Concise Natural History,* ed. Braund, 198–199).

19. Romans, *Concise Natural History,* ed. Braund, 94–95, 222.

ing to news that the first year's rice crop has been lost to inclement weather, John Bartram chides his son for his lack of industry: "I hope thee may plant some corn if not rice if it be but two or 3 acres it will help some and the hath been and is very indolent if the hath not planted much garde[n] truck." The change reflects widespread concerns that West Indian planters were too devoted to a narrow range of cash crops in a heedless attempt to maximize profits that led to escalating debt. The effects of William's profligacy threaten the paternal estate. Writing during a severe wartime depression, the father notes that a recent shipment of machinery and tools has "cost me dear and so much that I am still in debt for them: money being so very scarce that I cant get it when it is owing many years and ye expensive wall and bank of near half A mile is not near completed which must be done before winter or most of it will be washed away by the tide." In Crèvecoeur's letter on "John Bertram's" farm, this ambitious effort to alter the course of the Schuylkill River was chronicled in detail as evidence that improvement of the landscape through the synthesis of yeoman industry and enlightened knowledge would contribute to the continued diffusion of human happiness and well-being in the colony. In John Bartram's letter, much as in Crèvecoeur's "Sketches of Jamaica," the West Indian transit of a Pennsylvania youth threatens his virtue and reason.[20]

In seeking to cultivate virtue and reason in his son, John Bartram's letters to East Florida articulate a paradoxical position toward the colonial planter more generally. At numerous times in his correspondence, the father assists his son by attempting to transfer knowledge from the West Indies to the banks of the St. Johns River. In describing a group of slaves recently purchased on his son's behalf, John Bartram specifies that one is "cromantee." To designate slaves according to African ethnicity was customary in the Caribbean but comparatively rare in the southern mainland. Botanical and agricultural knowledge also circulates between the West Indies and Bartram's plantation. Precisely by better emulating the knowledgeable West Indian planter, his father implies, William might demonstrate his virtue through the material transformation of his surroundings: "I have procured 4 good yams two white and two red A present from the colonel [Laurens] and sent. A west india gentleman said thay cut of one half of the yam and

---

20. John Bartram to William Bartram, July 3, 1766, *CJB*, 669; J. Hector St. John de Crèvecoeur, *Letters from an American Farmer*, ed. Susan Manning (New York, 1997), 176. As Slaughter argues, although William Bartram had long been portrayed as a prodigal, that characterization intensified after his plantation venture. See Slaughter, *Natures of John and William Bartram*, 116–131, 155–163.

planted the upper part of it." At other times, however, slaveholding and plantation management are depicted as inherently incompatible with more virtuous and rational pursuits such as natural history: "All thy friends here laments thy resolute choice to live at St johns and leave off drawing or writeing thay say ye negros will run away or murder thee . . . thay are the greatest curse that ever came to america."[21]

Questions of cultural geography are integral to this imputed threat. The rhetoric of indolence and prodigality takes on particular valences owing to the tropical tableau of numerous letters. Writing to John Bartram in 1766, Henry Laurens bemoans the "unpleasant unhealthy situation" of the youth's plantation in terms that bear on the contemporary question of the colony's overall environmental character. The discourse of West Indian degeneracy saturates the letter, even as Laurens takes pains to deny it, maintaining that William's situation owes, not to the physical constitution of the region, but rather to his flawed character. Drawing on his knowledge of natural history and plantation management in Carolina, Laurens insists, "The swamp and adjoining marsh which I walked into, will, without doubt, produce good rice, when properly cleared and cultivated." But, given William's constitution, exacerbated by the effects of the local climate on his mind and body, he lacks sufficient vigor to improve the swamp. Laurens dwells on the disadvantages of William's situation, which he describes as "very hot, the only disagreeably hot place that I found in East Florida," surrounded by swamp waters that are "stagnated, exceedingly foul, and absolutely stank when stirred up by our oars." To organize the clearing and cultivation of such a spot, including coordinating the labor of "six negroes," is a job for men like Laurens and John Bartram, who "could surmount all those hardships without much chagrin." But a youth of William's "tender and delicate frame of body and intellects" stands little chance of success. Continued residence threatens to "drive him to despondency" and death. Laurens describes him as dwelling alone among "six negroes, rather plagues than aids to him, of whom one is so insolent as to threaten his life."[22]

---

21. John Bartram to William Bartram, Apr. 5, 1766, *CJB*, 661, 662; Michael Mullin, *Africa in America: Slave Acculturation and Resistance in the American South and the British Caribbean, 1736–1831* (Urbana, Ill., 1992), 23–27. Southerners identified slaves ethnically for only a brief period in the 1760s during the settlement of the Georgia and East Florida frontier. In the West Indies, careful demographic management of slaves (identified by ethnicity) was a familiar tactic for (ostensibly) reducing the risk of insurrection. It was employed to similar ends in the Florida borderland. Settlers (such as William Bartram) relied on agents (such as Laurens) to select slaves carefully according to ethnicity in Georgia and Florida because the area had historically been such fertile ground for uprisings.

22. Henry Laurens to John Bartram, Aug. 9, 1766, *CJB*, 670–673.

From these portraits of the prodigal planter, Bartram fashioned the narrative persona in the draft manuscript of two crucial chapters in *Travels through North and South Carolina, Georgia, East and West Florida*. Narrating his return to the epicenter of plantation development in East Florida in 1773 and 1774, a mere half decade after abandoning his own plantation, the manuscript chapters would be revised into the core of section 2 of the published *Travels*, covering such decisive incidents as his near-fatal encounters with predatory alligators and seasonal hurricanes in chapter 2 and his first visit to the seeming terrestrial paradise of the Alachua Savanna in chapter 3. Bartram began drafting those chapters during his travels in East Florida, supplementing his firsthand observations with botanical references upon his return to Charleston. As Thomas Slaughter argues, given its origin during the travels of the early 1770s, the draft manuscript is best understood as a botanical field journal, though one that challenges the conventions of this textual and empiricist praxis: "His 'notes' were more reveries, explications of states of mind, evocations of God in nature [than] . . . lists of flora and fauna that he saw as he crossed the landscape." These reveries are organized around the narrative persona of the "Philosophical Pilgrim." As recovered through the editorial labors of Nancy Everill Hoffmann, the "Philosophical Pilgrim" is a peculiarly ardent botanist, given to lengthy moralizing commentaries—excised from the published *Travels*—on the nature of man and the divinity of nature. Specimen collection is narrated within the temporal and epistemological conventions of the spiritual pilgrimage. A fallen and penitent individual progresses incrementally through a series of trials and visions that must be read for divinely revelatory meaning. In composing his field notes as spiritual history, Bartram hearkens back to early modern protocols of typological and emblematic reading even as he registers the emergence of sensibility as a necessary epistemological faculty.[23]

Themes of spiritual depravity and guilt are announced from the opening sentences, as Bartram crosses the threshold between temperate and tropical America. The narrator's delight, as he listens to the morning "anthems" of the surrounding birdlife, occasions a plea for divine grace: "O may I be

23. Slaughter, *Natures of John and William Bartram*, 188; Hoffmann, "Construction of William Bartram's Narrative Natural History." Hoffmann demonstrates that "natural history material, mostly botanical, was added or elaborated, with the core, or brief mention, of the material first occurring in the draft manuscript" (15). On the transformation of the draft manuscript, see also Hallock, *From the Fallen Tree*, 158. Hallock argues, "As the need for fair frontier policies collided with the politics of expansion, the manuscript persona of a 'philosophical pilgrim' would metamorphose into the book's 'Puc-Puggy'—his Seminole name, meaning 'flower gatherer,' and a socially benign figure that could straddle two worlds."

permitted to approach the throne of mercy! may these my humble and penitent supplications, amidst the universal shouts of homage, from thy creatures, meet with thy acceptance." Within the draft manuscript itself, the
penitent pilgrim never specifies the nature of his original sin. In revising
the chapter, however, Bartram invokes his past experiences in the region.
His travels with his father are inscribed into the landscape itself: "Ran by
Mount Hope, so named by my father John Bartram, when he ascended this
river, about fifteen years ago. . . . It was at that time a fine Orange grove, but
now cleared and converted into a large Indigo plantation, the property of an
English gentleman." In this fond reminiscence, the naming and mapping of
a place lead seamlessly to its beneficent material transformation. Long associated with the New World tropics, this accelerated form of environmental and historical change also raises unsettling implications. Though never
directly mentioned, Bartram's experiences as planter are evoked by other
traces in the landscape. Recollecting a verdant savanna, he laments: "But
that venerable grove is now no more. All has been cleared away and planted
with Indigo, Corn and Cotton, but since deserted: there was now scarcely
five acres of ground under fence. It appeared like a desart, to a great extent,
and terminated, on the land side, by frightful thickets, and open Pine forests." The pilgrim traverses an ominous and difficult landscape, both material and psychological, that springs from the ruins of plantations.[24]

Numerous moralizing passages omitted from the published *Travels* describe the narrator's sense of spiritual depravity and bondage. Framing
the practice of natural history as penance, they suggest that slaveholding
constitutes his original sin. In the opening paragraphs, Bartram prays for
divine wisdom in order to better fulfill his spiritual duty to "inferior" creatures. "And O Sovereign Lord if it be so that thou hast been pleased to endue
Man with power and preeminence on Earth and establish his dominion
over all creatures here," might he also inspire man with "a due sense of piety
and beneificence, that We may thereby be enabled to do thy Will and perform our duty to our fellow mortals thus submitted to our service and protection." Should they perform God's will in this manner, those submitted to
their service will be impressed with "the dignity and superiority of our high
and distinguished Station here on earth."[25]

24. "William Bartram's Journal, 1773–1777: Travels thro Carolinas, Georgia, and Florida," book 1,
MS, Bartram Papers, small Bartram volumes, HSP; Francis Harper, ed., *The Travels of William Bartram:
Naturalist's Edition* (Athens, Ga., 1998), 65.

25. "Bartram's Journal," book 1. For some sense of what Bartram had in mind in referring to his duty
to those "submitted to his service," see John Bartram to William Bartram, Apr. 5, 1766, *CJB*, 662. John

Questions of benevolent natural and social hierarchy are entwined throughout the manuscript. In a palm grove, Bartram meditates on the folly of earthly power. These "chiefs of the Vegitable Order of Nature" are subject to the same ignoble fate as "the Great and eminent chiefs amongst mankind," especially in a West Indian locale where "Tempests of wind . . . often turn them up by the roots and lay them prostrate upon the earth." The analogy between natural and social order goes only so far, for although botanical hierarchy is ordained by divine providence, the great man normally "establishes himself above his fellows, by unjust and Powerful means . . . infatuated by the false shew of momentary happiness and glory ever presented to his view by Pleasure Ambition and Avarice." Whereas the ongoing treaty negotiations between the British and Seminoles provide one obvious referent for this commentary on the pernicious social effects of avarice in East Florida, colonial slaveholding provides another. The delusive splendor of tropical nature inspires a lust for treasure that leads to spiritual and moral decline, lamented in terms that resemble the early abolitionism of radical Quakers such as John Woolman and Anthony Benezet, well known in the Bartrams' social circle. Because debates over plantation development in East Florida were public and spirited, Bartram need not mention slaveholding in order for his moral lesson to resonate.[26]

The narrative pattern of the first manuscript chapter further implies that slaveholder remorse occasions the pilgrimage. Bartram understands the potential outcomes of recent events in terms reminiscent of Catesby's *Natural History of Carolina*. Environmental transformation may culminate either in the chaotic violence of the swamp or the order and plenitude of the global botanical garden. Bartram returns to habitats and phenomena that fascinated Catesby in order to determine the likelihood of these futures. In outlining his own vision of universal violence, however, Bartram conveys more visceral sensations of personal peril, drawing on representational techniques well known to his readership from John Bunyan's *Pilgrim's Progress*. Having witnessed the "hellish combat" of male alligators during the spring breeding season and observed them gorging on fish at a

---

Bartram writes: "Doctor [Alexander] garden and others say that when the negroes pounds rice thay will be all in A sweat then thay run out or to the dore with thair brest open then they catch cold and often fall into A pleurisy . . . take great care of them and thair cloathes which thay are now well furnished with for thay will not take any care of themselves."

26. "Bartram's Journal," book 1, 137–140. On early Quaker abolitionism, see, for instance, Jean R. Soderlund, *Quakers and Slavery: A Divided Spirit* (Princeton, N.J., 1985); Thomas P. Slaughter, *The Beautiful Soul of John Woolman, Apostle of Abolition* (New York, 2008).

nearby lake ("the floods of Water blood and slime rushing out from their mouthes and nostrils"), Bartram narrowly escapes a nocturnal attack when he is awakened by the "terrifying screams of the Owls . . . which increast and spread every way, for miles round in dreadfull peals through the reverborating deep dark and endless forests, Meadows and Lakes." Such physical dangers do not dissuade Bartram from the spiritual imperative to study nature. Though mindful of the risk of a "furious and general Attack," the pilgrim leaves his canoe to study some curious mounds that serve as a "general breeding place or Nursery of crocodiles." His researches yield a renewed yet fragile appreciation for providential order as manifested in seemingly universal instincts for maternal care. Implicitly contesting Catesby's characterization of alligator reproduction in the mangrove swamps, where infants are abandoned and sometimes consumed by their parents, Bartram instead describes a female alligator, "leading about the shores numerous broods of young ones just like a hen leading her brood of chickens." Yet he must also acknowledge, "Few of a brood live to years of full growth or magnitude, as the Older feed on the Young as long as they can make prey of them."[27]

Having negotiated these physical and mental trials, the naturalist proceeds toward his destination at a working indigo plantation. As detailed in his written report to Fothergill, Bartram made two journeys along the St. Johns River, one in the spring and one in the fall, both culminating at the thriving Berresford Plantation. In the draft manuscript, Bartram condenses and rearranges biographical events to create a more compelling narrative frame. A single spring expedition concludes with the narrator's arrival at the plantation after a hurricane (which actually occurred during the fall journey). The draft chapter begins by evoking figurative tempests as divine retribution for violent domination. It ends with the effects of a literal hurricane on the livelihood of a prosperous planter. The narrative departs from a deserted plantation to arrive at one on the verge of ruin. Though the lives of all sixty slaves have been miraculously spared, the planter has lost "near One hundred acres of the Indigo plant almost ripe for the first cutting, which was almost ruined," and "likewise a very promising field of Sugar Cane almost ruind."[28]

The narrator's interactions with the planter raise questions about the link between slave-driven development and the sin of avarice. The use of slave labor is by no means depicted as inherently sinful. The plantation

27. "Bartram's Journal," book 1, 163, 175, 181, 183, 184, 187, 196.
28. Ibid., 207; Hoffmann, "Construction of William Bartram's Narrative Natural History," 53.

is also restorative and enlightening. Bartram uses his time there to "dry my Books and specimens of plants and with care and attention saved the most of them." He makes botanical forays into the surrounding savannas and groves, relying on the support and guidance of his "hospitable friend." Drawing on his authority as naturalist, he offers plans for a neglected portion of the estate. Berresford has yet to develop the "high, rich swamps [which] when properly drain'd trench't and other ways manure, are as proper for Indigo, Sugar cane, and every other article of agriculture as any lands in the So. states." The sin of avarice is associated less with slaveholding and agricultural development in and of itself than with the pursuit of a shortsighted vision for improvement. Despite his awareness that cultivating swampland is labor-intensive and potentially lethal for enslaved Africans, Bartram implies that a more natural and peaceable social order might emerge from the fusion of natural history and experimental agriculture to transform the swamp according to georgic ideals.[29]

Encounters with benevolent planters in the published *Travels* (in chapters for which no manuscript version is known to exist) imply that the peaceable kingdom is not so much the antithesis of the plantation as the result of its more rational and pious management. During his passage through Georgia, Bartram's planter host invites him to observe "some men at work squaring Pine and Cypress timber for the West-India market." To Bartram's eyes and ears, the manner of slave labor testifies to the "liberal spirit" in which it is organized: "The regular heavy strokes of their gleaming axes re-echo in the deep forest, at the same time contented and joyful the sooty sons of Afric forgetting their bondage, in chorus sing the virtues and beneficence of their master in songs of their own composing." Near the beginning of section 2, the narrator is received in "the most agreeable manner" by one Mr. Marshall, as his slaves repair Bartram's storm-battered boat. Marshall provides a tour of his "extensive improvements," including an orange grove where the two men retire during the "most sultry time of the day" and fields of thriving indigo plants. The hospitable exchange of specimens signals the fusion of commerce and polite learning: "Mr. Marshall presented me, with a specimen [of indigo] of his own manufacture, at this plantation: it was very little, if any inferior; to the best Prussian blue."[30]

Major rhetorical shifts in the second draft chapter (describing Bartram's visit to the Alachua Savanna) become difficult to interpret in light of these

29. "Bartram's Journal," book 1, 207–208.
30. Bartram, *Travels*, 49, 50, 197, 198.

idealizations of planter civility. The pilgrim's moralizing commentary on avarice and ambition begins to incorporate the language of antislavery. Surveying a pine grove, Bartram pleads:

> O may those unviolated retreats ever remain in their present state of Youthful Innocence unpolluted, by the violent hand of invidious industry avarice and ambition; false politeness, and cruel civilisation which refines and sublimates humanity quite away leaving in its place a subtile, restless firy Spirit ambitious powerful principle, continually watching to inslave mankind and destroy, the happiness of a future state.

Bartram's use of the language of slavery here, as a metaphor for political oppression and spiritual bondage, is in one sense conventional for the Revolutionary era, when protests against figurative enslavement frequently occluded critiques of slavery as an actual practice. Following his visits to working plantations, however, Bartram's sentences have the opposite effect, reattaching certain key terms in eighteenth-century moral and political debate (including enslavement and refinement) to their literal referents.[31]

A second moralizing passage produces similar effects. While traveling with a party of British officials and traders charged with initiating diplomatic talks with the Seminole leadership at Cuscowilla, Bartram is appalled by their wasteful culinary habits. A lengthy meditation on the need to associate more equitably with the "animal kingdom" ends with an apostrophe:

> O Men! The highly distinguished and favoured creature of God! Let us stop a little in our mad career, let us look back and examin our actions, our conduct; are we not bewildered and lost in error. . . . We labor continually for to enslave our own species, those visionary alluring scenes lead us wandering in a labyrinth of errors. and we are lost and led astray from the glorious eternal abodes of future tranquility.

Bartram's plea is self-referential. The pilgrim wanders in a labyrinth of errors because he, too, has been seduced by tropical plenitude. In pursuit of material riches, he has labored to enslave his own species. From the pilgrim's perspective, this is the single episode in his "mad career" that stands in greatest need of self-examination.[32]

---

31. "Bartram's Journal," book 2, 268–269.
32. Ibid., 278–279. Hoffman notes that the tone and language of such passages is "close to the radicalism of Quakers such as John Woolman whose preaching against slavery and the brutality of excess work

Direct observation of the natural world here provides the means to self-reflexive spiritual insight. This understanding of empiricism transforms the tradition outlined in Section 1 of this study, even as it derives from the hermeneutic strategies developed by Sloane, Catesby, and others. The authority of Catesby's theoretical speculations on climate depended on his itinerant travels in the plantation Americas. Direct experience of the natural world provided the only secure epistemological basis for speculations on universal natural laws. Bartram's manuscript shares this conviction. The narrator's incremental progress through Florida, via a series of encounters with its flora and fauna, yields universal knowledge. But Bartram places greater emphasis on the spiritual benefits of empirical practice as it reveals providential patterns. On one level, this returns natural history narrative to its early modern roots in the allegorical pilgrimage. In its desire for spiritual revelation, the emblematic method of the draft manuscript feels closer to the spirit of Protestant hermeneutics than earlier narrative experiments by natural historians such as Sloane. On another level, however, Bartram's novelization of natural history reflects the rise of sensibility. The text describes the psychology of the narrator as it unfolds in a secular chronology marked by the rise and fall of the colonial plantation. We detect a gradual but decisive shift in emphasis from the specimen perceived to the mind perceiving, as in Crèvecoeur's account of South Carolina.

Bartram's depictions of the Alachua Savanna culminate this shift. Within the pilgrimage structure of the draft manuscript, the narrator's saving vision of the savanna occurs just after his apostrophe to the reader, at a moment of peak spiritual despair, when, "at the forlorn extremity of hope, the wandering Pilgrim pours forth his last pious prayers." To continue tracing the narrative's ambivalent attitude toward the West Indian plantation, we must attend to Bartram's renderings of the savanna as a site of benign association between the tribes of man, vegetable, and animal. Before turning to these depictions, it bears emphasizing that Bartram explicitly conceived of the savanna as a site for plantation development. In his report to Fothergill, written just after his travels in East Florida, Bartram notes of the savanna "land about it very good and extremely proper for indigo."[33]

In section 2 of the published *Travels*, Bartram projects a similar vision.

---

for worldly gains might well have been a voice Bartram was following" ("Construction of William Bartram's Narrative Natural History," 29). For some of Bartram's unpublished antislavery writings, see Bartram Papers, I, 81, 83; Broadsides AB, n.d., 251, HSP.

33. "Bartram's Journal," book 2, 285; William Bartram to Lachlan McIntosh, July 15, 1775, Dreer Autograph Collection, HSP.

Describing a savanna in the Seminole territory in East Florida, he dwells on its scale, organic diversity, and beauty, concluding,

> This vast plain together with the forest contiguous to it, if permitted (by the Siminoles who are sovereigns of these realms) to be in possession and under the culture of industrious planters and mechanicks, would in a little time exhibit other scenes than it does at present, delightful as it is; for by the arts of agriculture and commerce, almost every desirable thing in life might be produced and made plentiful here, and thereby establish a rich, populous and delightful region; as this soil and climate appear to be of a nature favourable for the production of almost all the fruits of the earth, as Corn, Rice, Indigo, Sugar-cane, Flax, Cotton, Silk, Cochineal and all the varieties of esculent vegetables . . . and lying contiguous to one of the most beautiful navigable rivers in the world; and not more than thirty miles from St. Marks on the great bay of Mexico; is most conveniently situated for the West-India trade and the commerce of all the world.

As Myra Jehlen has characterized the passage, "Bartram looks once and sees the jungle marshes of Georgia's wetlands, looks twice and sees fields and markets, as if they had grown there, hardly even planted." The transformation of the cane field into a West Indian plantation, and subsequently into a providential global garden, results from a single act of purified perception, though this "act" only fulfills the material potential latent in the land. Such a vision would not be out of place in promotional tracts by Stork and Romans.[34]

This reconstituted promotional vision is stronger in the published *Travels* owing to Bartram's effacement of the Philosophical Pilgrim at his moments of most passionate self-examination and social critique. As detailed above, Bartram deleted many passages of this type in the mid-to-late 1780s. During the same years, he also inserted a number of natural history essays and descriptions into the manuscript while working steadily on a series of drawings that he hoped to include in the text. Although he preserved the architecture of the early modern pilgrimage narrative, that is, Bartram removed passages where emblematic morals are explicitly drawn, even as he included greater numbers of natural history specimens. Owing to their structural position in the text, those specimens almost demand to

---

34. Bartram, *Travels*, 148; Myra Jehlen, *American Incarnation: The Individual, the Nation, and the Continent* (Cambridge, Mass., 1986), 59.

be read emblematically as "stations" in the pilgrim's progress, through the traditional interpretive movement between word and image. Emblems proliferate in the published text at the same time that the omission of moralizing commentary renders them anything but transparent. To restore the allegorical dimensions of Bartram's writings, we must attend to the historical context in which the narrator's moral reflections were excised from the manuscript.

Creole Commerce and the Rise of Abolitionism

Despite the severing of commercial connections with the British West Indies, North American elites during the post-Revolutionary period maintained acute interest in the natural history of the Greater Caribbean. Commentators continued to view the sugar islands as part of a natural economic and social unit extending from New England through Barbados. As Thomas Jefferson declared of the French West Indies in 1793, "Their condition must always be interesting to the US. with whom nature has connected them by the strong link of mutual necessities." It was because of the prior labors of naturalists including Catesby, Du Simitière, and Romans, among many others, that Jefferson could proclaim this among the self-evident truths of New World experience.[35]

The relationship between the American Philosophical Society and the Cercle des Philadelphes illustrates this continued fascination with West Indian knowledge. During a postwar economic depression when American merchants hoped that increased trade with the French and Spanish Caribbean might compensate for the loss of British West Indian markets, and when French Caribbean resentments against the exclusif were growing, members of both societies forged connections through the exchange of letters, texts, specimens, and honorary memberships.[36]

Benjamin Franklin's 1786 letter to Charles Arthaud captures a cultural moment in which this new intellectual exchange was perceived as vital to the practical business of American Enlightenment. Acknowledging the receipt of printed copies of Arthaud's address to the Cercle during its public meeting of 1785, along with a detailed natural history of Cap Français and its environs, Franklin takes care to express a due sense of its personal,

35. Thomas Jefferson to Edmond Charles Genêt, Nov. 24, 1793, *PTJ*, XXVII, 429.
36. James E. McClellan III, *Colonialism and Science: Saint Domingue in the Old Regime* (Baltimore, 1992).

political, and economic importance: "I am very sensible of the great Honour done me by the Society of Philadelphians, in naming me among their Associates; and I beg they would accept my thankful Acknowledgements, together with the second Volume of the Transactions of our Society here. Your Account of the Cape, contains a Variety of knowledge respecting it that we had not before, and many Particular observations for preserving Health, that may be useful too our Northern People who visit your Island." The circulation of printed scientific knowledge between these emerging institutions, in Franklin's account, is necessary to the continued prosperity and refinement of two thriving societies.[37]

Through this emphasis on print circulation, Franklin and Arthaud call attention to what they perceive as a revolutionary transformation in the culture of New World natural history. As established in Chapter 2 of this study, over the course of the eighteenth century, colonial naturalists had grown dissatisfied with their appointed role as purveyors of raw empirical knowledge to the metropole, where this data would be synthesized and disseminated in printed form by the Royal Society and the Académie des sciences. The circulation of printed scientific texts within the hemisphere signals a new era of creole solidarity and autonomy, made explicit in Franklin's opening salutation to Arthaud: "It gave me great Pleasure to find that the Improvement of Science is attended to in a Country where the Climate was suppos'd naturally to occasion indolence, and an Unwillingness to take Pains except for immediate Profit." Franklin takes aim at a theory of degeneration that long had underwritten a hierarchical model of imperial knowledge production and scientific authorship in the Atlantic world and that had gained new prominence and prestige with the publication of the comte de Buffon's *Natural History*.[38]

In other ways, however, Franklin's greeting displaces this older cultural and epistemological hierarchy only to propose a new one. As both men were well aware, within the long tradition of early modern climate theory before Buffon, colonial indolence had been linked to the tropics, and West Indian planters had been its primary exemplars. With characteristic wit, Franklin's gesture of creole solidarity evokes a cultural geography distinguishing the mainland and the Caribbean, one with important roots in the correspondence of John Bartram and William Byrd II. In cultivating intellectual con-

37. Benjamin Franklin to Charles Arthaud, July 9, 1786, Manuscript Division, Library of Congress, Washington, D.C.
38. Ibid.

nections with the West Indian plantocracy, Franklin denies their crucial position within the early Republic itself.

The emergence of slave trade abolition as a social cause and cultural vogue in the late 1780s provides one impetus. Meditations on the potential effects of West Indian dependence were pervasive in a literary culture suffused with antislavery feeling. Consumption of tropical staples, commentators warned, might contaminate an otherwise temperate republic, enlightened nation, and continental empire. An antislavery contributor to Matthew Carey's *American Museum* argued that the cruelties of the slave ship and plantation were practiced "that we may have sugar to sweeten tea that debilitates us—Rum to make punch to intoxicate us—And indigo to dye our clothes." Such cries were a convention of the antislavery genre Philip Gould calls the "commercial jeremiad." Antislavery voices warned of a cyclical imperial history in which "commerce produces forms of cultural refinement that potentially become enervating 'Luxury.'" Once established as customs, these tastes for luxury items became monstrous appetites that in turn "enslaved" the consumer, nation, or republic. The genre emerged at a moment when antislavery societies in Britain and America had identified "the West Indian export economy—the sugar, rum, tobacco, and indigo that flooded into colonial and metropolitan ports—[as] their main target."[39]

As a result, ironies and tensions abound in the new hemispheric relationship between the American Philosophical Society and West Indian associations such as the Cercle. Though Benjamin Rush's antislavery writings included a scathing indictment of West Indian planters, he became an honorary member of the Cercle in 1786, at the very moment that the society had launched a survey of colonial agriculture, slavery, and rural economy. The survey marked the Cercle's "deepest institutional involvement in colonial slavery" and demonstrated its status as "a profoundly racist institution and an unquestioning supporter of the slave society out of which it emerged." Perhaps Rush had come to see the logic of the reply to his antislavery views by West Indian planter Richard Nisbet, then newly emigrated to Philadelphia. In 1773, Nisbet warned, "The inhabitants of this city will please to recollect, that the West-Indies form a considerable branch of their commerce."[40]

---

39. "Negro Trade—a Fragment," *American Museum*, I (1787), 46; Philip Gould, *Barbaric Traffic: Commerce and Antislavery in the Eighteenth-Century Atlantic World* (Cambridge, Mass., 2003), 21, 30.

40. McClellan, *Colonialism and Science*, 238–239; Richard Nisbet, *Slavery Not Forbidden by Scripture; or, A Defense of the West-India Planters . . .* (Philadelphia, 1773), ii.

The Published Travels and the
Natural History of the Peaceable Plantation

Bartram revised the draft manuscript of *Travels* during a decade when the planter-naturalist continued to play an integral role in the republic of science and letters but when the rise of abolitionist discourse had targeted his mental, moral, and physiological condition. By the mid-to-late 1780s, the ideological burden borne by the penitent West Indian planter, on his return pilgrimage to the scene of his original spiritual error, had become more onerous and unwieldy; the pilgrim's rigorous self-criticism of his prior actions was directed toward neither the abolition of the slave trade nor the reform of consumer appetites for tropical comestibles but rather toward the expansion of West Indian slavery into East Florida according to more rational and sensible principles. Although Bartram effaced the Philosophical Pilgrim from the manuscript draft during the revisions of the 1780s, however, he by no means rejected its basic vision of improvement. Indeed, that vision is in one sense more prominent in the published *Travels* than in the "spiritualized field notes" of the 1770s. The effects of Bartram's revisions are stranger than any simple negation of plantation settlement. Rather, while preserving the narrative telos of the draft manuscript, Bartram removes the individual subject who had enacted it. In the published *Travels,* the peaceable plantation appears to emerge spontaneously from the landscape itself.[41]

Bartram's prospect of the Alachua Savanna epitomizes the new importance of environmental agency to *Travels*. The naturalist dwells on the seemingly determinative relationship between landscape and animal behavior:

> The extensive Alachua savanna is a level, green plain, above fifteen miles over, fifty miles in circumference, and scarcely a tree or bush of any kind to be seen on it. It is encircled with high, sloping hills, covered with waving forests and fragrant Orange groves, rising from an exuberantly fertile soil. The towering Magnolia grandiflora and transcendent Palm, stand conspicuous amongst them. At the same

---

41. At least one contemporary reviewer noted that the narrative persona of the published *Travels* was at odds with the rationality and masculine vigor of colonial naturalists such as Romans: "In description, he is rather too luxuriant and florid, to merit the palm of chastity and correctness" (*Massachusetts Magazine,* IV [1792], 686–687 [quotation on 686]).

time are seen innumerable droves of cattle; the lordly bull, lowing cow and sleek capricious heifer. The hills and groves re-echo their cheerful, social voices. Herds of sprightly deer, squadrons of the beautiful, fleet Simonole horse, flocks of turkeys, civilized communities of the sonorous, watchful crane, mix together, appearing happy and contented in the enjoyment of peace, 'till disturbed and affrighted by the warrior man . . . See the different tribes and bands, how they draw towards each other! as it were deliberating upon the general good.

Foregrounding tropical species such as the orange, magnolia, and palm, Bartram characterizes the landscape, not as a scene of chaotic predation, but rather of natural sociability. The language of association is varied and insistent, including "droves . . . herds . . . squadrons . . . flocks . . . civilized communities . . . tribes and bands." The narrator details numerous examples of cooperation within and between species. We know from Bartram's meditation on a sinkhole fountain near Lake George that he regarded such forms of natural association and cooperation as possible only under extraordinary environmental conditions. Gazing down into the fountain, the naturalist perceived fish and alligators coexisting peacefully. Upon further scrutiny, however, he understands this aquatic utopia less as a challenge to the law of tropical predation (as a function of greater biodiversity) than the exception that proves the rule: "This paradise of fish, may seem to exhibit a just representation of the peaceable and happy state of nature which existed before the fall, yet in reality it is a mere representation." The remarkable transparency of the water renders predatory deception ineffective. By this logic, the Alachua Savanna is also a "mere representation" of prelapsarian nature. The absence of "a tree or bush of any kind" on a "level, green plain . . . fifty miles in circumference" creates ideal conditions of visibility.[42]

Themes of visibility and perception are further emphasized in Bartram's drawing of "The Great Alachua Savannah in East Florida" (Fig. 13), likely intended for inclusion in the published text. Cross-references between text and image are clear and deliberate. From his elevated vantage near the base of the palm tree in the lower left corner (the strong vertical of its trunk framing and stabilizing the image), the viewer gazes across the savanna toward a "civilized community" of large cranes in the upper right quadrant. The composition emphasizes the unity of the savanna as a habitat, almost a single organism. Using heavy pen strokes, Bartram inscribes the borders of

42. Bartram, *Travels*, 106, 119–120.

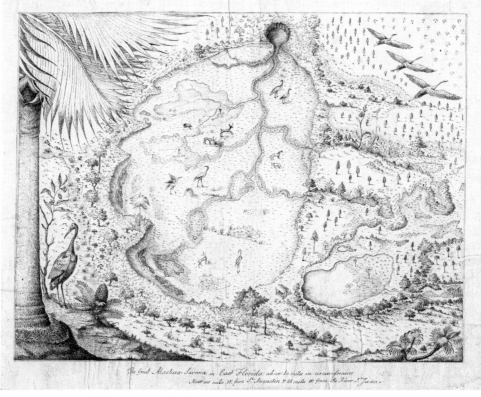

The Great Alachua Savanna in East Florida above to mile in circumference
Near 110 mile 11 from St. Augustin & 48 mile W from the River St. Juan

FIGURE 13. William Bartram, *The Great Alachua Savannah in East Florida.*
Permission, American Philosophical Society

the open plain in dark ink, thus highlighting its leaflike contours. Resembling the veins of a leaf, a network of streams radiates outward from the large fountain at the upper border. The drawing recalls Catesby's "Green Tree Frog and Arum Americanum," where a single, large leaf provided an encompassing habitat for the interaction between frog and spider. In emphasizing the organic unity and vitality of the savanna, the drawing also describes the limits of planter rationality and initiative. Details suggest the inability of the viewer to submit the landscape to cognitive management. Flowers are several times taller than the trees beside them. Whereas the foreground obeys the conventions of single-point perspective, the savanna is composed along a vertical axis, much like the large, circular leaf in Bartram's drawing of "Colocasia" (Fig. 10). The linguistic description provides a key for these compositional features as evidence of the naturalist's mental state: "How is the mind agitated and bewildered, at being thus, as it were, placed on the borders of a new world!"[43]

At moments such as these, we discern a gradual shift from Protestant to Romantic interpretations of the natural world. Drawing on Catesby's visual language of reflected form, Bartram's drawings and descriptions of the Alachua Savanna emphasize the organic unity of a landscape that is emphatically material yet embodies a transcendent law. To perceive the true nature of the landscape requires a synthesis of empiricism and idealism, combining accurate description of concrete particulars with the exercise of imagination or intuition. Bartram's mode of representing nature has as much in common with the Romantic symbol (as a tangible, external reality that can suddenly disclose some universal truth) as the Protestant emblem. To some extent, the emergence of these Romantic characteristics in the published *Travels* is contingent. Although Bartram's emphasis on the psychology of the observer is informed by the culture of sensibility (an important proto-Romantic development), his published representations of the savanna function as Romantic symbols only because the pilgrim's moral commentary has been deleted. In the palimpsest of *Travels*, however, the early modern specimen-as-emblem remains visible through the surface of the printed text.

The effacement of the Philosophical Pilgrim also transforms the representation of agency. The published *Travels* creates an unnerving impression that the land itself generates commercial prosperity and social harmony. This implies that the peaceable plantation is latent in the physical constitution of East Florida rather than a result of slave labor. But it necessarily suggests that the historical trajectory of the colony lies beyond imperial management. This is a version of the problem encountered in Catesby's portrayals of South Carolina, where seasonal rains, hurricanes, and floods threatened to create a primeval natural and social landscape characterized by cyclical violence. As discussed in Chapter 2, Catesby's meditations on slave agency are, for the most part, subsumed within his representations of organic relationships and natural processes. This occludes slavery as an explicit subject while making it pervasive as a subtext, especially as the question of environmental change takes on added importance. Relying on a reconstituted emblematic method, Bartram's landscapes address the question

43. Ibid., 120. My analysis of the drawing is indebted to Meyers, "Sketches from the Wilderness," 121, 137.

of slave agency together with the problem of native American sovereignty. In an environment characterized by instability, predatory deception, and secret mobility, his narrator confronts the possibility of organized insurrection and warfare.

The problem of agency surfaces prominently in Bartram's representations of sinkhole fountains. The so-called "Great Sink" dominates the top center of "The Great Alachua Savannah in East Florida" (Fig. 13). Like many rice planters of the Southeast, Bartram was preoccupied by problems of drainage and irrigation and considered the Great Sink in part as a wonder of natural engineering. He theorizes that the fertile lands between Cuscowilla and the Gulf Coast are watered by numerous "subterraneous rivers, which wander in darkness beneath the surface of the earth, by innumerable doublings, windings and secret labyrinths; no doubt in some places forming vast reservoirs and subterranean lakes." These "subterraneous courses" eventually surface in "surprising vast fountains" near the banks of distant rivers. The gothic imagery indicates that, although Bartram regarded sink hole fountains as sources of organic plenitude, he also feared them as signs of a secret underworld beyond the limits of empirical observation. In his analysis of Bartram's "View of the Alegator Hole in Isthmus Florida" (Fig. 14), art historian Michael Gaudio argues that this "secret underworld is evoked negatively through the black pit at the center of the image. . . . The sink hole is located at the threshold of natural history representation: beneath its dark, sunken surface is all that is unavailable to vision and therefore unavailable to Bartram as a naturalist." Such implications are highlighted in Bartram's description of the Great Sink. Tribes of fish appear to be swallowed up by the fountain. They descend through "vast perforations of the rocks, and from thence are conducted and carried away, by secret subterranean conduits and gloomy vaults." Many of those fish, Bartram speculates, are "strangers or adventurers, from other lakes, ponds, and rivers, [carried] by subterraneous rivulets and communications to this rocky, dark door."[44]

Bartram's depictions of these conduits suggest that human agents other than the colonial planter will determine the character of commercial intercourse in the region. His visit to the Seminole trading village of Talahasochte (on the Gulf of Mexico) discloses secret knowledge. In his ethno-

44. Bartram, *Travels*, 131, 142–143; Gaudio, "Swallowing the Evidence," *Winterthur Portfolio*, XXXVI (2001), 9.

FIGURE 14. William Bartram, *View of the Alegator Hole in Isthmus Florida.*
© Natural History Museum, London

graphic overview of the village, Bartram's description of some cypress
canoes takes an unexpected turn:

> In these large canoes they descend the river on trading and hunting
> expeditions on the sea coast, neighbouring islands and keys, quite to
> the point of Florida, and sometimes cross the gulph, extending their
> navigations to the Bahama islands and even to Cuba: a crew of these
> adventurers had just arrived, having returned from Cuba but a few
> days before our arrival, with a cargo of spirituous liquors, Coffee,
> Sugar and Tobacco. One of them politely presented me with a choice
> piece of Tobacco, which he told me he had received from the gover-
> nor of Cuba.

The stuttering syntax of the opening sentence—as it winds its way southward—is mimetic of the narrator's gradual awakening to a new and complicated geography, an archipelago of islands and keys linking the "backwater"
village to the booming metropolis of Havana. Bartram rediscovers the map

of the Americas articulated by Catesby's *Natural History of Carolina* but now clouded by darker implications. The governor of Cuba has given the Seminole mariners a choice plug of tobacco, a crucial symbol in Seminole diplomatic rituals centered on the Calumet pipe. The Seminoles, the vignette reveals, forged political alliances with Cuba at a moment when its explosive economic growth promised to revitalize the entire Spanish American empire and when the population of Havana outnumbered New York by some ten thousand residents. At a moment of persistent backcountry violence between the Seminoles and English, such alliances were especially threatening. Within the residual allegorical structure of *Travels,* forms of hidden subaltern agency such as this are linked to the agency of the environment itself, with the latter providing the material conditions for the former, which, in turn, transforms and fulfills the latter.[45]

As a former rice planter, Bartram was also preoccupied with East Florida's array of aquatic plants. In his drawing of the Alachua Savanna, the surface of a lake to the right is covered with a plant identified in the text as "Nymphea nilumbo." Eighteenth-century botanists often confused the species with colocasia. Reflecting on the "doubts and confusion" surrounding *Nymphaea nelumbo* in *The Civil and Natural History of Jamaica,* Patrick Browne blames "the ambiguous descriptions and accounts, left us by the ancient writers . . . who, under the title of *Faba Ægyptia,* have given a thorough description of the upper parts of this plant [*Nymphaea nelumbo*]; and as accurate an account of the roots of the lesser *Collocasia,* now commonly called *Caccos,* in *Jamaica.*" Bartram seems to have shared this confusion and to have used the terms interchangeably. Modern botanists agree that the plant identified as "Colocasia" by a handwritten notation on the back of the drawing (Fig. 10) is, in fact, *Nymphaea lutea,* commonly known as American lotus. But Bartram believed that he had observed colocasia throughout East Florida, including the Alachua Savanna. His 1773 report

45. Bartram, *Travels,* 143. On the growth of the Cuban economy, see James Gregory Cusick, "Spanish East Florida in the Atlantic Economy of the Late Eighteenth Century," in Jane G. Landers, ed., *Colonial Plantations and Economy in Florida* (Gainesville, Fla., 2000), 168–188. On Seminole contacts with Cuba, see Edward J. Cashin, *William Bartram and the American Revolution on the Southern Frontier* (Columbia, S.C., 2000), 102, 128, 169. The Seminole alliance with Cuba made the prospect of backcountry violence especially threatening. During Bartram's travels, the Southeast was filled with rumors of Spanish insurgency. Authorities in Cuba offered a commission to the rising Creek Lieutenant Escochabey, promising to provide ammunition and trade items should he open war on English settlements. Escochabey refused, but in the summer of 1774, just after Bartram's return from Talahasochte, he traveled to Havana to encourage expansion of the illegal Spanish trade to Florida.

to Fothergill notes, "Saw some leave, and dried Capsulae of the Colocacia Egyptian Bean Hybiscus, these grew in the water."[46]

Bartram knew that the history of the plant was bound up with the New World plantation. It was owing to prior interest by Sloane, Catesby, and others that he selected colocasia as the subject of one of the first Florida drawings shipped to his father's patron, Peter Collinson. At about the same time, William Stork annotated John Bartram's remarks on tanniers (*or Colocasia antiquorum*) in his Florida diary. In *Travels* itself, Bartram indicates his knowledge of West Indian botanical sources while inspecting a provision garden near Savannah, Georgia:

> Observed in a low wet place at the corner of the garden, the Ado (Arum esculentum) this plant is much cultivated in the maritime parts of Georgia, and Florida, for the sake of its large Turnip-like root, which when boiled or roasted, is excellent food, and tastes like the Yam; the leaves of this magnificent plant are very large, and of a beautiful green colour, the spatha large and circulated, the spadix terminates with a very long subulated tongue, naked and perfectly white: perhaps this may be the Arum Colocasia. They have likewise, another species of the esculent Arum, called Tannier, which is a large and beautiful plant, and much cultivated and esteemed for food, particularly by the Negroes.

Steeped in prior knowledge of colocasia, Bartram was also fascinated by interactions between multiple aquatics in a single habitat. Approaching the famed "Manate Spring" by boat, he chronicles the botanical colonization of a waterway by combining species: "As we gently descend floating fields of the Nymphea nilumbo, intersected with vistas of the yellow green Pista stratiotes [water lettuce] which cover a bay or cove of the river opposite the circular woodland hills."[47]

Composed around the same time as "The Great Alachua Savannah in East Florida," a drawing entitled "A Seed Vessell of the Calocasia" pictures such interrelationships (Fig. 15). The composition links the botanical speci-

46. Browne, *Civil and Natural History of Jamaica*, 243. For a discussion of the plant and drawing, see Joseph Ewan, *William Bartram: Botanical and Zoological Drawings, 1756-1788* (Philadelphia, 1968), 60-61; William Bartram, "Travels in Georgia and Florida, 1773-74," in Thomas P. Slaughter, ed., *William Bartram: Travels and Other Writings* (New York, 1996), 464-465.

47. Collinson to William Bartram, Apr. 10, 1768, Bartram Papers, box 3, file 73, HSP; Bartram, *Travels*, 145, 297.

FIGURE 15. William Bartram, *A Seed Vessell of the Calocasia.*
© Natural History Museum, London

mens in the right foreground and left background. Its tail visible beneath
the desiccated seed pod of a colocasia plant, the body of a scarlet snake
winds surreptitiously behind the ridge of a tangled river bank, its head
emerging from dense leaves of black root (*Pterocaulon pycnostachyum*),
arrow arum (*Peltandra virginica*), and water lettuce (*Pistia stratiotes*) to
devour an unsuspecting frog. The concealed form of the snake as it coils
through the landscape is mirrored by the two spiral snail shells, which cue
the viewer to contemplate the cyclical character of the relationships herein
portrayed. Seeds emerge and fall from the colocasia pod to take root in the
soil and eventually flourish. At the same time, two rectangular, stone fragments in the left foreground evoke the remains of prior human settlements
in the region, whether ancient native American civilizations or failed English plantations. (We find a similar fragment in the foreground of "Colocasia" [Fig. 10].) Bartram's juxtaposition of colocasia seeds and stone frag-

ments—both strewn across the earth—confuses the boundary between human and natural history. Both objects are human artifacts. In "Colocasia," Bartram associates the plant with themes of misperception and predation amid a semitropical habitat where expectations of natural hierarchy are drawn into question. These associations are underscored by "A Seed Vessell of the Calocasia." In a landscape evacuated of its prior human presence, colocasia continues to regenerate, creating the conditions ripe for artifice and ambush. A kind of human history proceeds apace, though absent the planter-naturalist who was ostensibly its primary subject.

Images of tangled aquatics provide a dark counterpoint to Bartram's fantasy that ordered plantations might emerge spontaneously from locales such as the Alachua Savanna. His description of *Pista stratiotes* returns to the language of natural association:

> I set sail early, and saw, this day, vast quantities of the Pistia stratiotes, a very singular aquatic plant. It associates in large communities, or floating islands, some of them a quarter of a mile in extent, and are impelled to and fro, as the wind and current may direct. They are first produced on, or close to the shore, in eddy water, where they gradually spread themselves into the river, forming most delightful green plains, several miles in length, and in some places a quarter of a mile in breadth. . . . It vegetates on the surface of the still stagnant water, and in its natural situation, is propagated from seed only. In great storms of wind and rain, when the river is suddenly raised, large masses of these floating plains are broken loose, and driven from the shores, into the wide water, where they have the appearance of islets, and float about, until broken to pieces by the winds and waves; or driven again to shore, on some distant coast of the river, where they again find footing, and there, forming new colonies, spread and extend themselves again, until again broken up and dispersed as before.

Like the "squadrons . . . herds . . . [and] tribes" inhabiting the Alachua Savanna, the floating pista organizes and reorganizes to form intricate, if ephemeral, "communities" and "colonies."[48]

This language of natural association also marks Bartram's description of another potential ambush near the conclusion of *Travels*. Bartram recalls his encounter with a "party of Negroes" upon his return to Carolina, dwelling on his anxiety and uncertainty:

48. Bartram, *Travels*, 57.

Observed a number of persons coming up a head which I soon perceived to be a party of Negroes: I had every reason to dread the consequence; for this being a desolate place, and I was by this time several
miles from any house or plantation, and had reason to apprehend this
to be a predatory band of Negroes: people being frequently attacked,
robbed, and sometimes murdered by them at this place. . . . As soon as
I saw them distinctly a mile or two off, I immediately alighted to rest,
and give breath to my horse, intending to attempt my safety by flight,
if upon near approach they should betray hostile designs, thus prepared, when we drew near to each other, I mounted and rode briskly
up, and though armed with clubs, axes and hoes, they opened to right
and left, and let me pass peaceably, their chief informed me whom
they belonged to, and said they were going to man a new quarter at
the West end of the bay, I however kept a sharp eye about me, appre-
hending that this might possibly have been an advanced division, and
their intentions were to ambuscade and surround me, but they kept
on quietly and I was no more alarmed by them.

Much like the previous depiction of Seminole mariners, this later image of
subaltern mobility and affiliation provides a key for interpreting the type of
environmental agency we have just been examining, already linked to slave
agency through Bartram's emphasis on the generative powers of colocasia.
This "predatory band" is as difficult to interpret and potentially as lethal
to the narrator as any of the semitropical tableaus that featured colocasia.
Conditions of ideal visibility (Bartram perceives the party "distinctly a mile
or two off") provide minimal protection against a sudden reversal of "natural" hierarchy. Common agricultural tools become menacing. Bartram's account of an "advanced division" organized into a possible "ambuscade" by
a "chief" resembles descriptions of Maroon tactics in the West Indies while
recalling the text's insistent imagery of improvised collectivity—animals
and plants reconfigured spontaneously amid precarious circumstances.[49]

Within the text's vestigial allegorical frame, the passage resolves that
imagery. At the conclusion of Bartram's travels in the Southeast, and with
near-hallucinatory intensity, the latent content of his emblematic narrative looms to the surface. In this final stage or trial of his progress, the narrator experiences a form of epistemic violence produced not only by the
ambivalent workings of his planter conscience but also by the minds and

49. Ibid., 298–299.

bodies of those supposedly "submitted to [his] service." The text confronts the possibility that the future of East Florida, as the new northern fringe of an interconnected social, economic, and environmental zone encompassing the Greater Caribbean, may be determined, not by the enlightened management of sensible and pious planters, but by the region's black majority. In Crèvecoeur's letter on Charleston, the narrator's leisurely observation of lowcountry flora yielded a sudden apprehension of the underlying violence of the plantation order. In Bartram's *Travels,* botanical inquiry results in new and vivid knowledge that the improvement of East Florida both fosters and is challenged by other kinds of revolutionary potential.

The conclusion of *Travels* in this way anticipates a theme that will play a central role in the writings addressed in the final two chapters of this study—Thomas Jefferson's epistolary revisions to *Notes on the State of Virginia* and John Audubon's *Birds of America* and *Ornithological Biography.* The discourse and literary genre of natural history, as wielded by these authors, became a medium for addressing the implications of the Haitian Revolution (1791–1804), the massive and successful slave insurrection that began the year *Travels* was published. Having traced the evolution of natural history in the Caribbean from Sloane's Jamaica to Bartram's Florida, we are now in a position to understand why figures such as Jefferson and Audubon conceived of the Haitian Revolution as an epistemological crisis. If the events of the Haitian Revolution constituted, as Michel-Rolph Trouillot argues, "'unthinkable' facts in the framework of Western thought," this is partly because the improvement of natural knowledge in the Greater Caribbean had contributed to establishing that framework, as part of the vital business of a new transnational republic of science and letters.[50]

50. Michel-Rolph Trouillot, *Silencing the Past: Power and the Production of History* (Boston, 1995), 82.

5

Notes on the State of Virginia, *the Haitian Revolution, and the Return of Epistolarity*

In April of 1797, as Toussaint L'Ouverture was establishing control over the revolution on Saint-Domingue, Thomas Jefferson received a polite letter from one Alexandre Giroud in Cap Français. A geologist and mineralogist of some repute in France, Giroud had only recently been assigned to Saint-Domingue as part of the Third Civil Commission under Léger Félicité Sonthonax. Since the temporary abolition of slavery in 1793–1794, Giroud had worked with the activist *homme de couleur libre* Julien Raimond, among others, to establish some limited form of multiracial *egalité* and *fraternité* on the island.[1]

Accompanying Giroud's letter to Jefferson were several seeds of breadfruit, a species that French and British colonial officials had, during the prior decade, taken pains to transplant from the East to the West Indies. In the latter islands, it was much sought after as a domestic food source for a restive black majority and as a sign of metropolitan support for an embattled plantocracy. That British desires for the plant had played a part in the organization of William Bligh's expedition to the South Pacific gives a sense of its geopolitical and geoeconomic importance. Addressing the "Philosophe et du Républicain de Monticello" in admiring tones, Giroud expresses the hope that "cette Plante précieuse," which had begun to thrive on Saint-Domingue, might also prosper in Virginia. He envisions a future in which groves of breadfruit trees will greet visitors to Monticello and in which he and Jefferson might continue to exchange botanical specimens from the Indies, guided by "Au Zèle des Philantropes, et des Botanistes pour multiplier, et répandre sur les divers points de la terre, les plantes utiles où agréables à l'homme" ["the zeal of Philanthropists and Botanists for cultivating, and shipping to all corners of the globe, plants useful or

---

1. On Giroud's career in Saint-Domingue, see James E. McClellan III, *Colonialism and Science: Saint Domingue in the Old Regime* (Baltimore, 1992), 286.

pleasurable to man"]. By initiating this exchange, Giroud insists on the bond between Jefferson and him as virtuous citizens of enlightened plantation societies.[2]

Despite its genial surface, the challenging implications of the letter were clear. For one thing, as Jefferson was undoubtedly aware, British and French Caribbean planters regarded the plant in part as a cheap and dependable substitute for imported foodstuffs from North America, at a time when the trade in staple grains to the French Caribbean was vital to the economy of the early Republic. Before the outbreak of the French and Haitian revolutions, Saint-Domingue stood not only as the wealthiest and most economically productive colony in the New World by far but also as the second largest trading partner of the United States, with some five hundred American ships carrying at least 10 percent of all American exports to its thriving ports and plantations. Owing to the continued British embargo against trade between the United States and the British West Indies, the commercial importance of the island increased in the 1790s.[3]

Far more unsettling were the implications of the letter for the future of New World slavery and race. As Jefferson also knew well, the political agenda of the Third Civil Commission went beyond improving plantation conditions by introducing adequate food sources. Giroud and his fellow administrators had set in motion an ambitious plan to dismantle colonial racial hierarchies in the first postslavery society in the Americas, with the conversion of *gens de couleur* and ex-slaves into formal citizens. Giroud's letter was addressed to "Citoyen Jefferson" from the home of "Citoyen [Julien] Raymond," the author of *Observations on the Origin and Progression of the White Colonists' Prejudice against Men of Color* (1791) and of a well-known speech in favor of mulatto rights to the royal government in Paris. In the previous year, Raimond and Giroud had together formed a scientific society in Cap Français, the short-lived Société libre des arts et des sciences, and the gift of breadfruit seeds to Jefferson was part of Giroud's broader effort to publicize the society and the spirit of cross-racial cooperation he claimed it embodied. In a contemporaneous letter to the Académie royale des sciences in Paris, Giroud proclaimed:

2. Alexandre Giroud to Thomas Jefferson, Apr. 9, 1797, *PTJ*, XXIX, 347–348.
3. On breadfruit, see Richard Drayton, *Nature's Government: Science, Imperial Britain, and the "Improvement" of the World* (New Haven, Conn., 2000), 111–115. On the importance of Saint-Domingue to the economy of the early Republic, see Alfred N. Hunt, *Haiti's Influence on Antebellum America: Slumbering Volcano in the Caribbean* (Baton Rouge, La., 1988), 30–34; Michael Zuckerman, *Almost Chosen People: Oblique Biographies in the American Grain* (Berkeley, Calif., 1993), 181.

You will receive . . . a letter from the Free Society of Arts and Sciences that has just formed here at Cap François through the efforts of your colleague, Raimond, and my own. You will see from the nominal list of members of this Society that it is composed of citizens from each of the three colors that nuance the human skin in this colony. A fairly large number of black and light-skinned citizens here are knowledgeable and very worthy of figuring in the Republic of Sciences and Letters.

Although declarations such as these were absent from the letter to Jefferson, there is little reason to doubt his ability to read between the lines or Giroud and Raimond's confidence that he would do so. In a 1797 letter to a new abolitionist society in Philadelphia, reprinted in *The Time Piece; and Literary Companion,* Giroud declared, "The ancient prejudices are daily wearing away, the creols and the Europeans become more united, as well by the marriages which confound and mix the black and white colours, as by the admission of the blacks and mulattoes to all offices." This included the admission of "blacks and mulattoes" to his new learned institution.[4]

Giroud's letter clarifies the importance of natural history within the ideological struggle over Saint-Domingue in the 1790s. It was in part through their exchange of specimens, seeds, and texts from the West Indies and through their rhetorical appeals to nature as the new secular ground of revolutionary authority that commentators from around the Atlantic rim debated the implications of the Haitian Revolution. By founding and publicizing the Société libre, Giroud and Raimond mounted an argument that the recent conflict on Saint-Domingue had creatively extended the principles for which the French and American revolutions ostensibly were waged (thus their effort to announce the society to revolutionary heroes on both sides of the Atlantic). The argument did not go uncontested. As discussed in Chapter 4, a number of accomplished, slaveholding naturalists were among the approximately ten thousand Saint-Dominguan exiles to find a temporary home in the new United States and among the five thousand French-speakers to settle in Philadelphia alone, comprising roughly 10

4. Giroud to the Académie royale des sciences, June 28, 1796, quoted in Alfred Lacroix, *Figures de savants,* 4 vols. (Paris, 1938), III, 113, translated in McClellan, *Colonialism and Science,* 286; Alexandre Giroud, "To the Society of the Friends of Humanity, Instituted at Philadelphia for the Abolition of Slavery, and the Improvement of the Condition of the Blacks," *The Time Piece; and Literary Companion,* July 19, 1797, 221. On the Société libre, see McClellan, *Colonialism and Science,* 4, 226–227, 302. On Raimond's conception of citizenship, see Laurent Dubois, *A Colony of Citizens: Revolution and Slave Emancipation in the French Caribbean, 1787–1804* (Chapel Hill, N.C., 2004), 184–187.

percent of the city's population. Trading on the institutional ties between the Cercle des Philadelphes and the American Philosophical Society, a number of these naturalists quickly integrated themselves into the intellectual life of their adopted port city. The society served as one institutional center from which they argued that the Haitian Revolution was a severe epistemological crisis, impeding the circulation of enlightened knowledge within the circumatlantic world.[5]

Giroud's letter also suggests that Jefferson's *Notes on the State of Virginia* (1787) became a prominent touchstone within this ideological contest. Giroud's correspondence on breadfruit can be understood as a response to Jefferson's call in Query XIV (on "Laws") for a natural history of black minds and bodies: "To our reproach it must be said, that though for a century and a half we have had under our eyes the races of black and of red men, they have never yet been viewed by us as subjects of natural history." The lack of empirical data did not prevent Jefferson from provisionally embracing an extreme theoretical position on racial inferiority, however diffident his phrasing:

> I advance it therefore as a suspicion only, that the blacks, whether originally a distinct race, or made distinct by time and circumstances, are inferior to the whites in the endowments both of body and mind. . . . Will not a lover of natural history then, one who views the gradations in all the races of animals with the eye of philosophy, excuse an effort to keep those in the department of man as distinct as nature has formed them?

During the years of the Haitian Revolution, lovers of natural history from throughout the hemisphere offered divergent answers.[6]

From its beginnings, *Notes on the State of Virginia* had always been a provisional and dialogic text. Written in response to a questionnaire circulated by François Marbois and in a polemic against the comte de Buffon and Abbé Raynal, its claims were challenged during subsequent decades by figures including the marquis de Chastellux, Benjamin Banneker, and, later, David Walker. In the 1790s, Caribbean interlocutors played a significant role in this dialogue because their writings placed pressure on the pub-

5. On Saint-Dominguan refugees to Philadelphia, see Ashli White, *Encountering Revolution: Haiti and the Making of the Early Republic* (Baltimore, 2010); Hunt, *Slumbering Volcano*. On the Cercle des Philadelphes, see McClellan, *Colonialism and Science*, 181–273.

6. Thomas Jefferson, *Notes on the State of Virginia*, ed. William Peden (1982; rpt. Chapel Hill, N.C., 1995), 143.

lished version of 1787, a text engaged in perhaps surprising ways (much like Crèvecoeur's *Letters* before it) in debates over the implications of West Indian commerce, slavery, and natural history for the future of enlightened republicanism.

For this reason, Jefferson began to revise his meditations on slavery from the published *Notes* in his personal correspondence during the early 1790s, as "intelligence" of the Haitian Revolution reached the early Republic. Over the next thirty years, in approximately a dozen letters on Saint-Domingue (later Haiti), Jefferson recast his published views on slave colonization and black intellectual capacity in Query XIV on "Laws" and his prediction of apocalyptic slave rebellion in Query XIX on "Manners." During the same period, he also continued to amass natural historical reports from informants throughout the Greater Caribbean for possible inclusion in an expanded edition of *Notes*. Jefferson's serial revisions of "Laws" and "Manners" in his personal correspondence are part of his effort to envision this updated edition, at a time when commentators from across the political spectrum and throughout the hemisphere appropriated and critiqued his published remarks on slavery for diverse ideological purposes. Jefferson's letters on Saint-Domingue and Haiti allow us to imagine a counterfactual text, an edition of *Notes* that would have assessed the implications of the Haitian Revolution for the idealized yeoman republic at the core of the published text of 1787. As literary critic Sibylle Fischer argues in her study of the "cultures of slavery" in Haiti, Cuba, and the Dominican Republic, "What happened in the Caribbean in the Age of Revolution was . . . a struggle over what it means to be modern, who can claim it, and on what grounds . . . over what would count as progress, what was meant by liberty, and how the two should relate." Jefferson's epistolary revisions of *Notes* during the 1790s and his rhetoric and practice of natural history in the period more broadly, occur in precisely this context of hemispheric ideological struggle over the meaning of modernity, liberty, and progress.[7]

---

7. Sibylle Fischer, *Modernity Disavowed: Haiti and the Cultures of Slavery in the Age of Revolution* (Durham, N.C., 2004), 24. For Jefferson's major epistolary revisions of "Laws" and "Manners," see Jefferson to marquis de Lafayette, June 16, 1792, Jefferson to James Monroe, July 14, 1793, Jefferson to St. George Tucker, Aug. 28, 1797, all in *PTJ*, XXIV, 85–86, XXVI, 501–503, XXIX, 519–520; Jefferson to Monroe, Nov. 24, 1801, June 2, 1802, Jefferson to Rufus King, July 13, 1802, Jefferson to John Lynch, Jan. 21, 1811, Jefferson to Edward Coles, Aug. 25, 1814, Jefferson to Jared Sparks, Feb. 4, 1824, Jefferson to Fanny Wright, Aug. 7, 1825, Jefferson to William Short, Jan. 18, 1826, all in *WTJ*, VIII, 103–106, 152–154, 161–162, IX, 303–304, 477–479, X, 289–293, 343, 361–362.

"Dilations Ending I Know Not Where"

Jefferson's most detailed clues about a revised edition occur in an 1813 letter to publisher John Melish. Jefferson appears to settle the question of whether an updated edition will ever materialize:

> You propose to me the preparation of a new edition of the Notes on Virginia. I formerly entertained the idea, and from time to time noted some new matter, which I thought I would arrange at leisure for a posthumous edition. But I now begin to see that it is impracticable for me. Nearly forty years of additional experience in the affairs of mankind would lead me into dilations ending I know not where. That experience indeed has not altered a single principle. But it has furnished matter of abundant development. Every moment too, which I have to spare from my daily exercise and affairs is engrossed by a correspondence, the results of the extensive relations which my course of life has necessarily occasioned. And now the act of writing itself is becoming slow, laborious and irksome. I consider, therefore, the idea of preparing a new copy of that work as no more to be entertained. The work itself indeed is nothing more than the measure of a shadow, never stationary, but lengthening as the sun advances, and to be taken anew from hour to hour. It must remain, therefore, for some other hand to sketch its appearance at another epoch, to furnish another element for calculating the course and motion of this member of our federal system.

Far more than a conventional expression of authorial humility, the passage articulates a theory of textuality and print. Through the concluding image of his text as a kind of solar clock—the momentary measure of a transient shadow—Jefferson argues that a new edition would be outdated almost at the instant of its publication. Because the issues of greatest import in *Notes* are subject to expansion and fluctuation (to "abundant development" as they "advance from hour to hour"), the printed book seems an inadequate medium.[8]

Jefferson concludes that future revisions must be entrusted to future generations, much like the U.S. Constitution. Earlier in the passage, however, he implies that his personal correspondence might provide an alternative

8. Jefferson to John Melish, Dec. 10, 1814, *WTJ*, III, 79–80.

medium for expanding the published original. Rather than undertake the quixotic task of compiling and publishing a second edition, he will instead devote himself to maintaining an ever-expanding network of correspondents. The multiplication of this network of "extensive relations" within the passage parallels and appears commensurate with the "dilation" and "development" of the material that any updated edition must contain. The passage indicates that correspondence might provide the necessary flexibility.

Correspondence did, indeed, provide a medium for revising *Notes*. Besides numerous letters in which Jefferson reworked passages from the 1787 edition, he also solicited natural historical reports from places including Cuba, Florida, lower Louisiana, and Darien. In 1797, he wrote to James Blake of his efforts to obtain a manuscript on the Isthmus of Darien: "My object was in some new edition of my Notes on Virginia to have said something on the subject of that Isthmus."[9]

Jefferson's letter to Melish connects the need for provisionality in any updated edition to the nation's geographic expansion. In describing a process of potentially limitless "dilation," the passage resonates strongly with some of Jefferson's best-known statements on the Louisiana Purchase. "Who can limit the extent to which the federative principle may operate effectively?" Jefferson asked in his second inaugural address, responding to Federalist criticisms of his expansionist agenda. The Mississippi Valley and Louisiana, as Jefferson predicted in a letter to the U.S. minister to France Robert Livingston in 1802, would soon encompass "three-eighths of our territory . . . and from its fertility it will ere long yield more than half of our whole produce and contain more than half our inhabitants," including significant numbers of gens de couleur libres and planters from Saint-Domingue in the commercial hub of New Orleans. Yet this was no reason to fear the fragmentation or degeneration of the Republic. Jefferson expressed similar sentiments in an 1823 letter to James Monroe on the annexation of Cuba, insisting that possession of the lucrative sugar colony would "fill up the measure of our political well-being." In instances such as these, he presents the incorporation of semitropical slave societies into the early Republic as potentially fulfilling his vision (first articulated in *Notes* in Query XX on "Manufactures") of an "empire of liberty" rooted in the virtue and industry of the yeoman farmer. Although the letter to Melish maintains that the "abundant development" of the nation's affairs since 1787 has not "altered a single

9. Jefferson to James Blake, Feb. 28, 1796, *PTJ*, XXVIII, 622.

principle" articulated in the original *Notes*, it also raises the possibility that the "dilation" of the Republic has intensified the ideological contradictions already embodied in his text.[10]

Jefferson's rhetorical posture in deferring the labor of a new edition suggests that the issue of slavery weighed heavily in his decision. As David Brion Davis has argued, tactics of deferral and delay were integral to Jefferson's characteristic locutions on abolition throughout his public life, from his "quietistic surrender to fate" after the vision of apocalyptic slave rebellion in *Notes* to the pose of senility and debility he would adopt during his "retirement" years. In the same year that he complained the labor of composing a new edition had grown too "slow, laborious and irksome" for a man of his advanced years, he protested in similar terms to Edward Coles that he was inadequate to the "arduous work" of forming a concrete plan for the emancipation and colonization of blacks currently residing in the United States, perhaps to Haiti. After referring to his early statements on colonization in *Notes*, Jefferson insists, "This enterprise is for the young; for those who can follow it up, and bear it through to its consummation. It shall have all my prayers, and these are the only weapons of an old man." During the same years that Jefferson avoided articulating a definitive policy on emancipation and colonization, he also demurred from publishing an edition touching on hemispheric matters.[11]

The letter to Melish allows us to infer the importance of circum-Caribbean concerns in Jefferson's decision to abandon the idea of a revised edition. Full comprehension of this decision, however, requires examination both of Jefferson's actual letters on Saint-Domingue and Haiti and of the published *Notes* itself.

Planter Enlightenment and the Problem of "Manners"

When Jefferson reluctantly agreed to publish *Notes* in Paris in 1787, he joined a growing chorus of colonial intellectuals defending plantation societies throughout the Americas against the comte de Buffon's thesis of New World degeneracy. Owing to the influence of an excessively humid climate, Buffon theorized, the flora and fauna of the Americas was not only less

---

10. Jefferson, "Second Inaugural Address," Mar. 4, 1805, *WTJ*, VIII, 344; Jefferson to Robert R. Livingston, Apr. 18, 1802, ibid., 144; Jefferson to Monroe, Oct. 24, 1823, ibid., X, 278.

11. David Brion Davis, *The Problem of Slavery in the Age of Revolution, 1770–1823* (1975; rpt. Ithaca, N.Y., 1999), 176; Jefferson to Coles, Aug. 25, 1814, *WTJ*, IX, 479.

various and abundant than in Europe but also in a state of gradual decline, with plants, animals, and human beings (including white creoles) growing smaller and less fertile with each generation. Though receiving scant attention in Antonello Gerbi's survey of the Buffon controversy, many of Buffon's most vocal antagonists were based in the Caribbean. These included Edward Long (whose *History of Jamaica* appeared in 1774), Moreau de Saint-Méry (who was hard at work on his *Description topographique ... de la partie française de l'isle Saint-Domingue* [1797] and had begun to circulate his researches on climate and law among Parisian intellectuals), and Bryan Edwards (who had been a member of the American Philosophical Society since 1780 and would publish *The History, Civil and Commercial, of the British Colonies in the West Indies* in 1793). These prominent thinkers were, among other things, accomplished natural historians. With what Davis describes as their "passion for measurement and for specific information on geography, meteorology, ethnology, and political economy," and with their acute observations on the physical and social constitution of particular New World colonies, their published writings bore a strong resemblance to *Notes*. At the moment of publication, Jefferson's treatise was not exclusively, or perhaps even primarily, a protonational text, part of a broader movement to extol the natural abundance of North America as the basis for a rising republic. By joining the polemic against Buffon, Jefferson also contributed to a "planter Enlightenment," no simple matter for a self-styled radical republican.[12]

A clearer sense of this context is provided by a survey of the Buffon controversy as it unfolded in France, Saint-Domingue, and the early Republic. Buffon developed his theory of New World degeneracy in a period marked by the rise of the French sugar planters, as Saint-Domingue came to provide 50 percent of the world's sugar and 40 percent of its coffee. In this new economic climate, French Enlightenment thinkers assessed the impact of the Caribbean environment on metropolitan economy and society.

12. On Moreau's response to Buffon, see Doris Garraway, *The Libertine Colony: Creolization in the Early French Caribbean* (Durham, N.C., 2005), 261, 267–268. On Long's response, see Roxann Wheeler, *The Complexion of Race: Categories of Difference in Eighteenth-Century British Culture* (Philadelphia, 2000), 209–233. On Edwards's response, see Olwyn M. Blouet, "Bryan Edwards and the Haitian Revolution," in David P. Geggus, ed., *The Impact of the Haitian Revolution in the Atlantic World* (Columbia, S.C., 2001), 44–57. For a consideration of *Notes* in the context of these Caribbean writings, see Davis, *Problem of Slavery*, 164–212 (quotation on 188–189). On the Buffon controversy, see Antonello Gerbi, *The Dispute of the New World: The History of a Polemic, 1750–1900*, trans. Jeremy Moyle (Pittsburgh, 1973). For an influential consideration of *Notes* in the context of the Buffon thesis, see Myra Jehlen, *American Incarnation: The Individual, the Nation, and the Continent* (Cambridge, Mass., 1986), 44–59.

Works by Raynal, Denis Diderot, and Georges Cuvier drew on prior natural history volumes by Jean-Baptiste Du Tertre, Le Per de Charlevoix, Charles Plumier, and Charles Rochefort, even as Louis XVI funded the creation of royal botanical gardens in Saint-Domingue and elsewhere. Much as in the British Atlantic, although the Caribbean environment was viewed as source of imperial prosperity, it was also understood as a cause of imminent decline. Buffon's theory lent new analytical rigor and theoretical scope to such notions. Discussions of racial specimens from Africa and the New World are significant to his theory. Through observations of "pied négresse[s]" and "white negroes," Buffon conjectures that Africans originally possessed white complexions and caucasian features but degenerated physically because of the tropical climate. Through an "accident" or "trick of nature," however, individuals such as the albino Dominican Genevieve had reverted to their "primitive color." Colin Dayan argues that such depictions expressed anxieties regarding the stability of racial identity in a colonial society where miscegenation was the rule. Buffon distinguished the physiology of "monstrous" specimens such as Genevieve from the characteristics of true whiteness. In so doing, however, he also questioned the racial identity of the creole elite. White and "pied negresse[s]" support his hypothesis that white creoles had also undergone something like a racial transformation, especially if they "adopted the manners, and used the food of the new country."[13]

By presenting the West Indian creole as a curious object of scrutiny, Buffon's theory of degeneracy gave new authority to the transoceanic system of knowledge production that Ralph Bauer calls "epistemic mercantilism." At a moment when the new wealth of the planters challenged the political and economic power of Paris, Buffon appeared to confirm beliefs that the creole planter could play only a circumscribed role within the republic of science and letters. His theory thus inspired a vigorous creole response. In the early 1780s, the Cercle des Philadelphes began soliciting empirical accounts of creole manners and physiology as part of their effort to refute the Buffon thesis. The 1784 prospectus for the Cercle announced, "We would like philosophical observations on the constitution and habits of people born in the colony [and] on the changes in temperament and in physical and moral constitution experienced by Europeans." By collecting this evidence, the Cercle

---

13. McClellan, *Colonialism and Science*, 112, 151–152, 155; Drayton, *Nature's Government*, 234–235; Joan [Colin] Dayan, *Haiti, History, and the Gods* (Berkeley, Calif., 1998), 238–241; George Louis Leclerc, comte de Buffon, *Natural History, General and Particular*, trans. William Smellie, 8 vols. (London, 1781), III, 164–165.

attempted to transform the white creole planter into an authoritative subject of natural history. The productions of their creole intellects testified that enlightenment could flourish in West Indian soil. In distributing materials from the Cercle to officials in Paris, the military administrator Cesar-Henri La Luzerne made such ambitions explicit: "I find it very interesting that this colony could study itself, that it would develop the ambition, and that enlightenment gathered here could be communicated to metropolitan France and all peoples."[14]

North American intellectuals were acutely conscious of these Caribbean dimensions of the Buffon controversy. As discussed in Chapter 4, Benjamin Franklin alluded to the new theory of degeneracy in his 1786 letter to Cercle founder Charles Arthaud, celebrating his attention to "the Improvement of Science . . . in a Country where the Climate was suppos'd naturally to occasion indolence." In so doing, Franklin refined a hemispheric cultural geography that had emerged as early as John Bartram's correspondence with J. Slingsby Cressy and William Byrd II's with Hans Sloane (see Chapter 2). By the 1780s, these cultural assumptions about the West Indies also had less flattering implications for mainland intellectuals. Responding to Jefferson's request for additional information on the question of North American humidity, Samuel Vaughan argued that most "European philosophers" formed erroneous impressions on the subject because they misapplied natural historical reports "from the cultivated parts of the West Indies (a supposed appendage of the part of America in question)." This perception of North America as an "appendage" of the Caribbean had a long and influential genealogy, dating at least from the publication of Mark Catesby's *Natural History of Carolina.*[15]

Recovering the circumatlantic contexts of the Buffon controversy illuminates Jefferson's remarks on slavery in *Notes.* As a number of critics have observed, the issue of slavery proved difficult to resolve within the structural and rhetorical framework of the treatise. Robert Ferguson argues that, whereas other major topics are considered within a single query, the examination of slavery constitutes "a structural incongruity in *Notes* spilling

14. Ralph Bauer, *The Cultural Geography of Colonial American Literatures: Empire, Travel, Modernity* (New York, 2003), 4; *Prospectus du Cercle des Philadelphes* (Cap Français, 1784), trans. in McClellan, *Colonialism and Science,* 209; Henri La Luzerne to Charles Arthaud, "Du 30 7bre 1787," "Correspondance du Cercle des Philadelphes depuis son établissement," letter 28, fol. 193v, Archives nationales, Paris, trans. in McClellan, *Colonialism and Science,* 238.

15. Benjamin Franklin to Arthaud, July 9, 1786, Manuscript Division, Library of Congress, Washington, D.C.; Benjamin Vaughan to Jefferson, Jan. 26, 1787, *PTJ,* XI, 72.

between and among sections." Moreover, Jefferson's rhetoric in the query on "Manners," containing his prophecy of a slave revolution assisted by the "supernatural interference" of a just god, challenges the text's governing logic. After "Manners," the final queries become "more haphazard organizationally." Betsy Erkkila understands that prophecy in similar terms as "a supreme moment of cultural recognition—a moment that registers the force of racial and ideological contradiction as formal rupture and narrative break." Though such analyses have clarified the formal contours of *Notes*, they assume that moments of incoherence and rupture derive from the practice of slaveholding within the early Republic's borders. Considered in its broader dimensions, slavery transgresses the formal boundaries of *Notes* ("spilling between and among sections") because it raises questions about the position of the early Republic within the plantation Americas and the triangle trade. The institution of slavery—so dependent on the circulation of bodies, luxury goods, and forms of knowledge across geographic and political boundaries—violates the text's philosophical premise. Jefferson arranged his treatise according to the Physiocratic principle that a society's political and legal systems must be harmonious with its climate. Shuffling the order of Marbois's queries so that his remarks on the natural history of Virginia would precede his meditations on civil affairs, Jefferson grounded his prospect of American republicanism in the physical constitution of Virginia.[16]

Powerful as it was, the vision sequestered some difficult realities. Dependent on West Indian trade, the early Republic was in jeopardy during the 1780s, as a cycle of slave revolts tore through the islands and European powers maintained embargoes against U.S. commerce in the region. As Jefferson wrote in a letter to James Monroe in 1785, while he was preparing *Notes* for publication, "Access to the West Indies is indispensably necessary to us." And, as he mentioned in his 1793 letter to Edmond Genêt, the West Indies' "condition must always be interesting to the US. with whom nature has connected them by the strong link of mutual necessities." Jefferson's published text advances a far different conception of American nature as it attempts to repudiate the need for West Indian affiliation. Yet this disavowal

---

16. Robert A. Ferguson, "'Mysterious Obligation': Jefferson's *Notes on the State of Virginia,*" *American Literature*, LII (1980), 381–406 (quotations on 399, 401); Betsy Erkkila, *Mixed Bloods and Other Crosses: Rethinking American Literature from the Revolution to the Culture Wars* (Philadelphia, 2005), 50. For studies of Jefferson that do attend to the transnational dimensions of his writings on slavery and colonization, see Peter Onuf, "'To Declare Them a Free and Independent People': Race, Slavery, and National Identity in Jefferson's Thought," *Journal of the Early Republic,* XVIII (1998), 1–46; David Kazanjian, *The Colonizing Trick: National Culture and Imperial Citizenship in Early America* (Minneapolis, 2003), 89–138.

cannot be sustained. The formal problems associated with the question of slavery in the text, as we will see below, constitute an oblique recognition of the region's vital role in sustaining the early Republic.[17]

Problems of boundary and scale beset the text from its opening pages. Demarcating the western border of Virginia in Query I, the narrator descends the Missouri and Mississippi rivers, arriving in places as far-flung as Spanish New Orleans and Mexico City. Similar problems resurface in Query VI on "Productions Mineral, Vegetable, and Animal," where Jefferson levels his first direct blow against the Buffon thesis, arguing that Virginia supports a greater variety of flora and fauna than Europe and is home to individual species far larger than any found in the Old World. Of fish and insects in Virginia, Jefferson observes, "Many are also to be found in Sir Hans Sloane's Jamaica, as being common to that and this country." On avian diversity, he notes, "Between ninety and an hundred of our birds have been described by Catesby" in the *Natural History of Carolina,* acknowledged as the source of Jefferson's ornithological chart on the following page. However unintended the effect, by referring the reader to these published natural histories, Jefferson situates Virginia within their influential geographic frame, not at the center of the emergent nation, but rather at the northern limit of the plantation Americas, as a kind of "appendage" of the West Indies.[18]

While West Indian specimens inhabit the opening sections of the text, West Indian voices contribute in contradictory ways to the discussion of "Laws" in Query XIV. Jefferson there proposes to colonize emancipated slaves to some unspecified location outside the nation's borders, forestalling an otherwise certain future of miscegenation, moral corruption, and racial violence. He rationalizes that proposal through his natural history of black minds and bodies. As noted previously, Jefferson complains that, at least among Virginians, "the races of black and of red men . . . have never yet been viewed by us as subjects of natural history." In formulating his own conjectural views on black physiology and intellectual capacity, he turns to Long's *History of Jamaica.* The majority of his "evidence" for the innate racial inferiority of New World blacks is derived more or less directly from Long, including his discussion of the "reticular membrane" as the permanent location of black skin color, his observations on black perspiration,

17. Jefferson to Monroe, June 17, 1785, *WTJ,* IV, 58; Jefferson to Edmond Charles Genêt, Nov. 24, 1793, *PTJ,* XXVII, 429.

18. Jefferson, *Notes,* ed. Peden, 65, 71.

body odor, and tolerance for heat, his claim that orangutans are attracted sexually to African women, and his consideration of writings by African American and Afro-British authors such as Phyllis Wheatley and Ignatius Sancho as specimens of black intellectual capacity. In 1787, such assertions were part of a controversial theory of racial difference, identified with the work of a particular West Indian author. On one hand, "Laws" seeks to remove Virginia from the corrupting influence of plantation slavery, whereas, on the other, it depends on the routine traffic in scientific "knowledge" between Jamaica and Monticello.[19]

This stark contradiction helps explain why the problem of slavery returns in "Manners." As Erkkila argues, Jefferson's prophecy of slave revolt catapults the text from a prior conceptual sphere of rationality and natural law into "a magical realm of unpredictability, unreason and the unknown." The intensity of Jefferson's rhetoric is striking, and the suddenness of his recourse to the supernatural cannot but surprise: "Indeed I tremble for my country when I reflect that God is just: that his justice cannot sleep for ever: that considering numbers, nature and natural means only, a revolution of the wheel of fortune, an exchange of situation, is among possible events: that it may become probable by supernatural interference!" This moment of epistemological and discursive rupture, however, becomes more legible when placed in the unfolding drama of the query, where Jefferson must judge "the manners of his own nation, familiarized to him by habit." As we have seen in Chapter 4, the manners and customs sketch had long posed special problems for creole naturalists of the Torrid Zone, who served as both subject and object of ethnological inquiry.[20]

Jefferson confronts this long-standing dilemma as he seeks to account for certain "odious peculiarities" in the moral character of the Virginian planter, which he attributes at first to the peculiar nature of slaveholding as a legal practice and social institution: "The whole commerce between master and slave is a perpetual exercise of the most boisterous passions, the most unremitting despotism on the one part, and degrading submissions on the other. . . . The man must be a prodigy who can retain his manners and morals undepraved in such circumstances." In a surprising turn of thought, however, Jefferson then links the moral depravity of the planter class to the influence of climate. "In a warm climate, no man will labour for himself who

19. Ibid., 143; [Edward Long], *The History of Jamaica; or, General Survey of the Antient and Modern State of That Island* . . . , 3 vols. (London, 1774), II, 351–364.
20. Jefferson, *Notes*, ed. Peden, 162; Erkkila, *Mixed Bloods*, 50.

can make another labour for him." This quasi-deterministic view of the relationship between climate and social organization, and thus of its indirect
influence on creole manners, is disconcerting in a text that has taken such
pains to contest Buffon. But such complications only increase in subsequent
passages. By virtue of his social position as a creole planter-naturalist, as
we have seen, Jefferson is of necessity both subject and object of his analysis of the relationship between plantation culture, moral corruption, and
climate. Thus the discursive and cognitive transformation within the query
takes on new meaning. The manners of the naturalist take center stage.
Having displayed his own "boisterous passions" through the apocalyptic
imagery, Jefferson descends to a lethargic conclusion, marked by a denial of
his capacity for rational contemplation, natural historical or otherwise: "It
is impossible to be temperate and to pursue this subject through the various
considerations of policy, of morals, of history natural and civil." Though he
supports emancipation in principle, he declines to advocate its implemen-
tation as a concrete policy: "We must be contented to hope they will force
their way into every one's mind. . . . The spirit of the master is abating, that
of the slave rising from the dust, his condition mollifying, the way I hope
preparing, under the auspices of heaven, for a total emancipation, and that
this is disposed, in the order of events, to be with the consent of the masters, rather than by their extirpation." With its multiple passive verbs and
obscure grammatical subject, the style and syntax of the passage attests
that, although emancipation may come with the consent of this planter, it
will not come through his action.[21]

When considered within a long history of colonial autoethnology, Jefferson's narrator displays some of the main traits of creole moral degeneracy
as defined by Abbé Raynal's *Philosophical and Political History of the Settlements and Trade of the Europeans in the East and West Indies*, one of the
specific texts targeted by Jefferson in his critique of the Buffon thesis in
Query VI. Jefferson there asserted (inaccurately) that Raynal was the first
to apply Buffon's ideas to "the race of whites, transplanted from Europe."
As he undoubtedly knew, however, Raynal's most extensive comments on
creole degeneracy occur, not in his remarks on North America, but in his
analysis of the West Indies. Though he does not himself subscribe to Buffon's theory of physiological transformation owing to climate, Raynal con-
cedes that, because a hot climate makes plantation slavery profitable, it contributes to a kind of moral degeneracy, with symptoms including excessive

21. Ibid., 162–163.

234 NOTES ON THE STATE OF VIRGINIA

passion, sensuousness, and indolence. Much like Jefferson, he describes the violent abuse of enslaved blacks by planters, the arrogance instilled in creole children attended constantly by slaves, and the lethargy induced by excess consumption in a hot climate. And he indicts the creole for a "warm imagination, incapable of any restraint." This excess of imagination makes Raynal's West Indian susceptible to supernatural belief and incapable of sustained rational thought. This incapacity, moreover, is one reason that Raynal holds little hope that creole planters will undertake the reforms necessary to avoid an otherwise certain future of slave revolution, a prediction that points to another intertextual connection between the *History* and *Notes.* Whatever his avowed antagonism toward Raynal, Jefferson found an important model for the apocalyptic rhetoric of "Manners" in the *History's* widely circulated call for a "Black Spartacus" capable of avenging the crime of slavery.[22]

We might explain Jefferson's repudiation of agency at the conclusion of "Manners" in a number of ways. We could note that Jefferson's prestige within a circumatlantic republic of letters depended on his image as a radical republican, and thus on his nominal support for abolition, whereas his domestic political standing depended on the support of a powerful planter constituency. The complex rhetorical posture of "Manners" provides a deft solution to the problem of how to oppose slavery in principle without challenging the interests of his slaveholding class. Whatever its motivations, however, what is notable here is the effect of this narrative rupture. The specter of West Indian degeneracy begins to haunt the treatise at precisely this moment, with the text thereafter descending into a state of formal incoherence. Even Ferguson, so adept at discerning the structural logic of the treatise, concludes that the final sections are "more haphazard organizationally." What he neglects to observe, however, is that these sections pay increased attention to transnational commerce. Query XX on "Subjects of Commerce" laments that, because the use of imported goods such as coffee and sugar has grown habitual, "we must go for them to those countries which are able to furnish them." Hard on the heels of "Manners," Jefferson situates the early Republic within a commercial network that radiates outward from the sugar mill. His explicit hope is that the rise of a new class of virtuous yeoman farmers, famously envisioned in the previous query

---

22. Ibid., 64; Abbé [Guillaume-Thomas François] Raynal, *A Philosophical and Political History of the Settlements and Trade of the Europeans in the East and West Indies* (1798), trans. J. O. Justamond, 6 vols. (New York, 1969), IV, 152–159.

on "Manufactures" as "the chosen people of God, if ever he had a chosen people," might diminish the danger of cultural corruption. Simplicity of manners all but defines the yeoman, in Jefferson's conception as in Crève-coeur's. But, in another sense, the rise of the yeomanry would only create additional opportunities for corrupting intercourse. As Jefferson acknowl-edged in his contemporaneous letters to Genêt and Monroe ("Access to the West Indies is indispensably necessary to us"), the Caribbean would con-tinue to provide an essential market for the staple foods cultivated by the yeomanry.[23]

The degenerate West Indian haunts the pages of "Manners" because they address an irresolvable state of affairs. Whatever imaginative or theoretical solution Jefferson proposed for the problem of mainland slavery, the new nation would remain deeply implicated within a global plantation econ-omy. The rhetorical strategies of "Manners" convey Jefferson's sense that he is powerless to extricate the emergent nation from a far-flung system of slave-driven commerce, at once a fatal corruption of the Republic and its necessary condition. This is why Jefferson would revise the query in his per-sonal correspondence with near-compulsive regularity over the next thirty-five years, as part of his effort to recast his thoughts on slavery in a period marked by the rise of abolitionist movements in the Atlantic world and slave revolution in Saint-Domingue.

Notes on the State of Sugar Maple and Mountain Rice

One of Jefferson's most cherished botanical projects of the late 1780s and early 1790s addressed the problem of West Indian dependence. By culti-

23. Ferguson, "Mysterious Obligation," *American Literature*, LII (1980), 399; Jefferson, *Notes*, ed. Peden, 165, 169. On the importance of trade between North America and the British Caribbean in the late-colonial period, see Andrew Jackson O'Shaughnessy, *An Empire Divided: The American Revolution and the British Caribbean* (Philadelphia, 2000), 69–76; John J. McCusker and Russell R. Menard, *The Economy of British America, 1607–1789* (Chapel Hill, N.C., 1985), 144–146. Concerns regarding Carib-bean exchange were prominent in Jefferson's diplomatic correspondence of the mid-1780s, the very years when the first editions of *Notes* began to appear. Jefferson is normally understood to have envisioned a far different political economy for the early Republic than his rival Alexander Hamilton. Whereas Hamilton worked tirelessly to create what Sean X. Goudie calls a hemispheric "Empire of Commerce," based on un-fettered access to the lucrative markets of the West Indies, Jefferson advocated a continental "Empire of Liberty" based on the agricultural labors of independent yeomen. It is important to stress, however, that Jefferson's correspondence throughout the 1780s emphasizes the importance of West India trade to the economy of the new nation. Focusing on the rhetorical contrast between Jefferson and Hamilton (at least in their published writings), Goudie overstates the distinction between their practical approaches to hemi-spheric political economy in the late eighteenth century. See Sean X. Goudie, *Creole America: The West Indies and the Formation of Literature and Culture in the New Republic* (Philadelphia, 2006), 64–110.

vating the sugar maple as a future source for domestic sugar consumption, Jefferson hoped to ensure that, even if the citizens of the early Republic failed to curb their appetites for tropical comestibles, they would no longer be compelled "[to] go for them those to countries which are able to furnish them." The scheme also counted William Cooper, Tench Coxe, and Benjamin Rush among its supporters and was discussed in *American Museum* and in the American Philosophical Society *Transactions*. In a 1791 letter to fellow planter and naturalist Thomas Mann Randolph, Jr., Jefferson speculated "that the U.S. may not only supply themselves the sugar for their own consumption but be great exporters." The same day, Jefferson sent similar letters to William Drayton and George Washington, who planted sugar maple trees at Mount Vernon the next year. Jefferson's enthusiasm for maple sugar reflects his desire to make the West Indies less "indispensably necessary" to the nation's economic prospects.[24]

The project also burnished Jefferson's abolitionist credentials. Like Benjamin Rush, he proposed that maple sugar could render the slave trade obsolete. Writing to the Jamaica-born intellectual Benjamin Vaughan in 1790, he concluded, "What a blessing to substitute a sugar which requires only the labour of children, for that which it is said renders the slavery of the blacks necessary." Although the narrator of "Manners" denied his ability to address the problem of slavery, by promoting sugar maple, Jefferson could reclaim a measure of yeoman independence while obscuring the degree to which "the slavery of the blacks" was made necessary by Virginia tobacco and Carolina rice. As declared by the author of a 1790 pamphlet entitled *Remarks on the Manufacture of Maple Sugar: With Directions for Its Further Improvement*, "He who enables another to obtain any necessary of life, either cheaper or more independently than heretofore, adds a new source of happiness to man; and becomes more or less useful, in proportion to the number of those who participate in the benefits of his discovery." In the eyes of Benjamin Rush, Jefferson's efforts made him an exemplary yeoman philosopher. In a letter to Jefferson republished in the American Philosophical Society's *Transactions*, Rush described a new orchard of sugar maples at Monticello, where Jefferson consumed "no other sugar in his family than that which is obtained from the sugar maple tree."[25]

24. "On Maple Sugar," *American Museum*, VII (1790), 303–304; "American Maple Sugar, and Melasses," ibid., VI (1789), 209–210; Jefferson to William Drayton, May 1, 1791, Jefferson to Thomas Mann Randolph, Jr., May 1, 1791, Jefferson to George Washington, May 1, 1791, all in *PTJ*, XX, 332–333, 341, 342–343.

25. Jefferson to Benjamin Vaughan, June 27, 1790, *PTJ*, XVI, 579; *Remarks on the Manufacture of*

This interest in the sugar maple was prompted by abolitionist writings that exposed the origins of West Indian comestibles in plantation violence. The narrator of William Cowper's popular poem "The Negro's Complaint" (1788) asks:

Why did all-creating nature
Make the plant, for which we toil?
Sighs must fan it, tears must water,
Sweat of ours must dress the soil.

The lines contest an idealized vision of the islands as source of a spontaneously generated superabundance. "All creating Nature" might have made the sugarcane, but its propagation required a brutal system of forced labor.[26]

Even as this antislavery discourse on Caribbean nature gained momentum, however, planter-naturalists defended their status within imperial politics and economics. During the same period when Saint-Dominguan planters founded the Cercle des Philadelphes, British planters also turned to natural history with renewed vigor. As Richard Drayton observes, though still an influential lobby in the decade after the American Revolution, the plantocracy nonetheless "faced a crisis of demand as well as supply." Owing to mercantilist restrictions on trade with the early Republic, the islands lost a crucial source of plantation supplies, including foodstuffs. Planter resentment grew as the British government rejected numerous requests for a suspension of the Navigation Acts, even as William Pitt bent a receptive ear to opponents of the slave trade. At the same time, British planters struggled to compete with the cheap, high quality sugar and coffee exported from Saint-Domingue and other French islands.[27]

Imperial officials moved to quiet planter resentments through a commitment to economic botany, financing projects with natural history societies throughout the islands. Up to that time, such societies had relied almost exclusively on creole initiative and funding. The formation of two botanical

---

Maple Sugar: With Directions for Its Further Improvement (Philadelphia, 1790), quoted in *PTJ*, XX, 344; Benjamin Rush to Jefferson, American Philosophical Society, *Transactions*, III (1793), 64–79.

26. William Cowper, "The Negro's Complaint," in John D. Baird and Charles Ryskamp, eds., *The Poems of William Cowper*, III, *1785–1800* (Oxford, 1995), 95–97. For a more extended analysis of the poem in the context of the poetics of antislavery, see Philip Gould, *Barbaric Traffic: Commerce and Antislavery in the Eighteenth-Century Atlantic World* (Cambridge, Mass., 2003), 71–73, 76, 77. On the critique of sugar consumption as an important aspect of British literary culture in the period, see Charlotte Sussman, *Consuming Anxieties: Consumer Protest, Gender, and British Slavery, 1713–1833* (Stanford, Calif., 2000).

27. Drayton, *Nature's Government*, 113

gardens by Jamaican planters in 1775 had been followed by the formation of the Society for the Encouragement of Natural History and of Useful Arts on Barbados in 1784 and the Physico-Medical Society on Grenada in 1791. The founders of these institutions began to see the introduction of Asian plants into the West Indies, and their acclimatization in well-funded botanical gardens, as a potential solution to chronic food shortages. They expressed particular interest in breadfruit. In response to such demands, metropolitan botanist Joseph Banks helped organize the voyages of William Bligh to the East Indies in 1787 and 1791–1793, seeking to transplant new food and cash crops to the botanical gardens of Jamaica and Saint Vincent. As Richard Drayton argues, such efforts amounted to "public gestures of solidarity with the West India interest. Economic botany had become a means of showing the benevolent interest of the 'mother country.'"[28]

The home nation also meant to demonstrate its benevolence toward enslaved blacks. Organizing a series of botanical transshipments, British officials implemented a new conception of colonial empire as the enlightened management of the natural world in the service of maximum human happiness. So, too, did prominent West Indian figures such as Bryan Edwards. Responding to the challenges of the abolitionist press, proslavery writers like Edwards returned to the same natural historical discourse that poems like "The Negro's Complaint" had appropriated. The botanical enthusiasms of creole elites like Hinton Este (owner of one of the Jamaican gardens to which Banks had shipped seeds from the Bligh expedition) were integral to the design of the *History, Civil and Commercial, of the British Colonies in the West Indies.* By collecting seeds from throughout Britain's global empire and transplanting them to the Caribbean, Edwards contended, Este had created a symbol not only of British mercantile and botanical mastery but also of his own benevolence and patriotism. To publicize this achievement, Edwards concluded the first volume of his history with a catalog of Este's garden, turning, as Richard Drayton puts it, "the botanic initiatives of his fellow planters into an emblem for the enlightened cast of their administration."[29]

That these sentiments were voiced in North American periodicals highlights the place of the Caribbean within the culture of natural history in the early Republic. Though distinctions between temperate continent and degenerate sugar islands had become familiar by the mid-1790s, favorable

28. Ibid., 115.
29. Ibid.

reviews of and excerpts from Edwards's text appeared in periodicals including the *American Monthly Review* and the *New York Magazine*. An anonymous contributer to the *American Monthly Review* claimed, "A history of the islands that so abundantly contribute, by their rich, and we had almost said invaluable, produce, to our national grandeur and opulence, must be a subject highly interesting to almost every class of readers." The writer praised Edwards for "displaying the blended knowledge of the naturalist, the politician, and the merchant" and provided a series of "specimens" from book 1 of the *History* on geography and natural history, concluding, "Nature has stocked these happy islands with every luxury that an epicure can desire: but she has principally exerted her power in the vegetable world, where the most luscious fruits spontaneously spring up, the juicy pulp of which at once delights and regales the parched inhabitant of the tropic."[30]

This context illuminates Jefferson's own practice of botany in the late 1780s and early 1790s. On the surface, Jefferson's efforts to cultivate a species of mountain rice appear to be motivated by his benevolent interest in the lives of enslaved blacks. His 1791 letter to William Drayton expressed the hope that mountain rice "may be a complete substitute for the pestiferous culture of the wet rice" in plantation societies including South Carolina. As he had written a year earlier, the transition to mountain rice would spare enslaved blacks in Carolina the labor of clearing and flooding lowcountry lands and thus remove the threat of yellow fever. It is ironic that Jefferson had received his first seeds of mountain rice from Samuel Vaughan, Jr., in St. James, Jamaica. Son of Benjamin Vaughan, Samuel had established temporary residence on the island to manage his family's properties. Like his grandfather Samuel, who had been vice president of the American Philosophical Society, the younger Vaughan took a keen interest in botany and natural history. His 1790 letter to Jefferson included a copy of a pamphlet entitled *The Objects and Rules of the Saint James's Mountain Club,* describing an "Agriculture Society just formed in the Mountains of this Parish." As part of the British Empire's renewed commitment to economic botany, Vaughan and the other members of the Mountain Club had received two hundred seeds of mountain rice from Sir Joseph Banks, then in the midst of disseminating plants brought back by Bligh from the East Indies.[31]

30. *American Monthly Review,* I (1795), 1–16; "Some Account of the Trees, Birds, etc. of the West-Indies," *New York Magazine,* I (1796), 198–200.

31. Jefferson to Drayton, May 1, 1791, *PTJ,* XX, 332–333; Samuel Vaughan, Jr., to Jefferson, Oct. 4, 1790, *PTJ,* XVII, 564–565.

By corresponding and exchanging seeds with Vaughan, in letters suffused with the language of candid friendship, Jefferson allied himself with his fellow planters in the West Indies. Asking Jefferson for any seeds he might cultivate in the Blue Mountains of Jamaica, Vaughan informs him, "I have often regretted that no Opportunity has given me the power of encreasing by a personal intercourse the pleasure and improvement I have derived from the Information you have given to the World" in *Notes on the State of Virginia*. In his reply, Jefferson sends Vaughan the seeds of a potato-pumpkin "of the Melon species," though he suspects that the species might be a native of the sugar islands. Because the plant is "well esteemed at our tables, and particularly valued by our negroes," he hopes it might "add to the catalogue of plants which will do as substitutes for bread." He continues, "I have always thought that if in the experiments to introduce or to communicate new plants, one species in an hundred is found useful and succeeds, the ninety nine found otherwise are more than paid for." In an earlier letter to Benjamin Vaughan on mountain rice, he expressed his plan "to write to Mr. Hinton Este of Jamaica on the subject." Jefferson sought guidance from the owner of the botanical garden celebrated by Edwards as an emblem for an enlightened plantocracy.[32]

Whereas Jefferson's promotion of sugar maple invoked the imaginative ideal of yeoman independence from the sugar islands, his interests in mountain rice and breadfruit depended on the forging and maintenance of connections with curious planters in the West Indies. In his practice of natural history in the late 1780s and early 1790s, Jefferson embodied the same contradictory conception of creole identity that had informed the original *Notes,* laboring to insulate the early Republic from hemispheric slavery (at least rhetorically) and to incorporate West Indian planters within a republic of science and letters imagined in hemispheric terms.

The Natural History of the Haitian Revolution

This posture became more difficult to maintain after the outbreak of the Haitian Revolution in 1791. Winthrop Jordan has summarized the ideological bind the revolution created for avowed republicans such as Jefferson.

---

32. Jefferson to Benjamin Vaughan, June 27, 1790, Samuel Vaughan, Jr., to Jefferson, Oct. 4, 1790, Jefferson to Samuel Vaughan, Jr., Nov. 27, 1790, all in *PTJ,* XVI, 578–580, XVII, 564–565, XVIII, 97–98. On the language of candid friendship in Atlantic correspondence networks, see Susan Scott Parrish, *American Curiosity: Cultures of Natural History in the Colonial British Atlantic World* (Chapel Hill, N.C., 2006), 136–173.

Whatever his personal horror at the prospect of black political autonomy at the heart of the sugar economy, Jefferson knew that "denial of the universal applicability of natural rights would have deprived their [American] Revolution of its broader meaning and of its claim upon the attention of the world." His revisions of "Manners" in response to this ideological conundrum begins with a June 1792 letter to the marquis de Lafayette. Despite the isolationist desires voiced in contemporaneous letters on the sugar maple, the letter to Lafayette reveals Jefferson's hope that recent unrest on Saint-Domingue might ease commercial access to the colony. For at least one of his correspondents, events on the island created an opportunity for political incorporation with Saint-Domingue. Before taking up temporary residence in Saint-Domingue, diplomat Nathaniel Cutting wrote excitedly to Jefferson that the colony "at some future period may possibly fall within the Jurisdiction of the Thirteen United States!"[33]

Jefferson grounds his argument for free trade in the hemisphere on the authority of natural history:

> What are you doing for your colonies? They will be lost if not more effectually succoured. Indeed no future efforts you can make will ever be able to reduce the blacks. All that can be done in my opinion will be to compound with them as has been done formerly in Jamaica. We have been less zealous in aiding them, lest your government should feel any jealousy on our account. But in truth we as sincerely wish their restoration, and their connection with you, as you do yourselves. We are satisfied that neither your justice nor their distresses will ever again permit their being forced to seek at dear and distant markets those first necessaries of life which they may have at cheaper markets placed by nature at their door, and formed by her for their support.

The letter depicts French imperial policy as opposed to the laws of nature and nature's God. Whereas "Manners" had asserted that "natural means only" (including the demographic dominance of the enslaved) made a "revolution of the wheel of fortune" in the plantation Americas probable, the letter to Lafayette claims that attempts to suppress the uprising on Saint-Domingue will prove futile. To avoid an apocalyptic race war, France must follow the example of Governor Trelawney in Jamaica, who had recognized the sovereignty of Maroon societies in the 1770s. The passage then shifts its

33. Winthrop D. Jordan, *White over Black: American Attitudes toward the Negro, 1550–1812* (Chapel Hill, N.C., 1968), 386–387; Nathaniel Cutting to Jefferson, Apr. 19, 1791, *PTJ*, XX, 240.

attention (without comment) from slave rebellion and maroonage to white creole rebellion against the exclusif. The justice of this second rebellion, in Jefferson's view, is made plain by the facts of New World geography and climate ("placed by nature at their door, and formed by her for their support"). As he had in the early 1790s, Jefferson maintains that nature has connected the United States and Saint-Domingue "by the strong link of mutual necessity."[34]

The letter appears to give slave rebellion a role in the expansion of republican liberty. Yet, by conflating white creole resistance against the exclusif with free colored and enslaved black resistance to racism and chattel bondage, the letter performs a characteristic appropriation. As in the rhetoric of the American Revolution, slavery is reduced to metaphor, whereas liberty is redefined as the ability to trade freely in slave-produced comestibles. At the same time, the 1792 letter allays Jefferson's fears that intercourse with the islands would yield moral and physical corruption. Whereas "Manners" had evoked the new nation's dependence on the West Indies through the figure of a creole planter devoid of will, the rhetoric of this letter places Saint-Domingue in a dependent position, in need of daily imports from North American farmers and merchants.

The letter to Lafayette thus provides a counterpart to Jefferson's epistle to James Monroe of the following year. Jefferson there provides a new geographic frame for the slave revolution in "Manners":

> I become daily more and more convinced that all the West India islands will remain in the hands of the people of colour, and a total expulsion of the whites sooner or later take place. It is high time we should foresee the bloody scenes which our children certainly, and possibly ourselves (South of Patowmac) have to wade through, and try to avert them.

The passage again combines a sensational prediction of hemispheric race warfare, a call for preventative action, and a disavowal of political agency. Jefferson offers concrete plans neither for emancipating mainland slaves nor for stemming the flow of West Indian commerce. The only policy discussed concerns state-sponsored assistance to refugee planters: "The situation of the St. Domingo fugitives (aristocrats as they are) calls aloud for pity and charity. Never was so deep a tragedy presented to the feelings of man."

34. Jefferson to Lafayette, June 16, 1792, *PTJ*, XXIV, 85–86.

Even as the letter outlines a racially segregated map of the hemisphere, pre-
dicting the expulsion of "the whites" from the sugar islands, Jefferson offers
sanctuary to Saint-Dominguan planters seeking both the reestablishment
of slavery in their former home and possession of their chattel property in
exile.[35]

This contradiction within Jefferson's response would grow in subsequent
years. Republicans struggled throughout the 1790s to maintain their status
as true defenders of the "spirit of '76" while distancing themselves from
radical revolutionaries in France and Saint-Domingue. Jefferson's writings
on Haiti were especially unstable because commentators from across the
political spectrum had begun to appropriate the language and imagery of
Notes in their accounts of the insurrection.[36]

Most Federalists were determined to maintain diplomatic and commercial ties with a Saint-Domingue controlled by L'Ouverture, a policy they
defended on moral as well as economic grounds. Theodore Dwight's *Oration, Spoken before "The Connecticut Society for the Promotion of Freedom
and the Relief of Persons Unlawfully Holden in Bondage"* (1794) justified
Caribbean slave rebellion by appealing to the same principles of natural
rights as had North American revolutionaries before them. Overthrow-
ing their "tyrannical masters" in the name of "oppressed human nature,"
Saint-Dominguan blacks had established themselves on the "firm pillars of
freedom and independence." Dwight's oratory resonates with the imagery
of divinely ordained natural destruction in British antislavery poems such
as Cowper's "Negro's Complaint" and with earlier images of divinely sanctioned slave rebellion in Raynal's *History* and Jefferson's *Notes*. So, too,
does David Everett's commencement day poem, "General Description of
America," delivered at Dartmouth College in 1795 and reprinted in Caleb
Bingham's *Columbian Orator* (1797). After a catalog of plantation horrors,
Everett intones:

But nature, wrong'd, appeals to nature's GOD.
The sun frowns angry at th' inhuman sight;
The stars offended, redden in the night:
In western skies, drear horror gathers round
And waking vengeance murmurs under ground.

35. Jefferson to Monroe, July 14, 1793, ibid., XXVI, 501–503.
36. Simon P. Newman, "American Political Culture and the French and Haitian Revolutions: Nathaniel
Cutting and the Jeffersonian Republicans," in Geggus, ed., *Impact of the Haitian Revolution*, 72–92.

Even as Dwight and Everett appropriated the imagery of *Notes,* they transformed the political import of its imagined rebellion. Despite their conservatism on domestic issues, Federalists lobbied energetically both for American aid to insurgent slaves and close commercial and diplomatic ties to the first postslavery, black majority society in the Americas.[37]

Federalist sympathy created the ideological climate in which Giroud promoted the Société libre. On the one hand, as noted at the beginning of the chapter, Giroud's letter on breadfruit challenges Jefferson's published views on multiracial republicanism. The gift confers an obligation to recognize free men of color and ex-slaves as citizens of the republic of sciences and letters rather than a danger to the state who must be colonized beyond its territorial bounds. At the same time, however, the letter also reassures Jefferson that the extension of political rights within Saint-Domingue poses little threat to hemispheric commerce. As Laurent Dubois argues, through "regimes of emancipation" such as the Third Civil Commission, individuals like Giroud and Raimond "developed new forms of governance that combined an antiracist and emancipatory agenda with forms of labor coercion and racial exclusion." Such views informed L'Ouverture's 1801 constitution (a document that Raimond might have assisted in drafting), with its commitment to the stability of the plantation economy. Through his gift of breadfruit, Giroud intimates that planter paternalism is alive and well on Saint-Domingue.[38]

During those same years, however, exiled planters envisioned a different model of hemispheric interdependence as they wove themselves into the political and cultural fabric of the United States. As noted above, several founding members of the Cercle des Philadelphes incorporated themselves within the natural history circles of Philadelphia and other port cities, including Moreau de Saint-Méry, Pierre-Louis Baudry des Lozières, Joseph Palisot de Beauvais, and Pierre-Louis Berquin-Duvallon. Articles by Baudry, Palisot, and the late Charles Arthaud began to appear in the American Philosophical Society *Transactions* by 1797. As the most energetic member of this cohort, Moreau established a printing press and

37. Theodore Dwight, *An Oration, Spoken before "The Connecticut Society for the Promotion of Freedom and the Relief of Persons Unlawfully Holden in Bondage"* (Hartford, Conn., 1794), 18–19; Caleb Bingham, *The Columbian Orator,* ed. David Blight (New York, 1998), 207–208.

38. Laurent Dubois, "'The Price of Liberty': Victor Hugues and the Administration of Freedom in Guadeloupe, 1794–1798," *William and Mary Quarterly,* 3d Ser., LVI (1999), 363–392 (quotation on 364). On Raimond's role in drafting the Constitution, see Dubois, *Avengers of the New World: The Story of the Haitian Revolution* (Cambridge, Mass., 2004), 242.

bookshop near the Philadelphia waterfront that served as a social hub for the exiled Antillean philosophes. In the back of his shop, Moreau printed his manuscripts from prerevolutionary Saint-Domingue. His *Description of the Spanish Part of Saint-Domingo* appeared in an English translation by William Cobbett in 1798, and *Description topographique . . . de la partie française de l'isle Saint-Domingue* appeared in two volumes the previous year.[39]

The American Philosophical Society thus provided one important institutional basis from which exiled Saint-Dominguans began to come to terms with recent events on their island, advancing a powerful interpretation of the uprising through their practice of natural history. Baudry's "Memoir on *Animal Cotton;* or, The Insect *Fly-Carrier,*" discussed in the introduction of this study, presents the loss of a valuable entomological specimen and its cost to hemispheric science and commerce as the basis of an affective bond with his learned audience. In forging that bond, Baudry emphasizes the shared value of archivization: "I thought that a fact of this nature deserved to be deposited among your archives, and I may perhaps request of you the permission of depositing there some other still more curious facts." Contrasting the destruction of natural knowledge during the burning of Cap Français with the efforts of the Cercle and the American Philosophical Society to store and disseminate specimens, Baudry defines the Haitian Revolution. The radical political and social aims of Toussaint L'Ouverture and his compatriots threaten to negate colonial Enlightenment.[40]

Moreau's treatises on Hispaniola advance related claims by refusing to depict the present condition of the island. Though the impending destruction of planter society was foremost in the thoughts of his readers, and though chroniclers such as Bryan Edwards had "documented" the insurrection and counterinsurgency in graphic detail, Moreau insisted on publishing two encyclopedic studies of prerevolutionary Caribbean societies. Cobbett's English translation of the *Description topographique* begins with an apology:

> I thought it necessary, in the description of Saint-Domingo, studiously to avoid touching on any thing relative to the revolution, since 1789. . . . Its object being to represent Saint-Domingo such as I had

---

39. Anna M. Roberts and Kenneth Roberts, eds., *Moreau de St. Méry's American Journey, 1793–1798* (Garden City, N.Y., 1947).

40. M. [Pierre-Louis] Baudry des Lozieres, "A Memoir on *Animal Cotton;* or, The Insect *Fly-Carrier,*" American Philosophical Society, *Transactions,* V (1802), 150–159 (quotation on 159).

seen it, it would have appeared whimsical in me to lay aside a true and interesting picture in order to take one that was every moment upon the change. I should have feared, in so doing, to resemble a painter, who, having undertaken to draw the portrait of a person celebrated for beauty and other advantages, should determine, at the moment of finishing it, not to represent the original in its natural state, but disfigured with the cruel effects of a convulsive malady.

Much like Baudry, Moreau attempts to recover the lost legacy of colonial Enlightenment before the unnatural history of insurrection. In the "Discours préliminaire" of his *Description topographique,* he conveys similar sentiments. Against claims that he has produced a useless and melancholic book, he contends that his portrait of prerevolutionary society will assist in restoring the ancien régime.[41]

This insistence on banishing slave revolution from representation made the *Description topographique* an unsettling text within the print culture of the early Republic. Much like Jefferson in "Manners," Moreau and his fellow exiles depicted slave revolution as a traumatic rupture in the history of Enlightenment progress. Yet they differed from Jefferson in their conviction that the trajectory of history could be reversed, that the splendors of the ancien régime could be resurrected. Their writings on prerevolutionary Saint-Domingue attempted to build enthusiasm for this cause, but, in so doing, they disrupted any simple equation between the practice of natural history and the rise of yeoman virtue and simplicity.

Moreau's analyses of race and racial difference are more unsettling. Like Giroud's letter, Moreau's *Description topographique* responds to Jefferson's call for a natural history of black minds and bodies. Doris Garraway describes Moreau's treatise as "a milestone in Enlightenment racial theory." Spread over nearly twenty pages of the text, Moreau provided a taxonomy of "human color variation" in the colony, charting an array of possible sexual liaisons between white men and nonwhite women on the island and stipulating the racial identity of each imagined couple's offspring. In so doing, he attempted to stabilize the boundary between white and *sang-mêlé* (mixed blood) individuals and to impede the social and political ambitions of free people of color such as Julien Raimond.[42]

41. [Méderic Louis-Élie] Moreau de Saint-Méry, *A Topographical and Political Description of the Spanish Part of Saint-Domingo . . .* , trans. William Cobbett, 2 vols. (Philadelphia, 1796), I, 1.
42. Doris Garraway, "Race, Reproduction, and Family Romance in Moreau de Saint-Méry's *Descrip-*

Moreau's racial taxonomy presented what Garraway calls "a fantasy of white sexual and political power in the context of an increasingly fragile system of racial domination." By imagining repeated instances of *métissage* between white men and black women—but never between their sang-mêlé offspring—Moreau represented Saint-Dominguan society as a family unit in which "white men are the real and symbolic fathers of the subaltern races in the colony." To concoct this "family romance," however, required candor regarding white male interracial desire. Having described the eyes, hips, arms, and teeth of a mulatta "Priestesses of Venus," in one passage, Moreau continued:

> The entire being of a *Mulâtresse* is dedicated to sensual pleasure, and the fire of that goddess burns in her heart until she dies. . . . There is nothing that most passionate imagination can conceive that she has not already sensed, foreseen, or experienced. Her single focus is to charm all the senses, to expose them to the most delicious ecstasies, to suspend them in the most seductive raptures. In addition, nature, pleasure's accomplice, has given her charm, appeal, sensitivity, and, what is far more dangerous, the ability to experience more keenly than her partner sensual pleasures whose secrets surpass those of Paphos.

The *Description* provides nothing like a congenial reply to Jefferson's call for a natural history of race. Moreau's tables and descriptions make public the forms of illicit desire that Jefferson's natural history attempted to suppress. Indeed, Moreau posits those desires as the very basis of planter authority. Such passages must have resonated strangely in a Philadelphia scandalized by the alien sexual practices of exiled Saint-Dominguans (and rife with gossip regarding Moreau's racial identity) and in a nation where anti-French feeling was on the rise. At the same moment that Federalists defended the natural rights of revolted Caribbean slaves—drawing in part on the prestige and authority of *Notes*—Moreau's meditation on race exposed fissures within the hemispheric Enlightenment. Divergent public attitudes toward interracial sex in the French Caribbean and the early United States contributed to rendering republican support for the refugees a nearly untenable position.[43]

tion . . . de la partie francaise de l'isle Saint-Domingue," *Eighteenth-Century Studies*, XXXVIII (2005), 227–246 (quotation on 227).

43. Ibid., 229–230; [Méderic Louis-Élie] Moreau de Saint-Méry, *Description topographique, physique, civile, politique, et historique de la partie française de l'isle Saint-Domingue . . .*, 3 vols. (Philadelphia,

"The Receptacle of the Blacks"

Within this complex ideological context, Jefferson refines his interpretation of the Haitian Revolution in another sequence of letters written between 1797 and 1801. Responding to St. George Tucker's manuscript "A Dissertation on Slavery: With a Proposal for the Gradual Abolition of It, in the State of Virginia" in 1796, Jefferson reminds the Bermuda-born jurist that his support for emancipation has been a matter of public record since the appearance of his treatise in 1787. He reformulates his thoughts in light of current events:

> Perhaps the first chapter of this history, which has begun in St. Domingo, and the next succeeding ones which will recount how all the whites were driven from all the other islands, may prepare our minds for a peaceable accommodation between justice, policy and necessity, and furnish an answer to the difficult question Whither shall the coloured emigrants go? And the sooner we put some plan under way, the greater hope there is that it may be permitted to proceed peaceably to it's ultimate effect. But if something is not done, and soon done, we shall be the murderers of our own children. The 'Murmura, venturos nautis prodentia ventos' has already reached us; the revolutionary storm now sweeping the globe will be upon us, and happy if we make timely provision to give it an easy passage over our land.

The letter appears to mark an emphatic foreclosure of the futures proposed by Baudry and the exiled planters on the one hand and Giroud, Raimond, L'Ouverture, and their Federalist sympathizers on the other. One is struck by Jefferson's prediction that the Haitian Revolution will degenerate into a form of outright race warfare, spreading throughout the Antilles. The letter underscores Jefferson's earlier proposition (in the query on "Laws") that multiracial republicanism is both morally undesirable and practically unfeasible, in part owing to the "real distinctions which nature has made" between black and white peoples. "Scientific" inquiry had only begun to delineate those differences in 1787. A decade later, Jefferson presents the Haitian

1797), I, 50–51, trans. in Laurent Dubois and John D. Garrigus, eds., *Slave Revolution in the Caribbean, 1789–1804: A Brief History with Documents* (New York, 2006), 58–59. On public scandals surrounding Moreau and his circle, including the sale of contraceptives in his bookshop and the public appearances of several refugees with mulatto mistresses, see Claire A. Lyons, *Sex among the Rabble: An Intimate History of Gender and Power in the Age of Revolution, Philadelphia, 1730–1830* (Chapel Hill, N.C., 2006), 188–189. On innuendo regarding Moreau's racial identity, see Davis, *Problem of Slavery*, 195.

Revolution as new evidence for his hypothesis of inevitable racial violence absent a plan for colonization. The image of a "revolutionary storm" sweeping northward is more than a conventional trope here; Jefferson draws on the discourse of meteorology to lend scientific authority to his bleak vision.[44]

But the letter also incorporates Saint-Domingue within the history of enlightened republicanism, addressing the problem that made "Manners" a disruptive section within the formal pattern of *Notes*. Whereas "Laws" had envisioned a racially homogenous republic created through an elaborate, though as yet unformulated, scheme of colonization, subsequent sections were shaped by the knowledge that the future prosperity of the nation depended on commercial and cultural connections with the West Indies. Though "Manners" held out hope that the rising spirits of slaves might provide critical momentum for abolition, such optimism was undermined by a rhetorical posture that highlighted the author's position within a degenerate plantocracy.

In the letter to Tucker, events on Saint-Domingue promise to create a suitable location for the resettlement of free blacks, making the proposal articulated in "Laws" a practical possibility. Much like his Federalist antagonists, and not entirely unlike Giroud, as well, Jefferson presents the American and Haitian revolutions as part of a progressive historical trajectory, with the actions of ex-slaves in the Caribbean allowing the United States to fulfill its commitment to universal equality and freedom while remaining a racially homogenous republic. The figure of a "revolutionary storm" passing safely over North America at once acknowledges the connections between the Caribbean and the early Republic while moving toward a less dystopic conception of their likely implications.

Similar designs explain the veneer of politeness in Jefferson's reply to Giroud during the same year. Having acknowledged the gift of breadfruit seeds, Jefferson describes his efforts to disseminate the species among southern planters. This exchange of natural historical knowledge, he maintains, surpasses the military triumphs of the American Revolution as a contribution to human happiness: "One service of this kind rendered to a nation is worth more to them than all the victories of the most splendid pages of their history, and becomes a source of exalted pleasure to those who have been instrumental to it. May that pleasure by yours, and your name be pro-

44. Jefferson to Tucker, Aug. 28, 1797, *PTJ*, XXIX, 519–520; Jefferson, *Notes*, ed. Peden, 138. For a consideration of Jefferson's Negrophobia, see Zuckerman, *Almost Chosen People*, 196–197.

nounced with gratitude by those who shall at some future day be tasting the sweets of the blessing you are now procuring them." Despite his effusive praise, however, Jefferson consigns Giroud to posterity. He will be part of the enlightened future projected by the letter only as an honored memory, not as a living participant. And he will be remembered solely for his contribution to plantation agriculture (by "introducing so precious a plant into our Southern states") rather than for his efforts to reshape the concepts of citizenship and rights in Saint-Domingue, even as Jefferson addresses his letter "chez le citoyen Raymond. Commissaire du Directoir executif au Cap Francois. Isle de St. Domingue."[45]

This same contradictory logic, more starkly expressed, structures a subsequent letter to James Monroe in 1801, during the first troubled year of Jefferson's presidency. In the wake of Gabriel Prosser's rebellion in Virginia, the letter addresses the perennial problem of colonization. After rejecting several proposed sites for a colony of free blacks in North America, Jefferson declares:

> The West Indies offer a more probable and practicable retreat for them. Inhabited already by a people of their own race and color; climates congenial with their natural constitution; insulated from the other descriptions of men; nature seems to have formed these islands to become the receptacle of the blacks transplanted into this hemisphere. . . . The most promising portion of them is the island of St. Domingo, where the blacks are established into a sovereignty *de facto*, and have organized themselves under regular laws and government.

The letter appeals once more to the authority of natural history as it imagines a radical reordering of hemispheric affairs, one that would find official expression in Jefferson's embargo against Haiti in 1805. Previous natural histories had depicted the islands as commercial crossroads connected to the rest of the planet through currents of wind and water and as gardens cultivated through a blend of creole learning and benevolent metropolitan management. Drawing on the discourses of geography, climatology, and racial science, Jefferson here portrays the West Indies as naturally isolated within the hemisphere, providing a more suitable climate for free blacks than a temperate North America. Jefferson displays his knowledge of Caribbean nature in order to cordon off revolutionary Saint-Domingue from an enlightened hemisphere. But this appeal to nature is bound up with his

45. Jefferson to Giroud, May 22, 1797, *PTJ*, XXIX, 387–388.

tentative recognition of black political sovereignty and self-determination, as articulated in L'Ouverture's constitution of the same year. The letter to Monroe experiments with a new set of terms for representing Saint-Domingue as both integral to the future of republicanism and external to Jefferson's "empire of liberty."[46]

This partial recognition of black sovereignty occurred solely at the level of discourse. As late as 1802, Jefferson still hoped for the reestablishment of French colonial rule and slavery in Saint-Domingue, lending tacit support to Napoleon Bonaparte's plans to regain possession of Haiti and New Orleans through the so-called Leclerc expedition, despite his knowledge that Napoleon's success would pose a formidable obstacle to U.S. westward expansion. Even at the level of discourse, moreover, Jefferson failed to arrive at a settled formula for representing events on the island. Over the next twenty years, he would continue to assess the implications of Haitian independence in two contexts: the development of lower Louisiana as a sugar territory and black majority society and the proposed annexation of Cuba, which had replaced Saint-Domingue as the world's leading sugar colony. As will be discussed in the next chapter on Audubon's early career in lower Louisiana, both developments owed to the influx of Saint-Dominguan refugees. Even as he elaborated the mythology of a racially purified yeoman empire, Jefferson labored to incorporate the Caribbean plantation and plantocracy within the body of the Republic. Just as the new nation could never close its borders with the Greater Caribbean, Jefferson could never efface the region from his rendering of American nature.[47]

46. Jefferson to Monroe, Nov. 24, 1801, *WTJ*, VII, 105.

47. On Jefferson's tacit support of the Leclerc expedition, see Zuckerman, *Almost Chosen People*, 205–210.

6

The Birds of America *and the*
Specter of Caribbean Accumulation

In 1834, as he approached the end of promoting, financing, and publishing *The Birds of America*, John Audubon began his autobiography. The idea had intrigued him since beginning his career as a professional ornithologist more than a decade earlier. Between 1820 and 1822, while living in near-indigence in New Orleans, Audubon kept a detailed journal of his efforts to collect and paint New World birdlife. During his travels in England and Scotland in 1826, he maintained a similar record of his attempt to collect prominent subscribers. The task of self-representation was not limited to these explicitly autobiographical writings. In dozens of so-called "ornithological biographies" drafted during the 1820s and 1830s and published in five volumes totaling nearly three thousand pages, Audubon developed a literary persona that transformed the standard natural history genre of the specimen description into a popular art form. Autobiographical writing had long been integral to Audubon's practice of natural history. The new celebrity he had achieved by 1834 lent new urgency to his desire to craft a coherent life story.[1]

It is notable that the opening pages of "Myself"—as the author's widow titled the autobiographical sketch when she published it—provide neither a stable point of departure for the subsequent life narrative nor an authoritative genealogy for the narrator. Rather, the opening foregrounds the difficulty of framing Audubon's creole origins. "The precise period of my birth is yet an enigma to me," the narrator commences, as he prepares his reader for the highly conjectural account of his birth and infancy that follows. In

---

1. John James Audubon, *Ornithological Biography; or, An Account of the Habits of the Birds of the United States of America . . .*, 5 vols. (Edinburgh, 1831–1839). On specimen description as a textual praxis, see Michel Foucault, *The Order of Things: An Archaeology of the Human Sciences* (New York, 1970), 132; Cynthia Sundberg Wall, *The Prose of Things: Transformations of Description in the Eighteenth Century* (Chicago, 2006), 70–80. On Audubon's fusion of specimen description and life writing, see Christoph Irmscher, *The Poetics of Natural History: From John Bartram to William James* (Piscataway, N.J., 1999), 188–235.

this version of events, which he "often heard [his] father repeat," Audubon was born and raised on his father's properties in Les Cayes, a thriving plantation region in southern Saint-Domingue, and had fled the island with his father and half-sister during the early stages of the Haitian Revolution. He describes how his father settled briefly, like many refugee planters from the island, in the polyglot port city of French colonial New Orleans, where he had years earlier met his first wife, Audubon's mother, during one of his frequent visits. Identified in this account only as "a lady of Spanish extraction, whom I have been led to understand was as beautiful as she was wealthy," the naturalist's alleged mother never escaped Saint-Domingue with the rest of her family but instead became "one of the victims during the ever-to-be-lamented period of the negro insurrection on that island."[2]

That Audubon's origins must remain conjectural lends gravity and import to the problem of self-narration. An irrevocable loss of origins is presented as a tragic consequence of the Age of Revolution in its disturbing drift toward political radicalism and the excesses of economic and racial violence: "How long my father remained in the service, it is impossible for me to say. The different changes occurring at the time of the American Revolution, and afterward during that in France, seem to have sent him from one place to another as if a foot-ball; his property in Santo Domingo augmenting, however, the while, and indeed till the liberation of the black slaves there." As the passage attests, because the routes of political radicalism in the period are seen to pass from the United States through France to Saint-Domingue—a triangle ironically mimicking the structure of trade that had secured the wealth of all three societies—Audubon's ignorance of his birth is presented as a legacy of slave revolution.[3]

The opening episodes of "Myself" advance a strikingly direct claim that the Haitian Revolution and its aftermath are the formative events in Audubon's ornithological career, the driving force behind his development of a distinctive visual and narrative aesthetic. The concluding sentence of the episodes, however, provides a convenient index of the narrative's broader and more complex meditation on the theme. As he turns from his early years in the Americas to a depiction of his adopted home in France, Audu-

2. A version of "Myself" was first published in *Scribner's* in March 1893, with an introduction by Maria R. Audubon. No manuscript is known to exist. Four years later, she published a corrected version in Maria R. Audubon, ed., *Audubon and His Journals* (New York, 1897). The text of the 1897 version is reprinted in Christoph Irmscher, ed., *John James Audubon: Writings and Drawings* (New York, 1999), 765–794 (quotation on 765).

3. Audubon, "Myself," in Irmscher, ed., *Writings and Drawings*, 767.

bon makes a theatrical gesture of banishing slave revolution from the field of representation: "The thunders of the Revolution still roared over the land, the Revolutionists covered the earth with the blood of man, woman, and child. But let me forever drop the curtain over the frightful aspect of this dire picture." Audubon insists that the problem of moving forward from an event as traumatic as slave revolution can only be resolved by effacing it. Nevertheless, to make such conspicuous theater of that effacement is to ensure that what is banished from the foreground maintains a strong presence.[4]

Here and elsewhere in his writings, Audubon signals that the defining features of his visual aesthetic should be understood within a specific historical frame. When finally completed, the original, "double elephant" folio edition of *The Birds of America* would be a work of extravagant violence. Christoph Irmscher argues that the images are "vortices of violent activity." In plate after plate, Audubon and his collaborators compose graphic and at times sensational images of scavenging and predation. Connected intimately with this thematic emphasis on violence is an aesthetic violation of the conventions governing subject-object relations in the tradition of natural history illustration, what Ann Shelby Blum calls "the conceptual separation" between bird and viewer. As Irmscher puts it, the reader is forced to "participate in an experience rather than, as had been the tradition, contemplate from a safe distance a scientific fact." Within the pictorial field of *The Birds of America*, objects transform into subjects with uncanny regularity.[5]

The formal organization of *The Birds of America* reflects back on the long and brutal history of "Caribbean accumulation." On one level, the term refers to a process of scientific collection and capitalist development, traced in prior chapters of this study, that extended from the sugar revolution of the late seventeenth century to the decline of the West Indian sugar economy in the mid-nineteenth century and that drew its principal energy from Caribbean colonialism and slavery. For the purposes of this

4. Ibid., 769. My thinking on this matter has been influenced by Sibylle Fischer's adaptation of Freudian theories of disavowal to describe a range of literary and cultural responses to the Haitian Revolution in Cuba and Santo Domingo. See Sibylle Fischer, *Modernity Disavowed: Haiti and the Cultures of Slavery in the Age of Revolution* (Durham, N.C., 2004).

5. Irmscher, *Poetics of Natural History*, 195–196; Ann Shelby Blum, *Picturing Nature: American Nineteenth-Century Zoological Illustration* (Princeton, N.J., 1993), 106; John James Audubon, *The Birds of America: From Original Drawings*, 4 vols. (London, 1827–1838). The double elephant folio was printed in the largest format then technically possible, with individual sheets measuring 29½" × 39½".

chapter, however, the term refers primarily to the temporal compression that results from this process, as the effects of past action—economic, ethical, and epistemological—accumulate in specific geographic locations, including the former slave societies of the Americas, and port cities and financial entrepôts around the Atlantic world. In *Specters of the Atlantic,* Ian Baucom proposes that we understand key developments in the literary and cultural history of eighteenth-century Britain—including the emergence of "liberal cosmopolitanism" and "melancholy romanticism" as modes of expression—within a protracted cycle of "Atlantic accumulation." Building on the insights of Caribbean and black Atlantic theorists and on Giovanni Arrighi's work in historical sociology, he uncovers a genealogy in which the expansion of slavery and the slave trade is bound to the ascendancy of speculative finance and in which their intensifying relationship provides the structure for our present-day financial system. Though this cycle can be divided into (overlapping) periods of national dominance—including Dutch (1560–1780), British (1750–1925), and American (1860–present) phases— it is nonetheless continuous and ongoing, such that slavery and the slave trade can in no way be consigned to a discrete past. As Caribbean theorists, poets, and novelists have long insisted, in a social world that continues to be shaped by the human catastrophe of slavery, "time does not pass, it accumulates." Audubon's writings prefigure this philosophy of history.[6]

We have seen how the accumulation of specimens, knowledge, and wealth in the circumatlantic world challenged Enlightenment notions of historical progress and chronology, whether in Sloane's and Catesby's perceptions of the West Indian plantation as a space of accelerated historical change that is at once modern and barbarous or in Crèvecoeur's and Jefferson's fantasies of Caribbean slave revolution as the collapse of New World republicanism. Drawing on this representational lineage and reflecting his varied experiences in the Greater Caribbean, Audubon's practice of natural history is also shaped by his sense that time can run backward.

Most considerations of Audubon locate him at one of a number of beginnings, finding in his aesthetics and environmental consciousness an antici-

6. Ian Baucom, *Specters of the Atlantic: Finance Capital, Slavery, and the Philosophy of History* (Durham, N.C., 2005), 325. Baucom argues that the Zong Massacre and the trials that followed it constitute the representative event of capitalist modernity, enshrining a form of "loss value" that had long been integral to the formation of a strange, new speculative culture in which enslaved people served as a form of currency. The Zong Massacre occurred when the British captain of a slave ship ordered the drowning of 132 enslaved Africans off the coast of Jamaica in 1781 so that the owners of the ship could collect insurance for their lost cargo. For Giovanni Arrighi's model of "Atlantic accumulation," see *The Long Twentieth Century: Money, Power, and the Origins of Our Times* (New York, 1994).

pation of mid-nineteenth-century romanticism or Darwin's evolutionary concepts of struggle, adaptation, and ecological relation. Modern studies similarly locate him at the beginnings of a nationalist discourse in which the chronicling of natural abundance within the United States became the motive of a new, self-consciously American literature. Audubon's own meditations on New World nature, however, are retrospective and circum-Caribbean. He represents his ornithological labors within a spatio-temporal frame that extends southward from Louisiana and Florida through the Greater Caribbean and ranges over the history of the slave plantation as a dominant New World institution.[7]

Whereas "Myself" represents one such moment of self-understanding, Audubon's *Mississippi River Journal* provides another. The journal details his efforts to compile specimens and paintings for *The Birds of America* in lower Louisiana and New Orleans. His journey to this region was an improbable attempt to recover his personal fortune after the Panic of 1819, described by historian Charles Sellers as, for many residents of the United States, a "traumatic awakening to the capitalist reality of boom-and-bust." Before the panic, Audubon had been a prosperous mill-owner in Kentucky. The economic downturn left him destitute and resulted in a brief jail term for unpaid debts. Read in conjunction with "Myself," and alongside Audubon's images from Louisiana, the journal depicts this formative phase in the composition of *The Birds of America* as a return to the Caribbean vortex—to a semitropical region shaped by plantation slavery, hemispheric mobility, French colonial métissage, and incipient slave revolution.[8]

In a period marked by mounting concerns about incorporating Louisiana and its creole inhabitants within the early Republic, Audubon's personal history presented difficulties. Audubon was one of several illegitimate children born to his father, Jean Audubon, and two women who resided with him on his plantation: the French servant Jeanne Rabine (identified as Audubon's birth mother) and the "quadroon" *ménagère* Sanitte Bouffard. The young Audubon's family history was hardly anomalous. In Saint-Dominguan society, the frequency of concubinage and other kinds

7. For some examples, see the introductory essays to Annette Blaugrund and Theodore E. Stebbins, Jr., eds., *John James Audubon: The Watercolors for the Birds of America* (New York, 1993), 3–68. For a useful discussion of this tendency, see Jennifer J. Baker, "The Making of John James Audubon," *William and Mary Quarterly*, 3d Ser., LXIII (2006), 176–183.

8. John James Audubon, "Mississippi River Journal," in Irmscher, ed., *Writings and Drawings*, 1–156; Charles Sellers, *The Market Revolution: Jacksonian America, 1815–1846* (New York, 1991), 137. For one of the many biographies that treat this period, see Shirley Streshinsky, *Audubon: Life and Art in the American Wilderness* (Athens, Ga., 1998).

of interracial relationships made the distinction between illegitimacy and miscegenation all but indiscernible. As Colin Dayan has argued, such arrangements inspired a voluminous colonial literature on Saint-Dominguan race that was at once quasi-scientific and protogothic in character: "The epistemology of whiteness, which was absolutely dependent for its effect on the detection of blackness, resulted in fantasies about secret histories and hidden taints that would then be backed up by physical, explicit codes of law." A similar discourse of hidden corruption took shape in lower Louisiana during the Americanization phase. French creoles as a class became an object of racialist scrutiny, as commentators asked whether they could be incorporated as citizens into the United States without rendering untenable the important legal category of whiteness—or exposing its fictionality. Encountering the dangers of his lineage during a decisive moment in the history of Americanization, Audubon develops and refines his aesthetic of violence. By portraying the natural history of the region as a scene of relentless predation and as a source of biologic diversity that is at once desired and feared, he positions the era we now call Jacksonian within a protracted history of circum-Caribbean slavery and trade.[9]

9. Joan [Colin] Dayan, *Haiti, History, and the Gods* (Berkeley, Calif., 1998), 229. For the definitive biography, which establishes Jeanne Rabine as the artist's birth mother and identifies her as a French chambermaid, see Alice Ford, *John James Audubon: A Biography* (New York, 1988). Ford goes to great lengths to contest claims by prior biographers that Audubon's birth mother can never be definitely established and that the most likely candidate, Rabine, was "a creole of Santo Domingo" (Francis Hobart Herrick, *Audubon the Naturalist: A History of His Life and Time* [New York, 1917]). In so doing, she strains the available evidence. Ford herself notes that, because of Audubon's illegitimacy, traditional sources such as baptismal records are unavailable: "Any record of the event, with particulars about parentage, was to be avoided at all costs on Saint Domingue" (14). What she does not make explicit is that they were to be avoided to protect Audubon from insinuations of racial impurity. To be born creole would create troubles in itself, but Jean Audubon's complex personal affairs created a second possibility, which seems to be Ford's real animus. Sanitte Bouffard, the "quadroon" daughter of a neighboring French sugar planter, was Jean's long-term companion and lived openly with him as ménagère of his plantation, where they raised their three daughters. She remained on the plantation even after Jean Audubon took Jeanne Rabine as his second mistress. Sanitte gave birth to at least one child, Rose, after Jeanne's death in 1785. Moreover, racial passing was an aspect of French colonial life well known to Audubon's family. In 1789, Audubon formulated a plan to flee the island with his eldest son and his favorite daughter. Ford writes, "Perhaps even his daughter Rose 'Bonnitte,' . . . a miracle of paleness, might also be brought out, and as white" (20). Upon arriving in Nantes, Jean Audubon carefully concealed his daughter's identity: "'Demoiselle Rabin, white,' she was described in the roll. . . . The conspicuous word 'white,' in a ledger where ordinarily only 'black' and 'mulatto' were designated, does not recur in a whole shelf of ledgers for the era. The long deceased Jeanne Rabine became an adventitious shield against the damning truth about the half-sister of her son" (23). Ford never entertains the possibility that she might have been a shield for John Audubon as well. On the reputation of Saint-Domingue as a "libertine colony," see Doris Garraway, *The Libertine Colony: Creolization in the Early French Caribbean* (Durham, N.C., 2005).

Emblematic Reading in The Birds of America

Since the late seventeenth century, as we have seen, natural histories of the Caribbean had relied on practices of emblematic reading to address the modernity of the Caribbean plantation, whether in Sloane's *Voyage . . . to Jamaica,* Catesby's *Natural History of Carolina,* Du Simitière's *American Museum,* or Bartram's draft manuscript of *Travels through North and South Carolina, Georgia, East and West Florida.* In the first two examples, the material format of the printed books was part of the texts' meditations on the relation between West Indian superabundance and violence. Urgent and long-standing questions regarding Caribbean slavery are embedded in the very aesthetics and format of Audubon's volumes—in the characteristic themes and compositional arrangements of the images and in the conspicuous size, technological sophistication, and expense of the printed volumes. The volumes were printed in an outlandishly large format (the so-called "double elephant" folio), were based on laborious firsthand observation of ornithological behavior in New World settings, and included some 435 lavish engravings produced through an expensive and technologically advanced printing process. The entire work sold for the then-staggering sum of one thousand dollars. The book was intended, on one level, as an expression of national self-confidence, a printed artifact commensurate with the nation's material and human potential. But because it is modeled on works by Sloane, Catesby, and others, the book also stands as visual testament to a history of West Indian plenitude.[10]

Understood from this vantage, the opening episodes of "Myself" appear less idiosyncratic. Although "Myself" and the *Mississippi River Journal* were published posthumously, Audubon surely intended that they appear in print. As a figure immersed in the conventions of colonial natural history, he assumed that his audience would read emblematically by linking the visual and the linguistic. (Indeed, he published the "ornithological biographies" separately from *The Birds of America* only to avoid expenses related to British copyright law.) What he hoped would emerge from this practice of reading was an awareness of the deep and multiple connections between naturalist and specimen, subject and object, the history and experience of

10. On the format and printing of *Birds of America,* see Annette Blaugrund, "The Artist as Entrepreneur," in Blaugrund and Stebbins, eds., *Watercolors for the Birds of America,* 27–42. On Catesby and Bartram as important precedents for Audubon, see Amy R. Weinstein Meyers, "Sketches from the Wilderness: Changing Conceptions of Nature in American Natural History Illustration, 1680–1880" (Ph.D. diss., Yale University, 1985).

the observer, and the natural scene or drama recorded—and encoded—as scientific image. As his biographers have observed, the success of *The Birds of America* owed as much to the artist's innovative marketing strategy as it did to the plates themselves. His autobiographical sketch—begun, we recall, as he completed *The Birds of America*—was a crucial component of that strategy.[11]

Taken together with the *Mississippi River Journal* and other autobiographical writings, "Myself" fashions an enigmatic persona. To some extent, all of these texts trade on the "Indianized" frontier identity that had made James Fenimore Cooper's first Leatherstocking novels a transatlantic sensation, fusing it with an emergent entrepreneurial savvy that would become a staple of Jacksonian narratives. "Myself," however, evokes less familiar aspects of Audubon's career—his birth in the notorious "libertine colony" of Saint-Domingue and his flight to French New Orleans after the loss of his mother. The thematic implication is clear. Interconnections between Saint-Domingue and New Orleans contribute to the rising cultural prestige of the new nation, for, without them, *The Birds of America* would never have been produced.

Just a few pages later, Audubon inserts a macabre narrative of vocational origins. After being settled in the thriving slave port of Nantes, where he was adopted by his father's French wife, the young Audubon is placed under the charge of "one or two black servants, who," he informs the reader, "had followed my father from Santo Domingo to New Orleans and afterward to Nantes." (These were likely the same "faithful servants"—undoubtedly slaves—who in the previous episode had helped his father escape "from Aux Cayes with a good portion of his plate and money.") Audubon recounts a scene of domestic upheaval involving one of the servants:

> One incident which is as perfect in my memory as if it had occurred this very day, I have thought of thousands of times since, and will

11. Writing to ethnologist John Bachman in 1834, Audubon announces: "This Coming Winter, I will Spend at Writing My *own Biography* to be published as soon as possible and to be Continued as God May be pleased to grant me Life!" (John James Audubon to John Bachman, Aug. 25, 1834, bMS Am 1482, Houghton Library, Harvard University, Cambridge, Mass., rpt. in Irmscher, ed., *Writings and Drawings*, 827). Audubon would have imbibed the conventions of emblematic reading through his study of colonial natural history books. It is probably for this reason that he was also drawn to the "delightful Mental fables of Lafontaine" (Audubon, "My Style of Drawing Birds," in Irmscher, ed., *Writings and Drawings*, 761). Joseph Sabin contends, "The plates were published without any text, to avoid the necessity of furnishing copies gratis to the public libraries in England, agreeably to the law of copyright." See Sabin, *Bibliotheca Americana: A Dictionary of Books Relating to America, from Its Discovery to the Present Time*, 29 vols. (New York, 1871), I, 315.

now put on paper as one of the curious things which perhaps did lead me in after times to love birds, and to finally study them with pleasure infinite. My mother had several beautiful parrots and some monkeys; one of the latter was a full-grown male of a very large species. One morning, while the servants were engaged in arranging the room I was in, "Pretty Polly" asking for her breakfast as usual, *"Du pain au lait pour le perroquet Migonne,"* the man of the woods probably thought the bird presuming upon his rights in the scale of nature; be this as it may, he certainly showed his supremacy in strength over the denizen of the air, for, walking deliberately and uprightly toward the poor bird, he at once killed it, with unnatural composure. The sensations of my infant heart at this cruel sight were agony to me. I prayed the servant to beat the monkey, but he, who for some reason preferred the monkey to the parrot, refused. I uttered long and piercing cries, my mother rushed into the room, I was tranquillized, the monkey was forever afterward chained, and Migonne buried with all the pomp of a cherished lost one.

Functioning as an allegory, this episode resonates with the speculative genealogy at the beginning of "Myself." Owing to its narrative placement, this depiction of sudden turmoil within a French bourgeois home reads as a recasting of the Haitian Revolution. The delicate parrot Migonne stands in both for Audubon's French-speaking adopted mother and for his creole birth mother, who, like the exotic bird, also fell victim to "unnatural" violence. The agent of that violence figures the insurrectionary slave an allegorical representation embedded in Audubon's use of colonial colloquialism. "Man of the woods" is Audubon's transliteration of the Latin binomial for orangutan *(Homus sylvestrus),* a species of primate routinely linked with Africans in natural histories of the late eighteenth and early nineteenth centuries.[12] Here, an orangutan that is seemingly conscious of its inherent dignity (the passage specifies its upright posture and deliberate gait) and outraged by the abrogation of its natural rights (its "rights in the scale of nature") murders in cold blood the feminized representative

---

12. Audubon, "Myself," in Irmscher, ed., *Writings and Drawings,* 765–766. On the substantial number of French West Indian blacks concentrated in Nantes on the eve of the French Revolution, see Pierre H. Boulle, *Race et esclavage dans la France de l'ancien régime* (Paris, 2007), 44. On comparisons between Africans and orangutans, see, for instance, [Edward Long], *The History of Jamaica; or General Survey of the Antient and Modern State of That Island . . . ,* 3 vols. (London, 1774), II, 356, 363 (discussed in Dayan, *Haiti, History, and the Gods,* 190–195).

of European refinement. The scene resembles planter narratives about the massacre of white women by vengeful ex-slaves. The episode is infused with a gothic sensibility that, as Dayan argues, was associated with the legacy of slave revolution in the period.[13]

Although the second episode presents an allegory of slave insurrection within Saint-Domingue itself, it also highlights the ways that the violence of revolution continues to travel with Audubon after his flight from the Caribbean. Despite, or perhaps because of, the fact that it cannot be remembered literally, that violence intrudes into the seeming tranquillity of France with all the force of the repressed. Just as disturbing to the young creole as Migonne's brutal murder is the revelation that a "faithful" black servant from Saint-Domingue has formed an alliance with the orangutan. Siding with "the man of the woods," the servant remains unmoved when Audubon—as displaced son of a deposed sugar planter—pleads for redress. The servant's refusal to punish the orangutan produces a second violent disruption of the "scale of nature." It is only with the entrance of Audubon's French mother that domestic order is restored, and the parrot properly mourned, "with all the pomp of a cherished loved one," as a surrogate for Audubon's birth mother. According to the logic of the episode, Audubon's subsequent career as natural historian, his study of New World birdlife with "pleasure infinite," both reenacts this scene of domestic insurrection and provides a sense of compensatory mastery.

As this reading implies, the repercussions of slave revolution within the narrative—both material and psychological—do not cease in France. Just as the violence of insurrection has traveled with Audubon to Nantes, following the routes of the triangle trade, so the memory of its intrusion into French domesticity has stayed with him throughout his career. Writing from Edinburgh, Scotland, some thirty-five years later, Audubon notes the incident is "as perfect in my memory as if it occurred this very day." It has been the subject of reflection "thousands of times since." One must assume that the memory recurred to Audubon in 1820, when he began compiling material for *The Birds of America* in Louisiana. The text of "Myself" makes this connection all but explicit. The sketch breaks off with a reference to the *Journal:* "In October of 1820 I left your mother and yourselves at Cincinnati, and went to New Orleans on board a flat-boat. . . . From this date my jour-

---

13. On refugee narratives, see Alfred N. Hunt, *Haiti's Influence on Antebellum America: Slumbering Volcano in the Caribbean* (Baton Rouge, La., 1988). On the gothic, see Dayan, *Haiti, History, and the Gods,* 187–268.

nals are kept with fair regularity, and if you read them you will easily find all that followed afterward." "Myself" now comes full circle. The opening episodes insisted on the historical ties between Saint-Domingue and New Orleans and the terrifying ease with which the memory and example of Saint-Domingue circulates with the exiled planter. The close of the sketch returns us to a lower Louisiana transformed in recent decades by the arrival of exiles in overwhelming numbers. Whereas the format of *The Birds of America* evokes a history of Caribbean abundance, the narrative structure of "Myself" insists that its author inhabits a decisive moment within that history—one in which the labors of New World naturalists are required urgently.[14]

A number of engravings respond more or less directly to this crisis. The folios are filled with specimens that Audubon collected in Louisiana and the Florida Keys. "American Flamingo" (Plate 6) provides a showcase for the scale and technological sophistication of the engravings as a whole. With deft compositional management, creating a sinuous line of the bird's neck as it extends downward, a double elephant sheet can accommodate something close to the actual dimensions of a flamingo, even as the image suggests that this tropical species scarcely can be contained or rendered, that it exceeds the bounds of even this largest of natural history books. The brazen pink of the bird's plumage, and the distribution and range of tones within it, likewise calls attention to the way that Audubon strains at the limits of the representable. These effects can be produced only through a cutting-edge technique that combines etching, aquatint, and line engraving. The ornithological biography emphasizes the transgression of boundaries, both epistemological and geographic. Dwelling on the cooperative labors necessary to collection, study, and representation of the New World tropics, it maps the tight connections between the Caribbean and the United States as a rising empire. Having observed migrating flamingos during an expedi-

14. Audubon, "Myself," in Irmscher, ed., *Writings and Drawings*, 765, 766, 793. Nathalie Dessens claims, "Between 1791 and 1810, at least 15,000 (and possibly close to 20,000) refugees from Saint-Domingue settled in the Lower Mississippi region, most of them (80 to 90 percent) in New Orleans and its vicinity." A second wave in 1809 added roughly 10,000 individuals. The demographic impact of this second wave was enormous, representing an increase of "43 percent for the white population, 134 percent for the free population of color, and 38 percent for the slave population of New Orleans Parish," which already included large numbers of refugees from the earlier wave. See Nathalie Dessens, "The Saint-Domingue Refugees and the Preservation of Gallic Culture in Early American New Orleans," *French Colonial History*, VIII (2007), 53–69 (quotation on 56). See also Paul Lachance, "The 1809 Immigration of Saint-Domingue Refugees to New Orleans: Reception, Integration, and Impact," *Louisiana History*, XXIX (1988), 109–141.

tion to the Florida Keys aboard a U.S. naval vessel—yet unable to approach close enough to shoot one—Audubon relied on Cuban correspondents to provide him not only with reports on the behaviors and characteristics of the species but also with preserved specimens (both part and whole). The specimen comes to him from an island that had quickly replaced Saint-Domingue as the leading producer of sugar after the Haitian Revolution, owing in large part to the arrival of exiled planters. The engraving bears the traces of this correspondence in the anatomical sketches of bill, tongue, and feet along the upper margin, which lend scientific authority to the image, as the product of an Enlightenment culture that remains vigorous throughout plantation America. Read according to emblematic protocols, the engraving maintains that Caribbean accumulation proceeds apace. Yet the image also makes visible its origin in a process of collection and composition construed as grotesque violence, not only through the dismembered body parts along the top margin but also by the bird's contorted posture. In a manuscript essay entitled "My Style of Drawing Birds," Audubon detailed his use of wires, skewers, and common pins to position dead specimens into lifelike attitudes (though his earliest efforts more often resulted in "grotesque figure[s]"). The viewer logically assumes that he used such techniques in sketching the preserved flamingo.[15]

This is by no means the only way that Audubon's engravings record the memory and threat of violence. The potential for violence from below is implied through the sequencing of sentimentalized engravings of bird "couples" and "families." In "Carolina Turtle Dove" (Fig. 16), Audubon depicts two pairs of doves linked through a narrative of courtship and mating. Should the male at the top persuade the "coy" and "virgin-like" female (who leans away, as she opens her wings and feathers to fly off), he will enjoy the same conjugal bliss as the pair at the bottom, where a female "embosomed among the thick foliage" receives food from her mate's bill. Lest the viewer miss these visual cues, the text points them out directly, explaining the moral significance of the botanical background in terms that sound distinctly early modern: it is a "branch of Stuartia . . . ornamented with a profusion of white blossoms, emblematic of purity and chastity." This is, the text insists, a form of chastity and domestic devotion specific to the "south-

---

15. On the details of this printing process, see Blaugrund, "Artist as Entrepreneur," in Blaugrund and Stebbins, eds., *Watercolors for the Birds of America*, 37; "American Flamingo," in Audubon, *Ornithological Biography*, V, 255–264; Audubon, "My Style of Drawing Birds," in Irmscher, ed., *Writings and Drawings*, 759–764.

PLATE XVII.

Carolina Turtle Dove, COLUMBA CAROLINENSIS *Linn.* Males 1 Females 2. White flowered Stuartia. Stuartia Malacodendron.

FIGURE 16. *Carolina Turtle Dove and White-Flowered Stuartia.* Engraved by Robert Havell in John James Audubon, *The Birds of America: From Original Drawings*, 4 vols. (London, 1827–1838), pl. 17. Special Collections, University Library System, University of Pittsburgh

ernmost fringes of the United States," where stuartia is found commonly in large clusters. The image thus presents a version of plantation pastoral. At the same time, however, the relationship between bird and plant introduces a note of eroticism. In language recalling Erasmus Darwin's writings on plant sexuality, Audubon informs us that the heart of the female dove at the top is "so warmed and so swelled by the ardour of her passion, that it feels as ready to expand as the buds on the trees are."[16]

The combination of chastity and eroticism associated with this plant is characteristic of a Louisianan landscape described elsewhere in terms of its exhilarating profusion and differentiated sharply from the rest of North America. Audubon opens his biography of the mockingbird with a tableau filled with magnolias, begonias, stuartia, and interlacing vines. Possessing a sublime "love-song," the species makes its home in a region where "Nature seems . . . to have strewed with unsparing hand the diversified seeds from which have sprung all the beautiful and splendid forms which I should in vain attempt to describe." Only at the end of the passage does the narrator disclose that this strange and "favoured land" is within the United States, in "that great continent to whose distant shores Europe has sent forth her adventurous sons."[17]

Crucial to the unfolding drama of *The Birds of America* is Audubon's orchestration of sudden transitions between images such as "Carolina Turtle Dove" and his engraving of the "Mocking Bird and Florida Jessamine" (Fig. 17), from pastoral courtship to tropical predation. The *1826 Journal* records an experiment conducted on two refined female visitors to his studio. Having prepared the women with a viewing of "Carolina Turtle Dove," he turns suddenly to "Mocking Bird," hoping that some "explosion might be produced" from the contrast and pleased when his visitors cry out in pained surprise. Here, it is as if the rattlesnake has exploded from within the center of the nest to strike the startled mockingbird to its left. This species frequents the margins of Louisiana plantations, where planters so admire its habits of conjugal devotion that they "generally protect" it from hunters and predators. The ornithological biography thus depicts a gesture of planter solicitude for delicate birdlife not unlike what the young Audubon of "Myself" had pleaded for. Yet, just as the domestic allegory of "Myself" broods over the potential for sudden violence at the heart of French

16. "Carolina Dove," in Audubon, *Ornithological Biography*, I, 91, 93; Erasmus Darwin, *The Botanic Garden: A Poem, in Two Parts* . . . (London, 1789–1791).

17. "Mocking Bird," in Audubon, *Ornithological Biography*, I, 108.

FIGURE 17. *Mocking Bird and Florida Jessamine.* Engraved by Robert Havell in Audubon, *Birds of America*, pl. 21. Special Collections, University Library System, University of Pittsburgh

family life, images of violated domesticity such as "Mocking Bird" stage its recurrence in lower Louisiana.[18]

The Natural History of the Haitian Revolution II

To register the full impact of this threat, we must turn briefly to another forgotten natural history corpus. As discussed in Chapter 5, among the thousands of French Caribbean refugees to Philadelphia in the 1790s were a number of prominent members of the Cercle des Philadelphes, who integrated themselves into the American Philosophical Society. During the final years of the Haitian Revolution, the members of this scientific community turned their gaze to lower Louisiana. The brief months between Spain's retrocession of Louisiana to France and Napoleon's sale of the territory to the United States inspired an outpouring of francophone writing on the region. Works by Pierre Louis Berquin-Duvallon, Pierre-Louis Baudry des Lozières, and C. C. Robin, among others, appeared between 1802 and 1809. So successful was Baudry's *Voyage à la Louisiane* of 1802 in France that he published a much longer *Second Voyage* in 1803.[19]

Baudry's *Second Voyage* is the most interesting of these works. The gathering of natural historical intelligence in Louisiana is framed throughout the volumes as a heroic attempt to counter the epistemological consequences of the ongoing insurrection on Saint-Domingue, to address the gap in natural historical knowledge that he sees as its only legacy. In numerous commentaries on the natural history of Saint-Domingue, Baudry claims that his published books are a first, tentative effort to reassemble his notes and drafts for a massive colonial encyclopedia, compiled during the heyday of the Cercle and lost amid the ashes of Cap Français:

> To the extent that I can recollect the items that comprised my Colonial Encyclopedia, upon which I labored for eighteen years, which filled 24 or 25 quarto volumes, and which the brigands robbed me of in their insurrection, I will share them with the public, because one may find

18. Audubon, "1826 Journal," in Irmscher, ed., *Writings and Drawings*, 180.

19. [Pierre Louis] B[erquin]-Duvallon, *Vue de la colonie espagnole du Mississipi, ou des provinces de Louisiane et Floride occidentale, en l'année 1802* (Paris, 1803); [Pierre-Louis Baudry des Lozières], *Voyage à la Louisiane, et sur le continent de L'Amérique septentrionale, fait dans les années 1794 à 1798* (Paris, 1802); Baudry des Lozières, *Second voyage à la Louisiane, faisant suite au premier de l'auteur de 1794 a 98*, 2 vols. (Paris, 1803); Charles César Robin, *Voyages dans l'intérieur de la Louisiane, de la Floride occidentale, et dans les isles de la Martinique et de Saint-Domingue, pendant les années 1802, 1803, 1804, 1805, et 1806*, 3 vols. (Paris, 1807).

in them many useful things for the present and future . . . I must console myself with the labor of beginning again, and, in the days that remain to me, providing some small idea of what I once accomplished.

In a period when graphic depictions of corporeal violence on Saint-Domingue were commonplace, Baudry highlights epistemic violence. Slave revolution is understood as a negation of Enlightenment knowledge rather than the creative extension of republican liberty.[20]

Other references to a lost colonial encyclopedia insist on the value of planter refugees to a second Franco-American empire. The reformation of empire must begin with the proper management of Louisiana and thus will depend on planter knowledge:

> Botany and natural history, which have been so neglected in this remote region, are the two breasts of the colonial state. Delight, riches, and virtue all flow from these sublime studies! I sought to give proof of this in my Colonial Encyclopedia, the loss of which, in my weakness, I have regretted for so long. Botany should be the first pursuit for the man of virtue in the colonies, living far from great cities.

The *Second Voyage* articulates a conception of natural history's role in a virtuous and prosperous empire shared by all French chroniclers of Louisiana in the early nineteenth century.[21]

Jefferson's acquisition of Louisiana inspired a second, almost simultaneous, effort to chronicle the region's natural history. That effort bore fruit in the American Philosophical Society *Transactions*, in an 1803 congressional report entitled *An Account of Louisiana*, in Jefferson's correspondence, and in a translation of refugee Berquin-Duvallon's travel narrative by Jefferson's supporter John Davis. The superficial distinctions between these bodies of writing are as obvious as they are striking. For the refugees, Louisiana provided a base from which to begin recuperating the losses of the Haitian Revolution and reforming a Franco-American empire based explicitly on a hemispheric slave economy. For Jefferson and his partisans (at least at the level of official discourse), Louisiana promised to fulfill their vision of a yeoman empire beyond the influence of Old World commerce and decadence. Within each body of writing, however, the Haitian Revolution is depicted as a crisis of Enlightenment epistemology and representa-

20. [Baudry des Lozières], *Second voyage à la Louisiane*, II, 4 (translation mine).
21. Ibid., 30–31 (translation mine).

tion. Baudry's portrayal of the planter-naturalist, as "the man of virtue . . . living far from great cities," resonates with Jefferson's vision of the yeoman farmer as guardian against civic corruption. The narrative persona of the *Mississippi River Journal* emerges from the collision between these two bodies of writing, between the planter-refugee and yeoman farmer they frame as the representative of New World progress.[22]

Ornithology and Ethnology in Lower Louisiana

Throughout the *Mississippi River Journal*, strangely, the ostensibly primary task of ornithology competes in importance with ethnology. Accounts of ornithological fieldwork flow seamlessly into scenes of ethnological inquiry. This rich interplay between ethnology and ornithology reflects the close relationship between these fields within the epistemological organization of eighteenth-century natural history. But, although this older epistemology still structures the fluid practice of natural history within the journal, it is counterbalanced by a new, more disciplinary understanding of the natural sciences. The journal was written at a moment when the American School of Ethnology had begun its rapid rise to international prominence. Figures such as Samuel George Morton had begun the work in craniology that would help consolidate a new theory of biologic race and polygenesis, and ethnology thus had emerged as a distinct discipline within a new, specialized terrain of professional science.[23]

The geography of the Louisiana Delta made both ornithology and ethnology difficult tasks. Currents of wind and water made it home to a startling array of migratory birdlife. Those same currents brought ships, people, and commodities from throughout the Caribbean basin, making New Orleans and the surrounding region indispensable to the nation's expansionist designs. Possession of the Delta enabled the profitable extension of plantation agriculture into the Gulf South while easing the access of backcountry farmers to global markets.

22. *An Account of Louisiana, Being an Abstract of Documents, in the Offices of the Departments of State, and of the Treasury* (Philadelphia, 1803); [Pierre Louis Berquin-Duvallon], *Travels in Louisiana and the Floridas, in the Year 1802: Giving a Correct Picture of Those Countries,* trans. John Davis (New York, 1806). For just a fraction of Jefferson's correspondence and official writing on the geography of Louisiana, see *WTJ*, VIII, 241, 243, 244, 294, 344.

23. George M. Fredrickson, *The Black Image in the White Mind: The Debate on Afro-American Character and Destiny, 1817–1914* (1971; rpt. Middletown, Conn., 1987). For an astute critical analysis of Morton's visual aesthetics, see Samuel Otter, *Melville's Anatomies* (Berkeley, Calif., 1999), 102–118.

Owing to its geographic location, the Delta occupied a paradoxical position for U.S. writers and thinkers. As a number of social and cultural historians have demonstrated, by the 1820s, New Orleans and the Delta were undergoing simultaneous processes of Americanization and Caribbeanization. Although the political incorporation of the region into the United States had begun in 1804, the ensuing two decades also witnessed a large influx of refugees from Saint-Domingue. The infusion of Saint-Dominguan capital, labor, and technology into lower Louisiana transformed it into a plantation society on a French Caribbean model, as numbers of thriving sugar plantations were established. By the time of Audubon's journey, which of these processes would determine the character of the region was still highly uncertain. To seize the material potential of the region entailed the risk of internalizing the Caribbean plantation.[24]

The transformation of racial demographics within the Delta made such questions urgent. Robert L. Paquette writes, "The relatively equal proportions of whites and slaves and the size of the free colored class . . . distinguished lower Louisiana from every state in the union." Demographically speaking, the region "bore a far greater resemblance . . . to the sugar plantation zone around the rising western Cuban port of Matanzas." Demographic change brought with it the possibility of a second successful slave revolt, on the model of Haiti's, within the boundaries of the new nation, and fears mounted with the discovery of a series of (alleged) conspiracies. But such change was disturbing to U.S. chroniclers for other reasons as well. A large population of "free coloreds" testified to a legacy of métissage. That history made the racial identity of the creole an object of scientific scrutiny.[25]

Indeed, as Gwendolyn Midlo Hall argues, scientific inquiry inspired a wholesale redefinition of the term "creole." During the French period, the term referred to "locally born people of at least partial African descent, slave and free." With American possession, common usage began to shift as French colonists struggled to preserve (or manufacture) a distinct cultural heritage. Creole was used to distinguish "that which was truly native to Louisiana from that which was Anglo." During the early phase of American-

24. Ashli White, "The Limits of Fear: The Saint Dominguan Challenge to Slave Trade Abolition in the United States," *Early American Studies*, II (2004), 362–397; Kimberly S. Hanger, "Conflicting Loyalties: The French Revolution and Free People of Color in Spanish New Orleans," and Robert L. Paquette, "Revolutionary Saint Domingue in the Making of Territorial Louisiana," both in David Barry Gaspar and David Patrick Geggus, eds., *A Turbulent Time: The French Revolution and the Greater Caribbean* (Bloomington, Ind., 1997), 178–203, 204–225.

25. Paquette, "Revolutionary Saint Domingue," in Gaspar and Geggus, eds., *Turbulent Time*, 214.

ization the term became racially inclusive, used to describe not only Africans but also Europeans born in the region. The inclusiveness of the term became problematic with the rise of ethnology and "scientific racism" in the nineteenth century, and, as a result, Louisianans of French or Spanish descent "rejected the racial openness of Louisiana's past, as well as, in some cases, their own racially mixed heritage, and redefined *creole* to mean exclusively white." By this logic, creole society engaged in a form of collective racial passing, one motivated by the emergence of a new form of ethnological discourse.[26]

In the *Mississippi River Journal,* Audubon fashions himself as an agent of Americanization, an individual whose finely attuned powers of observation are necessary to successful incorporation of the region. While docked near Bayou Lafourche (a few days upriver from New Orleans) on January 3, 1821, Audubon is interrupted by a group of curious locals as he works on some new sketches:

> We Were Visited by several *french Creoles* this is a Breed of Annimals, that Neither speak french English nor Spanish corectly but have a Jargon composed of the Impure parts of these three—they Stared at My Drawings, and when a litle Composed Gazed and Complimented Me very Highly—on asking them the names of about a dozen diferent Birds then lying on the Table they Made at once and without hesitating a Solid Mass of *Yellow Birds* of the whole = One of them a young Man told Me that he Could procure 3 or 4 dozen of them every Night by hunting the Orange trees with a Lantern—I Can said he "see the Rascalls' White bellies and knok them down with a Stick very handy" = few of these good Natured fools could answer any valuable account of the Country.

To Audubon's ears, his guests speak an impure dialect, embodying the region's history of successive colonization. Through an improvised experiment, he determines that creoles are unable to draw proper ornithological distinctions between the varieties of yellow birds. In Audubon's view, their disregard for the proper boundaries between languages and human populations renders them incapable of perceiving the demarcations between species. Audubon's ability to do so renders him distinct from the creole.[27]

26. Gwendolyn Midlo Hall, *Africans in Colonial Louisiana: The Development of Afro-Creole Culture in the Eighteenth Century* (Baton Rouge, La., 1992), 157.

27. Audubon, "Mississippi River Journal," in Irmscher, ed., *Writings and Drawings,* 67–68. Audubon's

Even as Audubon insists on this distinction, however, his journal portrays his journey to the Delta as a return to Saint-Domingue. As he descends the Mississippi, he notes, "The Plantations increase in number, and the Shores have Much the Appearance of those on Some of the Large river of France, their Lowness Excepted." Although the surrounding architecture recalls his boyhood home in the Loire Valley, it also conjures the less consoling memories passed down to him from his late father. A few pages earlier, Audubon provided a brief account of his ancestry, beginning with the rise and fall of his father's fortunes in Saint-Domingue. (He would later expand this account into the opening paragraphs of "Myself.") That same day, while passing Baton Rouge, he noted the orange trees, alligators, and "luxuriant verdure" around several "Rich planter's habitation[s]" while copying some of his father's old letters. His French Caribbean genealogy is prominent in his thoughts when, approaching New Orleans, he passes scenes such as *"Monsieur St. Amand's* Sugar Plantation." The journal commences with a double movement of prospect and retrospect, looking forward to the incorporation of Louisiana and its natural resources even as it looks backward on the tragic decline of the French Caribbean plantocracy. It fuses the optimism of Benjamin Franklin's *Autobiography* with Baudry's colonialist grief.[28]

This double movement reaches its crisis in New Orleans. Eleven of the fourteen months chronicled in the *Mississippi River Journal* are passed within the city. Unable to raise funds for exploring the backcountry, Audubon is stuck in the port city, at times without any fixed residence. Typical of these months are entries in which Audubon combs the New Orleans markets, teeming with fresh-killed fowl, for specimens to sketch and paint: "Having found No Work to do remained on Board the Keel Boat opposite the Market, the Dirtiest place in all the Cities of the United States." In several entries, he is frustrated to discover examples of undocumented species in the markets, too mangled to draw. Whereas the contemporaneous journals of Benjamin Latrobe establish the markets of New Orleans as spaces of interracial contact and Afro-Caribbean performance, Audubon's journals specify them as one characteristic site for his early practice of ornithology.[29]

use of the term "creole" in the journal reflects a transitional moment in its history, after it has been stigmatized but before it has been successfully redefined to exclude associations with blackness.

    28. Ibid., 65–66, 71.

    29. Ibid., 74, 78–79; Edward C. Carter II, John C. Van Horne, and Lee W. Formwalt, eds., *The Journals of Benjamin Henry Latrobe, 1799–1820: From Philadelphia to New Orleans* (New Haven, Conn., 1980), 171–172, 200–205.

In his account of a morning visit to the levee on January 14, Audubon provides a window into his bizarre circumstance as urban ornithologist. Just before the passage, he has been refused a menial position as assistant to the portraitist John Wesley Jarvis. His confidence shaken, he surveys the urban mob around him:

> The Levée early was Crowded by people of all Sorts as well as Colors, the Market, very aboundant, the Church Bells ringing the Billiard Balls knocking, the Guns heard all around, What a Display this is for a Steady quaker of Philada or Cincinnati — the day was beautifull and the crowd Increased considerably — I saw however no handsome Woman and the Citron hüe of allmost all is very disgusting to one who Likes the rosy Yankée or English Cheeks.

Audubon perceives the full spectrum of national, racial, and ethnic types in the city as a threatening and disorienting surplus. He recoils from the "Citron hüe" of its denizens as he conjures the consoling memory of a racially pure visage.[30]

In a narrative transition characteristic of the journal, Audubon responds to this social encounter by hunting birds in the surrounding wetlands:

> I took My Gun, rowed out to the edge of the Eddy and killed a Fish Crow, those Birds are plenty on the River every fair day — (when otherwise, the food is plenty in the swamps, the Crabs, Young Frogs, Watter Snakes, etc Shewing out in great numbers) — When the one I killed fell, hundreds flew to him, and appeared as if about to Carry him off, but they soon found it their Interest to let me have him, I drew Near and Loaded for another; they all rose in Circling Like Hawks extremely High.

Natural history provides a forum in which to reestablish distinction. On the levee, Audubon is subsumed within the creole mob. In the swamp, he reemerges, at least momentarily, as a heroic individual, possessing his proper "rights in the scale of nature."[31]

The entire narrative segment, however, concludes where it began — with a haunting evocation of racial multiplicity and of the artist's vagrancy. In a separate entry written the same evening, Audubon describes his effort to paint the fish crow:

30. Audubon, "Mississippi River Journal," in Irmscher, ed., *Writings and Drawings,* 77.
31. Audubon, "Mississippi River Journal," and "Myself," ibid., 77, 766.

I brought it on Board and began to Work imediatly—at Dusk took a Walk to Mr Gordon, from then on to Mr *Laville* where We saw some *White Ladies* and Good Looking ones—returning on Board the quartroon Ball attracted My View—but as it cost 1$ Entrance I Merely Listened a Short time to the Noise and came Home as We are pleased to Call it—.

In the light of day, on the levee and in the markets, a multiracial populace parades before Audubon's dismayed eyes. In his evening wanderings, the sources of métissage are revealed to him in social practices such as "quadroon balls."[32]

In passages such as these, natural history is driven by a rage for order amid the heterogeneity of the region. The natural and human diversity of lower Louisiana is collected, classified, and displayed in *The Birds of America* as national resource, the spoils of hemispheric expansion. Yet these passages are counterbalanced by an equal number in which Audubon reacts to being scrutinized: "Saw My Old Acquaintance John Gwathmey of Louisville, he was *a la guettée* on the Levée the appearance of My clothes, did Not please him we talk but Litle together." In a similar entry from New Orleans, he remarks: "Going through the Streets Not unlike (I dare Say) a Wild Man thinking too much to think at all My Eyes were attracted by a handsome faced Man, I knew it was My Old Acquaintance and Friend . . . We Met freely and I was eased." Walking the streets of New Orleans in a period of near indigence, Audubon fears that his former friend will fail to recognize him, confirming his loss of social identity after the Panic of 1819. More pointedly, he fears that his friend will misrecognize him as a member of the creole mob.[33]

Audubon's reference to himself as "a Wild Man" in the passage echoes his reference to the orangutan in "Myself" as "man of the woods." As Irmscher observes, Audubon's use of the terms "Wild Man" and "the woodsman" as favorite monikers throughout his career resonates with his description of the orangutan, betraying considerable ambivalence about his dual status as "preserver and destroyer of birds." If we read the episode from "Myself" as an allegory, with the orangutan as a representation of the insurrectionary slave, then Audubon's use of the terms also betrays uneasiness about his own racial identity, and, in the context of his reversal of fortunes after the

32. Audubon, "Mississippi River Journal," ibid., 77–78.
33. Ibid., 90, 97.

Panic of 1819, about how the loss of social station might, to the discerning eye, suggest a fall in the "scale of nature." Audubon is both subject and object of the ethnological gaze, taxonomist of racial multiplicity and living embodiment of it. Such passages are part of a tradition of writing on the creole naturalist's paradoxical position, which is detailed in prior chapters on Bartram's self-scrutiny in colonial East Florida and Jefferson's autoethnology of plantation manners. During a period marked by the rise of racialist science amid nationalism, however, the anxieties expressed within Audubon's journals are acute. Those anxieties are connected with the major aesthetic innovations of Audubon's early career. The challenge to "the conceptual separation" between bird and viewer depends on his gothicized images of birds of prey, with their focus on mutilated eyes and arresting gazes.[34]

From Subject to Specimen

Full-spread images of birds of prey play a prominent role in the visual drama of *The Birds of America*. Widening the frame of observation, they provide detailed renderings of interspecies violence. Most depict the bird of prey performing one (or both) of two characteristic behaviors: consuming the eyes of its prey and returning the gaze of the viewer.[35]

That these visual motifs emerge during the Louisiana period can be established through an analysis of "Great-Footed Hawk and Green-Winged Teal and Gadwal" (Plate 7). Audubon composed the original watercolor version in stages, sketching the female specimen on the right on the banks of the Mississippi River in 1820, just a few days after entering the Delta. A strong diagonal runs from the female's taut tail feathers through the bright drop of blood suspended from its beak. The rest of the image was composed in watercolor a few years after the original pastel and evinces the rapid development of Audubon's style. The floating feather near the center establishes a sense of temporal immediacy, augmenting the effect created by the drop of blood. The female has ripped open the torso of the gadwal and devoured its right eye. A bloody eye-socket punctuates the foreground. The talons of the male falcon penetrate the corpse of a second gadwal. Crouching over its prey, the falcon spreads its wings and splays its tail feathers to

34. Irmscher, *Poetics of Natural History*, 206; Shelby Blum, *Picturing Nature*, 106.
35. For further examples, see Audubon, "White-Headed Eagle, *Falco leucocephalus*," "Red-Shouldered Hawk and Virginian Partridge, *Perdix virginiana*," "Winter Hawk, *Falco hyemalis*," "Golden Eagle, *Aquila chrysaetos*," "Female Adult, Northern Hare," all in Audubon, *Birds of America*, pl. 31, 76, 71, 181. Though the engraving of "White-headed Eagle" does not contain a mutilated eye, the original watercolor does.

create dynamic points and angles. Its fierce gaze, meanwhile, is fixed on the viewer.[36]

Perhaps the most fascinating treatment of these same themes and formal strategies is found in "Black Vulture or Carrion Crow and American Deer" (Plate 8). Even in a corpus marked by graphic, at times morbid, scenes of scavenging and predation, the image stands out. The vulture on the right holds down the deer's antler, peering with an unnerving blend of disinterest and curiosity into a not-quite-lifeless eye. With the deer perhaps still breathing (its pink tongue hangs from its jaw), the vulture pauses in a seemingly reflective attitude as it prepares to consume the eye. The upheld black wings create a somber frame and lend an air of theatricality. It is as if the vulture has just retracted its wing to reveal this scene to us or is about to lower the wing and conceal it from our view.

The ornithological biography draws attention to these bleak visual details. Audubon includes testimonies from two South Carolina planters to support his hypothesis that the species feeds on live animals. In the first, a planter discovers two vultures atop a sick horse: "They had already plucked out the eyes of the horse, and picked a wound in the anus . . . he struggled considerably whilst the Buzzards were operating on him, but was unable to rise from the ground." In the second, a two-year-old cow is attacked by a carrion crow, which "picked out one of its eyes, and would have killed it by feeding on it while alive, if it had not been discovered."[37]

Foregrounding gory details, the ornithological biography also locates the species in plantation America. (So, too, does the placement of the sketch within the *Ornithological Biography,* just after a chapter entitled "The Runaway" describing Audubon's encounter with a fugitive slave in a Louisiana swamp.) It further insists that themes of ocular perception are crucial to the image. Audubon defends his theory that the black vulture locates its prey by sight rather than, as commonly thought, by smell. Surveying the plantation landscape from above, it can locate even the smallest dead animals. So acute are its powers of vision that the carrion crow can determine when an animal is about to die:

The power given to them by nature of discerning the approaching death of a wounded animal, is truly remarkable. They will watch each individual thus assailed by misfortune, and follow it with keen perse-

36. My reading of the engraving has been influenced by Blaugrund and Stebbins, eds., *Watercolors for the Birds of America*, 145.

37. "The Black Vulture, or Carrion Crow," in Audubon, *Ornithological Biography*, II, 48–49.

verance, until the loss of life has rendered it their prey . . . they often watch the young kid, the lamb and the pig issuing from the mother's womb, and attack it with direful success . . . judge then, how well they must see.

By specifying that the ocular powers of the species give it foreknowledge of death (and birth), the sketch creates a narrative frame around the image as a terrifying meditation on the prospect of death in life.[38]

Animals may not be alone in suffering such a fate, for the carrion crow can observe, remember, and recognize individual human beings: "The Carrion Crow and Turkey Buzzard possess great power of recollection, so as to recognise at a great distance a person who has shot at them, and even the horse on which he rides. On several occasions I have observed that they would fly off at my approach, after I had trapped several, when they took no notice of other individuals."[39]

What to make of this gothic blend of morbidity and recollection, of mutilated eyes and heightened ocular powers, within a plantation setting? We must turn to the *Mississippi River Journal* for a final interpretive context. Within the narrative progression of the journal, the carrion crow stands at the threshold between geographic zones—between the western backcountry of the United States and the Greater Caribbean. Audubon first describes the species upon his arrival in the slave market of Natchez, Mississippi, in the midst of observations on the climate of this strange, new region. For the American traveler, "Numberless prostrated Carrion Crows in the less frequented Streets prove to him the unhalthiness of the Atmosphere." Within the overarching narrative of his life provided by "Myself," then, the species also stands at a temporal threshold. The narrator's encounter with the carrion crow in Natchez marks the moment when his French Caribbean past returns to trouble his American future.[40]

Established at the outset of the *Journal*, the rich significance of the carrion crow is underscored in the ornithological biography by its association with the creole mob. Like the mob, its preferred place of congregation and recreation is the urban market: "Charleston, Savannah, New Orleans, Natchez, and other cities, are amply provided with these birds, which may be seen flying or walking about the streets the whole day in groups. They also regularly attend the markets and shambles, to pick up the pieces of

38. Ibid., 39–40.
39. Ibid., 50–51.
40. Audubon, "Mississippi River Journal," in Irmscher, ed., *Writings and Drawings*, 60.

flesh thrown away by the butchers." While in Natchez, Audubon remarks of the species "that many individuals known to me by particular marks made on them, and a *special cast of countenance,* were positively constant residents of town." There is a dynamic of identification and repudiation at work here. The passage presents both Audubon and the carrion crow as scavengers and vagrants. Audubon can only recognize the countenances of individual birds because the exigencies of his current financial situation make him a constant visitor to the markets. The passage thus makes palpable his anxiety that his own countenance might itself become an object of sustained examination.[41]

This is why Audubon's first description of the carrion crow in Natchez is followed by one of the scenes of nonrecognition characteristic of the journal: "I saw here a Gentleman with whom I travelled some distance down the Mississippi My first Voyage but as he did Not or Would Not recognize my features I spoke not to him." It is worth dwelling here on Audubon's specific complaint that the gentleman will not "recognize my features." The moment records Audubon's fear that he has been reduced to a set of phenotypes, his perception that, with his passage into a new geographic region, he has also entered a new social landscape organized around a different racial taxonomy, one with important implications for how his identity might be interpreted and classified. Running beneath the narrator's complaint is his realization that perhaps his features have been recognized too well.[42]

The issues of discernment and recollection in "Black Vulture" are linked in accompanying texts with the blank gaze Audubon so often receives from his former associates. Mutilated eyes and arresting gazes emerge as prominent motifs in his images from this period because his return to the Caribbean vortex brings with it a fear of his impending social death. He knows that the creole bears with him a long and tangled history, one that involves not only the accumulation of wealth and knowledge (desired so ardently by his adopted nation) but also of identities. And he knows that, in the eyes of this nation, the bearers of that history can exist only as living specters, troubling the collective fiction it calls historical progress.

41. Audubon, *Ornithological Biography,* II, 41, 48.
42. Audubon, "Mississippi River Journal," in Irmscher, ed., *Writings and Drawings,* 61.

Epilogue HUMBOLDT'S HAVANA

It is a widely known but generally underappreciated fact that Alexander von Humboldt visited Cuba twice during his extensive travels in the Americas from 1799 to 1804. Hosted by Havana's cosmopolitan scientific community and assisted throughout his travels by Aimé Bonpland, the celebrated naturalist and author compiled materials for what would become a fascinating physical and cultural geography of the island. Appearing first as part of his *Voyage aux régions équinoxiales du nouveau continent* (1805–1834)—his thirty-volume narrative of his researches in the tropics—Humboldt's writings on Cuba would be republished in a freestanding edition entitled *Essai politique sur l'île de Cuba* the following year. This was only the first of the text's afterlives, including its appearance over the next thirty years in two English translations—the first published by Helen Williams in 1829 as a chapter in the *Personal Narrative* (her translation of *Voyage aux régions équinoxiales)* and the second published in New York in 1856 by J. S. Thrasher, a southern proponent of Cuban annexation. Owing to its omission of Humboldt's essay on slavery near the conclusion of the text, with its strong abolitionist appeal, Thrasher's translation became a subject of immediate public controversy.[1]

By the time Thrasher's American edition of Humboldt's essay appeared in 1856, perhaps no other scientific author had achieved such wide acclaim. As Laura Dassow Walls argues, although "today Humboldt is forgotten in the United States," in the mid-nineteenth century, "he was the predominant intellectual of his age, the most famous scientist in the world, and, as was widely repeated, the most famous human being after Napoleon." Although Humboldt was undoubtedly best known for his voluminous writings on Central and South America, the broad circulation of his essay on Cuba demonstrates the continued importance of West Indian nature as an

---

1. Alexandre de Humboldt, *Voyage aux régions équinoxiales du nouveau continent, fait dans les années 1799 à 1804,* 30 vols. (Paris, 1805–1834); Humboldt, *Essai politique sur l'île de Cuba* (Paris, 1826); Humboldt, *Personal Narrative of Travels to the Equinoctial Regions of the New Continent during the Years 1799–1804,* trans. Helen Maria Williams, 7 vols. (London, 1814–1829); Humboldt, *The Island of Cuba,* trans. J. S. Thrasher (New York, 1856). On Humboldt's itinerary in Cuba and the controversy over Thrasher's translation, see Humboldt, *The Island of Cuba: A Political Essay,* ed. Luis Martínez-Fernández, trans. John S. Thrasher (Princeton, N.J, 2001), 1–17.

object of scientific knowledge and site of literary innovation in the early to mid-nineteenth century. At the same time, however, the decline of Humboldt's reputation reflects a number of historical transformations that contributed to foreclosing the hemispheric routes of American Enlightenment traced in this study: the decline of natural history due to the professionalization of natural science, the gradual separation between literary and scientific epistemologies, the diminished importance of the global commercial vision exemplified by Abbé Raynal's *Philosophical and Political History of the Settlements and Trade of the Europeans in the East and West Indies* as European imperial ambitions shifted toward South Asia and Africa.[2]

Humboldt's decision to devote a lengthy and minutely detailed volume to Cuba was informed by precisely the history of natural history that we have pursued from Hans Sloane to John James Audubon. Consider the following passage from the opening section of Humboldt's essay. The naturalist advances a novel argument that the importance of Cuba turns, not on the fertility of its soil (and thus not on its suitability for sugar cultivation), but on its geographic location, including the advantageous situation of Havana as its primary city and harbor:

> The Island of Cuba is not only the largest of the Antilles (its surface area differs little from that of England proper, without Wales); thanks to its narrow, elongated shape, it also has an extensive coastline. It neighbors on Haiti, Jamaica, the southernmost province of the United States (Florida), and the easternmost province of Mexico (Yucatán). This circumstance merits the most serious attention, because the countries that are accessible by sea in ten to twelve days—Jamaica, Haiti, Cuba, and the southern portion of the United States (from Louisiana to Virginia)—are home to more than 2.8 million Africans. Ever since Santo Domingo, Florida, and New Spain *broke away from the Spanish metropole,* the island of Cuba has been linked only by religion, language, and mores to the countries that surround it, countries that had been subject to the same laws for centuries.

From Mark Catesby's *Natural History of Carolina* through Audubon's *Ornithological Biography* and *Birds of America,* North American readers had been trained to regard the southern colonies (later, states) in precisely these terms—as part of an extended Caribbean region that was both a primary

---

2. Laura Dassow Walls, *The Passage to Cosmos: Alexander von Humboldt and the Shaping of America* (Chicago, 2009), ix.

source of national wealth and enlightened knowledge and a corrosive influence on national manners, borders, and beliefs. Humboldt heightens the
stakes of this cognitive geography. The fate of Cuba will determine whether
current historical developments in the Greater Caribbean tend toward the
formation of a "New World Mediterranean" or, as Humboldt proposes later
in the essay, "An African Confederation of the Free States of the Antilles."[3]

In proposing the latter possibility, Humboldt has an eye on influencing
political debates over slavery within the nineteenth-century United States.
In a period when expansionist desires focused on the prospect of Cuban annexation, Humboldt foregrounds its potential consequences for the nation's
territorial integrity:

> Florida forms the last link of this long chain of federal states whose
> northern reaches touch the basin of the Saint Lawrence River and
> which extends from the region of palms to a region of the most severe
> winters. The inhabitants of New England regard as public dangers
> the increasing growth of the black population, the larger number of
> *slave states*, and their appetite for cultivating colonial commodities.
> They vow that the *Straits of Florida*—the current border of the great
> American Federation—shall not be crossed save in the name of free
> trade founded upon equal rights. They fear that Havana might fall
> under the domination of a European power even more menacing than
> Spain. They are no less desirous that the political ties that once bound
> Louisiana, Pensacola, and Saint Augustine in Florida to the Island of
> Cuba should remain severed forever.

By reanimating the political connections between Cuba, Louisiana, and
Florida, Humboldt maintains, the annexation of the island may create dangers for the United States, especially given the possibility of black political
sovereignty in the extended region.[4]

Humboldt foregrounds this map of the Americas as a result of his familiarity with a hemispheric network of the curious and learned, one that the
itinerary of his travels put him in a position to experience in its full dimensions. When Humboldt arrived in the United States in 1804 for a brief visit
at the end of his New World travels, this network was considered vital to
the business of American Enlightenment. But Humboldt also composed

3. Alexander von Humboldt, *Political Essay on the Island of Cuba: A Critical Edition*, ed. Vera M.
Kutzinski and Ottmar Ette (Chicago, 2011), I, 3–4.
4. Ibid, 4–5.

his essay during a period when this older understanding of the hemisphere had been challenged over the preceding three decades by a new and strange vision for the future of enlightened modernity in the Americas, articulated most clearly by Humboldt's longtime correspondent Thomas Jefferson in *Notes on the State of Virginia*. As examined in Chapter 5 of this study, Jefferson's treatise obscured the necessity of West Indian trade for national prosperity. This is nowhere so clear as the query on "Sea-Ports," quoted here in full: "Having no ports but our rivers and creeks, this Query has been answered under the preceding one." Jefferson publishes such a sentence even as he knows that the food crops grown by Virginia's yeomanry will be exported to the West Indies.[5]

Jefferson's influential vision bears on the formal pattern of the *Essai politique sur l'île de Cuba*. The volume is normally experienced as a disappointment in formal terms, especially when compared with earlier volumes of the *Personal Narrative*. Modern scholarship has argued that the *Personal Narrative* challenges the prevailing epistemological assumptions of its time, experimenting with new protocols and forms of scientific inquiry that have been described as "empirical holism" or "social ecology." The narrative mode of those earlier volumes, moreover, is understood as a requisite feature of their challenge to epistemological conventions. Through the fusion of scientific inquiry and first-person travel narration, in a manner that bears analogy to the representational strategies of Sloane, William Bartram, Crèvecoeur, and Audubon, the act of perception is depicted as a dynamic process. Humboldt-as-narrator garners knowledge of the natural world through exposure to its psychological and corporeal impact. In the *Essai politique sur l'île de Cuba*, however, Humboldt eschews the organizing device of a single, concretely embodied narrator and instead provides a systematic and synchronic overview of a single locale, beginning with sections devoted to geology, climate, and geography before proceeding to questions of social organization, agriculture, and commerce.[6]

The organization of the essay mirrors Jefferson's *Notes* in order to critique a vision of American republicanism in which Caribbean affairs hold little place. Adhering to the Physiocratic principle that the political and legal systems of a society must be harmonious with its local climate, Jeffer-

5. Thomas Jefferson, *Notes on the State of Virginia*, ed. William Peden (1982; rpt. Chapel Hill, 1995), 17.

6. Laura Dassow Walls, *Seeing New Worlds: Henry David Thoreau and Nineteenth-Century Natural Science* (Madison, Wis., 1995), 84–93; Aaron Sachs, *The Humboldt Current: Nineteenth-Century Exploration and the Roots of American Environmentalism* (New York, 2007), 41–72.

son structures his treatise so that his remarks on geography, topography, climate, flora, and fauna precede his meditations on society, law, and culture. Conforming to the model, Humboldt's essay on Cuba proceeds incrementally from matters of physical geography and natural history to questions of social and political organization, reflecting not only Humboldt's immersion in Physiocratic thought but also his deep admiration for Jefferson's treatise. Humboldt makes central and explicit precisely what Jefferson repudiates in print—the hemispheric dimensions of slavery and the Caribbean routes of commercial prosperity.[7]

Humboldt advances this argument by infusing his natural history with psychological drama. In the final chapter, on slavery, Humboldt reflects back on his efforts as "an historian of America," describing his book as an "investigation of the facts, which borders on the obsessive." His remark captures the strangeness of a text that, in considering problems of social inequality and exploitation in Cuba, descends to details as minute as the mineral composition of its surrounding reefs and the chemistry of sugar manufacture. Within the overarching formal structure of the work, Humboldt's pursuit of such topics stems from the disorientation produced by Havana harbor:

> Havana's appearance from the entrance of the port is one of the most pleasant and picturesque on the coastline of tropical America north of the equator. Celebrated by travelers of all nations, this site has neither the luxurious vegetation that lines the banks of the Guayaquil, nor the wild majesty of Rio de Janeiro's rocky shoreline, two ports in the southern hemisphere. But it has the grace that, in our climates, embellishes scenes of cultivated nature, blending the majesty of vegetal forms with an organic vigor typical of the torrid zone. In this mixture of gentle impressions, the European forgets the dangers that threaten him at the heart of the Antilles' populous cities. He tries to take in the diverse elements of a vast landscape: the fortified castles that crown the rocks to the left of the port, an interior basin surrounded by villages and farms; the palm trees that grow to a prodigious height; the city half-hidden behind a forest of masts and sails.

This passage is best understood in the context of Humboldt's wider interest in the "view" as an epistemological instrument. A naïve European traveler

---

7. Helmut de Terra, "Alexander von Humboldt's Correspondence with Jefferson, Madison, and Gallatin," American Philosophical Society, *Proceedings*, CIII (1959), 783–806.

here surveys the harbor in a moment of heightened perception. In so doing, he initially "forgets" the dangers that await him in an urban center such as Havana. Within the overall drama of the passage, however, this moment of perceptual distortion is also enabling. By setting aside, for an instant, the dominant fact of Cuban society, Humboldt's viewer catches a glimpse of an alternative New World future, one no longer determined by the barbarity of the tropical plantation but by the synthesis of tropical fecundity with the civilizing potential of commerce. (The reader has been informed previously that Havana lies where "the trade routes of many people cross.") This potential future, latent in the material constitution of the harbor, finds figurative embodiment in the viewer's uncanny misperception of the waterfront as a "forest of masts and sails." The port city appears to merge with the palm trees dotting the surrounding landscape. Yet this misperception also culminates a shift from the picturesque to the sublime, for the "forest of masts and sails" is an image of disorienting surplus. In subsequent sections, Humboldt will strive to reduce this vision—as destabilizing as it is exhilarating—to its constituent parts. Whereas the arriving European catches sight of the rocky outcroppings east of the port, Humboldt will penetrate in subsequent pages to the limestone foundations of the island, as he seeks to account for its geographic orientation, fertility, and defensibility.[8]

Humboldt's description of the harbor exemplifies the long historical transformation, traced in this study, from emblematic to symbolic interpretations of nature. Humboldt still "reads" his natural surroundings to discern the patterns behind and within ordinary existence (in the manner of an early modern emblem), perceiving the harbor as a concrete reality that momentarily reveals something universal (in the manner of a Romantic symbol). In so doing, he situates his text in a distinguished tradition of Caribbean natural history writing. This formal strategy is consistent with Humboldt's ambition to restore Cuba in particular and the Caribbean region in general to a central position in geopolitical and geoeconomic thought. Humboldt draws on the authority of prior natural histories even as he strives to transform that discursive tradition from within. The early sections proceed against the grain of such histories, arguing that plantation agriculture represents, not the fulfillment of tropical ecology, but rather the tragic squandering of its potential to increase human happiness. This critical understanding builds steadily in the text, surfacing near the conclusion with Humboldt's eloquent antislavery polemic.

8. Humboldt, *Political Essay on the Island of Cuba*, ed. Kutzinski and Ette, I, 2, 9, 305.

The text's formal structure, however, also makes it susceptible to mistranslation by a proslavery annexationist such as Thrasher. The controversy over Thrasher's omission of the final chapter turns on a question of form. In responding to Humboldt's protests, in an 1856 letter to the *New York Daily Times*, Thrasher appeals to Romantic notions of aesthetic unity. Defending himself against the charge that he has "mutilated" Humboldt's text, he argues he has merely omitted a concluding chapter that seemed more like a "distinct essay," one in which "Cuba is only incidentally alluded to." Thrasher's claim here is surely disingenuous, but it is also revealing. His editorial manipulations clarify the risks of Humboldt's decision to separate his subjective responses to slavery from his scientific survey of Cuba, to reserve moral sentiment for a concluding polemic. Put another way, Thrasher's mistranslation forces Humboldt to pay the cost of abandoning the aesthetic innovations of earlier volumes in the *Personal Narrative*. Because science and sentiment are not integrated in the same manner in the *Essai politique sur l'île de Cuba* as in previous volumes, Thrasher can exploit structural affinities between Humboldt's essay and earlier natural histories of the region, which were also designed—though for different ideological purposes—to demonstrate the world-historical significance of particular West Indian islands.[9]

Humboldt was likely aware of this potential risk. In the final pages of the *Essai politique sur l'île de Cuba,* he returns to the narrative mode of his volumes on South America, incorporating his knowledge of slavery into his firsthand descriptions of his scientific practice. Here is the description of his final view of Cuba as he departs for the Spanish mainland:

By setting sail for the S¼SE, we lost sight of the palm-dotted shoreline, the hills in the town of Trinidad, and Cuba's high mountains. There is something solemn in the appearance of a land sinking, little by little, beneath the sea's horizon as one pulls away. This image had a special poignancy during a period when Saint-Domingue, a center of political unrest, threatened to engulf the other islands in one of these bloody fights that reveals the cruelty of the human species.

The passage provides a counterpoint to the view of Havana at the beginning of the essay, even as it mirrors Humboldt's well-known description

9. J. S. Thrasher, "Baron Humboldt and Mr. Thrasher," *New York Daily Times*, Aug. 16, 1856, 1. For Humboldt's previous letter to the editor, see "Baron Von Humboldt's Political Essay on Cuba—Letter from the Author on the Omission of a Chapter by the Translator," *New York Daily Times*, Aug. 12, 1856, 2.

of coastal Venezuela in the first volume of the *Personal Narrative*. Surveying the coast of terra firma for the first time, Humboldt there proposed a close relationship between empirical observation and individual memory and psychology: "The coasts from a distance are like clouds, where each observer sees the form of the objects that occupy his imagination." In a sense, then, Humboldt's final glimpse of Cuba brings us full circle to the beginning of his travels in the Americas, but this time with our imagination occupied by a new and formidable object. At the close of the *Essai politique sur l'île de Cuba*, we are invited to reread or recall the *Personal Narrative* in the new light afforded by Humboldt's obsessive inquiry into Cuban society, geography, and natural history, born of his traumatic awakening upon entering Havana Harbor to the extended ramifications of slavery.[10]

10. Humboldt, *Political Essay on the Island of Cuba*, ed. Kutzinski and Ette, II, 37–38; Alexander von Humboldt, *Personal Narrative of a Journey to the Equinoctial Regions of the New Continent*, ed. and trans. Jason Wilson (New York, 1995), 46.

Index